LETTERS

WRITTEN FROM

NEW-ENGLAND,

A. D. 1686.

BY

John Dunton.

IN WHICH ARE DESCRIBED

HIS VOYAGES BY SEA, HIS TRAVELS ON LAND,

AND THE CHARACTERS OF HIS FRIENDS
AND ACQUAINTANCES.

Now First Published from the Original Manuscript,
In the Bodleian Library, Oxford.

WITH NOTES AND AN APPENDIX,
BY W. H. WHITMORE.

Boston:
PUBLISHED FOR THE PRINCE SOCIETY.
1867.

Printing Statement:

Due to the very old age and scarcity of this book,
many of the pages may be hard to read due to the
blurring of the original text, possible missing pages,
missing text, dark backgrounds and other issues
beyond our control.

Because this is such an important and rare work, we
believe it is best to reproduce this book regardless of
its original condition.

Thank you for your understanding.

INTRODUCTION.

OHN DUNTON was born at Graffham, in Huntingtonſhire, the 14th of May, 1659. From the volume entitled "Dunton's Remains," in which our author piouſly preſerved thè record of his father's life and labors, we learn that the family had been for three generations devoted to the miniſtry. John Dunton, the father, was born 10th June, 1628, "at Little Miſſenden, in Buckinghamſhire, the place where his father and grandfather (both whoſe names were John Dunton) were miniſters." He had three ſiſters, viz: Anne, wife of William Reding, of Dungrove, in Cheſham, who had children, William, John, Nathaniel, Robert, Thomas and Anne; Mary, wife of Mr. Woolhouſe, miniſter at Prince-Reſbrow, co. Bucks, who had children, Mary, Margaret, Elizabeth, John, Anne, Richard and Sarah; and Mary, who married William Pratt, Eſq., and d. *s. p.*

The Rev. John Dunton, as we will term him to diſtinguiſh him from his ſon, was of Trinity College, Cambridge, and after travelling abroad was ſettled at St. Mary's, co. Bedford.
He

He was made Rector of Graffham, and there married Lydia, daughter of Mr. Daniel Carter, of Chesham. Their only child was John, and the mother died, 3 March, 1660. Soon after the father removed to Ireland, but after some seven years he returned to England, and was made Rector of Aston Clinton, co. Bucks. Here he married Mrs. Mary Lake, "daughter to the Rev. Mr. Mariot, and sister to that eminent citizen, Mr. Thomas Rolfe," by whom he had children, Sarah, Mary, Elizabeth and Lake. He died 4th November, 1676.

The autobiography of John Dunton, published in 1705, gives us a number of facts in regard to his life. He was intended for the ministry, but the design was abandoned in consequence of his dislike to study. He was then apprenticed to Thomas Parkhurst, a London bookseller, and found the business sufficiently to his taste to complete the term of his service. He then commenced the business of bookselling and publishing on his own account, and succeeded very well at first, so that he resolved upon being married. After various ineffectual attempts, which he very openly acknowledges, he was accepted by Elizabeth Annesley, daughter of Dr. Samuel Annesley, a distinguished non-conformist minister, and they were married, 3 August, 1682. Dunton says but little concerning the next three years, but it is probable that the prudence and diligence of his wife enabled him to maintain a good position in the trade.

In 1685 he resolved to visit New-England, and embarking in the "Susan and Thomas," of Boston, 150 tons burthen
Capt

Capt. Thomas Jenner, he failed from the Downs on the 2d of November of that year. His paffage was long and ftormy, and the veffel did not arrive at Bofton till about the 10th of February, 1686. This volume contains a full record of his entire trip, until he arrived back in London, on the 5th of Auguft, 1686, having been but one month on his return voyage. Having become refponfible for the debts of a brother-in-law, Dunton was expofed to arreft, and for ten months after his arrival in London, he was obliged to remain houfed.

His next undertaking was a vifit to Holland, and at Amfterdam he lived fome four months. He afterwards went up the Rhine, and, as he writes, having gratified his curiofity and fpent his money, he returned to London, 15 November, 1688. He took a fhop oppofite to the Poultrey Counter, its fign being the Black Raven, and opened it firft on the day the Prince of Orange entered London. Here he traded for ten years, with a variety of fucceffes and difappointments, putting into form fome of his numerous projects. The moft noticeable of thefe was the eftablifhment of the "Athenian Gazette," or "Athenian Mercury," as it was later entitled. This was a weekly publication, fomewhat of the nature of 'Notes and Queries,' wherein all kinds of queftions were afked and anfwered. The idea was Dunton's, and his principal affiftants were Mr. Richard Sault, Dr. Norris, and the Rev. Samuel Wefley. The latter had married another daughter of Dr. Annefley, and was fomewhat noted as a writer. He was the father of the famous founders of Methodifm, John and Charles Wefley. This publication reached nineteen

teen volumes, and a felection of the articles was republifhed in three volumes, under the title of the "Athenian Oracle."

Of this period of his life Dunton writes: "By the general acquaintance I now had with all ranks and degrees of men, and which daily increafed by the weekly fpreading of 'the Athenian Mercury,' trade enlarged fo much upon me, that I was quite cloyed with the crowd of bufinefs; and thereupon I began to bend my thoughts upon a quiet retreat from the world, that I might be more at leifure to get acquaintance with myfelf, and to devote my life more entirely to ftudy, which has been one of the beft pleafures I have met with. However, I could not reconcile myfelf to live altogether upon the main ftock; and therefore I thought it the moft prudent way to keep a warehoufe, which might be managed in privacy, without much hurry. After long fearching I found Mr. Shalcroffe's houfe, in Bull Head Court, near Jewin-ftreet, very fit for my purpofe; and there (as the Athenians jocularly faid) my Raven went to rooft." "I had a long time been making a choice collection of valuable Books from Mr. Shermerdine's fhop, and at all the noted auctions. . . . My nights were now divided betwixt fleep and ftudy. . . . I rofe ufually at four in the morning, and fhutting my clofet-door upon the vulgar world, and being encompaffed with fo many learned and great men, I thought myfelf in the very lap of Eternity."

"But, alas! the beft ftate of happinefs this world can afford is little more than an airy fcene of vanity, which we cannot keep from fhifting, which makes Life itfelf but little

better

better than mere knight-errantry. My happinefs was too fpirituous and fine to continue long; and the conclufion of it was a wounding tragedy, the ficknefs and death of IRIS." This fad event took place, May 28th, 1697; and notwithftanding the grief he fo loudly expreffed, Dunton in the fame year took a fecond wife. This was Sarah, daughter of Mrs. Jane Nicholas, a rich widow living at St. Albans. Soon after his fecond marriage he went to Ireland with a large collection of books, which were advantageoufly fold; and out of a quarrel in which he was involved, grew a characteriftic book which he entitled "The Dublin Scuffle."

We are not informed of the caufe of the embarraffments, pecuniary and matrimonial, in which he was foon involved, but he feems to have relied for affiftance upon his mother-in-law, and to have failed to receive it. NICHOLS, in his edition of the "Life and Errors," quotes a letter from Mrs. Dunton, which fhows that fhe was feparated from her hufband. It is dated at St. Albans, Feb. 28, 1701, and reads thus:—" I wifh to let you know that, if you think much of providing for me, I am very willing you fhould have all your yoke and burden, as you call it being married, removed, and return me my fortune, and we will be both fingle; and you fhall have your land if you will return me my money, and fure that will pleafe you, for I and all good people, think you never married me for love, but for my money, and fo you have had the ufe of it all this while to banter and laugh at me and my mother by your maggoty Printers."

In 1705 Dunton publifhed " The Life and Errors of John Dunton, Late Citizen of London; Written by Himfelf in Solitude.

Solitude. With an Idea of a New Life, Wherein is Shown How he'd Think, Speak and Act, might he Live over his Days again: Intermix'd with the New Difcoveries The Author has made In his Travels Abroad, And in his Private Converfation at Home. Together with the Lives and Char-acters of a Thoufand Perfons now Living in London, &c. Digefted into Seven Stages, with their Refpective Ideas. London: Printed for S. Malthus, 1705." Pp. 251.

This whimfical work has been undoubtedly the main fource of his reputation. His political tracts, and even the farcaftic praifes of Dean Swift, would hardly have preferved his memory; but this budget of goffip has proved irrefiftible to fucceeding generations. In it he has attempted to por-tray the characters and characteriftics of all the prominent printers, publifhers, engravers and even authors of his time. As an extenfive though poorly digefted collection of biogra-phies, it has been a fource of conftant reference. It is but juft to add that in many paffages we difcover a purity of thought not often feen in the pamphleteers of that time.

In the next year he publifhed "The Living Elegy," and from the reprint by NICHOLS, we will make a few quotations. "I had great loffes in trade (many of which have been owing to Malthus' telling me there was 400 fold of a Book, when there was not 60) and have had a much greater difappoint-ment in the fale of my Woods." "But now the mortgage being paid off, £200 is all I owe in the world; and could my fifter B—— now pay me that £200 I can prove fhe owes me, I would clear with the whole world before I flept."

In

In 1708 his mother-in-law, Mrs. Nicholas, died, without apparently altering her opinion of Dunton, or affording him any relief. In fact he had laid his family troubles before the public in a way which would naturally prevent a reconciliation, and had accufed Mrs. Nicholas of promifing him certain property which fhe refufed to deliver afterwards.

After this Dunton became a violent Whig, and probably became more deeply involved in debt by his numerous publications. In 1716 he made an appeal to George I. for fome recompenfe for his fervices, and, in 1723, he repeated his claims. From NICHOLS's reprint we quote the following paffages.

" That your petitioner, living in daily fear of a prifon, by reafon of the great fums of money which he freely fpent out of his own pocket in detecting your Majefty's Enemies, applied himfelf to his two good friends, the late Marquis of Wharton, and the Bifhop of Salifbury, who faithfully promifed to lay your Petitioner's wants and fervices before your Majefty, which two thoufand pounds would relieve." " That the expectation of fome reward . . . . has gained your Petitioner credit for fubfiftence for thefe feveral years, which is now withdrawn, and a jail threatened."

In return for the Royal bounty, Dunton promifed to republifh one thoufand valuable books for which he held the copyright, to attempt to reform the manners and morals of the people, to publifh a new book of his own, and to reprint the " Life and Errors." He adds a lift of forty political

tracts

tracts which he had iffued, in favor of the Hanoverian dynafty.

The induftry of NICHOLS has collected but few more facts concerning Dunton, than that his fecond wife was buried on March 21ft, 1720–1, and that he died in obfcurity, in 1733, aged 74.

The character of John Dunton is not eafily underftood, except upon the fuppofition that he was partially infane. He was vain and loquacious, and unfortunately for himfelf he had not only a ready pen at his fervice, but eafy accefs to the printing prefs. The unexpected fuccefs of his "Athenian Mercury," feems to have fo confirmed him in his oddities, that he did not perceive when the public had wearied of that fancy.

A letter addreffed to him in 1718, and cited by NICHOLS, expreffes this very fenfibly. " The reft I have to fay to you is merely to advife you for your own profit, and with the fame fincerity I would a friend. Such titles as ' Athenian Phœnix' and ' Pindarick Lady,' are fo fenfelefs and imper- tinent, that it would fpoil the credit of any Author that fhould ufe them ; and for Plato's Notions and Platonic Love, thofe terms have been fo juftly expofed by the SPECTATOR, and are fo very ridiculous and unfafhionable, that nothing of thofe chimeras and whimfies would fell in the genteel part of the world. . . . Frolic and merry conceits are defpifed in this nice age." " If you have Effays or Letters that are valuable, call them Effays and Letters in fhort and plain

language

language; and if you have any thing writ by men of fenfe, and on fubjects of importance, it may fell without your name to it." The advice was of courfe rejected, and to his lateft project the old catchword of Athenian was appended.

It would feem from many of his writings, that Dunton inherited a ftrong tafte for religious difcuffions and differtations. But for his unfortunate and miftaken defire to become a wit, he might have been a refpected and ufeful citizen. It was perhaps his defire to play a part for which he was unfitted which deftroyed the balance of his faculties. His works will remain as fources of information on many points, for in telling all that he knew or felt, he has occafionally preferved facts elfewhere unrecorded.

His writings often contain a random reference to matters which now provoke a defire for explanation. Thus in his Converfation in Ireland, (NICHOLS's edition of "Life and Errors," ii, 569,) he writes: "Having taken my leave of Sir Henry Ingolfby, in my way home I met with Lieutenant Downing, my former Fellow-traveller in New-England. You can hardly imagine, Madam, how agreeable a thing it is to meet with an old Friend in a Foreign Country. It was fome thoufands of miles off, that we were laft together; and we were equally furprized to meet each other here. There was in his company at that time Captain Annefley, Son to the late Earl of Anglefey, to whom I had the honor to be related by my firft Wife." "After a Health to the King and fome other of our friends in England, we talked over our New-England Ramble. After this I told the Lieutenant
of

of my Brother Annefley's death, at which he was highly concerned." "For the Lieutenant, my old fellow-traveller, I muft fay that he has much addrefs, and as great prefence of mind as was ever feen. He is moft agreeable company, and perhaps the beft friend I had in America." Yet this beft friend does not figure in Dunton's Letters, and we believe no genealogift has fucceeded in identifying him with any member of the well-known family here.

In regard to the volume now prefented to the public, it is thought that it will be confidered a valuable addition to our knowledge of affairs here at that period. We may regret that the writer was not more competent for the tafk, but we have at all events a lively picture of the man who actually lived here, and was well received by the leading inhabitants. If we cannot put full reliance in the reported converfations, we can be fure that fimilar ones did occur and were conducted on his part in that vein. There is no improbability in the affumption that Dunton has correctly reprefented the tone of fociety here, and we can at leaft realize that it was healthy and not unduly repreffive. As we follow Dunton on his various trips, we find evidences of a community well-ordered and profperous. The fubject of religion does not feem to have been unduly eftimated, and the portraits of Mrs. Breck, Mrs. Green, and Comfort Wilkins, are defcriptions of fuch Puritans as we' may be proud to claim for Maffachufetts.

Dunton has alfo the merit in our eyes of being favorably difpofed on the whole towards the colonifts. The few contemporary pamphlets treating upon our local affairs at this period

period were generally hoſtile in tone, and by no means truſt-
worthy. While this book has been in the printer's hands,
however, a moſt intereſting volume has been publiſhed by
the Long Iſland Hiſtorical Society, which contains new evidence in regard to affairs here. It is a tranſlation of a
journal written by Jaſper Dankers, who, with Peter Sluyter,
viſited this country in 1679, as agents for the Labadiſt community, landing at New York and exploring the country
with a view to purchaſing territory.

In June, 1680, they viſited Boſton, and ſtayed there a
month, ſailing thence to Europe, July 23d. This portion of
their journal covers nearly thirty pages and is of courſe very
intereſting as a new deſcription of Boſton and its inhabitants.
As compared with Dunton's account the picture they draw
is ſufficiently harſh; but it muſt be remembered that not only
were they ſtrangers, unable to ſpeak Engliſh with any flu-
ency, but they were regarded with ſuſpicion, as " Jeſuits who
had come here for no good." We may perhaps without im-
propriety copy from this volume a few paſſages which treat
of the topics that Dunton diſcuſſes.

Of Boſton they write, " The city is quite large, conſtitu-
ting about twelve companies. It has three churches, or
meeting-houſes, as they call them. All the houſes are made
of thin, ſmall cedar ſhingles, nailed againſt frames, and then
filled in with brick and other ſtuff; and ſo are their churches.
For this reaſon theſe towns are ſo liable to fires, as have
already happened ſeveral times ; and the wonder to me is,
that the whole city has not been burnt down, ſo light and
dry

dry are the materials. There is a large dock in front of it, conftructed of wooden piers, where the large fhips go to be careened and rigged; the fmaller veffels all come up to the city." "Upon the point of the bay, on the left hand, there is a block-houfe, along which a piece of water runs, called the Milk ditch. The whole place has been an ifland, but it is now joined to the main land by a low road to Roxbury." "There are many fmall iflands before Bofton, well on to fifty, I believe, between which you fail on to the city. A high one, or the higheft, is the firft that you meet. It is twelve miles from the city and has a light-houfe upon it, which you can fee from a great diftance, for it is in other refpects naked and bare." "There is a high hill in the city alfo with a light-houfe upon it, by which you can hold your courfe in entering."

Of Gov. Bradftreet they write, he "dwelt in only a common houfe, and that not the moft coftly. He is an old man, quiet and grave. He was dreffed in black filk, but not fumptuoufly."

They alfo went to vifit John Eliot, whom they term a very old man, " feventy-feven years old," who had been forty-eight years in thefe parts. Their fpecial defire was to obtain copies of his Indian books, and Eliot prefented them with fuch as he had then with him. They afked for an Indian Bible, but it feemed that during the "late Indian war all the Bibles and Teftaments were carried away and burnt or deftroyed, fo that he had not been able to fave any for himfelf; but a new edition was in prefs, which he hoped would
                                                        be

be much better than the firſt one, though that was not to be defpifed." However, he made up a copy from portions of the two editions, and in other ways ſhowed himſelf friendly to thefe miſſionaries.

One of the moſt curious items is the picture of Harvard College, then apparently not in a very flouriſhing condition. There were only about ten ſtudents and no profeſſors. On entering the College building they " found there eight or ten young fellows, fitting around, fmoking tobacco, with the fmoke of which the room was fo full that you could hardly fee; and the whole houfe fmelt fo ſtrong of it, that when I was going up ſtairs, I faid, this is certainly a tavern." " They could hardly fpeak a word of Latin, fo that my com-rade could not converfe with them. They took us to the library where there was nothing particular. We looked over it a little."

As to the fervices in the churches they write that attend-ing a day of faſting in a church, "in the firſt place a miniſter made a prayer in the pulpit, of full two hours in length; after which an old miniſter delivered a fermon an hour long, and after that a prayer was made, and fome verfes fung out of the pfalm. In the afternoon, three or four hours were confumed with nothing except prayers, three miniſters reliev-ing each other alternately: when one was tired, another went up into the pulpit."

As to the inhabitants generally, it is faid, "they are all Independent in matter of religion, if it can be called reli-gion;

gion; many of them perhaps more for the purpofes of enjoying the benefit of its privileges than for any regard to truth and godlinefs." "All their religion confifts in obferving Sunday by not working or going into the taverns on that day; but the houfes are worfe than the taverns." "There is a penalty for curfing and fwearing, fuch as they pleafe to impofe, the witneffes thereof being at liberty to infift upon it. Neverthelefs, you difcover little difference between this and other places. Drinking and fighting occur there not lefs than elfewhere; and as to truth and true godlinefs you muft not expect more of them than of others."

There are many other interefting particulars in this Journal, to which we refer our readers. As to the return voyage, they took paffage in the Dolphin, Capt. John Foy, paying therefor "the ufual price of fix pounds fterling for each perfon."

Thefe miffionaries were moft decidedly oppofed to the dominant fect here, and yet there is nothing in this record to which exception can be taken. The facts as ftated are not improbable, and though we may think it a prejudiced account, it is a very moderate attack, compared with others.

To revert to Dunton and his Letters, and the dates of various occurrences; the following points are eafily eftablifhed: 1685, October 14th, Dunton quits London, and November 17th is fairly at fea, out of fight of land. In 1686, within a day or two of February 10, he arrives at Bofton; February 16th, is allowed refidence here. On

March

March 7th and 11th, the fermons on Morgan were preached; April 4 and 10, the letter to his fervant Palmer, at Salem, is written and anfwered. May 15th is the date of the arrival of Randolph and Ratcliffe, and May 20th to 30th covers the time in which the arrival of Mr. Morton and Mrs. Hicks occurred. The Training, and the Natick lecture, were undoubtedly in May or June, and his vifit to Gloucefter was probably in the latter month. On the 5th July, he quits Bofton, and on the 5th Auguft, 1686, arrives in London. He was thus four months on the outward voyage, refident here nearly five months, and one month in returning.

One defect of our author may be here confeffed. In his accounts of the cuftoms and ideas of the Indians, he has profeffedly given information derived at fecond-hand. It is evident that his great fource of information was Roger Williams's " Key into the Language of America," originally publifhed in 1643. We cannot juftly accufe him of intentional plagiarifm, fince, had this volume been iffued in Dunton's life-time, he might have confeffed his indebtednefs. At the time he wrote, indeed, he was doing a good fervice, by republifhing information which had been out of reach for nearly forty years, and which he always confeffes he had 'from a friend.' Although this book by WILLIAMS has been twice reprinted, once in 1827, and again in 1866, very few perfons, comparatively, have accefs to it. In Dunton's verfion the matter is re-arranged, and is in a much more readable form. So, again, much of his effay on John Eliot is copied from Cotton Mather, but here we may not unfairly claim that Mather was the informant, as he was the friend,

of

of Dunton. Certainly it is not improbable that Mather was already collecting material for his life of Eliot, then a very aged man, and Dunton's admiration of the Indian Evangelist was too genuine and enthusiastic to admit of any hesitancy in seeking for information. With these imperfections, however, the Letters must remain as unique sketches of New-England life, honestly drawn, and defective rather than erroneous.

In printing from the manuscript of an author so long deceased, many difficult questions have necessarily arisen. For all exercise of the critical functions, for omissions and annotations, the editor is to be held solely responsible, and he will be fully repaid for his labors if they prove of any service to a single student.

W. H. W.

Boston, April, 1867.

JOHN DUNTON'S LETTERS

FROM

NEW-ENGLAND.

PREFATORY NOTE.

an introduction to "JOHN DUNTON'S LETTERS," the following extracts from his "LIFE AND ERRORS," concerning his firſt entertaining the idea of his voyage to New England, may be inſerted.

He was married, Auguſt 3, 1682, at the Pariſh Church of Allhallows-the-Wall, London, to Elizabeth, daughter of Rev. Samuel Anneſley. His account proceeds:

"When we had ſtayed a little time at my Father-in-law's, I carried dear Iris home, to the large houſe I had taken at the corner of Princes-ſtreet, where Mr. White had lived, who was ſo much noted for his courage in arreſting Juſtice Balch for ſending him to priſon from Dr. Anneſley's Meeting.   "We

"We now came (as they fay) to ftand upon our own legs, and to barter for fubfiftence among the reft of mankind; and dear Iris gave an early fpecimen of her prudence and diligence that way; and thereupon commenced Bookfeller, Cafh-keeper, managed all my affairs for me, and left me entirely to my own *rambling* and *fcribbling* humors. However, I always kept an eye over the main chance. But thefe were golden days. Profperity and fuccefs were the common courfe of Providence with me then, and I have often thought I was bleffed upon the account of Iris.

"We took feveral journeys together into the Country, and made vifits to both our Relations; but, look which way we would, the World was always fmiling on us. The piety and good-humour of Iris made our lives as it were one continued Courtfhip; but the Reader fhall have an impartial account of her Chriftianity towards the conclufion of this Stage.

"When I was thus feated to the beft advantage at the Black Raven, in Princes-ftreet, and as happy in my Marriage as I could wifh, there came an univerfal damp upon Trade, occafioned by the defeat of Monmouth in the Weft; and, at this time, having £500 owing me in New-England, I began to think it worth my while to make a voyage of it thither.

"I firft made a trial, how dear Iris would digeft the thoughts of parting with me; and I found that, though she had a very tender fenfe of all the dangers I fhould be expofed to, yet fhe was always perfectly refigned to the pleafure of her Hufband. I had no more than juft an opportunity to hint the matter to my honoured Father-in-law, in-law, Dr. Annesley, who was then going for Tunbridge; but immediately after I wrote him the following Letter:

"LONDON, AUGUST 7, 1685.

" *Much honoured Sir :*

"This comes to desire your free thoughts of my voyage to New-England. I have consulted several Friends upon it, who think it the best method I can take. I have a great number of Books that lie upon my hands, as the ' Continuation of the Morning Exercises,' and others, very proper for that place; besides the £500 which I have there in Debts. However, I will not move without your advice and consent. My dear Wife sends her duty to you; and we hope the Waters agree well with you.

" I am

" Your most affectionate and dutiful Son,

"J. DUNTON.

" To this Letter I had the following answer:

"TUNBRIDGE, AUG. 10, 1685.

" *Dear Son :*

"I received yours, but cannot give so particular and direct an answer as you may expect. You know I came hither presently after you mentioned this voyage, neither had I an opportunity to consider all the circumstances of it. I perceive those you have consulted are for it; and they are better able to foresee what may probably be the issue of such an undertaking, than I am, or can be. The infinitely wise God direct you, and give wisdom to those that advise you. I do as heartily desire your universal welfare as any Friend

you

you have in the World, and therefore dare not fay a word againft it.

"My prefent opinion is, that you do not (if you refolve upon the voyage) carry too great a Cargo; for I think it will be lefs trouble to you to wifh there that you had brought more, than to fret at the want of a market for too many. If you obferve the courfe of the World, the moft of all trouble is through fruftration of our expectation: where we look not for much, we eafily bear a difappointment. Moderation in all things but in love to God and ferious godlinefs, is highly commendable. Covet earneftly the beft Gifts, and the beft Graces and the beft Enjoyments; for which you fhall never, while I live, want the earneft Prayers of

"Your moft affectionate Father,

"S. ANNESLEY."

"I was very glad of any excufe that would make my friends more indulgent to my *rambling* humour. To make short of it, I got ready for my voyage with all poffible expedition, fent a great number of Books down the River to Gravefend, and followed them foon after, having bid a forrowful farewell to dear Iris and my other Relations."

[We now proceed with the copies of Dunton's Letters, as preferved in the Bodleian Library, Rawlinfon MS. Mifc. 71, which had evidently been prepared by him for publication, and to which he had prefixed the following title-page.]

A

SUMMER'S RAMBLE,

THROUGH TEN KINGDOMES,

OCCASIONALLY WRITTEN BY

JOHN DUNTON,

CITIZEN OF LONDON,

IN HIS TRAVELLS; AND SENT TO HIS FRIENDS IN ENGLAND.

WHEREIN HE RELATES

THE HISTORY OF HIS SEA-VOYAGES,

HIS CONVERSATION ON THE ROADS, AT THE INNS AND TOWNS

HE STAID ATT,

With Particular Characters of Men and Women, and almoft every thing
He saw : or converfed with.

MORE ESPECIALLY

IN HOLLAND, AMERICA, DUBLIN, &c.

Where 500 Perfons may find their Pictures, that at prefent little expect it.

The Whole writ in *A DIFFERENT METHOD* from other Travellers,
and difcovers the Miftakes of fome late Writers.

ILLUSTRATED WITH COPPER-PLATES REPRESENTING THE
MOST PLEASANT PASSAGES IN THE WHOLE ADVENTURE.

Hey Boys! She fcuds away, and by my head I know,
We *round the World* are failing now.—*Cowley*.

VOL. I.

LONDON:

Printed (FOR THE AUTHOR) and are to be fold by *A. Baldwin* near the Oxford
Armes in Warwick Lane, of whom is to be had THE DUBLIN SCUFFLE,
written by the fame Hand.

Price bound 5s.

LETTER I.

TO MRS. ELIZABETH DUNTON, AT MADAM
GODFRYE'S HOUSE, IN THE POULTRY, LONDON.

From Weft-Cowes, in the Ifle of Wight,
Octob. 25th, 1685.

Y Heart and more,—As I lay capering in[1] the winding chambers of nature, even there I was forming Ideas of long voyages and New Worlds. I was not born above 3 Houres but my eyes were offering at difcoveries. And by that time I could move my Tongue, it would be twattling of Forreign Countrys, and therefore (my Dear) you can't admire that *I leave England* (*to Ramble through Ten Kingdomes*) but may wonder that I leave you, for cou'd I goe and leave my felfe behind? (and without an Hyperbole, the beft part of my felfe, too.) Behind, did I fay? fooner fhall my foul forfake its dwelling than I can part with your Dear Image! you are with me (deareft Partner of my Life) wherever I ramble, and like my Guardian-Angell, keep my foul from every ftraying thought. That bond of Love in which our Hearts are tyed is indiffolvable, our Love is conftant. Many waters cannot
quench

---

[1] See a confirmation of this in my Juvenile travells lately publifhed in my Farwell to Dublin, p. 122, and in p. 148.—J. D.

quench[2] it, neither can place, time, or death it felfe, bring it to a Period. Nor is there any Reafon it fhou'd, for I have allways lov'd thee as the Indented counterpart of my foul, and I muft fay the Teares you fhed when I left London, affure the world you love me, not my Fortunes.

> Fair courfe of Paffions where two lovers ftart,
> And run together, Heart thus yok'd in Heart.

There's nothing in our Love that has been vulgar; our Paffions and Affections have been as pure as Æther, and all our Life has been nothing elfe but one continued fcene of Ecftacy and Rapture in the Mutuall Interchanges of our Love. In a word we are both fo happy in one another, that Adam and Eve in Paradife were fcarfe happyer. But, who can refift the laws of Fate? As happy as I am, I muft now leave you; 'tis true the man in the Gofpell had marryd a wife and he cou'd not leave her; but he was not born to ramble, or he muft have purfued his deftiny: fure I am, if any thing cou'd keep me at home, 'tis a Tender wife, fuch a one as your dear felfe. But my Starrs have decreed me a Rambler. Yet, my Dear, be chearfull, for I can live as well abfent as prefent. Then, feeing I've defign'd a Ramble through Ten Kingdomes, Ile now goe to America—Thence to Holland—Thence to Ireland—Thence to Scotland— Thence to France—Thence to Spain—Thence to Germany —Thence to Italy—Thence to Greece—Thence to Jeru- falem—and perhaps Thence to the Indyes, &c.; neither can I be ftop'd in this *long Adventure*, for being born under a Rambling-Planet, all that is done to fix me at home does but forward my Travells abroad. Even the Parfon[3] himfelfe (God bleffe him,) gave me a lifting hand, (and, Mr. H., I thank ye for't,) for as much as I love Iris, I can't but pity thofe that

are

---

[2] Cant. 8, 7.
[3] Mr. H— minifter of St. Chrifto- phers in Threadneedle-Street who was pleafed to excommunicate Mr. Aftwood, my felfe, and feverall others for not being of his opinion, or in plainer Termes for not comeing to Church.— J. D.

are meekly ty'd to a Petticoat. To fuch nothing is the
object of thefe fences, (except they get fuch a Spoufe as Iris,)
but that is common; they fee nothing furprizing or new; like
a horfe in a mill, they goe on in their conftant Round and
that they do to-day, that they do to-morrow; yet, (my Dear,)
as much as I love rambling, I ben't for goeing on fuch
errands as the Son of Kifh, only to feek his Father's Affes,
nor will I ramble like the Prodigall Son, only to feed upon
the Hufks of a Strange Country; nor need I travell with
Æfop to Iftria, thence to Africk, and fundry other kingdomes, only to find out the beft crabbs; or like him who
came to England from the furtheft parts of Hungary only
to eat *Oiflers*. Thefe Ramblers were better ha' ftaid at
home! but there are few Inftances of that nature — moft
men (like Alexander) travell for the Golden-Fleece.[4] And I
muft confeffe 'twas the Hopes of Gold (with a little pleafure
into the bargain) that has now engaged Ten merry boyes
of us[5] to plow the ocean and like fouldiers of fortune, to
run all hazards that we might obtain our end. 'Tis true,
had the valiant Monmouth fucceeded, I had deferred thefe
Rambles a year longer; but he was beaten (not to fay betray'd)
at Sedgmore, [there[6] were other parts firft to be acted, and
the great work of our deliverance was referv'd for a more
Noble and Illuftrious Arm; and Heavens peculiar Darling,
Great Naffaw, was only fit to be intrufted in it;] soe that
every thing this yeare confpired to fend me abroad, and
accordingly, Octob. 14, 1685, I took my folemn leave of
the

---

[4] Dunton has two drafts of this introductory matter, and we have ufed
the later one for our text. In the can-
celled part, however, is the following
claufe:

"At that time the Nation being in
a Ferment, and Trading bad to an
Extremity, and having there great fums
of money due to me at Bofton in New-
England, defpifing all the difficulties
that attended it, I took a Refolution to
Ramble thither."—ED.

[5] Mr. Stevens, Mr. Bolt, Mr. Roswell,
Mr. Charles Martin, Jun., Mr. Weaver,
Mr. Pain, Mr. Haffwell, Mr. Herrick,
Mr. Allen, a printer, my felfe and one
more.—J. D.

[6] The matter within this Brace was
added since the firft writeing of the
Letter.—J. D.

2

the good Doctor, (my Reverend Father in Law,) his wife and family. And now, my Dear, methought 'twas a little repre-sentation of a Funerall, to fee thee and my feverall friends, (like fo many mourners) marching with me to the water-fide; for I now fancyd my felfe as 'twere a Herfe and Coffin upon their fhoulders, and my weeping fpoufe decently attending the Ceremony; but we wanted Torches; and be-fides, it's not ufuall for any to waite upon their own Coffins. *However, your Dear Selfe,* Sifter Sarah, Teddy, Brother and Sifter Sudbury, Roger White, and a crowd of other friends, did not grudge me that fmall and laft office, to goe with me to the Boate that was to carry me to Graves-end. It lay at Ratcliffe, near one Mrs. Adams, where my fifter, Mary Dunton, then lived; fo takeing her with us (you may remember) we all went to the Ship-Tavern, in order to our laft Farwell. You ftaid here about Three Houres, drinking a Boon voyage to the young Traveller, for foe I was then, haveing as yet never feen the fea, nor fcarce a mariner's compaffe. But the deareft friends muft part, and as good at firft as at laft, and therefore takeing leave of my Dear, (which was the topping difficulty of my whole voyage,) and beckoning a fad farwell to my other friends, (as long as they cou'd fee hand or glove,) we parted.

(My Dear,) It was time now to commit and commend my felfe and Boate to the protection and conduct of that God who rules the winds and the waves; fo beckoning another Farwell to my friends at fhore, and wifhing you all (as long as you cou'd fee or hear me) as much happyneffe as cou'd be hoped for from a Popifh King, and you to Philaret as long a life as cou'd be expected by a man goeing to his Grave: We launch out on Wednefday about 2 of the Clock; an afternoon for ever to be remember'd by *Poor Phil:*—and the Bill of Lading is as followeth, viz.—

John Dunton, Samuell Herrick, and Roger White:

for I cant forget the generous love of honeft Roger, who
when

when all were gone ftill cling'd about me, and wou'd not leave me—till I was Embarked, and fo boated it with me to Erith, where we went afhore and lay that night. We lodg'd but in a poor Houfe, but our Landlady was refolv'd to crofs the Proverb, for tho' we had fcarce any thing but bare walls, fhe was no giddy Houfwife, but went more neat and lite in her patch't cloaths than lazy flatterns in their filks and fattins; She entertain'd us with an obliging Afpect, and waited upon us with a diligence fo peculiar to her, that tho' we might have gone to bigger Houfes (and had more variety) yet it could not have pleaf'd us better:

> To what fhe brought us, we were welcome ftill ;
> Good Entertainment, though the chear was ill.

The next morning, the Dawn fcarce drew the curtains of the Eaft, ere Herrick, Roger, and my felf got out of our Beds. We made Graves-End the Port to which we Rambled next; it is but two miles from Erith, where we lay;[1] and is a pretty little Town at the Mouth of the River Thames. Its Trading confifts chiefly, in entertaining thofe Paffengers that are either juft going to, or newly come from Sea; Such as the Graves-End Inkeepers never expect to fee again; and therefore make the moft of them while they have them: They make their cuftomers pay for every thing, juft as the Had'em Collegians fpeak, that is, through the Nofe. As foon as we had look'd a little about the Town, we went into an Inn, where we found our Hoft a man that confifted of Double Beds and fellowfhip; for as he was fure to fupply us with Drink even without afking, fo he would always thruft himfelf in for a snack, in helping to drink it; yet to fay the truth, he was a Man of great humility, and gave us power as well over himfelf as his houfe. I obferv'd him to be exceeding willing to anfwer all Mens Expectations to the utmoft of his Power, unlefs it were in the Reckoning, and there

---

[1] We have here omitted a long defcription of a milkmaid feen by the way.—ED.

there he would be abfolute; and had got that Trick of Court-Greatnefs, to lay all miftakes upon his Servants. His wife was like Cummin-seed to a Dove-houfe, and helpt to draw in the Cuftomers; and to be a good Gueft, was a fufficient Warrant for her Liberty. And to give you his character in few words, he is an abfolute flave, for he neither eats, drinks, nor thinks, but at other mens charges and Appointments. But he fells himfelf at an Extravagant rate, and makes all his Cuftomers pay dearly for the Purchafe. Nor was he at all fingular, for in the whole Town, there was never a Barrel better Herring.

In this Town, my Dear, I met with my old Neighbour and Friend, Mr. Thomas Malthus, (who is fince dead,) waiting for a wind for Holland. He liv'd, you know, at the Sun in the Poultry; but his Sun fetting in a cloud forc'd him to make a vertue of Neceffity. Tom being a Brother citizen and meeting me fo unexpectedly, was both pleaf't and furpriz'd, and therefore would needs attend me to my fhip, then riding at Graves-End; Her name was the Sufan and Thomas, belonging to Bofton in the Maffachufetts, a Colony of Englifh in New England, 150 Tuns Burden, mann'd with 16 faylers, the Mafters name Thomas Jenner, with about 30 Paffengers, the moft part of which were men flying for fafety after the Rout at Sedgemore: Being come to the fhip, after the Exchange of our good wifhes for each others wellfare, I took my leave of my True Friend Mr. Roger White, and of Mr. Malthus, who both went back to Graves-End in the Same Boat, not without feveral Huzza's to us, till we were out of hearing them. And now being on fhip-board, and having parted with all my Friends, I look'd upon my felf to be juft beginning my Rambles. We left Graves-End on the 16th of October, about three in the afternoon, and went down into the Hope; which (having never before feen fo great a Confluence of Waters,) appear'd to me a very hopelefs place; tho' this was
but

but like a little puddle, in comparifon of the mighty Ocean through which I afterwards fail'd. The 17th being Saturday, we fet fail out of the Hope : And this muft be a very difpairing circumftance : For

What worfer treatment can a Rambler find,
Than to be forced to leave e'en Hope behind ?

Having left the Hope, about 6 o'clock at night we came to an Anchor in Margaret Road, in 3 fathom and a half Water : the 18th we turn'd into the Downs, where a *New England Captain* came aboard us ; to whom the Mafter teftify'd his hearty Welcome by a Splendid Entertainment, in which there wanted no Dainties to fatiffie the moft curious Palate ; for befides thofe ftanding Difhes of Powder'd Bief, Peafe and Bacon, (a difh that's always welcome to the Saylers) there were all forts of Fowls and Fifhes ; three Elements at leaft contributed to furnifh out the Feaft ; nor wou'd the fourth have been excuf'd, could they have found a way to eat the Salamander. Neats Tongues, Weftphalia Hams, Runds of Sturgeon, with joles of salmon, Anchovies and Caveare, were [there.]   In brief, not Heljogabalus himfelf could fcarce boaft a more delicious table. Nor was there wanting to all this good chear, plenty of Wines to make it go down glibly.   But that which was the moft efteem'd by every one was a large Bowl of Punch, a Liquor of that Noble and Divine Original, that all the Gods and Goddeffes (or elfe the Poet lies) contributed to its Compofition.

The Wind proving contrary, we were forc'd to lie a confiderable time in the Downs, but nothing extraordinary occurr'd until the 23d of October (that Dismal Day wherein the Innocent Cornifh, and the Compaffionate Mrs. Gaunt, both fell a facrifice to Popifh Rage and Cruelty. Upon that dark and gloomy day there happen'd fuch a dreadful ftorm, that no mans memory cou'd produce its Parallel : 'twas attended both with Lightning and with Thunder : Thunder that rent the amazed Firmament, and tore in

pieces

pieces the wide cheek of air; Lightning fo flaming that it feem'd to open the Breft of Heaven, and let down fheets of fire: you cannot but remember how dreadful 'twas by Land: But in the Downs (where then I was) it was more difmall, for here the ftorm raif'd the proud Billows almoft to the fkies, and made the fhip's main-maft tilt at the ftars; fcarce a wave came rolling over us but what we thought the Meffenger of Death. How dreadful, think you, (deareft) muft it be, when even the Sailors, that but feldom pray, came to the Paffengers, defiring us, that for God's fake, we would go all to Prayer, for that the fhip [illegible] they could not hold out an hour. The feamen's defiring us to go to prayer put me in mind of that saying, He that would learn to pray, let him goe to fea, at the which feveral of us did.

But even in this confufion we had fome angry words, for upon the Seamen defiring us to goe to Prayers, one of our Paffengers pul'd out "*The Crumbs of Comfort*," (a prayer-book,) which difpleafed fome of the reft; which I was troubled at, for certainly fet Prayers are lawfull for any, otherwife God wou'd not have appointed the Priefts (prefumed of themfelves beft able to pray) a form of bleffing the people; nor need our Saviour have fet us His prayer, which (as the Town Bufhell is the ftandard both to meafure corn and other Bufhells by) is both a Prayer in it felfe and a Pattern and Platforme of Prayer. The cloaths of the Ifraelites whilft they wandered forty yeares in the Wildernneffe, never waxed old, as if made of Perpetuano indeed. So a Good Prayer often ufed is ftill frefh and faire in the Eares and Eyes of Heaven. Certainly a Form of Prayer (tho' ufed in a ftorm) is better than none. But tho' some in our fhip wanted fuch helps as thefe, yet there were others that did not, and particularly Mr. Charles Martin and Mr. Allen, who not only prayed with us extempore, but fung a Pfalm, which feemed like that at Tyburn, fung by Con-

demned

demned criminals before their Execution. I know not how 'twas with my fellow-Paſſengers, but for my ſelf I was too ſad to ſing.*

He whoſe word curbs the fury both of winds and ſeas, ſent us a Happy Calm. And 'twas our Equal wonder to ſee ſo great a ſtorm ſo ſoon ſucceeded by a Calm. Neptune now had wip'd his foamy Mouth, the Winds retir'd, and ſunk into their Caverns. The ſea-green Triton ſounded a Retreat. As ſtill as midnight were the Waves, as ſmooth as when the Halcyon builds her Neſt; and all the Sea lay proſtrate in ſlumbers. The Calm having thus ſucceeded, and given us ſome aſſurance of our Lives, ſome in our ſhip (I cant ſay they were ſeamen) begun to conſider that Prayer is not like a ſtratagem in war, to be uſed but once—no, the oftener the better, ſo our firſt work was to give God thanks for our Deliverance, which was perform'd by all with ſuch affection, (the ſenſe of Danger being ſcarcely off,) that I am ſure I never ſaw the like. This great Tempeſt was a lively and reall Comment on that place recorded in Ps. 107, 23 v. &c. They that go down to the Sea in ſhips, that do buſineſse in great waters—Theſe ſee the works of the Lord and his wonders in the Deep, and For he commandeth and raiſeth the ſtormie wind which lifteth up the waves thereof. They mount up to Heaven; they goe down again to the Depths; their ſoul is melted becauſe of Trouble. They reel to and fro, and ſtagger like a drunken-man, and are at their wit's end. Then they cry unto the Lord in their Trouble, and he bringeth them out of their diſtreſſes. He maketh the ſtorm a Calm; ſo that the Waves thereof are ſtill. Then are they glad becauſe they be quiet: ſo he bringeth them unto their deſired Haven. After this manner we were delivered.

But tho' the ſtorm was happily over, the wind kept ſtill in its old quarter, i. e., contrary to us; and therefore the

---

* We omit a long paſſage concerning ſtorms and prayer in general.—ED.

the next day, my felf and fervant Palmer, Who has fuch a Love for me that he tells me he'd goe with me round the world,—with four other Paffengers, took a Boat for Deal; for having been fo rudely toft upon the Sea, we hop'd to be more favorably treated on fhore.   But it was very near making good the Proverb, " Out of the Frying-Pan into the Fire," (tho' here 'twas into the water;) for juft as we were Landing, we had like to have been all drounded, and fo have found that Death a-fhore we had fo lately efcap'd at Sea; and tho' through the goodnefs of God, we were all pre-ferved, Yet did the dread of it fo feiz my fpirits, that, (to this hour,) I had rather go an Eaft India Voyage in a Tite Ship than Crofs the Thames in a Boat.   Being Landed at Deal, we left it the next morning, and fpent fome time in viewing the country, which was pleafant enough, confidering the feafon of the year.[9]

Having heard this ftory, we went back to our fhip highly pleaf'd with the diverfion we met with in fpending fome of our loofe Coins at Deal, which is the ufual fate attending thofe that are ftaid there by contrary winds.

On the 20th November, in the afternoon, we weighed out of the Downs, and fteered away for the Beachy.   About one of the clock in the morning, the wind took us a-ftays with a guft, rain, thunder and Lightning; and now we were in great danger of Rocks, but with much difficultie we Anchored at Cowes in the Ifle of Wight; the night proving very tem-peftuous, with much Thunder and Lightning.

The next morning, myfelf and Palmer, and 3 or 4 other Paffengers, went afhore, and rambled into Weft Cowes; but the multitude of fhamelefs women there, had like to have made us miftake it either for Rome or Venice, rather than for any place in a Reformed Country.[10]

There is, my Dear, both Weft Cows and Eaft Cows in this

---

[9] We here omit a ftory told by a cafual acquaintance to Dunton.—ED.

[10] We omit Dunton's more particular account of the inhabitants.—ED.

this Ifland. It is Weft Cows that we were in, and the entertainment we met with in Weft Cows quite turn'd our ftomachs againft Eaft Cows, that we refolv'd againft going thither, and fo rambled to Newport, which was three miles from Weft Cowes, and the Principal Market Town in the whole Ifland: Being come thither, I went to fee Martha Lambert, my old Correfpondent there, who treated me with a generofity worthy of her felf; her Perfon was (not to fay deform'd) but very indifferent, but her Soul was Great and Noble; and the Internal Virtues and Endowments of her Mind, did more than compenfate for all that was wanting in her Perfon; Her difcourfe and Notions, were fo pure and cleare, and fo great and Uncommon, that they juftly exacted my Admiration; And when I had reflected both on them and her Perfon, it brought the following lines to my remembrance:

> They oft mif-judge, that by the Front Divine,
> The brighteft Bufhes better not the Wine,
> Nor does the Garment of a gilded Pill,
> Add Health unto the Patient that is ill:
> I love to know the in-fide of a Man,
> Let who will gaze o'th' fhadow of him there,
> For fometimes does a Doltifh afs appear
> In fhew a very Learn'd Philofopher;
> And where without but little has-been feen,
> The greateft Treafures have been found within.

While we were difcourfing with Mrs. Lambert, we underftood that there was in the Town a Famous Aftrologer, one that pretended to be Regifter of Heaven, and Privy Counfellor to all the Planets, that took upon him to underftand the ftars' Prophetick Language, and with his Jacob's ftaff to walk to Heaven, and dive into the fecrets of Futurity. My curiofity to difcourfe him, made me ramble to give him a vifit, which he accepted with civility, as hoping I was come to be his Cuftomer; and he would fain have been telling me the fuccefs of my voyage; but I excuf'd my felf from giving him that Trouble for this Reafon, That what
the

3

the Stars (according to his Notion) did forfhow, was either
Fate, or not; if it was Fate, it won't to be Reverf'd, and
therefore the fore-knowledge of it might anticipate an Evil
without Remedy; which brought a man into the worft
condition that was poffible; but if it was not Fate, and fo
might be reverfible, then there was nothing certain in his
Art, and his Prognoftications were but vain.   For fhou'd a
Woman that's with Child, defire to know whether the
Burden of her Pregnant womb be Male or Female, all that
this Starry Notary can tell her, is that the Stars prognofticate a Boy, but not fo certainly, but that it yet may chance
to be a Girl; how idle and ridiculous wou'd this appear, and
who wou'd credit fuch uncertain ftories?   This Star-Divine,
my Dear, was not aware that my Defign was to attack
his Art, and therefore did defire a longer time to anfwer me,
but my occafions not permitting any further ftay, I left him
to confult the Stars about it; and fhall only give you my
Obfervations on him, which is, That he is the worft part of
an Aftronomer, and a meer compafs of Figures, Characters,
and Cyphers, out of which he proves a Horary-Queftion not
fo profitably as doubtfully; He is Tenant by Cuftom to the
Planets, of whom he holds the Twelve Houfes by Leafe
Parole, paying the yearly Rent of his Study and Time; His
Life is meerly contemplative, for his practice is nothing
worth, or at leaft not worthy of credit; Ptolemy and Tycho
Brahe are his Patrons, whofe volumes he underftands not,
but admires; and the rather becaufe they are ftrangers, and
fo eafier to be believ'd than difprov'd: Yet I muft needs fay
his Life is upright, for he is always looking upwards; yet
dares believe nothing above Primum Mobile, for 'tis out of
the reach of his Jacob's Staff.   The reft of him you fhall
know when I return from New England; for what he will
be then, he himfelf knows not now.

Having taken my leave of the Star-Gazer, and given
my good Friend Mrs. Lambert a Thoufand Thanks for our

generous

generous Entertainment, we return'd back to our Ship, which is now ready to fail, as foon as the wind prefents; which according to the Obfervation of the Seamen will be before the Blooming Light buds from the blufhing Eaft.

Thus (my Dear) have I fent you the account of my firft embarking and the Hiftory of my fea voyage fo far as to Weft Cowes; In which I've inferted the manner of my leave-ing London, which you may think needleffe as 'tis what you were prefent att, but I fend it, fee ye, to remind ye endear-ments that paft then, and as 'tis neceffary to render the Hiftory of my Rambles perfect, which I defign to print, and therefore defire you'd keep all the Letters I fend either to you or my friends. To-morrow if a gale prefents we faile on for a new-world (for foe they call America): at my firft arrivall I'le fend an account of the wonders I meet on the Great *Herring-Pond* and a Particular Character of it. My Servant Palmer has been very ufefull to me and doe prefent his humble fervice to you. But hark! The Seamen are hoifing faile and I muft be gone. A long Adieu to your dear Selfe which with my dayly prayers for our meeting agen at the Black-Raven is all at prefent (for we are under-fail) from

Yrs Entirely

JOHN: DUNTON.

LETTER II.

TO MY ONLY BROTHER MR. LAKE DUNTON.

LATELY RETURN'D FROM SURAT IN THE EAST-INDIES.

From Boſton in New England.

ONEST Lake!—My laſt letter, (to my Deareſt Spouſe), relates the Rambling Fate that I was born to; (I ſay born to, for you know, Brother, we are of a Rambling Generation; which my Father's Rambling through a great part of England, and then croſſing St. George's Channel to the Hibernian Shore, and your great Travels to the furtheſt Eaſt, to meet the morning Sun in his own Aromatick Indies, ſufficiently evince, tho' I had never Rambled to America, nor waited on the Sun till he lies down in the ſoft Bed of Thetis:) And tells the Melancholy ſtory of my leaving England; with my own obſervations on what I met with in my Paſſage to the Iſle of Wight, for 'twas from thence you had the lateſt News of Philaret; till like a Duck that had been Diving in the Aqueous Element, I popt up my head again above Water in New England, after having been four months out of ſight—So that now, I am next in Order, (that I may obſerve a Method in Writing my Rambles), to ſend the Hiſtory of my Sea-Voyage: And to which of my Friends can I ſo properly direct this, as your ſelf? Your

long

long Eaſt-India-Voyage, making you both a Competent Judge, and a good Witneſs, of the Truth of what I here relate.

Bro, I know there be ſome that cenſure the Relations of all Travellers. It was a good proviſo of a learned man never to expeꜩ wonders, for in ſo doeing of the greateſt he will be ſure not to be believed but laughed at, which certainly betrays their Ignorance and want of diſcretion of fools and mad men. Then I ſhall take no care: this Letter is only deſigned for you, who perhaps have ſeen all I relate, or at leaſt have lern'd enough to believe that you can't diſprove. For you know, my Brother, from your own Experience, That they that go down to the Sea in Ships, and do Buſineſs in great Waters, that theſe ſee the Works of the Lord, and his Wonders in the Deep: So that on two Accounts you are Entituled to this Letter; the one, as I can mention no Wonders in the Sea that you're a ſtranger to; and the other as you deſired this Voyage of me; And 't's both pleaſant to me, and reaſonable alſo, not only to ſatiffie, but exceed the deſires of a Brother, who like you, by a thouſand good offices in my Abſence perſwade me (for I am not thinking of Truſtees) that the Bonds of our Friendſhip are ſtronger, as well as ſweeter, than thoſe of our Birth: And ſince I have mention'd Friendſhip, I muſt put you in mind, Brother, that an honeſt Boldneſs in Noting of Errors, is the Trueſt Teſtimony of a Faithful Friend: And therefore if the following account of my voyage be ſtuff'd with Wonders of my own Invention, and ſuch as never were in rerum natura, it is your duty to deteꜩ and find them out; And tho' your good Nature is as ready to forgive Faults, as your Wiſdom is able to diſcover 'em, yet let me beg of you, when you Anſwer this, to tell me my Errors, Miſtakes, and Omiſſions; not with the flattering Tongue of a Courtier, but with the honeſt ſeverity of a true Friend: and remember, tho' you are a Traveller (and a great one too) yet you have no
Authority

Authority to fubfcribe to the Lyes (if any fuch you meet with) even of your Elder Brother.—

To proceed then to the Hiftory of my Sea-Voyage; Having fet out from Weft Cows in the Ifle of Wight, with a fair Gale, and my dear brother, my Fair Spoufe's beft wifhes for my good voyage and fafe Return, I dreamt of nothing but of fporting Winds and Halcyon Weather; but alas! I quickly found my felf miftaken; and all my teeming hopes foon prov'd abortive; for in this Voyage, Brother, which kept us on the furface of the Angry Main four Months together, (which is two more than ufually Men make their Voyage thither in) you'll find the hardfhip of my whole life.

It was on Friday, the 29th of October, we began to fail from the Ifle of Wight, dreffing our felves with Aurora; Nay, before fhe had put on her Indian Gown; and Sol himfelf juft rofe from Thetis' Lap, did with his all-reviving Light and Heat accompany us: But what difguft we gave this glorious Luminary I know not; but fo it was, that in a little time he took occafion to with-draw himfelf behind a Cloud, and afterwards would hardly give us one kind Ray in our whole Voyage; nor was this all, for on the Sun's with-drawing, the face of Heaven was chang'd, and with a frowning and contracted Brow, fhew'd its Refentment in dreadful Storms of Thunder and of Lightning; and fo difconfolate it was at the Sun's abfence, that it fcarce kept from Weeping till we had reach'd America; infomuch that our whole voyage feem'd unto me but one continued ftorm—So that our Captain (who had for many years been Rambling on thofe Seas) told us he ne'er had feen the like before. This was but cold Encouragement, my Brother, you may imagine, to poor Trembling Philaret, who ne'er had feen fuch Waves as thofe before. Nor need you difbelieve me, if I tell you, I wifh'd my felf i' th' Arms of my dear Iris (for 'twas fafe Anchor there) as often as I view'd the Ocean, or

durft

durſt peep out of my Cabin, to order Palmer to aſſiſt me in my Spewing: For now the Sea began to work upon me; and the fighting of my Humors with Each other, ſoon made it evident the Harmony of Nature was quite out of Tune, which made as great a Tempeſt in my Microcoſm as on the boyling Gulf on which we floated. And had I not been comforted by ſome experienced Paſſengers, that I ſhould be the better for it afterwards, I ſhould have fear'd the Diſſolution of the Bodies League had been at hand. For I was ſo diſorder'd by it, that at every heave, it ſet me on the Borders of the other World, and made me ſenſibly to touch the Extremities of Life: So violent my ſickneſs was, that to undergo it long, requir'd a greater Remedy than Patience, and better helps than thoſe that Man afforded; which as I wanted, ſo I alſo found; for which I on my bended knees adore that Soveraign Hand by which I was ſupported: Ah! had my deareſt Iris ſeen me then, how much would ſhe have been afflicted, and how much have pitied me! and ſo I doubt not but your ſelf would have done alſo. But, my dear Brother, Tho' I cann't Say that I was well till I arriv'd at Boſton, yet I had between whiles thoſe lucid intervals, that gave me opportunity to look about me, and make my Obſervations of ſuch things as paſſ'd; or elſe I had been incapacitated to give you this Relation of my Voyage.

On the 2d of November (being Monday) at Ten in the morning, the Lizard was about five Leagues from us; The Lizard (ſo called by Mariners) is a high Promontory near the Lands End of Cornwal, edg'd and pointed like a Cone, or Pyramid. Near this place there was a great Ridge of Sand, which the Winds and Waters had laid there, which made the maſter Examine how the Tide ſtood affected, for that we ſhou'd need a Tide of Flood to carry us over it.[11]

On the 4th of Novemb. the furthermoſt part of Scilly
was

---

[11] We omit a long diſſertation on the Cauſe of Tides.—ED.

was 9 Leagues off N. W.   Here we faw great quantities of Sea-fowl flying, which feem'd ftrange to me fo far off of Land, tho' not quite out of fight of it.   But the Mariners told me, that was very ordinary, even when out of fight of Land; for that thefe Fowls live generally upon Fifhes, and indeed they wou'd be often-times popping at 'em: While we were thus obferving the Flying Fowles, one of the Seamen affirm'd that he had feen Flying Fifhes, and that they had wings like a Rere-Moufe, but of a filver-colour; and that under the Tropick of Capricorn they fly in fhoals like ftares. Nature has given this fifh Wings (as he affirm'd) for the prefervation of its Life, for being often purfued by the Beneto, Porpoife, and other ravenous Fifh, with the fame Eagernefs as the hungry Hound purfues the timorous Hare, it is oftentimes forced to fave it felf by flying.   It is obferved by the Mariners, That this fifh will rather chufe to fly into a Ship or Boat, if any be near, than be taken by its Enemies; tho' this only makes good the Proverb, Out of the Frying-Pan into the Fire.   If in your Voyage to Surat, you have happen'd to fee any of 'em, you can the better judge of the defcription I have given, and of the truth of what the Mariner affirm'd.   Brother, I have feen a Dial Piece of a Clock in the Collegiate Church of Glou-cefter, whereon was pourtray'd four Angels, each of them feeming to fay fomething to thofe that look'd up to obferve the hour of the day: This I remembred, being at Sea, and it put me upon Improving what I faw and heard in my Voyage; a Recital of which Improvements upon feveral occafions will fhew you how I fpent my time.   And even upon the Relation of this Flying Fifh, I could not but reflect upon the great folly that we often run our felves into, that to efcape an outward danger, which is but temporal, venture upon Sin, and thereby run the hazard of Eternal Ruine.

Novemb. 6.   We made the Ship to be in the Latitude

of

of 48 degrees 32 min. having a great Sea all Night; and the next Morning being out of fight of Land, the Ships Crew were all very jocund, and drank a Chearful Cup to our good Voyage, which brought to my remembrance the following Ode of the Immortal Cowley:

> Chear up, my Mates : the Wind does fairly blow ;
> Clap on more fail, and never fpare ;
> Farewel all Lands, for now we are
> In the wide Sea of Drink, and merrily we go.
> Blefs me 'tis hot ! another Bowl of Wine,
> And we fhall cut the Burning Line :
> Hey Boys ! fhe fcuds away, and by my head I know,
> We round the World are failing Now.

And now Brother, being come into the great and Wide Sea, give me leave to prefent you with a Particular Character, firft of the Sea, itfelf, and fecondly of our Leaky Ship; Thirdly, the Ship's Crew from the Mafter to the Cabin-Boy; Fourthly, What I faw and obferv'd during the whole voyage; and laftly an account of our Landing at Bofton in New England.[12]

Having thus given you fome brief Account of the Ocean, I am in the next place, Brother, according to the Method I before prefcrib'd to my felf, to give you fome account of our Leaky Ship: And fure the very Name of Leaky, wou'd be fufficient to frighten a Young Rambler from adventuring in it: Nor can I but efteem it as fome degree of Daring, (if not of valour,) to expofe my Life in a veffel where the Avenues to Ruine were left fo unguarded: If he that fails within the ftancheft fhip, is yet within the Verge of Death, and but four Inches diftant from it, how near muft he be to thofe difmal fhades, that lets the Enemy into his Bowels every moment, and does by every drop of Water fhe receives, make frefh Advances towards it. And yet, my Brother, this was our fad cafe; we had a fhip that Leak'd inceffantly, and tho' our Seamen ftoutly ply'd the Pump, fhe would be

letting

---

[12] We venture to omit the general defcription of the fea.—ED.

letting in the Enemy: And were it not that a peculiar Providence protected us, 'twas little lefs than Miracle we had not perifh'd in that great Abyfs.

But I have been too long within this Leaky Veffel; and therefore, Brother, will entertain you next with an account of our Ship's Crew: And Decency and Order leads me firft to tell you what our Captain was: His name was Thomas Jenner,[13] a gruff Tarpaulin, but never bred a Courtiour, nor fcarcely underftood Civility: And yet he had fome fmatterings of Divinity (as moft of the New England Captains have) and went not only conftantly to Prayers (which was a thing very Commendable) but alfo took upon him to Expound the Scriptures, which gave offence to feveral of the Paffengers, who thought he took upon him more than belong'd to his Employment. However, I believe he meant no hurt in't; for being brought up in New England, where for a man to be Religious is the Fafhion, he muft be either a fincere Profeffor, or a Hypocrite; 'Tis not my Bufinefs, Brother, to judge men for their Principles, I only wifh that we had found his Practice more correfpondent to 'em. Yet had not Covetoufnefs been his Idol, he had done well enough. The next in Order was his Mate, George Monk, who to fay truth was a good failor, and a good condition'd Fellow; or to give you his Character in Sea-terms, he is a pitch'd Piece of Reafon, calckt and tackl'ct, and only ftudied to difpute with Tempefts; and which is ftranger, he's part of his own Provifion, for he's always pickl'd in Salt Water: The next Man is the Boat-fwain, his Name Charles King, an Able Seaman, and as far from Fear, as Brokers are from Honefty; a Fore-Wind is the fubftance of his Creed, and frefh Water the Burden of his Prayers. He is naturally ambitious, for he is ever climbing: Time and he are every where, and always contending

---

[13] As Dunton afterwards vifited his houfe we referve mention of him till later.
—ED.

tending who fhall arrive firft. He is extream long-winded, for he tires the Day, and outruns Darknefs.—But enough of him. The Cook is the next Man, a Tawney-more Indian; a neceffary man in a fhip, efpecially if he chance to be ones Friend, which I found it was my Intereft to make him; and to that end, Employ'd my Servant Palmer, who had fo infinuated himfelf into his affection, that he could have procur'd anything from him; I have alfo this further to fay of him, That tho' he was a Tawney-more Indian, yet he was a Converted one, and in the main, a very honeft Fellow. The next was George Drinkewater, the Gunner, a Man fo pufillanimous, that he had rather creep into a fcabbard, than draw a Sword, the moft unfit man in the World for a Gunner, for fear had that afcendant over him, that he Cou'd fcarce endure the Noife of his own Guns; and like K. James the firft, the very fight of a naked Sword wou'd almoft caufe him to be—t himfelf: Yet was he wonderful exceptious and Cholerick, when he faw men were loth to give him an occafion: but then there was no better way to allay his anger than by quarelling with him; for how hot and violent foever he appear'd, he might be eafily threaten'd into a very pacifick Temper. The next Man was the Purfer, an old, dull, fleeping Fellow, and fo abandon'd to obftinacy and felf-will, that there was no perfwading of him; And if one had a mind to have him do a thing, the only way was to declaim againft it. As for the common Sailors, they were in generall Men that underftood their Bufinefs, and very Courteous to the Paffengers; But in the ftorm we met with, it was very difputable whether they or the Elements made moft noife, and which wou'd firft leave off fcolding. Nor muft the Cabbin-Boy be here forgotten, who was a very neceffary inftrument in the Ship, efpecially to fuch a one as I, who was fo very ill and indifpof'd, that I often wanted his affiftance, notwithftanding all the Help that I receiv'd from Palmer: When I have feen the poor willing Boy beaten
                                                                    and

and abuf'd by every one, even the Common Seamen, without caufe; I have reflected on the Curfe of Ham, what an uncomfortable thing it was, to be thus the Servant of Servants. But for my own part, I always treated him with that Compaffion that I thought the Boys good Humour merited. And thus, my Brother, I have given you an account of our whole fhips Crew.

After we had got into the main Ocean, as I told you before, one of the firft things our Captain did, was to fettle the Ships Family, and divide us into our feveral Meffes: which Divifion was thus made; My Self, Captain Belcher, Mr. Bolt, Mr. Stephens, and Mr. Charles Marten, Junior, were all the Charge of being of the Captain's Mefs: Mr. John Allen the Printer, and Monmouth's Forlorn Hope were of the Second Mefs, and the Sailors and Seamen of (Hellin?).[14] We had always a ftated hour for Dinner-time; but fometimes when the cloth was laid, and Dinner on the Table, a boifterous Puff of Wind would give the Ship fo great a tofs, as would both over-turn the Table, and put us all into Confufion, converting our feveral Difhes into one, and making a meer Ollapodrida. This, Brother, has made me often to reflect on the Uncertainty of every fublunary thing, even the moft promifing, and that which moft appear'd to be within the compafs of our Power: And that which was the Natural refult of thofe Reflections was, To get an Intereft in, and place the Anchor of my Hope upon thofe things that are above the Power of Chance and Fortune; things that fhall be immutable and permanent, when the whole World fhall fhake, and be reduc'd again to its firft nothing.

And now, Brother, being about 50 Leagues off the Lizard, and in 86 Fathom Water, we began to fail by the Log, (a Phrafe you cann't but underftand, having been fo long at Sea)

---

[14] *Sic* in MS., but probably it fhould read, " of the third."

Sea) When on a fudden we were furpriz'd by the Sudden
Cry of a Sayl! a Sayl! This was occafion'd by one of the
Seamen having defcry'd to the S. W. a fhip which he took
for a Sally-Man; which being after confirm'd by the mate,
who by his Profpective-Glafs could make a more clear
difcovery, and bring the Ship nearer, tho' we all thought
fhe was too near already: Upon this, Orders were giving
for clearing the Gun-room, and making all things ready for
an Incounter; For to ufe our Boatfwain's Words (fince
made a Captain for his valour) we were refolv'd to fink by
her fide, rather than be taken captive. Nay, as much an
enemy to fighting as I am, began to grow valiant: For
flavery, methought, had fomething in it of I know not what
harfhnefs, which I could not brook; Fetters, tho' of Gold,
do not lofe their nature, they are Fetters ftill: Had the
fierce Bajazet's cage been made of Gold, as 'twas of Iron,
yet it was a Cage, and that was provocation enough to fuch
a haughty Spirit to beat out his Brains againft its Bars:
Thefe thoughts, my Brother, infpir'd me with New Courage,
and I was now grown fierce, and as forward for fighting
as the beft of 'em. But after all this forwardnefs to fight,
being come nearer to the Pyrate, our Captain thought fhe
was an Over-match for us, and that we could not deal with
her; and therefore the Ships company alter'd their Counfels,
let their Refolutions die, and refolv'd to run for it: Uncertain Counfels never produce better Succefs: And therefore
we fneak'd away under the Protection of a Mift; Which,
brought to my remembrance that of the Ingenious Marvel,
in a like cafe:

> Old Homer yet, did never introduce,
> To fave his Heros, Mifts of better Ufe:
> Worfhip the Sun, who dwell where he doth rife,
> This mift doth more deferve our Sacrifice.

By the Protection of this Mift, and fteering a contrary
courfe, we did not doubt but we had loft our Pyrate; but
the

the next morning by two a Clock we were fenfible of our being miftaken; and were awak'd out of our fleep by the Cry of Arife! Arife! The Sally-man's upon us! This Allarm fet every man to his Gun but poor Philaret, Who being loth to dye fo early in the morning, would not leave his Cabin, or come above Deck, till he had found his Ruffles: (a bad Excufe, you know, Brother, is better than none) or rather, 'till he had feen the iffue of the Sally-man's Adventure: Thus you fee the Valiant dare face their Danger, but Cowards wink when they fight. But after all this Noife about the Sally-man, it was but like the Devil's Sheering Hogs, according to the Proverb; A great Cry, and a little Wool; for this Suppofed Sally-Rover prov'd nothing elfe but a Virginia Merchant Man, as much affraid of us as we of them. And fo our Danger being thus blown over, Philaret appears above Deck, and was as valiant now, as any of 'em; wifhing almoft that this Virginia Ship had been a Sally-man, that fo he might have had an opportunity of fhewing them his Valour, for had they come to engage 'em, he wou'd—have ftill been looking for his Ruffles, I'm afraid. Well, Brother, whatever you may think it, I have given but too true a Character, of fome that make a greater figure in the World than Philaret.[16]

After a fortnight's being out at Sea, we cou'd not find one of our Sailors, whom we call'd Father Shepherd: So that it was fuppof'd by the Ship's Crew, that going to unburden Nature, a boifterous Wave took him from off the fhip, and Wafted him into Eternity.

Had

[16] In his "Life and Errors" Dunton gives a little more dramatic verfion. "Upon this fecond alarm, every man was fet to his gun in an inftant, but as for myfelf, I kept out of fight as well as I could, till I heard them afking, 'Where is Mr. Dunton, that was fo valiant overnight?' This, I confefs, put me in a cold fweat, and I cried, 'Coming! Coming! I am only feeking my ruffles;' a bad excufe is better than none. I made my appearance at laft, but looked nine ways at once; for I was afraid Death might come in amongft the boards, or nobody knew where. This is the only inftance I can give, when my courage failed me."—ED.

Had Father Shepherd not ftole out of the World fo unfufpectedly, but made his Exit in his Cabin, he had had that Formality of Burial, which his precipitated Death depriv'd him of: For we had then ty'd a Bullet to his Neck, and another to his Legs, and fo turn'd him out at a Port-hole, firing a great Gun after him; which is, you know, the manner of our Burials at Sea. However he made his own grave as all dead bodyes do, buryed not in duft but water, which fhall one day as well as the earth give up its dead. Rev. 20 : 13.

On the next Day, in the Captain's Cabin, we had hot debates about a Flame, which fometimes fettles upon the main maft of a Ship (for we began to reckon all our Dangers.) I fuppofe, Brother, your felf has feen of 'em in your Eaft-India-Voyage). It is about the bignefs of a good large Candle, and was call'd by the Seamen St. Ellines Fire; it ufually comes before a ftorm, and is commonly thought to be a Spirit; and here's the conjuration of it, that tho' one is look'd upon as an ill Omen, yet if two appear, they are faid to Prognofticate Safety. Thefe are known to the Learned by the Names of Caftor and Pollux: to the Italians, by St. Nicholas and St. Hermes, and are by the Spaniards called Corpus Santos.

Being by the help of Palmer got out of my Cabin, and crawl'd up upon the Deck, I found the weather very thick and hazy, infomuch that we could fcarce fee the Ship's length before us; upon which one of the Paffengers afk'd the Mafter whether he was fure that they went right; To which the Mafter anfwer'd, That 'twas not by the Weather, but the Compafs that they fayl'd: This occafion'd a Difcourfe about the finding out of the Loadftone, with its ufe and vertues. * * * * * * * * * * * *
* * * * * * * * * * * * * *

That night, my Brother, and the next day, the Wind blew directly againft us; but we kept on our Courfe notwithftanding

ing; and this contrary wind ferv'd only as a foyl to make our Captain's Skill and Conduct appear the more confpicuous·: For to give him his due, he knew how to make all winds ferviceable to him in his Voyage; and turn every gale that blew to his advantage: I confefs I have many times wonder'd to fee two fhips failing in a direct Countermotion by one and the fame Wind: But this is one of the Evidences of a fkilful Sayler.

The weather being a little clear, feveral Fifhes were feen playing above-water, not far from our Ship, which made me do my utmoft with the affiftance of Palmer and another of the Paffengers, to get above deck again; and indeed I did not lofe my labour, for I faw a vaft number of Fifhes called Sea-hogs, or Porpoifes. They were headed much like a Hog, and tooth'd and tufk'd much like a Boar; Thefe Sea-hogs take fuch delight in one anothers Company, that they fwim together in great Numbers, exceeding the largeft herd of Swine I ever faw by Land, for thofe by Land are far inferior for multitude, to thofe that are in the Seas. [And as the Porpoifes ufually appear at Sea in very great Sholes or companyes]—Thefe Porpoifes, or Hog-fifh, are very fwift in their motion (as if they came of the race of the Gadaren fwine that ran violently into the fea)—and are like a company marching in rank and file; they leap or mount very nimbly over the waves and fo down and up again, makeing a melancholy noyfe when they are above the water: when they appear they are certain prefagers of foul weather. There is one thing very remarkable about this Fifh, and that is, That if one of them happen to be wounded, either by fhott or Harping Iron; the whole Herd purfue him with the greateft fury and violence that may be, feeming to contend who fhou'd fall upon him firft, and have their Teeth deepeft in his Carcafe.

* * * * * * * * * * * * * *
* * * * * * * * * * * * * *

My

My conftant indifpofition would not fuffer me to ftay long upon the Deck at a time, and therefore having view'd thofe Sea-Hogs, I was forc'd to retire again into my Cabin: but Palmer afterwards brought me word that they had feen a Fifh called Shark, a very dangerous and ravenous Fifh, as the Mariners told me, of whom they are more afraid than of all the Fifhes in the Sea befide; for if he chance to meet with any of them in the Water, he feldom fuffers them to Efcape without the lofs of a Limb at leaft and many times devours the Whole Body; fo great a Lover is this Fifh of Humane Flefh; infomuch that fome have obferv'd that they have endeavour'd to clamber up the fides of the Ship, out of a greedy defire of Preying on the Sailors: This Fifh, it feems, is of a very great Bulk, with a double or treble fet of Teeth, as fharp as Needles: But Nature has fo order'd it, that as an allay to his Devouring Nature, he is forc'd to turn himfelf upon his Back, before he can take his prey, by which means many efcape him which elfe would fall into his Clutches. It is, my Brother, from the Devouring Nature of this Fifh, that we call thofe Men Sharks, who having nothing of their own, make it their bufinefs to live upon other Men, and devour their Subftance.

My Sicknefs had now render'd me fo weak, that I was altogether unable to help my felf, and therefore for feveral Days together was forc'd to be taken out of my Bed by Palmer, and laid upon the Bench like a Child, while he made my Bed.

My Deareft Love, out of her Tender Affection to me, the better to regale me in my Voyage, had laid out about £8 in Sweet-meats, Preferv'd Damorins, Cherry-Brandy, and the like Knick-knacks; but it fo fell out I was not much the better for them, for being fo long fick, my Man Palmer was afraid they wou'd turn Sour, and fo be fpoil'd, which he took a good courfe to prevent, for finding of 'em toothfome, he fed on 'em like common food, and eat 'em all up before I

got

got well; So that, when I wou'd have eat fome of 'em, I had
none to eat; I call'd Palmer to an account for it, but he
alledging he did it out of a good intent to prevent their
being fpoil'd, I eafily pardon'd him.   And the rather, becaufe
during my whole voyage he had a conftant care of me; and
would never leave my Cabin unlefs I bid him: So that as
Alexander the Great told one, that afk'd him how he could
fleep fo foundly in the midft of fo great danger, That Par-
menio watch'd, and when he watch'd not, he durft not fleep
fo foundly; I may in like manner fay of Palmer, while he
was watching by me, I thought my felf fecure: Nor was
it more than reafon, for there were Sharpers, (not to fay
Sharks) that had not Palmer watch'd, would have been
nibling at what I had.   But his care prevented 'em.

Being a little better, I got upon the Deck again, and the
weather being pretty clear, the mariners difcovered a Fifh
called the Sun-fifh, of a lovely bright and fhining colour,
whofe property it is in Calm weather to come out of the
Depths, and lie fleeping and bafking itfelf upon the Surface
of the Waters, by which means often-times the Mariners
have an opportunity of taking them.   This, my Brother,
made me refleét how dangerous a thing it is for any one to
fleep unguarded in the midft of Enemies, efpecially fo
induftrious and indefatigable an Enemy as the Scripture
reprefents the Great Enemy of our Souls to be, who goes
about continually like a roaring Lion, feeking whom he
may devour.

I had now, thro' the Divine Goodnefs, attain'd a Competent degree of Health again; my Stomach was return'd, and
I cou'd now eat like a Horfe; our ordinary Meals wou'd not
fuffice me, and therefore I was forc'd to Employ Palmer
(who for his own fake, as well as mine had uf'd the Art of
Wheedling with the Cook, and by that means had got into
his Favour) to get me now and then a Dumpling between
Meals; but being once difcover'd, as he was privately
                                                conveying

conveying the (as it were) ſtolen Morſel to my Cabin, where I always eat it, he was in danger of the Baſtinado, which I reſented very ill, becauſe the Captain's Meſs (of which I was a Member) had eat up all my part of Fowls, tho' they were near Ten dozen.

Being laid down upon the Bed one Day to repoſe my ſelf, Palmer comes down to me, and tells me, I had loſt the ſight of a very great and ſtrange Creature, which our Captain call'd an Alligator; this Creature is of a vaſt length and breadth, (ſome ſay many yards in length:) in colour he is of a dark brown, which makes him the more imperceptable when he lies as a Trapan in the Waters. He is of ſo vaſt a ſtrength that no Creature is able to make his Eſcape from him, if he gets but his Chaps faſtened in them; for he has three Tere of Teeth in his Chaps and ſo firmly ſealed and armed with Coat of Male, that you may as well ſhoot at a Rock, or ſtrike againſt Bars of Iron, as offer to wound him.

We were now, my Brother, got near the Bay of Biſcay; and ſure the mighty Noiſe by the Waters of that rowling Sea, might have ſufficiently fore-warn'd us of our Impending Danger: For, Brother, we were no ſooner come upon that Bay, But the whole Face of Heaven was muffled up in Clouds, and all the Winds let looſe upon the Sea, which cauſ'd ſo great a ſtorm, as that we met with all when in the Down, was nothing in Compariſon of this. That in the Downs was but a Tranſient Storm, and quickly over, tho' 'twas violent: But this was both more violent, and far more laſting, continuing ſeveral Days together: Upon its firſt approach, I got into my Cabin, and laid me down upon my Bed: where tho' I was ſoftly enough . lodged, yet won't I much at eaſe: At Land, you know, we rock our Children in a Cradle, the ſooner to lull 'em aſleep; but here it was quite contrary, for the more I was rock'd, the leſs I cou'd ſleep. *

After

After this Storm was over, (which every one expeƈted would have landed us in the Immenſe and boundleſs Regions of Eternity) our Maſter and the Mariners had time to look about 'em, and to examine in what Latitude they were ſailing; and this was the Account they gave us, that we were every way 500 Leagues from Land: And really Brother, I cannot but acknowledge, that in all the occurrences of this Long Voyage, there was nothing appear'd to me with a more formidable Aſpeƈt, than to be ſailing thus upon the Ocean, at ſuch a mighty diſtance from the Land: Bleſs me! cry'd I; ſtill fifteen hundred miles to ſail, before we come to Land! And in a Leaky veſſel too! How ſhall we ever weather out this voyage? And that which made it (unto me at leaſt) appear more diſmal was, That we weren't only ſailing in a Trackleſs Path, but in an unfrequented Wat'ry Deſart: For cou'd we but have ſeen a ſail, (which we ſcarce did for three Weeks time together,) it would have been a Cordial to us, tho' ſailing a Contrary courſe to ours; but to have no other proſpeƈt, which way ſo e'er we look'd about us, but Seas and Skies, and Skies and Seas, was I thought very diſmal; eſpecially when that Expanded Canopy of Heaven was muffled up in Darkneſs and thick clouds all Day,

> ——and every Night,
> Its Twinkling Tapers kept out of our ſight.

Theſe difficulties, Brother, were enough to ſtagger a more reſolved Rambler, than poor Philaret, And when I have confider'd the ſeveral circumſtances of all the Paſſengers, I found my Caſe was ·worſe than any of them: The Maſter and the Mariners were about their buſineſs and going to their ſeveral Relations: Mr. Allen the Printer was going to his Uncle, who had invited him over, and from whom he expeƈted Preferment: And Monmouth's forlorn Hope had all their hopes of Safety in their Flight, and by this Voyage
                                                                had

had efcap'd their Hands who wou'd have fhew'd no Mercy:
But for my felf, the cafe was vaftly different, for every League
we fail'd, I ftill went farther from the Centre of my Happinefs, and left a Thoufand Joys behind me, in the Perfon of
my Charming Iris.   How wou'd one fight of her upon this
Wat'ry Wildernefs, have fupported me, and made me fearlefs
pafs Ten thoufand Dangers: The very thoughts of Iris,
even in this difmal profpect of Affairs, was fight of Land,
and Fire, and every thing: Like Manna, ftill it anfwer'd all
my wants: I know to whom it is I write; even to you, my
Brother, who fo well know my Iris, that you are fenfible fhe
lofes ftill by all that I can fay: for Praife can come no nearer
to her Worth, than can a Painter with his Mimick Sun,
exprefs the Beauty of Hyperion.   Think then, my Brother,
at this Vaft Diftance from her, Encompaff'd with a World
of Water on each fide, what comfort I cou'd take: It made
me even hate the Sea, for wafting me fo far from my dear
Iris: I could have almoft been of his Opinion, abating only
for the Profanity of it, who thus gave way to his Unbridled
Paffion:

> Noah be Damn'd, and all his Race accurf'd,　·
> That in Sea-brine did Pickle Timber firft:
> What tho' he planted Vines, he Pines cut down;
> He taught us how to Drink, and how to Drown:
> He firft built Ships, and in his Wooden Wall,
> Saving but Eight, e'er fince, Endanger'd All.

But whither has the thoughts of Iris carry'd me? It is
indeed a fubject that I could dwell upon for ever.   But
I muft leave her, and attend my Voyage. Only I muft
acquaint you, That whilft I thus lay mufing in my Cabin,
one of the Seamen came, and told me that they had had a
Dolphin fwiming a pretty while by the Ship fide, as if it did
intend to vye with them in failing: I made what hafte I
cou'd upon the Deck, but came too late to fee it, for the
fociable Fifh had now withdrawn himfelf: But the account

I

I had of it from them that faw it, was, This Fifh takes great
Delight in failing along by those Ships that pafs through the
Seas ; and one of the mariners affirm'd that in fome voyages
he had feen feveral of them accompanying their fhip, for a
long time together; fome fwimming a head, and fome a
ftern, fome on the Starboard, and others on the Larboard
fide, like fo many Sea-Pages attending them, feeming to tell
us we were welcome into their Territories; or as if they were
refolved to be our fafe-conduct thorow 'em.   But this is not
fo much, I think, for the love they bear unto man, (as fome
write,) as to feed themfelves with what they find caft over-
board, whence it comes to pafs, that many times they feed
us, for when they fwim clofe to our fhips we often ftrike
them with a broad inftrument, full of barbs, called an
Harping-iron.   The Dolphin may be a fit emblem of an ill
race of people who under fweet countenances carry fharp
tongues.   As to their being generally reprefented as a
Crooked Fifh, I enquir'd about it, and am inform'd it is only
a vulgar errour of the Painters, for 'tis a ftraight a Fifh as
any fwims the Ocean : If I am in an Errour, Brother, I hope
you'll rectifie me, for I am fure you muft have feen of 'em
in your Voyage to Suratt: Dubartas records of this Fifh,
that he's a great Delighter in Mufick : on which he has
thefe Verfes :

> Among the Fifhes that did fwiftly throng
> To dance the meafures of his Mournful Song,
> There was a Dolphin that did beft afford
> His Nimble Motions to the Trembling Chord :

But whether that in the Story of Arion be true I cannot
fay :—However, very remarkable is the Story related by
Pliny, of a Boy feeding a Dolphin, and carried on his back
over the Waters to School : They did fwim fometimes fide
by fide, and at laft, grew fo familiar, that fometimes the Boy
would get upon the Dolphin's Back, and ride in Triumph
through Neptunes Wat'ry Kingdom, as upon fome proud
Prancing

Prancing Horfe: At laft, it fo unhappily fell out, that the Boy carelefs how he fat upon the Fifhes Back, was by his Sharp and brifly Fins wounded to Death; which the commiferating Dolphin ftraight perceiving fwam to the Land, and there laid down his wounded Burden, and for very forrow Died. In memory whereof, a Poet writes,

> The Fifh would Live, but that the Boy muft Dye,
>   The Dying Boy, the Living Fifh Torments :
> The Fifh tormented hath no time to cry,
>   But with his Grief, his Life he fadly vents.

The Storm, my Brother, which we fo lately were deliver'd from, and which had given us fo much Terrour, and Affrightment, had by its rapid motion brought us near the Banks of New-found Land: but why 'tis call'd The Banks of New-found Land, I underftand not, for there was nothing to be feen but a vaft world of Water: However, being got thither it let us into a New World of Wonders, and Every Day made frefh Difcoveries of various forts of Fifhes, which we before were utter ftrangers to: And to make this good, we had not fail'd a day upon thofe Seas, but the Mariners difcover'd two Fifhes of a different fort and fize, which they inform'd us were the Sword-fifh and the Threfher: and told us they believ'd the Whale was not far off; and when I afk'd what reafon they had to fuppofe fo, they told me, That thofe two Fifhes were always at a Truce between themfelves, but always at open Wars with the Leviathan: And that nothing was more pleafant, than to fee the combat between the Three, i. e. The Sword-fifh and the Threfher upon one fide, and the Whale on the other. For this Sword-fifh is fo well weapon'd, and arm'd for an Incounter with its mighty Enemy, that he has upon his Head a Fifh-Bone, that's both as long and as like to a two-edged fword, as any two things can refemble one another, fave only that there are a great many fharp fpikes on either edge of it: Nature has it feems inftructed this Fifh what ufe to make of it; for being thus

arm'd

arm'd, the property of this Fifh is to get underneath the Whale, and with his Two-edg'd Sword to rake and riple him all over's Belly, which caufes him to roar and bellow at fuch a prodigious rate, as if a Thoufand Darts were fticking in his heart, and then the Threfher, (when by the bellowing of the Whale he underftands the Sword-fifh is affaulting him below) ftraight get a top of him and there plays his part, affaulting him with fuch thick and maffy blows, as may be plainly heard at two or three miles diftance; and this rage and fury is fo great againft the Whale, that one wou'd think they'd cut and thrafh him all to pieces. * * * * *

The fight of thefe two Ffhes, and the relation that the Seamen gave us of 'em, gave me the curiofity to afk 'em, If any of 'em had e'er feen a Mermaid or a Merman; and one of the moft ancient of 'em told me, That he had formerly been uf'd to Sail to the Eaft Indies, and in thofe Voyages he had feen them frequently (and therefore Brother you muft needs have feen 'em in your Voyage to Surat) but that they never car'd for fuch a fight, for that they were the certain Fore-boders of a Storm, and that they always look'd on their appearance as Ominous and Unfortunate. They may perhaps forefhew, but I don't think 'tis their power to raife a Storm; they may perhaps Know when a Storm is near, by certain secret Sympathies of Nature; and 'tis like thofe fort of Creatures which love to fifh in troubled Waters: They are, however, very beautiful Creatures it feems; their upper parts bearing a perfect Symmetry to thofe of a Young Virgin, but their lower parts are purely Fifh: The Poets feign there were but three of them, whom they call'd Syrens: And the Neitherland Hiftory tells us of a Meermaid that was taken there, that was both Taught to fpin, and perform feveral other petty offices of Women. And fince I have been naming Hiftory, pray give me leave to tell you, Brother, (for tho' you have been a far greater Traveller, yet I don't think you ever read fo much as Philaret) That in the year 1576,

there

there was taken in Norway a certain Fish refembling a
Mitred Bishop. Cou'd fuch a Fish but now be found, 'twou'd
be a Natural and Living Argument for Epifcopacy.

But now, my Brother, I am Entring on a New Scene of
Sorrows; For being in the Latitude of .   .   .   I fcarce
cou'd forbear thinking our Captain had miftook his Compafs,
and brought Us to the Frozen Zone; for even there, it
hardly cou'd be colder: For the very   .   . were bound
with Icy fetters, and the   .   .   Frofts had chain'd up all
the Deep: Our very breath was prefently congeal'd and
attom'd mifts turn'd inftantly to Hail. 'Twas colder here
than in the middle of January in England; even when it
happens to be moft fevere: Not that great bitter Froft in
London, Brother, which happen'd in the year 1683-4, and
which made the Thames as common and as much beaten a
Road for Coaches to drive on, as it had been before ufual for
Boats to row in; that had I know not how many thoufand
People ftill going and returning on the Thames, and fo
many hundred Booths built thereon, felling all forts of goods,
as defervedly gave it the Name of Blanket-Fair: I fay this
mighty and unprefidented Froft was but a Flea-biting to
what we met with on the Banks of New-found-Land. You
are not able to imagine, Brother, how much I was furpriz'd
one morning (and I believe you wou'd have been the fame)
to fee two mighty chriftal Mountains of congealed Water
incorporated as it were, into the Stern and Poop of our Ship,
which was judged by the Captain to be about feven Tun of
Ice, and fo continued feveral Nights together; fo that had
not the Warm Southern Winds, and the hot Sun by Day,
reduc'd thofe Chriftal Mountains into their firft original, as
often as they froze by Night, this had alone perform'd, what
Winds, and Storms, and Raging Billows, hard rocks and
angry fkies, had hitherto in vain attempted: This made me,
Brother, to reflect, That when our Danger grew to fuch a
height, it feem'd impoffible to be prevented, Then interpofing
Mercy

6

Mercy ftept between and brought us off : So that I cou'd not bear crying out with the Royal Pfalmift, O that men wou'd praife the Lord for his Goodnefs, and for his Wonderful Works to the Children of Men !

I told you, Brother, in the Day time, we were reliev'd from thofe vaft Piles of Ice that like 4 Remora cleav'd to our Ship, by the Salubrious Southern Briezes, and the Suns hot Beams ; This Kindnefs of the Sun thus to affift us in our greateft need, who had fo long abfconded and kept out of fight before, did fo affect us, that we went all upon the Deck to make a Vifit to him ; where whilft we all were walking up and down, it was my hap to fix my Eye on fomething I knew not what, which unto me feem'd like a moving Rock ; and fhewing of it to a Seaman, we foon difcover'd it to be one of thofe floating Mountains of the Sea, the Whale : As we came nearer him, I faw his very Breath put all the Water round in fuch a ferment, as made the very fea boyl like a Pot.   I do confefs I had a very great defire to take a more particular view of him, becaufe GOD gives him fuch an Elaborate and accurate Defcription in the 41ft of Job : And this I particularly obferv'd, That the Sun fhining upon him, caft a very orient Reflection upon the Water ; which is alfo confirm'd by the Defcription given of him, Job 41 : 32.   He maketh a path to fhine after him, one wou'd think the Deep to be hoary : Another thing I obferv'd was, That there was fo great a fmoak where he was, that it feem'd to me as if there had been a Town full of Smoaking Chimneys in the midft of the Sea.   I do confefs I never faw fo large and formidable Creature in my Life.   He appear'd to me as big as either of the Holmes's, two little Iflands that lie at the mouth of the Severn, near Briftol in England.   It was im-poffible for me to take the True Dimenfions of him : His Eyes are as large as two great Pewter-Difhes, and there's room enough in his Mouth for many People to fit round in, as thofe that have been at the Taking of them affirm.   His

teeth

teeth are terrible, and his Tongue is above two yards in breadth, and in length exceeds the talleſt man on Earth, out of which they extract above a Hogshead of Oyl. Ex pede Hercules. I have been told that the Whale is of ſuch incredible ſtrength, that in Greenland (where moſt of them are taken) when they come once to dart an Harping-iron into 'em, they rage and rend at ſo extravagant a rate, that if there were an hundred Shallops near him, he'd make 'em fly into a thouſand ſhivers, and ſend 'em up into the Skies. When the victory is got over 'em, and the mighty victim lies at their Conquering Feet, they fearleſs then ſurvey his huge and maſſy Body, and tell all his goodly Fins, which like ſo many Oars in a great Gally do ſerve to row his Carcaſe through the Seas at his own pleaſure : and they are reckoned by the moſt curious Anatomiſts of him to be above three hundred, and by theſe he can go, if he pleaſes, with that ſwiftneſs and violence, as Arrows ſcarce fly ſwifter from a Bow, nor Bullet from a piece of Ordnance. The Seamen tell me, That in ſmooth Water and calm weather, they are often ſeen ſporting of themſelves, and ſhewing their great and maſſy Bodies upon the Surface of the Waters, eaſily diſcernible by Ships that ſail hard by 'em in the Seas, one while riſing up, and in a little time fall down again and diſappear. Some whales in calm weather often ariſe and ſhew themſelves on the top of the water, where they appear like unto great Rocks, in their riſe, ſpouting up into the Ayr with noyſe, a great quantity of water which falls down again about them like a ſhowr. The Whale may well challenge the Principalitie of the Sea, yet I ſuppoſe that he hath many enemies in this his large Dominion ; for inſtance, a little long Fiſh called a Threſher often encounters with him, who by his agilitie vexeth him as much in the Sea, as a little Bee in Summer, doth a great Beaſt on the ſhore. Munſter writeth, That near unto Ireland, there be great Whales whoſe bigneſs equalizeth the Hills and mighty Mountains;
and

and thefe, faith he, will drown and overthrow the greateft fhips, except they be afrighted with the found of Drums and Trumpets.

Pliny writes of a little Fifh called Mufculus, which is a great Friend to the Whale; for the Whale being big, wou'd many times endanger her felf between Rocks and narrow ftraits, were it not for this little Fifh which fwimmeth as a Guide before her.   Whereupon Dubartus defcants thus:

> A little Fifh, that fwimming ftill before,
> Directs him fafe, from Rock, from Shelf, from Shore:
> Much like a Child, that living Leads about
> His Aged Father when his eyes are out:
> Still wafting him through every way fo right,
> That reft of Eyes, he feems not reft of fight.

Which office of that little Fifh, may ferve as a fit Emblem to teach Great Ones that they ought not to contemn their Inferiours: There may come a time when the meaneft Perfon may do a Man fome good; and therefore there is no time wherein we ought to fcorn fuch a one.   To conclude, my Brother, and fum up all I have to fay of him in one word, That what the Spirit of God fays of Behemoth, I may fay of the Leviathan, as to the Sea at leaft, He is the Chief of the Ways of God.

And now, Brother, we had another fcene of Mifery Entering in upon us; which feem'd more formidable, and concern'd us nearer than all the reft: For as the Poet has it,

> Nor is this all; for lo, our Troubles find,
> No calm nor Truce, as if they had combin'd,
> Like th' Ocean's reftlefs Billows, when they fmother
> Themfelves, one riding on the Neck of th' other.

The cafe, Brother, was this, our Voyage being much longer, and our Paffengers more, than our Captain expected, our Provifion began to fall fhort, and we were brought to an Allowance even to a pint of Water a Day, and our Bread

in

in proportion: and tho' this Frugality was fo neceffary, that
without it we had all been ftarv'd, it was yet worft in my
cafe, becaufe being newly recover'd from my Sea-ficknefs, I
had the ftomach of a Horfe; and to have my ftomach in-
creaf'd, and an Embargo laid on our Provifion, was extreamly hard upon me: And I never found anything more difficult
than to ftop the Importunate Cravings of that grand Incen-
diary of all my Bowels, Colon: And I am fure I had been
quite choak'd for Liquor, had not the Generous HERRICK
(whofe fingular Friendfhip to me for the whole Voyage,
and particularly in this Extremity, I fhall never forget,)
given me a Bottle of Water, out of his own Allowance,
which ferv'd me for three days, (by melting it gradually over
the Candle, as we did almoft all we drank) after my own
was gone; for 'twas fo long before hand that I out-drank
my Allowance, which was ftill given for a week, and I drank
it in three days. This Gentleman giving this Bottle in my
great Extremity, made me then think of what I had read of
one of the Eastern Princes, who in a like Extremity cry'd
out, A Kingdom for a Drop of Water! Many purfue the
World, as if a great deal on't cou'd make 'em happy: But,
alas! 'Tis no further valuable, but as it fuits our Neceffities
of Body and Mind, or anfwers our Prefent Occafions: Our
Englifh Richard the Third, being feiz'd with an immoderate
defire of Poffeffing the Kingdom fwam to it through a Sea
of Innocent Blood, and yet at what eafie value would he
have parted from this Dear-bought Purchafe, at Bofwel
Field, when he cry'd out, A Kingdom for a Horfe! Tho'
inftead of obtaining that, he loft his Kingdom, and his Life
to boot.

About this time we difcover'd another Sea-Wonder, to wit,
a Fifh called a Calamorie; which fome call the Ink-horn-
Fifh, becaufe he hath a black Skin like Ink, which Serveth
him inftead of Blood: When they are like to be taken, they
then caft their Ink into the Water, and fo by colouring it,
they

they obſcure and darken it, and the Water being darken'd, they eſcape.

> For through the Clouds of this dark Inky Night,
> They dazling paſs the greedy Fiſhers Sight.

But we had not yet encounter'd with all our Enemies, and almoſt every thing we had to do with, prov'd ſo: You will eaſily grant, Brother, that Winds and Storms, and Tempeſts may paſs for ſuch; but will not perhaps agree, that a Calm cou'd be an Enemy, at leaſt not a formidable one: For, Brother, we had about this time for ſeveral Days together ſo great a Calm, that not one breath of Air was ſtirring: 'Tis true, the Sea was far from ſtill, although there was no Wind, but ſtill kept rowling up and down, and rock't our Ship as if 't had been a Cradle; but without making the leaſt way at all; ſo that in Six Days time, we had not ſail'd a League: This was to me, the moſt uncomfortable thing that cou'd be, Brother; and I believe you muſt conclude it reaſonable that it ſhou'd be ſo; For if you but conſider, that now, notwith-ſtanding all our good Huſbandry, in the prudent Manage-ment of our Proviſions, we were reduc'd to that low Ebb, we had but juſt Enough to ſerve a Fortnight, and that we were ſtill out of ſight of Land: and knew not when a gale of Wind wou'd riſe to carry us out of that Standing Lake, wherein our Ship ſeem'd to be fix'd for ever; you will not wonder that it made our hearts ake.

During the time that we were lolling and rowling thus upon the reſtleſs Ocean, our Mariners diſcover'd that ad-mirable Wonder of the Torpedo, or Cramfiſh, a Fiſh much better to behold than handle, for it has this prodigious, yet clandeſtine quality, that if it be but touch'd or handled, the perſon touching it is preſently benummed, as a Hand or Leg, that is Dead, and without feeling: In which condition they ſometimes continue for two or three Days together; and with difficulty obtaining the uſe of their Limbs again.

But

But that which brought us the firſt Dawning of Hope, with reſpect to the Diſcovery of Land, was the Diſcovery which one of the Seamen made, of three or four great Fiſhes, which he call'd Sea-Horſes; and not without reaſon, for their fore-parts were the perfect figure of a Horſe, but their hinder parts perfect Fiſh; when the reſt of the Sea-men ſaw theſe Creatures, they all rejoyc'd, and ſaid we were not far from Land; the reaſon of which was, That theſe Sea-Horſes were Creatures that took a great delight in ſleeping on the Shore, and therefore were never ſeen but near the Shore: This was but a collateral Comfort, for tho' theſe Sea-Horſes delight in Sleeping on the Shore, yet they might ſwim two or three hundred Leagues into the Sea for all that: But we that look'd upon our ſelves in a periſhing Condition, were willing to lay hold on any little Twigg of Hope, to keep our Spirits up. One of the Seamen that had formerly made a Greenland Voyage for Whale-Fiſhing, told us that in that Country he had ſeen very great Troops of thoſe Sea-Horſes ranging upon Land, ſometimes three or four hundred in a Troop: Their great deſire, he ſays, is to rooſt themſelves on Land in the Warm Sun; and Whilſt they ſleep, they appoint one to ſtand Centinel, and watch a certain time; and when that time's expir'd, another takes his place of Watching, and the firſt Centinel goes to ſleep, &c. obſerving the ſtrict Diſcipline, as a Body of Well-regulated Troops. And if it happen that at any time an Enemy approach, the Centinel will neigh, and beat, and kick, and ſtrike upon their Bodies, and never leave till he has wak'd 'em; and then they run together into the Seas for ſhelter. But for all this Caution, the Sailors are, it ſeems too cunning for them; and get between them and the Sea, and beat out the Brains of the firſt that comes to hand; and ſo have done, till they have kill'd ſo long, that they have wanted ſtrength to kill another; and that which moves the Seamen to this cruelty, is, becauſe their Teeth are of great worth

and

and value, and are a very vendible Commodity in the Southern parts of the World. And fince it is the Shore on which thefe Creatures meet with this Deftruction; and that if they had kept at Sea, they had been fafe: I cou'd not but reflect, That thofe who leave their fettled ftations, whether out of Principles of Profit or of Pleafure, and will be trying New Experiments, and putting of New Projects on the Tenters, do often times make very poor Returns; and are convinc'd it had been better for 'em to have kept that ftation which Providence at firft had put 'em in.

Whilft thus, my Brother, we were lying between Hope and Defpair, and Fearful Famine ftar'd in the face, we were upon a fudden, encompaff'd round with a whole world of Fifh; the vafteft fhoals of Codfifh were fwiming round about us, that I ever yet beheld: The Seamens hunger, and the ftraightnefs of our Provifions, fet them foon a work to catch 'em: which they foon did in that abundance, that prov'd a very feafonable mercy to us. Thus we cou'd ftill experience, JEHOVAH JIREH, in the Mount of the Lord, i. e. in the Time of greateft Extremity, Deliverance fhall appear.

The next day after our Codfifhing was over, and they were all gone out of fight, I know not whither, we difcover'd a Fifh call'd the Sea-calf, whofe Head and Hair's exactly like a Calf's: This Creature's an amphibious Animal, living fome-times at Sea, and fometimes on Land: I am told there are feveral of this kind of Creatures in the Iflands about Scot-land, (but more of that in my Rambles thither,) and that at night they will come on Shore to fleep and reft themfelves; and early in the morning return to Sea, not daring to ftay on Land, for fear of furprifals. This Fifh was a further Inducement to our Sea-men to believe that we were upon the Coaft of America, and very neer Land: And thefe diftant Hopes we Emprov'd for our fupport the beft we cou'd.

But that which gave us greateft ground of hope, was,

That

That we had now a fine freſh gale of Wind that blew directly for us. And the next Morning we thought, at leaſt, that we diſcover'd Land. And tho' we yet were but in a ſuſpence about it, we wou'd not let go thoſe ſmall hopes we had for the whole Spaniſh Plate fleet. A fight of Land had been a great rarity with us a long time: It was a Novelty of Providence; and really it wonderfully refreſh'd our Spirits, repaired our decayed ſtrength, and recruited Nature; at leaſt poor Exhauſted Nature was willing to be cheated, and fancy her ſelf recruited. But there was no Cheat in 't: We were really refreſh'd: for about noon, we Diſcover'd, or at leaſt thought we diſcover'd Land: 'Tis impoſſible, my Brother, to expreſs the Joy and Triumph of our raiſed Souls at this Apprehenſion. The Poets tell us, That as often as Hercules threw the great Gyant againſt the Earth, his mother Earth gave him new ſtrength againſt the next encounter: It was new ſtrength, new Life to us, tho' not to Touch, yet to ſee; or if not to ſee to think we ſaw the Earth: It brought freſh Blood into our Veins, and a freſh Colour into our late Pale Checks: We looked not like Men preſerv'd in Tempeſts, under want of Bread and Water: But like Perſons raiſ'd from the Dead, in all the ſtrength and vigour of our Youthful Bloom. Hope and Fear made a ſtrange medley Paſſion in our Souls. We had ſeen nothing but Air and Sea, and Sea and Air, in almoſt four months time: That though our Reaſon and Experience too, had fully certify'd us, that there was ſuch a thing as Land, yet the Impreſſions Fear had made upon us, made it extreamly queſtionable whether ever we ſhou'd ſee it. Yet Hope, by much the kindeſt of the Two, did us this Favour, to put us on a ſtricter Scrutiny whether we were deceiv'd or no: And ſince it is Reward gives Wings to Vertue, we by a voluntary Contribution from each Paſſenger, made up a Purſe of Money, and then proclaim'd that it was the juſt Guerdon of their Induſtry, who firſt ſhould bring the happy Tydings of a True Diſcovery of Land: We ſcarce had

7 .

had fail'd an hour longer, before one cry'd out from the Top-
maft Head, Land! Land! A true Difcovery of Land! Our
Captain and the Mate did both run up the Cords with equal
Swiftnefs, and having ftaid fome time, came down and told
us, They cou'd fee plainly the New-England Coaft, and that
they doubted not but by God's grace, they fhou'd all lie in
Bofton to-morrow night: This was, methought, the moft
reviving News I ever heard, and was

> More Welcome, than to greedy Mifers, Wealth ;
> To Rebels, Pardon ; or to sick Men, Health :—For
> As when the Sun, after a ftormy Night,
> Difplays o'er Eaftern Hills the Morning Light,
> Nature revives, and fmiles, and thinks no more
> On the Black Tempeft of the Night before ;
> So the Defir'd approach of Land, now chears,
> Our Drooping Souls, and diffipates our Fears :
> Commands of every Paffenger, that he,
> Shou'd unto God, himfelf a Victim be :
> And offer up a Pyramid of Praife
> To Him whofe Wondrous Goodnefs crowns our Days.

Being now fatisfied that we were within fight of New-
England, we call'd the firft Difcoverer among us, and gave
him firft a double Portion of the Defign'd Gratuity : and
then Divided the reft among the Seamen, including him
again within that Number : So that all were very well pleaf'd.

> And now the Seamen got the Hatches under,
> And to the Ocean told their joys in Thunder.

This was to us the joyfulleft Day that we had feen in all
our voyage ; and every man might now fet up his Eben-Ezer,
and fay, That hitherto the LORD had been our Help. And
yet, methought this Day that I had long'd fo much to fee,
and wifh'd and pray'd fo often for; now 'twas arriv'd, brought
it's Alloy along with it. I cou'd not but reflect upon my
Deareft Iris ; and when I thought that Providence had now
Divided us into two Diftant Worlds ; and that thofe Rocks
and

and Shelves, thofe mighty Storms and Tempefts, thofe dreadful ficknesses, thofe fights of meagre Famine, and Pale Death that ftar'd us in the Face fo often, muft all be new Trod o'er again, before I cou'd behold my charming Iris! That very thought had almoft broke my heart: I'm fure it made me melancholy, (in fpite of all thofe weak Effects my Feeble Refolution cou'd fet up againft it) even on that general and publick Day of Joy. Altho' our Climate was extreamly chang'd, being in 42 Degrees of Northern Latitude, yet it had made no change in my Affection, but Love retain'd his Old Dominion ftill; and the fierce tranfports of my Love to the dear object of it, did rather ftill burn fiercer, than abate. Which made me cry,

> O cruel Love! how great a Power is thine!
> Under the Poles, altho' we lie,
> Thou mak'ft us Fry;
> And thou canft make us Freeze beneath the Line.

And now the Paffengers[16] cou'd all plainly difcern the Coaft upon the Lar-board fide; and every one was now Preparing for a Difembarkment the next Day, if Wind and Weather, (or to fpeak better, He who rules them) favour'd us. But for my own part, I was more taken up in viewing of the Miracles of Nature; who now came crowding in fo faft upon us, as if (as Once they did to Adam in the happy Garden) they wou'd a fecond time prefent themfelves, to receive Names according to their various Natures. * * * *
* * * * * * * * * * * * *

The Sun was now making a vifit to th' Antipodes, and all the feveral watches of this Night were run with much more Joy and Satisfaction than was ufual, fo acceptable was the fight of Land unto us: And this Night, becaufe I hop'd it
was

---

[16] The only one of Dunton's fellow-paffengers not mentioned by him, whom we can identify, is defcribed in the following item in the book of 'Warnings out of Town.' 'Feb. 22, 1685-6. Andrew Wood, cooper, came from England with Jenner, at widow Sedwicks; —has a wife and feveral children.'—ED.

was to be my laſt, I ſlept more ſweetly in my Cabin, than I had done for many Nights before. And yet, as ſoundly and contentedly as I had ſlept, the Sun it ſelf had ſcarce got up before me, ſo earneſtly did I deſire to take a view of the New England ſhore, which now appear'd as plain as cou'd be to us; And tho' it was a ſight ſo much deſir'd, it look'd to me with but a poor appearance: A mighty Wilderneſs of Trees it look'd like; and here and there a little ſpot of clearer Ground, that look'd like a Plantation; and ſuch the Mariners inform'd me that they were: Bleſs me! thought I, have I ſail'd from my Deareſt Iris, ſo many hundred Leagues, to viſit ſuch a Wilderneſs as this? And yet for all this ſtuff, I muſt ingenuouſly acknowledge, Brother, I was as glad to ſee my ſelf ſo near the Land, as any of 'em; and I am ſure I had more reaſon for it: for my long ſickneſs had made the Sea more unſupportable to me than any of them.

This morning we ſaw a Sea-Turtle, or Tortoiſe, (which it ſeems are frequent on the New-England Coaſt:) And its fleſh is a very delicious Food. It is the property of this Creature at one time in the year conſtantly to leave the Seas, and betake her ſelf to the Shore, where ſhe will lay an infinite number of Eggs, and cover them in the Sand; and as ſoon as ſhe has done, ſhe leaves them, and goes to Sea again, not daring to ſit and hatch them, as other Birds will do, becauſe ſhe has no wings to fly away, in caſe of an attack. And when her young ones by the Heat of the Sun are hatch'd, they'll all go as directly to the Sea, as if they had been there before, or that they had been bred in't; yea, tho' ſometimes the old one leaves her eggs a mile or two from Sea, and quite out of ſight on't; ſuch is the mighty Power of Natural Inſtinct. It is obſervable, that if any of theſe Sea-fowl be taken on the Land, as oftentimes they are by Sea-Men, that they will never give over ſighing, ſobbing, and weeping, as long as Life is in them; yea, even Tears will trickle from their Eyes in great abundance. *   *   *   *   *   *

But

But now 'tis time to leave the Sea, and its Inhabitants, for we were now gott pretty near the Shore, and within ken of Boſton. We all drew near the Land with joyful hearts; and yet we durſt not give too great a Looſe unto thoſe Pleaſing Paſſions, becauſe Extreams do equally annoy, and ſometimes do infatuate our Minds. We went out into the Long-boat, and Landed near the Caſtle, within a mile of Boſton, where we lay that Night; and tho' the Country ſhew'd at firſt but like a Barbarous Wilderneſs, yet by the Generous Treatment the Governour was pleaſ'd to give us, we found it wan't inhabited by Salvages. And now that wee were come to Land, we were not inſenſible of God's great Goodneſs in our Deliverance at Sea; tho' like men newly awaken'd out of a Dream, we had not the true Dimenſions of it. We conſeſſ'd God had done Great things for us, but how great, was beyond our apprehenſion. We had eſcap'd the Sea, but yet Death might be found at Land, and therefore we ſhou'd moderate our Joy. But one thing I remember, Brother, tho' we had been ſo long at Sea, and conſequently weary of our Ship, yet when I came to leave it, it was not without ſome Reluctance; for I conſider'd it as that Faithful Inſtrument of God's Providence, that had ſo long preſerv'd us, and therefore it cou'd not but recoil upon my ſpirit, that I ſhou'd ſo much as in appearance imitate the ingratitude of thoſe who having ſerv'd their private Ends upon their Friends, and have now no further uſe of them, moſt ungratefully ſhake them off: That I ſhou'd be like the Water-Dog, which uſes the Water to purſue his Game; and when he comes to Land, ſhakes it off, as Troubleſome and Burdenſome: Unlike the Generous Lion I have read of, who having got a Thorn into his Foot, which cauſ'd exceeding pain, he made after a foot Traveller which he had eſpied in the Foreſt, and made ſigns to him that he was in diſtreſs, which the Traveller ſeeing, and apprehending that his caſe was dangerous if he ran, he ſtood ſtill to know the Lion's Pleaſure, who by

holding

holding up his Foot having declar'd his Grief, the poor man quickly gave him Eafe by pulling forth the Thorn; which having done, the Lion to requite him became his Guardian, and fav'd him from the wrongs that might be offered by other Wild Beafts there, and was his Safe-Conduct through the Foreft.

Having refrefh'd our felves the firft Night at the Caftle, where (as I have already told you) we were very civilly treated by the Governour, the next morning we bent our Courfe for Bofton; but differ'd at our fetting out about the Way: O what a felf-will'd, obftinate, frail thing is Man! That they whom Common Dangers by Sea had fo united, fhou'd for a Trifle differ and fall out by Land! And yet thus we did.

Our way from the Caftle to Bofton, was over the Ice, which was, me thought, but a cold fort of Rambling, efpecially for thofe that had fo long been mew'd up in a Cabin. But fince without the Rambling this one mile more, the many hundred Leagues we had already Rambled, had been in vain, we were refolved that this fhou'd break no Squares: And fo, tho it was over Ice, we went it chearfully, and found a good Reception there.

And thus my Reader, I am come at laft, through God's good Providence, to the End of my Long Voyage: in which I do believe you'll fee made good what I afferted at the beginning of it, That in this Voyage (when I publifh the Hiftory of my Travells) you'll find the hardfhips of my whole Life; hardfhips fo very great and difficult, that, were they to be acted over-again, rather than I wou'd undergo 'em, I'd part with both the Indies, were they mine; Yes, and fhou'd think I parted with 'em to advantage too. My next, which I intend for my Friend Mr. George Larkin, fhall give you an account both as to the City it felf, its Publick Structures, Inhabitants and Trade: Their Cuftoms and Way of Living, Marriages, Burials, &c. The Characters of their Minifters, and in brief whatever is Remarkable in
Bofton.

Bofton. And as I doubt not, but that you will communicate this Letter to my Dear; So I will in like manner defire my Friend to communicate that which I fend him next, to you. And thus, Dear Lake, not Doubting but you will in my abfence be ready to perform all good offices to your Sifter, that fhe fhall defire of you; and fubmitting the Relation of this my Long Sea-Voyage, to your more accurate Correction, with the Remembrance of my Sincere and cordial Love, I reft,

Your truly Loving and

Affectionate Brother,

PHILARET.

Bofton, Febr. 17, 1685–6.

LETTER III.

TO MR. GEORGE LARKIN, PRINTER, AT THE
TWO SWANS, WITHOUT BISHOPSGATE, LONDON."

Boſton in New-England, March 25, 1686.

Y Dear Friend!—After a long and hazardous Voyage, I am now in the New World called America. We were longer in our Ramble to this Countrey, by reaſon of bad Weather, than is uſually ſeen in an Eaſt India Voyage. But having ſent my Sea-Adventures (from my leaving Weſt Cows in the Iſle of Wight to my Arrival in Boſton) to my Brother Lake, I ſhall repeat nothing of that Letter (which you may ſee at any time) but proceed to the further Account of my Rambles. And here I ſhall obſerve this method:

1. Give you an Account of my Reception at Boſton:

2. The

"Of George Larkin, Dunton has twice given a charaćter in his Life and Errors. "He has been my conſtant friend for Twenty-five Years, and the firſt Printer I had in London." "He is a particular Votary of the Muſes, and I have ſeen ſome of his Poems, eſpecially that upon Friendſhip, that cannot be equalled. He formerly wrote 'A Viſion of Heaven,' &c. (which contains many nice and curious thoughts) and has lately publiſhed an ingenious 'Eſſay on the Noble Art and Myſtery of Printing,' which will immortalize his name amongſt all the Profeſſors of that Art, as much as his Eſſay will the Art itſelf." "Mr. Larkin has a Son now living, of the ſame name and trade with himſelf; and four Grandſons (beſides Larkin How, his Grandſon by his Daughter) which, humanly ſpeaking, will tranſmit his name to the end of time."—Ed.

2. The Character of my Bofton Landlord, his Wife and Daughter:

3. Give you an Account of my being admitted into the Freedom of this City:

4. I fhall next defcribe the Town of Bofton, it being the Metropolis of New-England; and fay fomething of the Government, Law, and Cuftoms thereof.

5. I fhall relate the Vifits I made, the Remarkable Friendfhips I contracted, and fhall conclude with the character of Madam Brick as the Flower of Bofton, and fome other Ladyes, And I'll omit nothing that happened (if remarkable) during my ftay here. And in all this I will not copy from others, as is ufual with moft Travellers, but relate my own Obfervations.

Thefe General Heads will be the Subject of this Letter: And I think myfelf obliged to fend this part of my Rambles to you, my dear Friend, Mr. Larkin, both as your Letter to Mr. John Allen, your quondam Servant (and my Fellow-Traveller hither) fpeaks fo kindly of me, and engages me to this tafk; as alfo as a Teftimony of the Refpect I have for you, for your fo boldly appearing for the True Englifh Liberties and Proteftant Religion, even at a time when it could not be done without Danger, and for which you have likewife been fo great a fufferer; Befides, you know, my Friend, that in Days of Yore we uf'd to trade together, and I wou'd not have you think that a far Country can make me to forget my old Friends.

But perhaps you'll wonder that this Letter was not fent to my Dear, as it relates to my Private Affairs, as well as my Rambles in Bofton:—O Sir! She's aforehand w' ye in this matter! for ftill as I've a kind thought rifes in my Breft, 'tis the fubject of a letter to Iris; And when Fairweather left Bofton (which was a week ago) he had no lefs than fixty Letters of mine in his Bag (a whole Cargo of Love!) and all Directed to Iris: If every fhip fhou'd bring her as many till

I leave

8

I leave Bofton, fhe'il receive a Thoufand in three Months time: But thefe being Letters of Tendernefs, are not fo proper for Publick View—Not but that fhe'ill have a hand in my Printed Rambles; and therefore 'twas I fent her my Voyage from London to the Ifle of Wight, and defign to fend her my Rambles to Salem (a Town in New-England), and another from Holland, when I get thither; but I cull out my He-Friends, when I relate matters of State; and that's the reafon, together with the Obligations you have laid upon me, that I have fent this Letter to you: but you love much in a little, and therefore to avoid any further Preamble, I fhall give you an Account of my Reception at Bofton.[18]

The

[18] About half a page has been cut out and is miffing in the original. The " Life and Errors " fupplies us with the following letters written at this time, and inferted by Dunton at this point in his narrative. He writes thus:

" The Air of New-England was fharper than at London, which, with the Temptation of frefh Provifions, made me eat like a fecond Mariot of Gray's-Inn.

" After I got fafe upon _Terra-firma_, I could fcarce Keep my Feet under me for feveral Days; the Univerfe appeared to be one common Whirl-Pool, and one would think that Cartes had contrived his Vortices immediately after fome tedious Voyage. The firft Perfon that welcomed me to Bofton was Mr. Burroughs, formerly a Hearer of my Reverend Father-in-Law, Dr. Annefley. He heaped more Civilities upon me than I can reckon up, offered to lend me Moneys, and made me his bed-fellow till I had provided Lodgings.

" After I had been fome Days in Bofton, there was a Ship ready to fail for England, with which I fent the following Letter to my Reverend Father-in-Law, Dr. Annefley.

" Reverend and Dear Sir,

" I am at laft, through merciful Providence, arrived fafe at Bofton in New-England. We were above Four Months at fea, and very often in extreme Danger by Storms; and, which added to our Misfortunes, our Provifions were almoft fpent before we Landed. For fome time we had no more than the Allowance of one Bottle of Water a Man for four Days. Since my Arrival, I have met with many Kindneffes from Mr. Burroughs, and others of your Acquaintance in Bofton. I am now, Sir, in great fufpenfe whether to part with my _Venture_ of Books by Wholefale to fome of the Trade in Town here, or to fell them by Retale. If this Letter comes fhortly after the Date of it to your Hands, pray let me have your Advice in this Matter.

" I am, Your moft Affectionate and

" Dutiful Son,

" JOHN DUNTON.

" Bofton, March 25, 1686.

" Some Time after, I received the following Anfwer:

" Dear Son!

" I Was very glad to hear of your fafe Arrival after your Tedious

and

The firſt perſon that welcomed me to Boſton was Mr. Burroughs, a Merchant in Boſton, formerly a hearer, and ſtill a great Lover, of my Reverend Father in Law, Dr. Samuel

and Hazardous Paſſage. Thoſe Mercies are moſt obſerv'd, and through Grace the beſt improv'd, that are beſtowed with ſome grievous Circumſtances. I hope the Impreſſion of your Voyage will abide, tho the Danger be over. I know not what to ſay to you about your Trading. Preſent Providences upon preſent Circumſtances muſt be obſerved; and therefore I ſhall often (in prayer) recommend your Caſe to GOD: who alone can, and I hope will, do both in you, and for you, exceeding abundantly beyond what can be aſk'd, or thought by

"Your moſt Affectionate Father,
"S. A.
" London, May 10, 1686.

" With the ſame Ship that brought over my Letter to Dr. Anneſley, I ſent a whole Packquet to Dear Iris; but the greater part of them being upon Buſineſs, I ſhall only tranſcribe that which follows :

" My Dear!
" I am at laſt got ſafe aſhoar, after an uncomfortable Voyage, that had nothing in it but Misfortune and Hardſhip. Half of my Venture hither was caſt away in the Downs ; however, don't ſuffer that to make you Melancholy, in Regard the other Half is now ſafe with me at Boſton. I was very often upon the Edge of Death in my Paſſage over hither, beſides all the Hazards of our Ship, &c. Palmer, indeed, was very diligent to ſerve me : he took me out and put me into my Cabin, for almoſt four Months. It wou'd be endleſs to tell over the Extremities I was in, which lay Double upon my Hands, becauſe you, my Dear, were not there

to tend me, and to give a Reſurrection to my Spirits with one Kind Look, and with ſome ſoft Word or other, which, you know, would ſignifie ſo much to me.

" Dear Iris! I am now and then tormented with a Thouſand Fears. The Ocean that lyes betwixt us ſeems lowering and unkind. Had I Wings, I'd rather ſteer myſelf a Paſſage through the Air, than commit myſelf a ſecond Time to the Dangers of the Sea. My Thoughts, now I am at Boſton, are however all running upon Iris ; and, be aſſur'd, that with all imaginable Diſpatch I'll reſign my ſelf to God and Providence, and the Conduct of my guardian Angel, to bring me Home again in ſafety. Our Pleaſures and Satisfactions will be freſh and new when I'm reſtored t'ye, as it were from another World, and methinks upon the Proſpect of that very Advantage, I could undertake another New-England-Voyage. After all, my Dear, our compleat and our final Happineſs is not the growth of this World ; 'tis more exalted, and far above the Nature of our beſt Enjoyments. I would not have you in the leaſt ſolicitous about me. I have met with many Kindneſſes from the Inhabitants of Boſton. You'll take Care to read over the Letters that relate to Buſineſs. I am as much yours as Affection can make me.
" PHILARET.
" Boſton, March 25th, 1686.

" To this Letter Iris returned me the following Anſwer :

" Moſt endeared Heart!
" I received your moſt Wellcome Letter of March 25th, which acquainted me

Samuel Annefly. On whofe account I had the Civilitys I cann't properly fay, for he heap'd and crowded 'em upon me at that rate that he at firft fight offers to lend me money (the true Touchftone of Friendfhip); Then has me to his own quarters (to Mr. ——), and I being as yet unprovided of a Lodging, makes me his Bedfellow, and would fcarce fuffer me to be out of his fight, tho' 'twere to make a private Vifit to

me with your Tedious and Sick Voyage; I was very much overjoy'd for your fafe Arrival at Bofton, tho' much troubled for your Illnefs in the way to it. Thofe Mercies are the fweeteft, that we enjoy after waiting and praying for them. I pray GOD help us both to improve them for his Glory. I think I have Sympathiz'd with you very much; for I don't remember I have ever had fo much Illnefs in my whole Life as I have had this Winter.

When I firft received your Letters, My Dear, I was refolv'd upon coming over t'ye, if my Friends approv'd of it; but, upon Difcourfe with them, they concluded I cou'd not bear the Voyage; and I, having had fo large an Experience of your growing and lafting affections, could not believe but that you had rather have a living Wife in England, than a Dead one in the Sea. Befides, I cannot leave London till I have paid down the Money you were bound for, to Nevet,* upon my Sifter's Account. I have receiv'd more Kindneffes from your Coufin R——†(who was your Bail at leaving England) than from all your other Friends and Acquaintance. I am not able to exprefs how great a Trouble it has been to me this Winter, that you fhou'd be brought into fo many Troubles and Bondfhips by Marrying of me. If there is any Encouragement for fettling in New-Eng-

land, I will joyfully come over t'ye; but am rather for your going to Holland to trade there. Pray GOD direct you what to do, and in the mean time take great Care of your Health, and want for nothing. I do affure you, My Dear, yourfelf alone is all the Riches I defire; and if ever I am fo happy as to enjoy your Company again, I will travel to the fartheft Part of the World, rather than to part with you any more; Nothing but Cruel Death fhall ever make the Separation. I had rather have your Company, with Bread and Water, than enjoy without you the Riches of both Indies. I have read your Private Letter, and fhall do that which will be both for your Comfort and your Honour. I take it as the higheft Demonftration of your Love, that you intruft me with your Secret Affairs. Affure yourfelf I do as earneftly defire the Welfare of your Soul and Body as I do my own; Therefore let nothing trouble you, for were you in London, you cou'd not take more Care of your Bufinefs than I fhall do. I can't exprefs how much I long to fee you. Oh, this Cruel Ocean that lies between us! But, I blefs GOD, I am as well at prefent as I can be when feparated from you. I muft conclude, begging of GOD to keep you from the Sins and Temptations which every Place and every Condition do expofe us to. So, wifhing you a fpeedy and a fafe Voyage back again to England,

"I remain yours beyond Expreffion,

"IRIS.

"London, May 14th, 1686."

* This was "for £50 to one Nevet, a Surgeon." LIFE AND ERRORS, p. 82.

† "Mr. R——, and Mr. Aftwood offered themfelves to be bail for me."—IBID.

to Dame Nature ; and where'er I went, wou'd not fuffer me to *fee* (as they call it) that is, not fpend a Penny for nine days. In brief, his kindneffes were fo great, fo many, and fo fincere and uninterefted, that he out-did all I can fay. So great a Man he was that he indeed hid himfelf with the Garb of the Vulgar, and that was all that was Vulgar in him. His Looks are according to Nature, and fo is his Behaviour, as far from Deceit and guile even as Nathaniel himfelf, who was told by One that cou'd tell, That he was an Ifraelite indeed, in whom there was no guile. Truth is the prize he aims at, and he takes care to get her, and is not content only to look like her. But why fhou'd [I] go about to commend him, whofe juft Praife exceeds all Commendation ?

Mr. Larkin, I remember you are a great Admirer of Verfe; and I have feen feveral of your own making, far from being defpifable, to fay no more in their Commendation. For that Reafon I have chofen to conclude the Character of my Friend with the following Poem, as knowing it will be diverting to you, for fo I wou'd have all my Letters to my Friend : Tho' the Verfes are none of the moft modern, yet they well enough comprehend the Character of a happy Life.

THE CHARACTER OF A HAPPY LIFE.

How happy is he born or Taught
  That ferveth not another's will,
Whofe Armour is his honeft Thought
  And Upright Truth his higheft fkill.

Whofe Paffions not his Mafters are,
  Whofe Soul is ftill prepar'd for Death ;
Unty'd unto the World with Care
  Of Princes Love, or Vulgar Breath :

Who hath his Life from Rumours freed,
  Whofe Confcience is his ftrong Retreat ;
Whofe ftate can neither Flatterers need,
  Nor Ruine make Accufers Great.

Who

Who envieth none whom Chance doth raife,
  Or Vice: who never underftood
How deepeft Wounds are given with Praife;
  Not Rules of State, but Rules of Good:

Who Goᴅ doth late and early pray
  More of his Grace than Gifts to lend:
Who Entertains the harmlefs Day
  With a well chofen Book and Friend.

This Man is free from Servile Bands,
  Of hope to rife, or fear to fall;
Lord of Himfelf, tho' not of Lands;
  And having Nothing, he hath All.

Having thus offered fomething as a grateful acknowledgment to my good Friend Mr. Burrows,[19] I cannot pafs by in filence his Worthy Landlord: who for a Zealous Profeffor, and a fincere Practicer of True Piety, was one of the moft eminent in the whole Town of Bofton: He was one that efteem'd Godlinefs his greateft Gain, and fo was far from making a Gain of Godlinefs, which is too much the fault of the generallity of the Boftoneers. But what need I fpeak of that, his Reputation is too bright to need a foyl to fett it off, and the conftant exercife of Religion in his Family, and the general Influence it had on all the Actions of his Life, fufficiently fignaliz'd him for a truly Religious Man.

Meeting with fo good Friends, Mr. Larkin, I began to think myfelf at home agen; and cou'd I have put Iris and yourfelf out of my mind, I might perhaps have forgot London—But Iris had got fo firm a poffeffion of my whole heart, and you fo great a Right to my Friendfhip, that ftill the Name of Native Country bewitch'd me. 'Twas that dazl'd my eyes: And 'twas thus with the firft Planters of this Country, who were, even to their 80th year, ftill pleafing
themfelves

---

[19] Francis Burroughs was a merchant from London. He m. for fecond wife 29 Dec. 1709, Elizabeth, widow of Thomas Grofs, who was then a widow Heath. He probably had no child by her, as his will mentions only a daughter Sarah, wife of Capt. John Brown of Salem.—Eᴅ.

themſelves with hopes of their Returning to England. But 'twas now my Duty, (and the Diſcharge of my preſent Duty I thought would help me to the better performance of my future Duties,) to look upon that as my Native Country where I cou'd thrive and proſper—For I had married a Wife (and a very kind one too) and 'twas my Duty to provide for her, and in that way, as well as by Writing, and other Endearments, to ſhew my Love for her. But now Exit Spouſe, that is, till I am ſettled ſo very well as to have nothing to think of elſe: And this brings me 4000 miles back in a Moment, even to the Door of Mr. Richard Wilkins,[20] (oppoſite to the Town-Houſe in Boſton). 'Twas here in Capital Letters I found

LODGINGS TO BE LET, WITH A CONVENIENT WAREHOUSE.

I found 'twas convenient for my Purpoſe, and ſo wee ſoon made a Bargain, and entred into ſuch a Friendſhip as will ſcarce end with our Lives. Mr. Wilkins' Family was only— Himſelf—his Wife—and Daughter—who I muſt ſay deſerve better from me than all New England beſides (Mr. Burroughs only excepted). And therefore in pure Gratitude I have Attempted their Characters.

My Landlord, Mr. Richard Wilkins, like good old Jacob, is a plain good man. He was formerly a Bookſeller in Limerick, and fled hither on the account of conſcience, with two Divines, Mr. John and Mr. Thomas Bayly. But to go on with his Character: His Perſon is tall, his Aſpect ſweet and ſmiling; and tho' but fifty years old, his Hair's as white as Snow. He is a Man of good ſence, very generous to his
Friend;

[20] Of Richard Wilkins we learn little in addition to Dunton's account, but that he was nominated for poſtmaſter after the overthrow of Andros, and died at Milton, 10 Dec. 1704, aged 80. By the Boſton Records it ſeems that he was admitted to a reſidence here on the 28th Nov. 1684, with William Stewart, John Adams, John Langdon, Samuel Gray, John Simon, Thomas Atkinſon and Archibald Eraſkiħ; their ſureties being Timothy Prout, Edward Willy and Edward Wyllys.—ED.

Friend; Talks well, keeps up the Practice of Religion in his Family, and is now a Member of Mr. Willard's Church.

I come next to his Wife, my kind and obliging Landlady, who is a Perfon of fo agreeable a temper, and withal fo eafie Company, that 'tis a pleafure to be in it; which renders her Converfation Chearfuller than thofe that laugh more, but fmile lefs : Some there are who fpend more fpirits in ftraining for an hour's Mirth than they can recover in a month after, which renders 'em fo unequal company; whilft fhe is always equal and the fame. It is indeed Vertue to know her, wifdom to converfe with her, joy to behold her, and a fpecies of the beatitude of the other World, only to enjoy her Converfation in this. Or to fpeak all in a few words, She is the Counterpart of her Hufband, who without her is but half himfelf.

Having faid fomething of my Landlord and Landlady, You, Mrs. Comfort, (for fo was their Daughter call'd) may well take it amifs, if I fhou'd forget your Favours; Your Smiles by Day, *and the Warming-Pan by Night;* your Affiftance when I was ill, and the *rich Looking-glafs* you fent my Dear; and all this with a world of Innocence—For tho' I had fair Opportunities to try your Vertue, yet I never was fo wicked : 'Tis true, Platonick Love has ruin'd many of your fex, yet you muft fay (when you fpeak of me) that you found me a True Platonick : And when I think of you, I fhall ftill fay, There may be Maids at 15, 20, 30, 40, 50, 60, 70; But I'll go no further, for there's no Danger of 'em after that.

Being thus fix'd to my Heart's content, I began to vifit my Friends, and the next Ramble I took was to deliver fome Letters of Recommendation : Mr. Stretton, a Reverend Divine in London, fent one to Mr. Stoughton[21] the Deputy-Governour;

[21] This Mr. Stoughton was William, fon of Col. Ifrael Stoughton. He was born in 1631, H. C. 1650, was a preacher in Suffex, England, and a fellow of New College, Oxford. Returning here he held various high offices and died unm. 7 July, 1701.—Ed.

Governour; and Mr. Morton of Newington-Green fent another to Major Dudley,[22] afterwards Prefident; And I had fome letters to other Magiftrates; which had that effect, that in three or four Days after, I opened my Warehoufes and was made a Freeman of Bofton;[23] for which I thank my good Friend Mr. Burroughs; For by his means I am now free of Two parts of the World.

I was invited by Captain Hutchinfon[24] (the talleft man that I ever beheld) to dine with the Governour and Magiftrates of Bofton; the Place of Entertainment was the Town-Hall, and the Feaft Rich and Noble: As I enter'd the Room where the Dinner was, the Governour in Perfon, the Deputy-Governour, Major Dudley, and the other Magiftrates, did me the Honour to give me a particular Welcome to Bofton, and to wifh me Succefs in my Undertaking.

And

[22] Jofeph Dudley, fon of Gov. Thomas Dudley, was born 23 Sept. 1647, and died 2 Apr. 1720. He was Governor of the Colony from 1702 till 1715 and held many other offices.—ED.

[23] As our readers may like to fee the mode in which Dunton was made a freeman of the town, we tranfcribe the only document we have found or prefume ever exifted. It is in a book at the City Clerk's Office.—ED.

"Witneffe thefe prefents, that I, Francis Burrowes, of Boftone, Merchant, doe binde myfelfe, my Executors and Adminiftrators to Edward Willis, Treasurer of the Towne of Boftone, in the fume of fortie pounds in mony, that John Dunton, booke-feller, nor any of his familie, fhall not be chargeable to this towne duringe his or any [of] there abode therein. Witneffe my hand the 16th of February, 1685.

"That is, fd. Burrowes binds himfelfe as above to fd. Willis and his fucceffors in the office of Treasurer, omitted in the due place above."

Frun: Burroughs

John Dunton

[24] This was doubtlefs Capt. Elifha Hutchinfon, born in 1641, fon of Edward, and grandfon of William and Anne H. He was Capt. in 1676, and a Counfellor from 1684 till his death in 1715. His grandfon was the noted Governor Thomas Hutchinfon.

9

And now, Mr. Larkin, having proceeded thus far in making good the Promife I made ye,—I fhall next defcribe the Town of Bofton, and fhall fay fomething of the Inhabitants, Government, Laws, and Cuftoms of the City and Kingdom. And here, my Friend, when I come to fpeak of the Inhabitants of Bofton, I muft entreat your Candour in Diftinguifhing; Or elfe you will not know what to make of what I fay; To which End, I ought to premife, That the firft Englifh that came over hither, in the latter end of Queen Elizabeth's, and the Beginning of King James's Reign, forced thereto by the fevere Treatment they met with from the Bifhops in England, were certainly the moft Pious and Religious Men in the World, Men that had experienc'd the Power of Divine Grace upon their own Souls, and were the lively Patterns of Primitive Zeal and Integrity; and wou'd have converted all the World, if they cou'd; efpecially their own Pofterity: But alas! this bleffed Wind of the Spirit blows where it lifteth; Many of them were converted and made truly Gracious, and thefe walk to this Day in the fteps of their Pious Fore-fathers: But there are others of them, who never knew the Power of Converting Grace, who yet retain a form of Godlinefs, and make a ftrict Profeffion of the out-fide of Religion, tho' they never knew what the Power of Godlinefs was; and thefe are the moft Profligate and Debauched Wretches in the World; their Profeffion of Religion teaching them only how to fin (as they think) more refinedly. Having premifed thus much, you will foon know how to difcern what is fpoken of thefe Hypocrites, from what belongs to the Truly Religious; of which there are many, tho' the others are the far greater Number.

Bofton[25] is fituated in the Bottom of the Maffachufets Bay, in the Latitude of 42 degrees and 10 minutes, (its Longitude

tude

---

[25] This defcription of Bofton is copied almoft exactly from Joffelyn's Account of Two Voyages to New-England, 1675. Compare p. 124–6 of Veazie's edition. (Bofton, 1865.)—ED.

tude being 315 degrees, or, as others affirm, 322 degrees and 30 feconds.) So called from a Town in Lincolnfhire. It is the Metropolis, not only of this Colony, but of the whole Country: And is built on the South-Weft-fide of a Bay large enough for the Anchorage of 500 Sail of Ships. Situated upon a Peninfula about four miles in compafs, almoft Square, and inviron'd with the Sea, having one fmall ifthmus, which gives accefs to other Towns by Land on the South.

The Town hath two hills[28] of equal height on the Frontire part thereof, next the fea; the one well fortified on the Superficies with fome Artillery mounted, commanding any Ship as fhe fails into the Harbour within the Bay: The other Hill hath a very ftrong Battery, built with whole Timber, and fill'd with Earth. At the Defcent of the Hill, in the extreameft part thereof, betwixt thefe two Strong Arms, lies a large Cove or Bay, on which the chiefeft part of the Town is built. To the North-weft is a high Mountain that over-tops all, with its three little rifing Hills on the fummit, called Tramount: This is furnifhed with a Beacon and Great Guns: from hence you may overlook all the Iflands in the Bay, and defcry fuch fhips as are upon the Coaft.

The Houfes are for the moft part raifed on the Sea-Banks, and wharfed out with great Induftry and Coft; many of them ftanding upon Piles, clofe together on each fide the ftreets, as in London, and furnifhed with many fair Shops; where all forts of Comodities are fold. Their ftreets are many and large, paved with Pebbles; the Materials of their Houfes are Brick, Stone, Lime, handfomely contrived, and when any New Houfes are built, they are made conformable to our New Buildings in London fince the fire. Mr. Shrimpton

[28] Thefe two hills will be recognized as Copp's Hill and Fort Hill; the North Battery was where Battery Wharf now ftands, and the South Battery was on the fhore in front of Batterymarch Street. The water line is now greatly altered.—ED.

Shrimpton[77] has a very ſtately houſe there, with a Braſs Kettle atop, to ſhew his Father was not aſham'd of his Original: Mr. John Uſher (to the honour of our Trade) is judg'd to be worth above £20,000, and hath one of the beſt Houſes in Boſton; They have Three[28] Fair and Large Meeting-Houſes or Churches, commodiouſly built in ſeveral parts of the Town, which yet are hardly ſufficient to receive the Inhabitants, and ſtrangers that come in from all Parts.

Their Town-Houſe[29] is built upon Pillars in the middle of the Town, where their Merchants meet and confer every Day. In the Chambers above they keep their Monthly Courts. The South-ſide of the Town is adorned with Gardens and Orchards. The Town is rich and very populous,[30] much frequented by ſtrangers. Here is the Dwelling of [Mr.] Broadſtreet, Esq., their preſent Governour. On the North-weſt and North-Eaſt, two conſtant Fairs are kept, for daily Traffick thereunto. On the South, there is a ſmall

but

---

[77] Samuel Shrimpton, born in 1643, was the ſon of Henry Shrimpton, of Boſton, who had been a brazier in London. A brother of this Henry was Edward S., of Bednall-Green. Henry Shrimpton died in July, 1666, leaving a large eſtate to his ſon and four daughters. Samuel was captain of the Artillery company, a member of Androſſe's Council, and of the Council of Safety in 1689, and died of apoplexy, 9th Feb. 1698. His large eſtate paſſed to his ſon Samuel.—Ed.

[28] The three churches were the following: The Firſt Church, founded in 1632 by Rev. John Wilſon, and of which James Allen was miniſter from 1668 to 1710, and Joſhua Moody aſſiſtant 1684-1692; it ſtood where Joy's Building now is on Waſhington St. The Second Church, or Old North, eſtabliſhed in 1650 by Samuel Mather, brother of Increaſe. It ſtood at the head of North Square, and the ſecond edifice, built in 1677, was deſtroyed by the Britiſh troops

in 1775. Increaſe Mather preached here from 1669 to 1723, Cotton Mather 1685 to 1728, and Samuel Mather (ſon of Cotton) 1732 to 1741. The Third Church was the Old South, of which Thomas Thatcher was inſtalled the firſt paſtor in 1670. Samuel Willard ſucceeded him in April, 1678, and died in 1707.—Ed.

[29] The Town Houſe was built about 1657. Drake writes (p. 350) "At what time it was completed does not clearly appear. It is incidentally mentioned a few years later, as being entered by a flight of ſeveral ſteps. It was where the old State houſe now ſtands, at the head of State Street, and ſtood until the great fire of 1711, in which it was conſumed."—Ed.

[30] Drake ſtates that in 1686 the rateable polls were 1447; in 1698 there were above 1000 houſes, and over 7000 inhabitants after 1000 were eſtimated to have died in that year.—Ed.

but pleasant Common, where the Gallants a little before sun-
set walk with their Marmalet Madams, as we do in Moorfield,
&c., till the Nine-a-Clock Bell rings them home; after which
the Constables walk their Rounds to see good orders kept,
and to take up loose people.   In the high-street towards the
Common, there are very fair Buildings, some of which are
of stone.   And at the East end of the Town, one amongst
the rest built by the shore, by Mr. Gibbs,[31] a Merchant, being
a very stately Edifice.[32]   But I need give you no further a
Description of Boston; for I remember you have been at
Bristol, which bears a very near Resemblance to Boston.

But I shall say something of the Inhabitants, as 10 months
of my Life was spent amongst 'em.   There is no Trading
for a stranger with them but with a Grecian Faith, which is,
not to part with your Ware without ready Money; for they
are generally very backward in their Payments, great Censors
of other Men's Manners, but extreamly careless of their own,
yet they have a ready correction for every vice.   As to their
Religion,[33] I cannot perfectly distinguish it; but it is such
that

[31] Robert Gibbs, son of Sir Henry
Gibbs, of Honington, Co. Warwick, was
a prominent merchant here, and died
7 Dec. 1673, aged 37.   His son, Robert
Gibbs, died 7 Dec. 1702, leaving issue.
—ED.

[32] Gibbs's house is also referred to by
Josselyn in his New England's Rarities,
1672, (Veazie's reprint, Boston, 1865.)
Here it is added, "it is thought it will
stand him in little less than 3000 £ before it be fully finished."   It stood on
Fort Hill.—ED.

[33] "As to their Religion," &c.   The
next few lines are copied by Dunton
from a folio pamphlet of only 9 pages,
signed J. W., issued with the following
title: "A Letter from New-England
Concerning their Customs, Manners,
and Religion.   Written upon occasion
of a Report about a Quo Warranto

Brought against that Government. London, Printed for Randolph Taylor near
Stationers Hall, 1682."   This little
pamphlet, of which a copy is in the
possession of William S. Appleton, Esq.,
is doubtless extremely rare.   It contains
the most disgusting charges against the
colonists, so gross indeed as to require
no refutation.   Dunton was evidently
acquainted with it, and has copied some
things from it.   The only items of the
slightest value now noticed are these:
"I have seen them whip several of the
Anabaptist Principle in one day at the
Gun, (the usual Whipping place here)."
"A sixth Instance I shall give you of a
Lay Elder, one W——ll, as he prayed
in the old Conventicle: 'Lord,' (says he)
'thy mercies have been to us manifold,
for behold formerly it was but a mere
Bog and a Swamp, where our stately

that nothing keeps 'em friends but only the fear of expofing one another's knavery. As for the Rabble, their Religion lies in cheating all they deal with. When you are dealing with 'em, you muft look upon 'em as at crofs purpofes, and read 'em like Hebrew backward; for they feldom fpeak and mean the fame thing, but like Water-men, Look one Way, and Row another. The Quakers here have been a fuffering Generation; and there's hardly any of the Yea-and-Nay Perfuafion but will give you a fevere Account of it; for the Boftonians, tho' their Forefathers fled thither to enjoy Liberty of Confcience, are very unwilling any fhould enjoy it but themfelves: But they are now grown more moderate. Thofe were the Heats of fome Perfons among 'em whofe zeal outran their knowledge, and was the effect of their Ignorance: For you and I, Mr. Larkin, are I am fure both of this Opinion, as our fufferings for it fufficiently Teftifie, That Liberty of Confcience is the Birth-Right of all Men by a Charter Divine.

The Government both Civil and Ecclefiaftical is in the hands of the Independents and Prefbyterians, or at leaft of thofe that pretend to be fuch.

On Sundays in the After-noon, after Sermon is ended, the People in the Galleries come down and march two a Breft, up one Ifle and down the other, until they come before the Defk, for Pulpit they have none: Before the Defk is a long Pew, where the Elders and Deacons fit, one of them with a Money-Box in his hand, into which the People as they pafs put their Offerings, fome a fhilling, fome two fhillings, and fome half a Crown, or five fhillings, according to the Ability or Liberality of the Perfon giving. This I look upon to be a Praife-worthy Practice. This Money is diftributed to

fupply

Townhoufe ftands; yea (Lord) the Sea and the Tide came up where now our Boys play at Football.'"

The hiftorical value of this pamphlet is abfolutely nothing, and whoever this J. W. may have been, it is an unmerited charity which leaves him in obfcurity.— ED.

fupply the Neceffities of the Poor, according to their feveral wants, for they have no Beggars there.

Every Church (for fo they call their particular Congregations) have one Paftor, one Teacher, Ruling Elders and Deacons.

They that are Members of their Churches have the Sacrament adminiftered to them. Thofe that are not actually joyned to them, may look on, but partake not thereof, till they are fo joyn'd.

As to their Laws,[34] This Colony is a Body Corporate and Politick in Fact, by the Name of, The Governour and Company of the Maffachufets Bay in New-England. Their Conftitution is, That there fhall be one Governour and Deputy-Governour, and eighteen Affiftants of the fame Company, from time to time. That the Governour and Deputy-Governour, (who for this year are Efq: Broadftreet and Efq: Staughton,) Affiftants and all other Officers, to be chofen from among the Freemen the laft Wednefday in Eafter Term, yearly, in the General Court. The Governour to take his corporal oath to be True and Faithful to the Government, and to give the fame Oath to the other Officers. They are to hold a Court once a month, and any Seven to be a fufficient Quorum. They are to have four General Courts kept in Term-Time, and one great General and Solemn Affembly, to make Laws and Ordinances; Provided, They be not contrary or repugnant to the Laws and Statutes of the Realm of England. In Anno 1646, They drew up a Body of their Laws for the benefit of the People. Every Town fends two Burgeffes to their Great and Solem General Court.

Their Laws for Reformation of Manners, are very fevere, yet but little regarded by the People, fo at leaft as to make 'em better, or caufe 'em to mend their manners.

For

---

[34] Dunton again copies from Joffelyn's Two Voyages, p. 134-7, enlarging fomewhat upon the text, but evidently depending upon this as authority.—ED.

For being drunk, they either Whip or impose a Fine of Five shillings: And yet notwithstanding this Law, there are several of them so addicted to it, that they begin to doubt whether it be a Sin or no; and seldom go to Bed without Muddy Brains.

For Curfing and Swearing, they bore through the Tongue with a hot Iron.

For kissing a woman in the Street, though but in way of Civil Salute, Whipping or a Fine. [Their way of Whipping Criminals is by Tying them to a Gun at the Town-House, and when so Ty'd whipping them at the pleasure of the Magistrate, and according to the Nature of the Offence.]

For Single Fornication, whipping or a Fine. And yet for all this Law, the Chastity of some of 'em, for I do not Condemn all the People, may be guess'd at by the Number of Delinquents in this kind: For there hardly passes a Court Day, but some are convened for Fornication; and Convictions of this Nature are very frequent: One instance lately told me, will make this matter yet more plain: There happened to be a Murder'd Infant to be found in the Town Dock: The Infant being taken up by the Magistrates Command, orders were immediately given by them for the search of all the Women of the Town, to see if thereby they cou'd find out the Murdress: Now in this Search, tho' the Murdress cou'd not be found out, yet several of the Bostonian Young Women, that went under the Denomination of Maids, were found with Child.

For Adultery they are put to Death, and so for Witchcraft; For that there are a great many Witches in this Country, the late Tryals of 20 New England Witches is a sufficient Proof.

An English Woman suffering an Indian to have carnal knowledge of her, had an Indian cut out exactly in red cloth, and sewed upon her right Arm, and enjoyned to wear it Twelve Months.

Scolds

Scolds they gag, and fet them at their own Doors, for certain hours together, for all comers and goers to gaze at. Were this a Law in England, and well Executed, it wou'd in a little Time prove an Effectual Remedy to cure the Noife that is in many Women's heads.

Stealing is punifhed with Reftoring four-fold, if able; if not, they are fold for fome years, and fo are poor Debtors. I have not heard of many Criminals of this fort. But for Lying and Cheating,[35] they out-vye Judas, and all the falfe other cheats in Hell. Nay, they make a Sport of it: Looking upon Cheating as a commendable Piece of Ingenuity, commending him that has the moft fkill to commit a piece of Roguery; which in their Dialect (like thofe of our Yea-and-Nay-Friends in England) they call by the genteel Name of Out-Witting a Man, and won't own it to be cheating. As an Inftance of what I have faid, I was fhewn a Man of fuch a Kidney as I have been fpeaking on, in Bofton (whofe Name for a Special Reafon I fhall here omit), who (as I was told by Mr. Gouge, Son to the Charitable Divine of that Name) agreed with a Country-man for a Horfe, and was to pay him Four Pounds of Maffachufet Money, and that to become due upon the Day of the Election for Magiftrates, which is held yearly. But our witty Boftonian underftanding that the Country-man cou'd not read, makes the Bill payable under his hand, at the Day of the Refurrection of the Magiftrates; willing belike to take Time enough to pay his Debts; or elfe poffibly in good hopes that the Magiftrates had no fhare in that Day. But he carry'd the Jeft a little too far, for the Country-Man fu'd him, and tho' with much Trouble and Charge recover'd his Money.

In fhort, Thefe Boftonians enrich themfelves by the ruine
of

---

[35] " But for Lying," &c. From this fentence through the paffage " I am holier than thou," Dunton has copied again from the obfcene pamphlet of J. W. already cited. The anecdote is therein attributed to H——n L——tt, but in connection with fuch other improbable ftories as make us doubt this one, even though endorfed by Mr. Gouge.—ED.

10

of Strangers; and like ravenous Birds of Prey, ſtrive who
ſhall faſten his Tallons firſt upon 'em.   For my own ſhare I
have already truſted out £400, and know not where to get
in 2d. of it.   But all theſe things paſs under the Notion of
Self-Preſervation and Chriſtian-Policy.

I had not given you the Trouble of ſo large an Account
of the manners of the Boſtonians, nor rak'd in ſuch a
Dunghil of Filth, but that this ſort of People are ſo apt to
ſay, Stand off, for I am holier than Thou.³⁶   *   *   *   *
*   *   *   *   *   *   *   *   *   *

And thus, my Friend, I have given you an Account of
Boſton: But as I ſaid before, ſo I ſay again, You muſt make
a Diſtinction: For amongſt all this Droſs, there runs here
and there a vein of pure Gold: And though the Generality
are what I have deſcrib'd 'em, yet is there as ſincere a Pious
and truly Religious People among them, as is any where in
the Whole World to be found.

The next thing I have to do is to proceed to give you
ſome account of the Viſits I made: For having gotten a
Warehouſe, and my Books ready for ſale, (for you know
mine was a Learned Venture,) 'twas my Buſineſs next to ſeek
out the Buyers: So I made my firſt Viſit to that Reverend
and Learned Divine, Mr. Increaſe Mather:³⁷ He's the Preſent
Rector of Harvard College: He is deſervedly called, The
Metropolitan Clergy-Man of the Kingdom.   And the next
to him in Fame, (whom I likewiſe viſited at the ſame time)
is

<hr/>

³⁶ We here omit a ſtory concerning
the ſign of a Vintner at the " Roſe and
Crown," as it is copied from J. W.'s
pamphlet, and poſſeſſes no hiſtorical in-
tereſt to counterbalance its indecency.
One anecdote we will copy from the
pamphlet as an addition to the ſtock
ſtories concerning the Puritans. "Another was at his Exerciſe, and a Cuſ-
tomer Knock'd at the door for a Penyworth of Nails : the Brother ſends the
Boy to the door to enquire who it was ;

he returns and tells him, 'twas a Cuſ-
tomer for a Penyworth of Nails ; aſk
him, (ſays the Good Man,) if he will
joyn with us in prayer ; he goes and
returns with a No : why then, (ſays the
Good Man,) ſerve him, John, ſerve
him."—ED.

³⁷ Increaſe Mather, ſon of Rev. Richard Mather, of Dorcheſter, Maſs., was
born 21 June, 1639, and died 23 Aug.,
1723. He was Preſident of Harvard
College from 1685 till 1701.—ED.

is his fon Mr. Cotton Mather,[38] an Excellent Preacher, a great Writer; He has very lately finifh'd the Church-Hiftory of New-England, which I'm going to print; And which is more than all, He Lives the Doctrine he Preaches. After an hour fpent in his company (which I took for Heaven) he fhew'd me his Study: And I do think he has one of the beft (for a Private Library) that I ever faw: Nay, I may go farther, and affirm, That as the Famous Bodleian Library at Oxford, is the Glory of that Univerfity, if not of all Europe, (for it exceeds the Vatican,) fo I may fay, That Mr. Mather's Library is the Glory of New-England, if not of all America. I am fure it was the beft fight that I had in Bofton. As to the Difcourfes that paft between us, 'tis not proper to infert 'em here; but I muft fay, I am greatly wanting to myfelf, if I did not learn more in that hour I enjoy'd his Company, than I cou'd in an Age fpent in other Mens. Having taken my leave of Mr. Cotton and Nathaniel Mather[39] (whofe Life I afterwards Printed) and after that, of their Reverend Father, I return'd home hugely pleaf'd with my firft Vifit.

Early the next morning (before the Sun could fhew his Face) I went to wait upon Mr. Willard: He's Minifter of the South Meeting in Bofton: He's a Man of Profound Notions: Can fay what he will, and prove what he fays: I darken his Merits if I call him lefs than a Walking Library. The Civilities I receiv'd from him, both at his own Houfe, and in other places, might (had I any Gratitude) engage me further to write his Character; but he's too great a Man for me

---

[38] Cotton Mather was born 12 Feb., 1663, and died 13 Feb., 1728. In regard to his library, DRAKE, in the Introduction to his edition of Mather's "Hiftory of King Philip's War," (Bofton, 1862,) makes the following citation from a letter written by Rev. Samuel Mather. "My Father's Library was by far the moft valuable Part of the family Property. It confifted of 7000 @ 8000 Volumes of the moft curious and chofen Authors, and a prodigious Number of valuable Manufcripts which had been collected by my Anceftors for five Generations." Thefe he confidered worth at leaft eight thoufand pounds fterling.—ED.

[39] Nathaniel Mather, who was fix years younger than Cotton, died Oct. 17, 1688.—ED.

me to Attempt it; (and Mrs. Abigal, your Father's too modeft to read it.) So I fhall leave his Houfe, with only admiring what I cann't Defcribe.

From hence I Rambled with John Allen,[40] to Dine with his Reverend Unckle of that Name: He's a grave Antient Divine, and now Paftor of the New Church in Bofton: All that I fhall fay of him more, is, That he's very Humble, and very Rich, and can be Generous if he pleafes. As I left him, he urg'd me to vifit him often. And his Son was not lefs obliging, with whom I contracted a particular Friendfhip: [His fon came afterwards for England, and prov'd an Eminent Preacher, but dy'd at Northampton.]

Leaving Mr. Allen's Houfe, your fervant Johnny left me to vifit Mr. Green (the Chief Printer in Bofton), but we were no fooner parted, but Mr. Wilkins, my Landlord, meets me, as I was going to Mr. [Reve] Pierce,[41] another Printer in this Town, and takes me with him to vifit Mr. John and Mr. Thomas Bayly:[42] Thefe two are Popular Preachers, and very generous to Strangers: I heard Mr. John laft Sunday, on thefe words, LOOKING UNTO JESUS; and I thought he fpoke like an Angel: They exprefs a more than Ordinary Kindnefs to Mr. Wilkins; and (as I told you before) came over with

him

[40] John Allen, the printer, we thus learn was the nephew of Rev. James Allen, paftor of the Firft Church. This clergyman was fon of a minifter in Hampfhire and was born 24 June, 1632. He was a fellow of the New College, Oxford, was an ejected minifter, and arrived here in June. 1662. He married three wives, Hannah Dummer, widow Elizabeth Endicott, and Sarah, widow of Robert Breck, the laft in 1673. Of his fons, Jeremiah was Treafurer of the Province, and James, H. C. 1689, is the one faid to have fettled in England. Rev. James Allen died 22 Sept., 1710. —ED.

[41] Of Richard Pierce little feems known, fave that he married, 27 Aug., 1680, Sarah, daughter of Rev. Seaborn Cotton. In 1691, (a later date than THOMAS records,) he printed Cotton Mather's Scriptural Catechifm, and in 1695, his "Johannes in Eremo."—ED.

[42] John and Thomas Bayley were both fettled at Watertown. Rev. John, born at Blackburn, co. Lanc., 24 Feb., 1644, came here in 1683, and after preaching at the Old South, was fettled at Watertown in 1686. In 1693 he became Affiftant at the Firft Church, and died s. p. 12 Dec., 1697. Rev. Thomas, of Watertown, died 21 Jan'y, 1689, aged 35, poffibly leaving a fon Thomas. He had a brother, Henry Bayley, living in Manchefter in 1688, and his mother and fifter Lydia were then living alfo.—ED.

him from Ireland: I might be large in their Chara&er, but when I tell you they are true Pi&ures of Dr. Annefly (who they count a fecond St. Paul) 'tis as high as I need go.

The Sun being gone to Bed, (for tho' we were up before him, he got to his Lodging firft,) we bid Good-Night to the Two Brothers, and in our way home made a vifit to Mr. Moody⁴⁵ (Affiftant to Mr. Allen). His Houfe ftands on the fide of a Hill, ('tis called [Dean] Deacon-Hill,⁴⁶ of which more hereafter,) and gave me at one glimpfe a view of the whole City: 'tis furrounded with fhady Trees, has a pleafant Garden before it: So that he that's a Lover of a good Profpe&, wou'd call this Houfe an Earthly Paradice, and the very Elizium of Bofton. But that which gives it the greateft Ornament, is that Learned Perfon that lives in it: I may fay of him, as a fon of the Church did of the Great Owen, That he's both a Gentleman and a Schollar: In the Pulpit he's a Boanerges, and in his Family a true Nathaniel: His Printed Advice to a condemned Criminal, who I faw Executed, as you'll hear anon, fhews his Compaf-fionate Temper: And his Sermons on ONE DAY IN THY HOUSE IS BETTER THAN A THOUSAND, fhows where his Heart lies. No wonder then Pifcateway was fo loth to lofe him; for if there be a good Man in the World, 'tis He.

And now My Friend, having firft paid my Vifits to the Reverend Clergy of Bofton, and given a fhort account what they are, which may ferve only ex pede Hercules: Pray give me leave to afk my Brethren the Bookfellers how they do, and that fhall be all: For, tho' I know they love to be refpe&ed, yet at the fame time I am fatisfy'd that I'm as welcome

---

⁴⁵Rev. Jofhua Moody was fon of William Moody, of Newbury, a faddler from Ipfwich, co. Suff. He was of H. C. 1653, preached at Portfmouth (or Pifcataqua) in 1671, was involved in a difpute with Gov. Cranfield in 1683, and unjuftly imprifoned. He came to Bofton and was chofen Affiftant at the Firft Church. He returned to Portfmouth, but died at Bofton, 4 July, 1697, aged 64. He was honorably diftin-guifhed by his oppofition to the witch-craft delufion.—ED.

⁴⁶ Deacon-Hill is furely a miftake for Beacon-hill. It bore that name in 1689. See DRAKE, p. 482.—ED.

welcome to 'em as Sowr Ale in Summer; they Look upon my Gain to be their Lofs, and do make good the Truth of that old Proverb, That Intereft will not lie. But I muft begin to make my Addreffes to 'em.

Mr. Ufher,[44] your humble Servant: He's very rich, and Merchandizes; very witty; and has got a great Eftate by Bookfelling. He propof'd to me the buying my whole Venture; but yet wou'd give but £30 per cent. which wou'd not do with me by a great deal; and therefore the Treaty being over, I fell to planting of my Cannon, and making my Redoubts, and fo made far better Advances.

Mr. Phillips,[45] my old Correfpondent! 'Tis reafon I fhou'd make

---

[44] John Ufher, fon of Hezekiah and Frances Ufher, was born at Bofton, 17 Apr., 1648. He was a bookfeller as we have feen, and was early interefted in public affairs. In 1676 he was Agent for the Colony to purchafe the Province of Maine, and vifited England in 1679. He was one of Androffe's Council and chofen friends. In a letter dated Salem, 17th June, 1686, to Jofeph Dudley, is the following item: "Sir, I did forgett to fpeak to Monck for your dinner, butt hope you will order your officer to doe itt"; this is not without intereft, in connection with Dunton.

When Androffe was feized by the people in April, 1689, he was fent under guard to Ufher's houfe; and foon after Ufher went to London, where he ftayed until 1692. He married, probably during this vifit, Elizabeth, daughter of Samuel Allen.

Allen bought in 1691, from the heirs of Capt. John Mafon, all their right to the Province of New-Hampfhire. Ufher accordingly was appointed, 1 Mch., 1692, Lieutenant - Governor, and returned to this country. Here he was involved in perpetual difputes with the actual fettlers, and was fuperfeded by William Partridge in 1697. Afterwards Allen came over himfelf, and Ufher

acted as one of the Council. In 1699, the Earl of Bellomont became Royal Governor, and in 1703 Ufher was again commiffioned as Lieutenant-Governor. The claims of Allen produced endlefs difputes; Ufher however feems to have acted as a faithful officer, and to have exerted himfelf to fecure the fafety of the colony during the French war. In 1715 Col. Samuel Shute was made Governor and George Vaughan, Lieutenant, and Ufher, thus fuperfeded, retired to Medford, Mafs., where he had a fine eftate. Here he died, 5 Sept., 1726, leaving feveral children, one of whom was Rev. John, of Briftol, R. I. Defcendants of the name are ftill remaining.—ED.

[45] Samuel Phillips, who died in October, 1720, aged 58, married probably in 1681, Hannah, daughter of Capt. Benjamin Gillam. The match connected him with many wealthy families here, as I have fhown in the "New-England Hiftorical and Genealogical Regifter," xix. 254. There were feveral other families of the name in Maffachufetts, and the defcendants of Rev. George Phillips, of Watertown, have been diftinguifhed in our political hiftory. No connection however is traced between the bookfeller and his namefakes, and

make you the next Vifit.⁴⁷ He dealt with me before; has a pretty and obliging Wife; Treated me with a noble Dinner, and good Store of Excellent Cyder; (and his maid then, was an Old Englifh Woman, and has fince liv'd with Mr. Laurence, Bookfeller in the Poultry, and my Neighbour.) He's young, witty, and the moft Beautiful Man in the whole Town of Bofton; He's very Juft, and (as an effect of that) Thriving.

But leaving him, I Rambled next to vifit Mynheer Bruning,⁴⁸ at the corner of Prifon-Lane; a Dutch Bookfeller from Holland; he is a man that's fcrupuloufly juft, plain in his cloaths, and upright in his Dealing: And fo exact therein, that he wou'd not wrong a man of the hundredth part of a Farthing if he knew it, and fo very careful that nothing can efcape his knowledge: and fo well verf'd in the knowledge of all forts of Books, that he may well be ftil'd, A Compleat Bookfeller. He was more generous than to decry whatever Book he fees, fowerly becaufe 'twas not of his own Printing: There are a fort of Men like Bafilifks, that dart an Eye empoyfon'd with the Dregs of Pining Envy, who when they fee another's Happinefs, do wifh the Organs of their fight were crack'd, and that the Engines of their grief wou'd caft their

THOMAS, in his "Hiftory of Printing," undoubtedly errs in faying that Samuel Phillips's defcendants continued bookfelling; he having miftaken the true anceftry of thefe later merchants. Samuel Phillips had three fons, Gillam, Samuel and Henry; and three daughters, two of whom married relatives named Savage.

Gillam Phillips, who was for a fhort time a bookfeller, died 18 Oct., 1770. His wife was Marie, fifter of famous Peter Faneuil, with whom he received quite a large dowry. Henry Phillips, the youngeft fon, was the unfortunate man who killed Benjamin Woodbridge in a duel, July 3, 1728. The furvivor efcaped, but died in France, in May, 1729. Mr. L. M. Sargent, in his "Deal-

ings with the Dead," has given a very full and interefting account of this deplorable affair.—ED.

⁴⁷ In his "Life and Errors" Dunton alters this fentence as follows: "He treated me with a noble Dinner, and (if I may truft my Eyes,) is bleft with a Pretty obliging Wife; I'll fay this for SAM (after dealing with him for fome Hundred Pounds) he's very juft, and (as an Effect of that) very Thriving. I fhall add to his Character, that he's Young and Witty," &c., &c.—ED.

⁴⁸ Mynheer Bruning, was Jofeph Bruning, or Browning, his name being varioufly fpelt. He was of Bofton in 1682, but his name does not occur in the Bofton Cenfus of 1695.—ED.

their Eye-Balls, like two Globes of Wildfire forth, to melt the unproportion'd frame of Nature: Thefe are the Men that will run down the moft elaborate and well-writ Treatifes, only becaufe it had none of their Midwifery to bring it into public view; And yet fhall give the greateft Elogies to the moft naufeous and infipid Trafh that e're was made the Burthen of the Prefs, when they have had the hap to be concern'd in't. But our Dutch Bookfeller was none of thofe; he valu'd a good Book, who-ever printed it; nor wou'd he praife an Idle Pamphlet tho' it fhou'd happen to be done for him. He was my Partner in Printing Mr. Mather's and Mr. Moody's Sermon on condemned Morgan.

But from the Dutch, I rambled to the Scotch Bookfeller, one Campbel: He is a brifk young Fellow, that dreffes All-a-mode, and fets himfelf off to the beft Advantage; and yet thrives apace. I am told (and for his fake I wifh it may be true) that a Young Lady of a Great Fortune[49] has married him. He's an Induftrious Man, and faw me often.

And

[49] As to this wealthy damfel we find the following particulars:

By a deed, recorded Suffolk Deeds xxiv. 110, it feems that Sufanna, widow of Duncan Campbell, by order of Court, dated 4 May, 1708, fold a houfe and a lot of land meafuring over one hundred feet fquare, on Summer Street, one half being part of her husband's eftate, and one half being her inheritance from her mother, Mrs. Grace Oxford, widow, deceafed.

By another deed, dated 30 Apr., 1679, (Suff. Deeds xii. 252,) William Pitt, merchant of Marblehead, granted this land to truftees for his daughter Grace, now wife of Thomas Oxford, and her children Sufanna and Margaret Porter, whom fhe had by her former husband, William Porter, deceafed. This was one half of the property belonging to Pitts' late wife Sufanna, formerly wife of Philip Eley, deceafed. The other half by a fimilar deed, recorded at Salem, (Effex Deeds v. 308,) Pitts gave to his daugher Mary, wife of Chrifto-pher Latimore, vintner. Thefe details are not to be found in SAVAGE, nor the faﬅ that, 25 Nov., 1670, (Suff. Wills vii. 48) adminiftration was granted "on the eftate of Sufanna Ely (fince Sufanna Pitts)" to John Bundy, of Taunton, in the colony of Plymouth, he being near-eft of kin.

Duncan Campbell had by this wife five children, William, born 27 May, 1687; Archibald, b, 10 Feb., 1688–9; Mathew, 14 Feb., 1690–1; Sufanna, 1 Feb., 1695–6; and Agnes, 2 Mch., 1699–1700.

Campbell feems to have given up bookfelling and have become a merchant, being fo denominated in his inventory of 7 April, 1703, when his property was valued at about £900, one third being in bills of exchange on bottomry. His widow at that time renders her return on his eftate as infolvent.—ED.

And now my Friend, having thus vifited the Bookfellers, I'll give you next a brief account of what Acquaintance I had among the Town : And will begin with Mr. Willy,[20] who fled hither on the Account of Confcience, (and is Brother-in-Law to the Reverend Mr. Bayly, of whom I've fpoke before.) He is a man of a large heart, and an extenfive Charity ; And one who in Relieving others Wants, confiders not fo much his own Ability, as their Neceffity. This Monmouth's Forlorn Fugitives experienc'd largely, to whom he was the common Refuge and Affylum.

The next that I fhall mention is Mr. White,[21] a Worthy Merchant, who croffes both the Torrid and the frozen Zone, midft Rocks and fwallowing Gulfs for gainful Trade ; piercing the Center for the fhining Oar, and th' Oceans Bofom to rake Pearly Sands ; a Merchant who by Trading has clafp'd Iflands to the Continent, and tack'd one Countrey to another : Nor was his fkill in Merchandizing all : His Knowledge both of Men and Things, was Univerfal : And to have heard him talk of any fubject, you wou'd have thought he had engroff'd all Knowledge ; and that the feven Liberal Sciences took up their Refidence within his Breft.

The next was Mr. Green[22] the Printer : I need do no more than to name his Trade, to convince you that he was a Man
of

---

[20] Mr. Willy was no doubt Edward Willy, already mentioned, (note 20, p. 63,) as fecurity for feveral new-comers. His name alfo occurs on documents at the State Houfe, dated in 1687. He is there called "fhop-keeper." The name muft not be confounded with that of Willys or Willis.—ED.

[21] This may poffibly have been Capt. Samuel White, of Weymouth, who married Mary Dyer, and d. s. p. in 1698–9. His widow's will, of 30 Oct., 1705, mentions two negroes, plate, &c. SAVAGE mentions a William White, of Bofton, as a friend of Andros in 1688. —ED.

[22] Mr. Green, the printer, was doubtlefs Samuel Green, jr., fon of Samuel Green, of Cambridge, Mafs., a printer there, and grandfon of Bartholomew, who died here in 1635. SAVAGE would make Dunton's friend to be the father ; but as Samuel, jr., was born in 1648, and was thus 36 years old at this time, the defcription feems more fuited to him. I am affured on good authority that this Samuel did not marry Elizabeth Sill, of Cambridge, but that her husband was of another branch of the family, poffibly allied to this.—ED.

11

of good Senfe and Underftanding: and here likewife was Mr. John Allen,[55] your quondam fervant, who was fo well known to you, that I need fay the lefs of him; But yet being both my Friend and Fellow-Traveller, that for four Months together run the fame rifque of Fortune with me, I cannot but fay fomething of him: His Afpect has fomething fo extraordinary in it, that whoever does but look upon him, will make no Scruple to give him the Title of My Lord: He is Mafter of an Excellent Mediocrity of Temper, for if Fortune fmile, it never elates him; neither is he caft down if fhe Frowns. And under fome more than ordinary Dif-appointment, I have known him to drown his Sorrows in a glafs of Cyder: Fortune has plaid him fome flippery Tricks fo that he'll never Truft her: and if any thing falls out, better than he expects, 'tis Welcome.

But being got among the Printers, Mr. Larkin, You may juftly expect that I fhou'd fay fomething of Printing: Which certainly is an Art (or Myftery, as I think you call it) which deferves a greater Encomium than the narrow Limits of this Letter will permit me to give it. It is without doubt the moft compendious and eafie Way of Communicating Mens Inward Sentiments to one another, tho' at never fo remote a Diftance, as was ever found out in the World. But before I fpeak of the Ufe and Benefit of Printing, It is neceffary that I fpeak fomething of its Original and firft finding out: For it wou'd be a great Pity that that Noble Art that gives Im-mortality to all other Sciences, fhould it felf be buried in the Dark Womb of Oblivion. It is generally agreed that it is a German Invention, found out about the year 1440; tho' whether it was John Guttenburg, or Laurence Cofter, (by fome called Laurence John,) or whether it was firft found

out

---

[55] John Allen, the Printer, is duly mentioned by THOMAS, as the printer of the Bofton News-Letter from 1707 to 1711. He kept in Pudding-Lane, near the Poft-Office, being thus a near neighbor of George Monck. The laft book printed by him which Thomas had feen, was dated in 1724.—ED.

out at Mentz in High Germany, or at Haerlem in the Netherlands, is yet a Difpute among Hiftorians. But all agree that the firft Occafion of this Noble Invention was the Inventers cutting of the Letters of his Name out of the Bark of a Tree, and then putting them into a fine Linnen Handkerchief, he found upon the taking of them out, the Characters of thofe Types he had cut, imprinted on the Handkerchief: This fet him at work, firft to cut feveral Alphabets of great and fmall Letters in Wood, to Print upon Paper; which fucceeding according to his Defire, he afterwards improv'd it further, in making his Letters of Metal, and for the more quick Difpatch, found out a way of cafting them. This was very fair for the beginning, tho' all muft grant it was Improv'd vaftly by thofe that came after. It is great Pity that the Original Inventer was no more carefully tranfmitted down to Pofterity: The beft Reafon I have heard affign'd for it is,—

> Brave Men more ftudious were in former Days,
> Of Doing good, than of Obtaining Praife.

But whoever was the Inventer, certain it is that it is an Excellent Invention, and has made us acquainted with the World, and with all thofe Remarkable Actions that have happened in the Remoteft Parts and Ages of it. This brings frefh to my Remembrance the Sermon Preach'd to the Society of Printers in 1682, at St. Sepulchre's Church in London, when you were one of the Stewards that kept that Feaft. The words of the Text I remember were, *Thefe are the Men that have turn'd the World upfide down, and now they are come hither alfo:* and Mr. Stoughton the Lecturer (for he it was that preach'd the Sermon) affirm'd, That tho' the Charge was falfe againft the Apoftles in the Senfe by them intended; yet it was true in a better fenfe, and they had turn'd the World up-fide-down in that, that is, They had turn'd the World from Heathenifh Idolatry and Paganifm

to

to the Worfhip of the True and Living God: And his
Application was, That the Enemies of Religion and Learn-
ing had Traduc'd Printing as turning the World up-fide-
down in a bad fenfe; tho' it was really True that Printing
had turn'd the world upfide-down in a good, which was,
That it had Turn'd it from a World of Darknefs, Ignorance,
Irreligion and Atheifm, to a World of Light, Knowledge,
Erudition, Learning, and the Knowledge of God and the
True Religion; and what can be faid more in its praife, I
know not.

But having faid enough of Printing, I muft return again
to Mr. Green, one of the New-England Printers: Who was
a very honeft and a very fenfible Man, and fo facetious and
obliging in his Converfation, that I took a great delight in
his Company, and made ufe of his Houfe to while away my
Melancholy Hours. His wife is a fine Woman, and of a
very affable and obliging Temper.   But fhe needs no higher
commendation than this, that fhe was an Intimate of, and
brought me acquainted with, Madam Brick, one of the fineft
and moft accomplifh'd Women in Bofton, of whom more
anon.

Another of my acquaintance was Captain Geery,[54] an
honeft and a worthy Gentleman, who is remarkable, and
very much efteem'd in Bofton for a True Lover of his
Lover, and perhaps Junius Brutus, and the famous Scævola
among the Romans, were not more eminent for their Love
to their Countrey then was Captain Geery in New-England.

Another of 'em was Mr. George Monke,[55] a Perfon fo
remarkable

[54] Capt. Geery. As we fhall fee by Letter VII., Dunton vifited at Wenham a Mr. Geery, who had a fine eftate there, and whofe father was a Captain in Bofton. We fhall therefore probably be fafe to identify this gentleman with Capt. William Gerrifh, of Newbury, and after 1678, of Bofton. He had a large family, and his immediate defcendants attained high pofitions here, as recorded by SAVAGE. Capt. Gerrifh died at Salem, 9 Auguft, 1687, aged probably 67 years.—ED.

[55] George Monke was the landlord of the Blue Anchor Tavern. He married Lucy, daughter of Thomas Gardner, and widow of John Turner, by whom he had George, b. 7 Nov., 1683, and

remarkable that, had I not been acquainted with him, it wou'd be a difficult matter to make any New-England Man believe

William, 17 Aug., 1686. By his fecond wife, Elizabeth, widow of John Woodmanfey, he probably had no children. He died 5 Sept., 1698. His will, dated in 1698, mentions only fon George, and ftep-daughter, Margaret Woodmanfey. It alfo mentions "one meffuage or tenement lying or being in the county of Effex, within four miles of Rumford, in the Kingdom of England, containing two acres of land, formerly the eftate of my father, William Monck, and the place where faid eftate is, goes by the name of Naveftock."

George Monck

As to the Blue Anchor Tavern, it undoubtedly ftood very near the fpot now covered by the Tranfcript Building on Wafhington St. As will be fhown in the appendix to this volume, the eftate was only feparated by a lot forty feet wide from the eftate belonging to Harvard College, now occupied by Little, Brown & Co., bookfellers.

George Monck bought this eftate, 28 July, 1691, of his ftep-daughter Hannah, wife of John Edwards, and daughter of John Turner, deceafed. It was moft probably the houfe which Robert Turner built in 1652, when he had liberty to "let his new houfe jet into the ftreet further than his old one is, and to pay, 2s. 6d. a year for ever," as DRAKE records (p. 332). SAVAGE fays of Robert Turner, that "at the fign of the Anchor he furnifhed lodgings and refrefhments to the members of the government frequently, to the Commiffioners of the United Colonies of New England, to juries, and to the clergy when fummoned into fynod by our General Court." In his will he left "to fon Ephraim my new-built houfe, a part whereof he now dwelleth in ; alfo my garden, running from the houfe down to the lane, running upon a ftraight line home to John Toppins' houfe." "To fon John the other part of my dwelling houfe and the ground below it, bounded by Mr. Cole's fence, the other fide to be fo left as my fon Ephraim may have paffage to the yard and garden."

After Robert Turner died, probably in 1664, his fon John followed the fame bufinefs of vintner, and died before Oct., 1681. His inventory of 12 Apr., 1681, (Suff. Wills, vi. 360,) mentions "one houfe with a piece of land fronting to the highway, and fo running down to the land of Mr. Wharton's pafture, and Mr. Middlecutts, and running to the corner-poft of Mr. Fayerweather's land, and fo down in a ftraight line to Mr. Wharton's land." It mentions a little room, court chamber, fore-ftreet rooms, garret and parlor. The wines enumerated were Canary, Madeira and Claret.

As a proof that our forefathers brought their home cuftoms, we may here copy from the inventory of Nicholas Wilmott, in 1684, the lift of the apartments in an inn fimilar to the "Blue Anchor." It mentions the chamber called the 'Crofs Keyes,' that called the 'Green Dragon,' the 'Anchor' Chamber, the 'Caftle' Chamber, the low room called the 'Sun,' and the 'Rofe' low room.

We may imagine that Dunton as a favored gueft at the Blue Anchor occupied the "Court chamber," or one of the rooms on the Fore-ftreet.

It is probable that the Blue Anchor Tavern efcaped the great fire of October, 1711, but we have not traced its later hiftory.—ED.

believe that I had been in Bofton: For there was no one Houfe in all the Town more noted, or where a Man might meet with better accommodation: Befides he was a brifk and Jolly Man, whofe Converfation was coveted by all his guefts, as being the Life and Spirit of the Company, animating all with a certain Vivacity and Cheerfulnefs, which chaf'd away all Melancholy as the Sun does clouds; fo that it was almoft impoffible not to be Merry in his Company.

Another was Captain Towenfend,[56] a fine Gentleman, courteous and Affable in his Converfation: For as the Sword of the beft temper'd Metal is moft flexible, fo the truly Generous (like him) are moft pliant and courteous in their Behaviours.

I might next Ramble to Mr. Jollyff, Juftice Lines, Macarty,[57] and fome others; But leaft I tire you quite, I'll next come to another diftinct Head, which fhall be, of thofe of my Countrey-Men that have Rambled into this Countrey as well as myfelf; fuch of them, I mean, as I came acquainted with in the courfe of my Bufinefs: And of them, Firft,

Mr. Mortimer,[58] who came from Ireland; a Gentleman fo modeft that the leaft Commendation wou'd make his Rofie Cheeks to blufh, as if Modefty itfelf lay there within a bed of corral. A bawdy jeft fpoke in his company wou'd fhame him more than if another had a Baftard laid to him. And yet there was none that underftood fenfe better than himfelf;

or

---

[56] This was probably Penn Townfend, born in 1651, fon of William T., by his wife, Hannah Penn. He was a wine merchant, and a prominent citizen. He was Speaker, and Counfellor for many years, and ferved through all the ranks in the militia from enfign to colonel, and died 21 Aug., 1727.—ED.

[57] John Joyliffe died in 1702; Juftice Lines may be Benjamin, fon of Simon Lynde, or Jofeph Lynde, of Charleftown, of a different family, who was a promi-nent man at this date; Florence Maccarty and Thaddeus Maccarty were both of Bofton, in 1686.—ED.

[58] An Edward Mortimer, of Bofton, had quite a family born here between 1674 and 1688. Yet as Dunton records that he and Mr. King were his two fellow-paffengers on his return, it is poffible that the two friends here noticed never returned to Bofton, and that their names do not appear on our record.—ED.

or that cou'd with more readinefs anfwer the moft abftrufe and knotty queftions. And 'twas my happinefs to have this Gentleman for one of my fellow Travellers home.

The next of thefe was Mr. King,[58] who was my daily companion; an Ingenious and good Natur'd Perfon; Heir to a good Eftate;—But

> Love ! Cruel Love ! Thou Source of all his Tears ;
> Unhappy he in whom thy Power appears :
> But happy he in whofe untroubled Breft
> No Storms of Love difturb his Halcyon Reft ;
> Not bleft with Pleafure, but fecure from Wo,
> And Jealoufie and Rayes which with it go ;
> Then fhou'd we not by clear Experience fee
> What fits of Heat and Cold in Love there be :
> How near the Brink of Death and dire Defpair,
> Th' Imagined Sweets of Love and Pleafure are ;
> Nor thofe Tormenting Tortures fhou'd we know,
> Which who left merit, moft do undergo ;
> For ftill the more fome pay profound refpect,
> Their flighted Service finds the more neglect.

Love was the fad fweet caufe of this young Gentleman's long Ramble hither; My Cafe and his, you know, are mighty different; for I am happy, as far as Love can at this Diftance make me fo: But yet methinks I cann't but fympathize with him, and bear a part in his unhappinefs; And unto me the reafon's obvious: The Breafts I fuck'd were neither Wolves nor Tygers, and I am fure I have a heart of Wax, foft and foon melting: But whither has the thoughts of Love cauf'd me to Ramble? But there's another Excellency in this Gentleman that muft not be omitted; He has a Voice that wou'd have charm'd the Sphears; and had he but been a Contemporary with the Thracian Harper, the ftones had follow'd him, and not Orpheus. And laft of all, he had a mighty Kindnefs ftill for Philaret.

The

---

[58] Benjamin and William King occur in the lift for 1687; but the previous note fhows that the Mr. King mentioned returned home in 1686.—ED.

The next of thefe was Mr. York,[59] an induftrious Merchant, who fought uncertain Treafure with a certain Care: One that wou'd proudly Plow the foaming Main, and climb fteep Mountains for the fparkling ftone. And yet for all his Induftry in Merchandizing, he had his Lucida Intervalla, when he unbent the Bow (for too long keeping of it bent is the high way to fpoil it, as the Archers tell us), and then he treated the Fair Sex with fo much Courtfhip and Addrefs, as if it had been all his Study, and he had never minded any other Bufinefs. His Garb was always neat and fpruce, fuch as might make him Acceptable to the Ladies.

The next I'll mention fhall be Mr. Andrew Thorncomb, a Bookfeller from London, and who fometime kept a fhop on London-Bridge. He's an Ingenious Man, and one that underftands himfelf fo well, and is fo facetious in his converfation, that his Company is coveted by the beft Gentlemen in Bofton, and they efteem themfelves the happieft that can get it. Nor is he unacceptable to the Fair Sex, for he has fomething in him fo extreamly charming as makes 'em very fond of being in his Company; for which perhaps his excellent finging and variety of Songs is none of the leaft motives. He is a perfon whofe humour I like very well, and one that vifited me often. But I need fay no more, becaufe I'm fure you know him very well.

The next I'll mention fhall be Mr. Heath[60]—a grave and fober Merchant: And were I now to write the Character of a good Merchant, I wou'd as foon take him for the Exemplar of one, as any Man I know. This I am fure, he never wrongs the Man that buys of him, in Number, Weight or Meafure. For 'tis his Judgment that thefe are the Statute

Laws

---

[59] John York is on the tax lift of 1687. —ED.

[60] Elias Heath is on a petition in 1700, (fee DRAKE, 518,) figned by feveral "merchants and traders," for a bankrupt law. Other figners were Penn Townfend, Francis Burroughs, Thaddeus Maccarty. Elias Heath died 19 Oct., 1706, aged 55. He had a fifter, Ann Turner, of Buckland, co. Surrey. —ED.

Laws of Trade, which, like thofe of the Medes and Perfians, muft never be remov'd; and I have heard him fay that fuch a Cozenage is worfe than open Felony; becaufe they rob a Man of 's Purfe, and never bid him ftand; and befides that they Endeavour to make God acceffory to their cozenage by falfe weights: For God is the Principal Clerk of the Market: All the Weights of the Bag (as Solomon tells us, Prov. 16, 11,) being his Work. There are two things remarkable in him, (and I will inftance no more.) One is, That he never warrants any Ware for good, but what is fo indeed: And the other, That he makes no Advantage of his Chapman's ignorance, efpecially if he referrs himfelf to his Honefty. Where the Confcience of the Seller is all the Skill of the Buyer, the Seller is made the Judge, fo that he doth not fo much afk as Order what he muft pay. I have read that old Bifhop Latimer once bought a knife that coft him two pence (which was it feems accounted a great Price in thofe days), and fhewing it unto his Friend, he told him, The Cutler had cozen'd him, for the knife was not worth a penny: No, replied Latimer, he cozen'd not me, but his own Confcience. So far from that was this honeft Gentleman, that when a Bookfeller (that fhall be namelefs) did out of Ignorance demand lefs for a Book than it was truly worth, he of his own accord gave him the full value of it. This honeft Gentleman did me the favour to be my daily Vifitor, and has brought me acquainted with one Mr. Gore of New York, with whom I trade, which I hope will be to my advantage.

Mr. Watfon fhall be the next, formerly a Merchant in London; but not thriving on it, he left the Exchange for Weftminfter Hall; (obferving that the Lawyers get moft Money), and fo in Bofton paffes for a Solicitor; And is become as dextrous at fplitting of Caufes as if he had been bred up an Attorneys Clerk. And now his Pen's the Plough, and Parliament is the foil from whence he reaps both Coyn, and fometimes Curfes; as often is the fate of

other

other Lawyers. But I muſt do him the Juſtice to affirm, That he knows how to be as honeſt as the beſt Lawyer of 'em all. He is full of fancy, ſo that the Quirks of the Law are become familiar to him; but what is more ſtrange, is, That Broken Titles make him whole. I ſhall only add more, That he has the Reputation of a Wit.

The next is Mr. C——, [Cook,] a Young Beau; One that has boaſted of more Villany than ever he committed; [However as he bought a great many Books, I cannot diſown my acquaintance with him. And I here publiſh his matchleſs impudence, in hopes to ſhame him into better morals.][61]   *

* * * * * * * * * * * * *

What I have to ſay more of this Young Spark, is this, He brought over a great Venture; but at his rate of managing his matters, 'tis well if he can ſave enough to bring him back again; For he does all by his Proxy, Mr. Watſon, while he Wenches: which is a thing ſo chargeable, that if he had the Wealth of Creſus, it wou'd make him Bankrupt.

Another of my Fellow-Ramblers is Mr. Maſon,[62] a grave, ſober Merchant, a good Man, and well reſpected; amongſt honeſt Men downright honeſt, but very blunt: One that wou'd ſpeak his Mind, howe're Men took it. I remember once, that when he went to Viſit a Boſtonian Gentlewoman, ſhe told him ſhe was glad to ſee him, but ſorry that he came at ſuch a time when her Houſe lay ſo dirty, and ſo much out of Order. To which Mr. Maſon only return'd, Why, prithee, when was't otherwiſe? Which blunt Expreſſion (which perhaps carry'd too much Truth in't) the Gentlewoman

---

[61] This paſſage thus ſtands in the "Life and Errors," and it ſeems preferable to the page or two of general moralizing which Dunton wrote in the preſent MS., and which we have omitted. —Ed.

[62] Arthur Maſon, of Boſton, a baker, died 4 March, 1708, aged 77. He lived on School St. His children and heirs were David, Arthur, Jonathan, Alice, wife of Sam. Shepherd, Joanna, (the widow Breck,) Mary, wife of Rev. John Norton, and Abigail Gillam. As will be afterwards ſhown, he was the father of Dunton's famous "widow Brick." —Ed.

woman took as an affront. But 'twas all one to him, for he wou'd make no Retraction. He is lately gone for England.

Another was Mr. Mallinson; He is one of thofe unfortunate Gentlemen that fled from Monmouth: One that is a great Fencer, who yet found there was no Fence againſt a Flail: And was in England, ſo ſenſible that the Weakeſt goes to the Wall, that he rather truſted to his Flight than to his ſkill in fencing, for his ſafety. He is a very confcientious, good Man, (which is rare in one of that Profeſſion,) and ſo great a Critick, that he wou'd even find a knot in a Bulruſh.

But it is time now to deſcend to my Particular Friends, (who tho' laſt named, yet being ſuch, will the more readily pardon it.) For tho' I had now Acquaintance with moſt of the confiderable Traders in Boſton, yet particular Friendſhips are neceſſary for ſeveral Reaſons: And, if we will believe the wifeſt of Men, ought to be preferr'd not only before Acquaintance, but Relations; and that for a good Reaſon too, Even becauſe they are nearer; for, (ſays he,) *There is a Friend that is nearer than a Brother:* And therefore his Counſel is, Thy Friend, and thy Father's Friend, forget not. And the Truth is, tho' 'tis good to have the reſpeⅽt of all, and to live generally belov'd; yet every Man has his particular Wants, which he finds it neceſſary to Communicate to ſome Particular Friend; for a ſecret is ſafe, lodg'd in the Boſom of one, which is many times improper to be communicated to one more; at leaſt not to ſeveral. So that a ſolid and true Friend, founded upon Vertue and ſincere Religion, (which are the only Ligaments that will make it hold,) is one of the greateſt Sweetneſſes of Human Life. How pleaſant is it to communicate our Misfortunes to a Friend, who will both alleviate our Griefs, and Sympathize with us in our Sorrows: And even our Joys themſelves, unleſs imparted to a Friend, ſwell to that height, that it proves dangerous, and often fatal. But I confeſs ſuch

Friends

Friends are rarely to be found, tho' fuch there are; and former Ages afford us feveral Examples of them: There has been in the World, a David and a Jonathan, a Cranmer and a Cromwel; a Eufebius and a Pamphilius. As to Cranmer, he was faithful to the Lord Cromwel even in his Difgrace, infomuch that he Ventur'd the Difpleafure of King Henry VIII., to Excufe for Him; and abfented from the Parliament when he was condemned; thereby fhewing himfelf a True Friend; for fuch a one is born for Adverfity, and Changes not as Fortune Changes. Eufebius, Bifhop of Cefarea, for his great Love to his Friend Pamphilus, was firnamed Pamphilius. Minutius Felix faith, That he and his Friend Octavius did both will and will the fame thing.

Memorable is the Story of Audarnidas, a Corinthian by Birth, who had two Friends, Aretæus and Charixcenus; both Wealthy, but himfelf very poor: This Man at his Death made this his laft Will and Teftament, viz.: I bequeath my Mother to Aretæus, to be nourifhed and Cherifhed by him in her old Age: Mem., I bequeath my Daughter to Charixcenus, to be placed out by him, with as big a Portion as poffibly he can give her. The Girl was at that time Marriageable. Thofe two Friends to Audarnidas, as foon as they heard of the Will, came forth-with, and accepted thofe things that were given in charge; but Charixcenus dying within five Days, Aretæus undertook the whole Charge, maintained the old Woman during Life, and marry'd the Daughter, together with his own, on the fame Day, allowing them out of five Talents, Two Talents a piece for their Portion.

But notwithftanding this inftance, and fome others, of Remarkable Friendfhips, yet a pair of true Friends are feldomer to be found, than a Club of Knaves, or a herd of Brutes agreeing together. Cowley tells us, There are fewer Friends on Earth than Kings. Yet I was fo happy as to
find

find fome even in Bofton, whofe Characters I fhall next prefent you with. And fhall begin with

Dr. Oaks,[63] whofe great Abilities and Extraordinary Skill in Phyfick, has juftly render'd him the greateft Æfculapius of the Countrey: His wife and fafe Prefcriptions have expell'd more Difeafes, and refcu'd Languifhing Patients from the Jaws of Death, than Mountebanks and Quack-Salvers have fent to thofe dark Regions: And on that fcore, Death has declar'd himfelf his Mortal Enemy: Whereas Death claims a Relation to thofe Pretenders to Phyfick, as being both of one Occupation, viz.: that of killing Men. But to give you his more particular Character: As touching his Perfwafion in Religion, he is a great Diffenter; and fo far from being a Ceremony-monger, that he believes in the Days of the Gofpel, the Worfhip of GOD confifts not in outward Pomp and Ceremony, but in Spirit and Truth: He is a modeft, humble, and good Man; as will fufficiently appear by this, That at his firft coming to a Patient, he perfwades him to put his Truft in GOD the Fountain of Health: The want whereof, hath cauf'd the bad fuccefs of moft Phyficians; For they that w'ont acknowledge GOD in all their Applications, GOD won't acknowledge them, in that fuccefs which they might otherwife expect. His Civilities to me, were fo many and great, that not to acknowledge them, were to be guilty of Ingratitude. He is one that in this degenerate Age, retains the Piety of the firft Planters: He has Treated me very kindly at his Houfe, and has manifefted a great refpect to his Relation in Ratcliff, who fent by me a Letter of Recommendation to him, and to Mr. Gibfon, a young Divine. I cou'd be much larger in his Character; but after all, muft come far fhort of it; and therefore fhall conclude with

[63] Thomas Oakes, fon of Edward Oakes, of Cambridge, Mafs., and brother of Urian Oakes, the Prefident of Harvard College, was a phyfician. He was Speaker, Affiftant and Agent to England. He died at Eaftham, where his fon Jofiah was minifter, 15 July, 1719.—ED.

with what I have already faid. From him, I pafs to my good Friend

Dr. Bullivant,[64] formerly my fellow-citizen in London. His Skill in Pharmacy was fuch, as rendered him the moft

compleat

[64] Benjamin Bullivant was Androffe's Attorney-General. SAVAGE fays that he had a daughter Hannah, bapt. 3 Jany., 1686, at the Old South ; but that he was afterwards, in 1687, a Warden of King's Chapel. Though a friend of Androffe's, and imprifoned at the Revolution, he remained doubtlefs in Bofton, where he was in 1699, when the Governor, the Earl of Bellomont, had an encounter with him, thus recorded by Hutchinfon, ii. 113: "Among the more liberal was one Bullivant, an apothecary, who had been a juftice of peace, under Andros. Lord Bellamont, going from the lecture to his houfe, with a great crowd round him, paffed by Bullivant ftanding at his fhop door, loitering. '*Doctor*,' fays his lordfhip with an audible voice, '*you have loft a precious fermon to-day.*' Bullivant whifpered to one of his companions who ftood by him, '*If I could have got as much by being there as his lordfhip will, I would have been there too.*'"

By the following letter, copied for us from the original in the Bodleian Library, (Rawlinfon MS. Mifc. 72, f. 74.) it feems that Bullivant was living in England, it being in reply to one of Dunton's dated three days previous.

Letter addreffed :
"For Mr. John Dunton,
    "at Mrs. Tomkins, the laft houfe
    "next the feilds in Grayes-Inn Lane,
        "In London."
"My moft worthy Ultra-diluvian friend !
"The great paynes you have taken in your very large and patheticall epiftle of the 15th prefent, give me a full affurance of your continued, and very loveing refpects to your fellow wanderer,

and I wifh I could perfwade my felfe to be a partner with you in this your fo much applauded new-adventure, but fo it is (my kind friend) that haveing 10 Tickets in the laft yeares Lottery, and all turned up *blanc*, I am reduced to the eftate of Æfops fhepheard, (who had been a Merchant and loft by his adventures,) when attending his flock upon the fhore, viewing a calm fea, and the ftately fhips ploughing the back of the furly ocean, cried out, Ne'r flatter, I have no more dates and almonds for you. And though this is excufe enough to a reafonable mind that my fpare crums are gone, and Ne Sutor ultra, &c. yet I will tell you a very truth, that my indifpofition of the Stone in the Bladder, doth fo frequently and fiercely affault me, that I have my grave in View, and am ready to cry out with the Trojan, Poft varios cafus, poft tot difcrimina rerum, tendimus in——fepulchrum——and have little courage at 65 to entertain a project not like to Iffue in Leffe than 32 yeares. I own the hook is well guilt, but ictus pifcator fapit, fo much for Lotteries : yet I will not part till I tell you I thinke you do well to joyn forces in good company ; it is a likely way to advantage ; and I heartily wifh it you. And now to fhew you, I am not weary of a correfpondence with you, I muft pray you give me your opinion of Mr. Cotton Mather's Magnalia Chrifti Americana in folio, printed .for Parkhurft, and what cenfure it hath from the Learned world. I have read it Over and over, and fome things are very takeing in itt, (Epigrams, Punns, Gingles, &c., excepted,) efpecially Sir Wm. Phips and Eliots life. I fancie myfelfe amongft them when I have it in

my

compleat Pharmacopean, not only in all Bofton, but in all New-England; and is befide, as much a Gentleman as any one in all the Countrey. And to do him right, I muft confider him both as a Gentleman and a Phyfician. As a Gentleman, his Birth was generous, but his Qualities exceeded his Birth: He cou'd not indeed boaft of a large Genealogy of Lords and Barons defcended from his Anceftors; but this he cou'd boaft, (which was far greater,) That he had Ennobled himfelf by his own Merits: His Valour makes him Son to Cefar, and his Learning and Oratory gives him a Title to claim Kindred to Tully. His knowledge of the Laws fitted him for the Office of Attorny-General in this country, which was conferr'd upon him, on the Revolution here. 'Tis true, he fought it not, tho' he accepted of it when 'twas offer'd: The Countrey knew his worth, and knew how to prize it, altho' himfelf feem'd ignorant of it: And while he held it, he was fo far from pufhing things to

that

my hand. I muft alfo, my friend, take upon me fo farr as to requeft you will ferioufly Let me know if you are really the author of fuch Compofitions as carry your name, or whither you are (according to the cuftom of your faculty) only the publifher. I have feen feverall, as the Bull-baiteing, &c. and wonder at your paynes, and where you have Leafure; it would pleafe me alfo if I did know, how the warr iffued betwixt you and your mother-in-Law's ghoft; that other of her flattering Doctor and you; if your late fpowfe be on this fide eternity: and what elce you thinke fitt to empart to a rufty Bumpkin, hanging his head over a fmoaky fire as unregarded, as unmolefted, (though not fo obfcure as your Cripplegate friend,) yet more happy then Cæfar who often wifhed for, but never obtained a Quietus from the fatigues of the publick, till a Brutus figned his pafs-port with a dagger; much happier was Scipio, that retired to his Neapolitan villa after his great

fervices for his ungratefull country, a part of whofe monument (faith a Late Voyadger to the Mediterranean) is yet to be Seen, and known by the only legible words on the infcription, ingrata patria. I have now and then A Letter from Bofton from fuch furviveing friends as I have there, and more particularly from Collonell Dudley theyr prefent gouvernour, they were lately in peace at home, and full of conqueft abroad. Nova Scotia, and the Eaftern (and the beft) part of N. England being refcued from French and Indian tyranny. And now my friend I thinke I have matched your 2 fided letter; come againe and welcom, and be pleafed to believe I fhall be glad to know your health and profperity, and will be proud if you fhall thinke fitt to allow me the Character of

"Sir, Your affured friend and
"moft humble Serv't,
"BEN: BULLIVANT.
"Northampton, February 18, 1710-11."

that Extremity, that fome hot fpirits wou'd have had him, that he was for accommodating things, and making Peace. His Eloquence is admirable: He never fpeaks but 'tis a Sentence; and no man ever cloath'd his words in finer or more proper Epithets; and all flow from him with that natural fimplicity, that there is nothing looks like Bombaft in it. But thus much as a Gentleman; I now muft reprefent him to you as a Phyfician. He is as intimate with Gallen and Hypocrates, (at leaft ways with their works,) as ever I have been with you, Even in our moft Familiar Converfe. And is fo converfant with all the great variety of Nature, that not a Drug or Simple can Efcape him; whofe Power and Vertues are known fo well to him, he needs not Practice new Experiments upon his Patients, except it be in defperate Cafes, when Death muft be expell'd by Death. This alfo is Praife-worthy in him, That to the Poor he always prefcribes cheap, but wholefome Medicines, not curing them of a Confumption in their Bodies, and fending it into their Purfes; nor yet directing them to the Eaft-Indies to look for Drugs, when they may have far better out of their Gardens. This Gentleman was my particular Friend; and both himfelf and Wife have often treated me. (I am very much troubled at his Wives misfortune, who was lately kill'd in St. Martins le Grand in London.) But I proceed in the next place to

Mr. Gouge,[65] a Linnen-Draper from London, (Son to the Charitable Divine of that Name,) an Ingenuous and Witty Perfon; fo that you'd take him for a Mafter of the Mint of Wit; and that his Brain was only a Quiver of Smart Jefts. He's an old Batchelor, and yet (as I am told) a Secret Friend to the Fair Sex. He is a Church of England-Man in his Perfwafion, and yet wou'd often buy his Father's Books to
give

[65] Edward Gouge, draper. It feems that he was probably unfortunate in his bufinefs. Adminiftration was granted on his eftate, 6 March, 1704-5; and in June, 1708, his widow, Frances Gouge, paid four fhillings in the pound to his various creditors.—ED.

give away, that fo he might (as he was uf'd to fay) make the Boftonians better, that fo much needed it. This was a noted Quality in him, that he wou'd always tell the Truth, a Quality well worthy of a Friend. But I muft not forget

Mr. Tryon, a young Merchant, and mightily given to ftudy; and as a Confequent of that, a great Admirer of Books, one of a fingular good Nature, and extraordinary Generofity of Temper; affable and courteous, and ready upon all occafions both to Advife and Help his Friend, or indeed any one that ftood in need on't, if it lay within his Power. Dr. Bullivant, Mr. Gouge, Mr. Tryon, and my felf were fo wrapt up in one another's Company, that it was rare to find us parted. The next I fhall mention is

Mr. Barns,⁴⁶ A great Arithmetician, whofe Skill in Numbers none can Excell, nor hardly any Equal; He's of a Perfon of great Generofity to Strangers: He at firft fight of me, exprefs'd a mighty kindnefs for me, which made him vifit me often, and Promote my Trade, being a mighty Bookifh Man himfelf. He is Clerk to the Government, and a Perfon of very great worth.

But perhaps, Mr. Larkin, you'll afk whether I had not my foft hours as well as other Men? Or in plain Terms, Whether I only was for a Friendfhip with my own Sex? I anfwer, No, by no means; for I ever thought Women as fit for Friendfhip as Men; And I lov'd Iris too well, ever to fear the Sex fhou'd creep in for a fhare: No, Mr. Larkin, The Sun fhall change his Courfe, and find New Paths to drive his Chariot in; the Loadftone leave his Faith unto the North; the Vine withdraw thofe ftrict Embraces that infold the Elm in her kind Arms, before I'll wrong my Iris in a Thought. Having faid this, why fhou'd I be afham'd to own that I have found fome Female Friends in Bofton: For they were all fo ftrictly vertuous, that for their Sakes, I
cou'd

---

⁴⁶ Mr. Barnes, clerk to the Government, was moft probably Nathaniel B., who was Town Clerk in 1679, and for fome years later.—ED.

13

cou'd become an Advocate for the whole Sex; which in the general are the moſt excellent.[67] *   *   *   *   *   *   *
*   *   *   *   *   *   *   *   *   *   *   *   *

Thus much, my Friend, for Women in General: I come now to give you the Particular Characters of thoſe few Female Friends I found in Boſton: I ſay, My few Female Friends: becauſe tho' I was acquainted with many of the Fair Sex, yet they were but few with whom I contracted a Friendſhip.

The Principal and moſt Diſtinct Scenes in which a Woman can regularly act a Part, are either as a Virgin, a Wife, or a Widow; and in theſe three Capacities, you'll find my Female Friends of this Town: For the Damſel (one Eminently known by that Name) was a Virgin, Mrs. Green a Wife, and Madam Brick a Widow, and Mrs. Toy, Parte per Pale, as the Lawyers ſay; that is, half Wife, half Widow; her Huſband, a Captain, having been long at Sea.

I ſhall firſt Speak of the Damſel,[68] for Virginity is firſt in order of Time; and if we will take St. Paul's Judgment, in reſpect of Excellence alſo; 1 *Cor.* VII. and (as a late Writer tells us) ſhe that preſerves her ſelf in that ſtate, upon the account he mentions, vers. 34, *That ſhe may care for the things that are of the Lord, that ſhe may be holy both in Body and in Spirit*, deſerves a great deal of Veneration, as making one of the neareſt approaches to the Angelical ſtate. In the Primitive Times, Virginity had a Particular Coronet of Glory belonging to it, and the Roman Veſtals had Extraordinary Priviledges allow'd them by the State. In the Papal Church there is a Religious Order virgins, they call Nuns; but tho' there be not among us ſuch Societies, yet there may be Nuns which are not Profeſt; and ſuch I eſteem my Friend the Damſel; for ſhe Devoted her heart to GOD, and
perhaps

---

[67] We here omit ſome four-ſcore lines, in praiſe of the ſex in general.—ED.

[68] The Damſel was evidently Comfort Wilkins, daughter of his landlord, Richard Wilkins. She was born, it ſeems, about 1660.—ED.

perhaps this was more acceptable to him, than if her Prefumption had made her more Pofitive, and Engag'd her in a vow that fhe is not fure to perform.—She was little Tranfported with this Zeal of Voluntary Virginity as knowing there's few Practice it. But tho' an old (or Super-annuated) Maid, in Bofton, is thought fuch a curfe as nothing can exceed it, and look'd on as a Difmal Spectacle, yet fhe by her good Nature, Gravity, and ftrict Vertue, convinces all (fo much as the Fleering Beaus) that 'tis not her Neceffity, but her Choice, that keeps her a Virgin. Mr. Larkin, fhe's now about Twenty Six years (the Age which they call a *Thornback*) yet fhe never difguifes her felf by the Gayetys of a Youthful Drefs, and talks as little as fhe thinks of Love: She goes to no Balls or Dancing Match, as they do who go (to fuch Fairs) in order to meet with Chapmen. The two great vertues effential to the Virgin-State, are Modefty and Obedience; and thefe are as remarkable in her, as if fhe was made of nothing elfe. Modefty appears in her in the higheft elevation and comes unto fhamefac'dnefs: Her Looks, her Speech, her whole behaviour are fo very chafte, that but once going to kifs her, I thought fhe'd ha' blufh'd to Death. And indeed (as a Friend tells us) The very name of Virgin imports a moft Critical Nicenefs in that point.—Every indecent Curiofity, or impure Fancy, is a deflouring of the Mind, and every, the leaft, Corruption of them, gives fome degrees of defilement to the Body too: She that liftens to lewd Talk, has defil'd her Ears; fhe that fpeaks any, her Tongue; and every wanton glance leaves a ftain behind it. Nothing is more nice and delicate than a Maiden Vertue. Our Damofel knowing this, (for fhe's a Virgin of great Senfe) fhe avoids ill Company and Idlenefs; and her Converfation being generally amongft the Women, (as there's leaft Danger from that Sex) I found it no eafie matter to Enjoy her Company: Moft of her time but what's taken up in Religious Worfhip, is fpent in acquiring thofe

Accomplifhments

Accomplifhments which become her Quality, as finging, Writing, Needleworks, Learning French, and the like. And I muft tell you, fhe has fo well learnt the Art of Domeftick Government, as to be able to manage (cou'd Mr. L—— per- fwade her to it) a large Houfe of her own. As to Plays and Romances (which are thought a fit Study for Ladies) fhe tells me fhe never reads 'em: She knows thofe Amorous Paffions, which 'tis their defign to paint to the Life, are apt to infinuate themfelves into their unwary Readers; and by an unhappy Inverfion a Copy fhall Produce an Original.

When a Young Lady (as a late Author expreffes it) fhall read there of fome Triumphant Beauty, that has I know not how many captive Knights proftrate at her feet, fhe will probably be tempted to think it a fine thing; and may refleft how much fhe lofes time, that has not yet fubdu'd one heart; and then her bufinefs will be to fpread her Nets, lay her Toils, to catch fome Body who will more fatally infnare her. And indeed 'tis very hard to imagine what vaft Mifchief is done to the World, by the Falfe Notions and Images of things; particularly of Love and Honour, thofe Nobleft Concerns of Humane Life, reprefented in thefe Memoirs. But to return to our Damfel; I fhall next fpeak of her vifits abroad, and they are all Innocent: I think my felf and Mr. King, (who I told you was a Loving Soul) were an hour perfwading her to take a Ramble with us to Governours Ifland, to accept of a fmall Treat; but on no other terms cou'd we prevail, but this, That fhe might have the Company of Madam Brick, and Mr. Green, and Mrs. Toy, (of whom more anon) to go along with her. Not that fhe was a Nun, as I told you before, or lov'd to confine her felf to a Cloifter: She knew to be always wandering, is the Condition of a Vagabond; but the common Entercourfe of civility is a Debt, and vifits now and then are neceffary.

But fhe went but feldom abroad; as believing that thofe Dinahs that are ftill gadding, tho' on pretence only to fee
the

the Daughters of the Land, (*Gen.* 34,) may at laft meet
with a Son of Hamor. Neither did fhe wafte much of her
time in Dreffing her felf; They that love to be feen much
abroad, (which fhe does not) will be fure to be feen in the
moft exact form. She knew Time was a Dreffing-Room
for Eternity, and therefore referves moft of her Hours for
better ufes than thofe of the Comb, the Toylet, and the
Glafs.

[*] [Having fpoken of the Damfels Modefty, &c. I fhall fay
fomething of her Matchlefs Obedience. And here I fhall tell
you fhe thinks it as much her Intereft as her Duty to obferve
her Parents Commands. Her Obedience extends itfelf to
all things that are either Good or Indifferent, and has no
Claufe of Exception but only where the Command is unlaw-
ful. I have known her Scruple to go to Roxbury (not a
Mile from Bofton) without her Fathers Confent. But now
a days fhe that goes with her Parent (unlefs it be a Parent
as Wild as herfelf) thinks fhe does but walk abroad with her
Gaoler. But the Right of the Parent is fo undoubted, that
we find GOD Himfelf gives way to it, and will not fuffer the
moft Holy Pretence, no, not that of a Vow to Invade it, as
we fee in *Numb.* 30. How will He then refent it, to have
this Law violated upon the Impulfe of a gay Paffion, and an
amorous Fancy? Neither did I ever know a Child in my
Life that married againft his Parents Confent (and I have
known feveral) but the Curfe of GOD has followed either
them or their Off-fpring. Let all Virgins, therefore, beftow
themfelves with their Parents leave, that they may not only
have their Benediction, but GOD's. And I am fure this is
moft agreeable to the Virgin Modefty which fhou'd make
Marriage an Act rather of their Obedience than their
Choice. And they that think their Friends too flow-pac'd
in

[*]Pages 77–80 of the original manufcript are wanting. The following pages
are copied from Dunton's " Life and Errors," and from his ufual mode of writing, this is doubtlefs but a flightly con-
denfed copy of the loft original.—ED.

in the Matter give certain proof that luſt is the ſole motive. But, as the Damſel I've been deſcribing wou'd neither anticipate nor contradict the Will of her Parents, ſo, I do aſſure you, ſhe's againſt forcing her own by marrying where ſhe cannot love ; and that's the Reaſon ſhe's ſtill a Virgin.

Thus, Reader, having Characteriz'd my Virgin-Friend, I ſhall ſhift the Scene, and give you the Picture of the beſt of Wives (Iris ſtill excepted.) This is another of my Friends, with whom I uſ'd to ſpend ſome of my leaſure Hours. And when you hear her Character, you'd wonder indeed if her Huſband was Jealous.—The Perſon whoſe Character I am going to give is Mrs. Green, a Printers Wife, in Boſton.

A Wife is the next Change that a Virgin can lawfully make, and draws many other Relations after it. Which Mrs. Green was ſenſible of ; For I have heard her ſay, " That when ſhe married Mr. Green, ſhe eſpouſ'd his Obligations alſo ! and where-ever her Huſband, either by Tyes of Nature or ſqueezing of Wax, owed either Money or Love, ſhe eſteem'd herſelf to be no leſs a Debtor." She knew her Marriage was an Adoption into his Family, and therefore paid to every Branch of it what their reſpective Stations requir'd. She is ſenſible that the Duty of her place has ſeveral Aſpects. Firſt, As it relates to her Huſbands Perſon, and next to his Relations, and thirdly to his Fortune. As to his Perſon, ſhe well enough knew that the great Duty of a Wife is Love. Love was the reaſon that ſhe marry'd him ; for ſhe knew, where Love is wanting, it is but the Carcaſe of a Marriage. It was her ſtudy therefore, to preſerve this Flame of Love, that, like the Veſtal Fire, it never might go out ; and therefore ſhe took care to guard it from all thoſe things that might Extinguiſh it. Mrs. Green knew very well how fatal Jealouſie had been to many ; and therefore as ſhe took care never to harbour it in her own Breaſt, ſo ſhe was nicely careful never to give her Huſband the leaſt umbrage

for

for it. She knew, fhou'd fhe give way to Jealoufie, fhe
fhou'd not only lofe her Eafe, but run the hazard of parting
alfo with fomewhat of her Innocence; for Jealoufie is very
apt to mufter up the Forces of our irafcible part to abet its
quarrel. Another Debt that Mrs. Green was fenfible fhe
ow'd, and was careful to pay to her Hufband, was Fidelity.
She knew that as fhe had efpouf'd his Interefts, fo fhe ought
to be true to 'em, keep all his Secrets, inform him of his
Dangers, and in a mild and gentle manner admonifh him of
his Faults. And this fhe knew (how ill foever many take it)
is one of the moft genuine Acts of Faithfulnefs; and to be
wanting in it wou'd be a Failure in her Duty. And fhe was
fenfible that, if fhe did not do it, fhe fhou'd be unfaithful to
herfelf; as well knowing nothing does fo much fecure the
Happinefs of a Wife, as the Vertue and Piety of her Hufband. But Matrimonial Fidelity has a fpecial Relation to
the Marriage-Bed; and in this Mrs. Green was fo feverely
fcrupulous, that fhe wou'd never fuffer any light Expreffions,
or wanton Difcourfe in her Company; and this was fo
remarkable in her, that, there being an invitation of feveral
Perfons to a Gentleman's Houfe in Bofton, and fome that
were invited refolving to be very merry; one of the company
made this an Objection "that Mrs. Green wou'd be there,
which wou'd fpoil their Mirth." To which another wild
Spark in the Company replied, " It is but fpeaking two or
three words of Bawdy, and fhe'll be gone prefently."

Another thing that was very remarkable in Mrs. Green
was her Obedience to her Husband; to whofe will fhe was
fo exactly obfervant, that he cou'd not be more ready to
Command, than fhe was to obey; and when fome of his
Commands feem'd not to be fo kind as fhe might have
expected, fhe wou'd not only obey 'em, but wifely diffemble
the Unkindnefs of them, as knowing where Men have not
wholly put off humanity, there is a native Compaffion to a
meek-fufferer. She was alfo extreamly tender of her Hufbands

bands Reputation, fetting his Worth in the cleareft Light, putting his Infirmities (for where is the Man that lives without 'em?) in the Shade.   And as fhe was this way tender of his Reputation, fo fhe was alfo in another refpect more particularly relating to herfelf; for, knowing that the mif-behaviour of the Wife reflects upon the Husband, fhe took care to abftain even from all appearance of evil, and refolved to be (what Cæfar defir'd of his Wife) not only free from Fault, but from all fufpicion of it.

But Mrs. Green was not only a Loving, a Faithful, and an Obedient Wife, but an Induftrious Wife too; managing that part of his Bufinefs which he had deputed to her, with fo much Application and Dexterity as if fhe had never come into the Houfe; and yet fo manag'd her Houfe as if fhe had never gone into the Ware-houfe.   The Emperour Auguftus himfelf fcarce wore anything but what was the Manufacture of his Wife, his Sifter, his Daughter, or his Nieces.   Should our gay Englifh Ladies, thofe Lilies of our Fields, which neither fow nor fpin, nor gather into Barns, be exempted from furnifhing others, and only left to Cloath themfelves, 'tis to be doubted they wou'd reverfe Our Saviour's Parallel of Solomon's Glories, and no Begger in all his Rags, wou'd be array'd like one of thefe.

But Mrs. Green follow'd the Example of Solomon's Ver-tuous Wife, who rifeth while it is yet Night, giving Meat to her Houfhold, and a Portion to her Maidens; and as fhe is a good Wife to her Husband, fo fhe is alfo a good Mother to her Children, whom fhe brings up with that fweetnefs and Facility as is admirable, not keeping them at too great a diftance, (as fome do) thereby Difcouraging their good Parts; nor by an Over-Fondnefs (a fault moft Mothers are guilty of) betraying 'em into a thoufand Inconveniences, which oftentimes proves fatal to 'em.

In brief, fhe takes care of their Education, and whatever elfe belongs to 'em; fo that Mr. Green enjoys the comfort

of

of his Children, without knowing anything of the trouble of 'em.

Nor is fhe lefs a Good Miftrefs than a good Mother; Treating her Servants with that Love and Gentlenefs as if fhe were their Mother; taking care both of their Souls and Bodies, and not letting them want any thing neceffary for either. I one Day told her, That I believ'd fhe was an extraordinary Wife; but Mr. Green was fo good a Man, fhe cou'd not well be otherwife. To which fhe anfwer'd "That fhe had fo good a Husband, was her Mercy; but had her Hufband been as bad a Man as any in the World, her Duty wou'd have been the fame, and fo fhe hop'd her Practice fhou'd have been too." Which, as it is a great Truth, it wants to be more known and Practic'd.]

And thus, Reader, I have given you the Character of another of my Female Friends in Bofton, and in her, the Character of a good Wife. I have only to add, That thefe Vertues are all found in my Iris, as 'twere in a *New Edition*, more Correct and Enlarg'd: Or rather, Iris is that bright Original which all good Wives fhou'd imitate.—Then no wonder I name her fo often; when to think of her, is my Bufinefs, my Life, my Everything.—But having given a Farewell to Mrs. Green[70] I fhall next prefent you with the Character of

The

---

[70] Mrs. Green. In our note on Mr. Green, the printer, (*ante*, p. 81) we expreffed the opinion that Samuel Green, Sr., who was born about A. D. 1615, could not be Dunton's friend, but that this was evidently Samuel Green, Jr. It was alfo faid that this Samuel did not marry Elizabeth Sill, in 1685, as SAVAGE has recorded. This is evident if THOMAS be correct in faying that Timothy Green, a noted printer here, was born in 1679, and was the fon of Samuel, Jr.

We have fince found fome confirmation of the fuppofition that Samuel Green, Jr., married in Bofton. A deed, recorded in Middlefex Deeds, vol. xiv, and dated Auguft 2, 1707, is figned by Jonas Green, of New London, Conn., mariner, Bartholomew Green, of Bofton, printer, Jofeph Green, of Bofton, tailor, Timothy Green, of Bofton, printer, and Sarah, widow of Capt. Samuel Green, of Cambridge. We have here plainly the widow and heirs of Samuel Green, Senior.

We learn from SAVAGE that Jonas and Bartholomew were the fons of Capt. Samuel,

The Widow Brick,[71] the very Flower of Bofton; That of a Widow is the next ftate or change that can fucceed to that of marriage. And I have chofen my Friend the Widow Brick, as an Exemplar to fhew you what a Widow is: Madam Brick is a Gentlewoman whofe *Head* (i. e. her Husband) has been cut off, and yet fhe lives and Walks: But don't be frighted, for fhe's Flefh and Blood ftill, and perhaps fome of the *finefl* that you ever faw. She has fufficiently evidenc'd that her Love to her late Husband is as ftrong

Samuel, and that Jofeph may poffibly have been; yet there is more reafon we think to believe that both Jofeph and Timothy were the fons of Samuel, Jr., and reprefented their father's fhare of the eftate.

We find that Samuel and Hannah Green, of Bofton, had at Bofton, Jofeph, born 21 Feb., 1682, and Jane, b. 12 June, 1685, and we know of no other Samuel Green at this date to have been fo married. We therefore are of the opinion that Dunton's "Mrs. Green" was named Hannah, and was probably born about 1660. It must be added that the identification of her family muft be left to future genealogists. We only know that according to THOMAS, (i, 282,) in July, 1690, 'Printer Green died of the fmall pox, in three days, and his wife alfo is dead with it.' No record remains of any fettlement of the eftate, nor have we found any other clue to the name of Green's children.

The Green family has been connected with printing for feveral generations, as will be feen by the following abftract from THOMAS' Hiftory. Samuel Green, Sr., fon of Bartholomew Green, of Cambridge, commenced printing as early as 1649, and continued the bufinefs till he was aged. His fons, Samuel and Bartholomew, were alfo printers. Samuel, Jr., was the father of Timothy Green, who married Mary Flint, in 1702, was a printer in Bofton, and removed to

New London, Conn., in 1714. He died there, 5 May, 1757, aged 78, leaving fix fons, of whom three, Timothy, Jonas and Samuel, were printers.

Of thefe, Samuel had Timothy, a printer, who left two fons, alfo printers. Jonas removed to Maryland and had three fons who were printers. We believe that in the prefent generation feveral purfue this fame bufinefs.—ED.

[71] The Widow Brick was without doubt, Joanna, daughter of Arthur Mafon, who married firft Robert Breck, and fecondly Michael Perry. From Dunton we have the following items for identification: She was a widow, twenty-two years old in 1686, the mother of two children, and a member of Rev. James Allen's church. We find that Robert and Joanna Breck had children, Joanna, b. 12 June, 1681, and Robert, b. 6 May, 1683. That Joanna Breck m. Michael Perry, 12 July, 1694, and this could only be the widow of Robert Breck; and that Joanna Perry, widow, (Michael having died 9 Oct., 1700, aged 34,) was, in 1708, one of Arthur Mafon's children and heirs. Laftly, Joanna Mafon was born 26 March, 1664. It is impoffible to doubt that we have identified the "Flower of Bofton."

By her fecond husband fhe had Elizabeth, b. 6 Sept., 1695. Rev. James Allen m. for his third wife, in 1673, Sarah, widow of Robert Breck, and mother of Joanna's firft husband.—ED.

ſtrong as Death, becauſe Death has not been able to Extinguiſh it, but it ſtill burns like the Funeral Lamps of old, even in Vaults and Charnel-Houſes; But her Conjugal Love, being Tranſplanted into the Grave, has improv'd it ſelf into Piety, and laid an Obligation upon her to perform all offices of Reſpect and Kindneſs to his Remains, which they are capable of.

As to his Body, ſhe gave it a decent Enterment, ſuitable to his quality; or rather above it, as I have been inform'd; for Mr. Brick was Dead and Buried before I came to Boſton. And that this was the Effect of that dear love ſhe had for him, appears in this, That ſhe wou'd not ſuffer the Funeral Charges to make any Abatement from the Children's Portions. Her grief for his Death was ſuch as became her, great but moderate, not like a haſty Shower, but a ſtill Rain: She knew nothing of thoſe Tragical Furies wherewith ſome Women ſeem Tranſported towards their Dead Husbands; thoſe frantick Embraces and Careſſes of a Carcaſs, betray a little too much the Senſuality of their Love. Such violent Paſſions quickly ſpend themſelves, and ſeem rather to Vaniſh than Conſume. But Madam Brick griev'd more moderately, and more laſtingly. She knew there was a better way of Expreſſing her Love to him, and therefore made it her Buſineſs to Embalm his Memory, and keep that from Periſhing. And I always obſerv'd, That whenever ſhe ſpoke of her Husband, it was in the moſt Endearing manner. Nor cou'd ſhe ever mention him, without paying the Tribute of a Tear to his Memory. She wou'd often be reviving the remembrance of ſome Praiſe-worthy Quality or other in him; and if any happen'd to ſay ſomething of him not ſo commendable, ſhe wou'd excuſe it with a world of Sweetneſs, and by a frowning glance at the Relator, declare how much ſhe was diſpleaſ'd. And tho' I cannot think it her deſign, yet I believe ſhe was ſenſible enough that ſhe cou'd no way better provide for her own Honour, than by this Tenderneſs

ſhe

ſhe ſhew'd for her Husband's.   But Madam Brick ſhew'd a better way of expreſſing the Honour ſhe had for her Huſband's Memory, and that is, She ſet ſuch a value on her Relation to her Husband, as to do nothing that might ſeem unworthy of it.

Hiſtorians inform us, That 'twas the Dying Charge of Auguſtus to the Empreſs Livia, Behave thy ſelf well, and remember our Marriage. This Madam Brick made her Care; For having been the Wife of a Gentleman of good Quality, ſhe ſo remember'd it, as not to do any thing below her ſelf, or which Mr. Brick (cou'd he have fore-ſeen it) might juſtly have been aſham'd of. But Madam Brick had yet another way of Expreſſing the Value ſhe had for Mr. Brick, and that is, by the kindneſs ſhe ſhow'd to the Children which he left behind him, which were only two: And this was ſo remarkably Eminent in her, that I have heard her ſay, Her Children might now claim a double Portion in her love, one on their Native Right, as being Hers; and the other on the Right of their dead Father, who had left them to her: "And truly," ſaid ſhe, "ſince I muſt ſupply the place of both Parents, 'tis but neceſſary that I ſhou'd put on the Affections of both; and to the Tenderneſs of a Mother, add the Care and Conduct of a Father." She was as good as her Word, both in a ſedulous care of their Education, and in a Prudent Management of their Fortunes. As to their Education ſhe took care that they might have that Learning that was proper for them, and above all, that they might be furniſhed with ingenuous and vertuous Principles, founded on the Fear of God, which is the beginning of all true Wiſdom. And as to their Fortunes, ſhe was ſo far from Embeziling them, a Practice too common with ſome Widows, that ſhe augmented them, while it was in the Power of her hand to do it. (For Madam Brick is but a Young Widow, tho' ſhe is the Mother of two Children.)

But

But Madam Brick is one that has yet more refined and Exalted Thoughts: She is highly fenfible that God, who has plac'd us in this World to purfue the Interefts of a better, directs all the fignal Acts of his Providence to that end, and intends we fhou'd fo interprett them; And therefore fhe wifely reflected that when God took away from her the Mate of her Bofom, and fo reduc'd her to a folitude, he thereby, as it were, Sounded a Retreat to her from the lighter Jollities and Gayeties of the World; and therefore in Compliance to the Divine Will, and that fhe might the better Anfwer the Requirement of the Almighty, tho put on a more retired Temper of Mind, and a more ftrict[72] * * * * *
* * * * * * * * * * * * *

Neither did fhe fuffer Her Pious behaviour, to be caft off with her Widow's Vail, but made it the conftant Drefs both of her Widowhood and Life; and as a confequence hereof, fhe became a Member of Mr. Allen's Congregation; and liv'd a Life of Sincere Piety: And yet was fo far from Sowrnefs either in her Countenance or Converfation, that nothing was ever more fweet or agreeable: Making it evident that Piety did not confift in Morofenefs, nor Sincere Devotion in a fupercilious Carriage; 'twas the *Vitals* of Religion that fhe minded, and not Forms and Modes; and if fhe found the Power of it in her heart, fhe did not think her felf oblig'd to fuch a *ftarch'dnefs* of Carriage as is ufual amongft the Boftonians, who value themfelves thereby fo much, that they are ready to fay to all others, Stand off, for I am holier than thou. She did not think herfelf concern'd to put on a Sorrowful Countenance, when the Joy of the Lord was her ftrength.

I had much the greater value for Madam Brick, on the Account of a Difcourfe that paft between Mrs. Green and her, which (as Mrs. Green related it to me) was to this effect: Mrs. Green commended her very much, in
that

---

[72] Here the manufcript is imperfect.—ED.

that being a Young Widow, in the bloom of all her Youth and Beauty, (for fhe was but twenty-two) fhe had given up fo much of her time to the Exercife of Devotion, and the Worfhip of GOD; To which fhe reply'd, 'She had done but what fhe ought; for in her Married ftate fhe found many things which yet are but the due Compliances of a Wife, which were great Avocations to a ftrict Devotion; but being now manumitted from that Subjection, and having lefs of Martha's Care of Serving, it was but reafonable fhe fhou'd chufe Mary's better part.' "And thofe hours (added fhe) which were before my Husband's Right, are now devolv'd on GOD, the Great Proprietor of all my time: And that Difcourfe and free Converfe with which I uf'd to entertain Mr. Brick, ought now to be in Colloquies and heavenly Entercourfes with My dear Redeemer." Nor was her Piety and Devotion barren, but fruitful and abounding in the Works of *Charity*, and fhe cloath'd the Naked as far as her Ability permitted. And tho' my felf and Mr. King went thither often (for fhe wou'd fcarce permit a fingle vifit) we never found her without fome poor but honeft Chriftian with her, always difcourfing of the things of Heaven, and ere fhe went, fupplying of her with the things of Earth. How long fhe may remain a Widow, I have not yet confulted with the Stars to know, but that fhe has continu'd fo two years, is evident to all that are in Bofton.

To conclude her Character, the *Beauty* of her Perfon, the *Sweetnefs* and Affability of her Temper, the *Gravity* of her Carriage, and her Exalted Piety, gave me fo juft a value for her, that Mrs. Green wou'd often fay, Shou'd Iris Dye (which Heaven forbid) there's none was fit to fucceed her but Madam Brick: But Mrs. Green was partial, for my poor Pretences to fecure vertue, wou'd ne'er have anfwer'd to her Towring heighths. 'Tis true, Madam Brick did me the Honour to treat me very kindly at her Houfe, and to admit me often into her Converfation, but I am

fure

fure it was not on Love's, but on Vertue's fcore. For fhe well knows (at leaft as well as I do) that Iris is alive : And therefore I muft juftifie her Innocence on that account. And tho' fome have been pleaf'd to fay, That were I in a fingle ftate, they do believe fhe wou'd not be difpleaf'd with my Addreffes, As this is without any ground but groundlefs Conjectures, fo I hope I fhall never be in a capacity to make a Tryal of it.

But, I'm fure our Friendfhip was all Platonick (fo Angels lov'd) and full as Innocent as that of the Philofopher who gave it the name; but if Plato was not very much wrong'd he never lov'd vertue fo refinedly, as to like to court her fo paffionately in a foul or homely habitation as he did in thofe that were more Beautiful and Lovely; and this fufficiently juftifies my Friendfhip to Madam Brick and her Spotlefs Innocence in accepting of it. Thus, Reader, I have given you the Character of another of my Friends of the Fair Sex in Bofton; and leave you to judge whether or no fhe deferve the Title of *the Flower of Bofton*, which at firft fight I gave her.

But can I forget Mrs. Toy,[73] who is another of my Friends and one that I am *proud* of having fo; for fhe is an Epitomy

of

[73] This Mrs. Toy was probably Mercy, wife of Jeremiah Tay or Toy, a mariner of Bofton. The name is more commonly fpelled Tay on our records, and in Drake's Hiftory of Bofton has been perverted to Foy; a miftake the more natural fince the Foyes were a contemporary family, and eminently maritime. William Tay, of Bofton, 1643, and Billerica, was the father of Jeremiah Tay, who married Mercy, only child of Nathaniel Woodward, and had children in 1685, 1687, 1689, 1693, 1696, and 1703. There can be little doubt that Dunton's laborious pleafantry only fignified that Mrs. Tay's husband was a failor, and Jeremiah alone of the family feems to have been fuch. His brother Ifaiah was a fhop-keeper, and probably was not married in 1686.

1 Nov. 1711, Mercy Tay, widow, figns a deed recorded in Suffolk Deeds, calling herfelf the only child of Nathaniel Woodward, who was the oldeft fon of Robert Woodward, of Bofton. The other party was Mehitable Ince, only daughter of Benjamin Harwood, who was the fon of Thomas Harwood by wife Rachel (Smith), widow of Robert Woodward. Jeremiah Tay was living in 1709, and died before Nov., 1711. Poffibly his widow married, 4 April, 1715, John Euftis.—ED.

of the other Three: She has the Bafhfulnefs and Modefty of the Damfell; the Love and Fidelity of Mrs. Green, the Wife; and the Piety and Sweetnefs of the Widow Brick. But perhaps you'll afk me (If fhe's neither maid, wife nor widow) What I call her?

> Is fhe a Maid ?—*Phil.*—What Man can anfwer that!
> Or Widow ?—*Phil.*—No.—What then ?—*Phil.*—I know not what.
> Saint-like fhe looks; a Syren, if fhe fing:
> Her Eyes are Stars; Her Mind is every thing.

And well may I fay her Mind is every thing, fince everything is contain'd in it: It is the Habitation of the Graces, the Refidence of the Mufes, and the general Rendezvous of all the Vertues. And as to that Queftion, What is fhe? I told you before fhe was *parte per pale*, as the Lawyers fpeak; that is, half a Wife and half a Widow.

And now, Sir Daniel, I fuppofe you'll give fome grains of Allowance to Sir John: For I believe fuch Females as thefe, wou'd fet even a Gentleman of more Reformation, a longing for further Acquaintance with 'em, without making it a Crime. And that will be of the fame Opinion with me, That it is happinefs to have the Honour of having Converfation with fuch Friends. But perhaps you'll fay, Are all your Female Friends Perfons of fuch Exalted Worth, and had you none of a Coarfer Alloy?

I anfwer, My Friends are fuch as I've here recited; but I had feveral Acquaintance with Perfons of a far different character: For all forts of Perfons came to my Warehoufe to buy Books, according to their feveral Inclinations. And I'll give you the Characters of fome of them:

I'll begin with Mrs. Ab—l, (a Perfon of Quality:) A well-wifher to the Mathematics: A young Proficient, but willing to learn, and therefore came to Enquire for the *School of Venus;* She was one of the firft that pof'd me, in afking for a Book I cou'd not help her to; I told her however, I had

the

the *School of Vertue;* but that was a Book fhe had no occafion for. Her Love is a Blank, wherein fhe writes the next Man that tenders his Affection. As fhe fees, fo alfo fhe is feen by her own Eyes: Sometimes fhe ftares on Men with full fix'd Eyes; Sometimes fhe dejects her Eyes in a feeming Civility, and makes many miftake that for Modefty, which is only Cunning. But as thofe Bullets which graze on the ground, do moft hurt to an Army, fo fhe does moft mifchief with thofe glances that are fhot from a down-caft Eye.

But 'tis not with her Eyes only fhe draws in Cuftomers, but with her feet alfo, for fhe writes Characters of wantonnefs as fhe walks. But then it vexes her, when from an affected Dullnefs [you] won't underftand the Language of her Behaviour. And yet fhe has a ftrange affected kind of Coynefs; which yet differs from Modefty as much as Hemlock from Parfley. She'll deny Common Favours, becaufe they are too fmall to be granted: She will part with all or none; and it is eafier to obtain from her the laft favour in private, than a kifs in Public. I will only add, It is a Proverbial Phrafe, of ill People, That they have been better bred than taught; but of Mrs. A——l I muft fay, fhe has been both well bred, and well taught, but has not learn'd well: for as I faid before, fhe left the *School of Vertue,* for the *School of Venus.* Yet as bad as fhe is, for her Father's fake, I hope fhe'll live to repent.

Another of thefe Female Acquaintance (for fo they wou'd be, whether I wou'd or no) was Mrs. F——y, who had the Cafe of a Gentlewoman, but little elfe to fhew fhe was a Rational Creature, befides Speech and laughter. When I firft faw her, I was not long to guefs what fhe was, for Nature had hung out the fign of Simplicity in her Face. When fhe came into my Warehoufe, I wonder'd what Book fhe intended to buy; at laft I perceiv'd fhe intended to buy none, becaufe fhe knew not what to afk for; yet fhe took up feveral, look'd in

15

in 'em, and laid 'em down again.   Perceiving her Simplicity, I afk'd her in Joque, Whether fhe wou'd not buy the Hiftory of Tom Thumb?   She told me "Yes;" upon which, I afk'd her whether fhe'd have it in folio, with Marginal Notes; to which fhe only faid, " The beft, the beft."   Then looking amongft my Pamphlets and Penny Books, and by Chance I found one of that Worfhipful Hiftory, which I prefented to this Overfight of Nature, who both paid for't, and I believe Efteem'd it as highly as fhe wou'd have done the beft Book in my Ware-houfe.

In looking upon her, I cou'd not but reflect how much I ow'd to the Divine Goodnefs that had given me the ufe of my Senfes, who might have made me like her; It being only His pleafure that put the Difference between us: And this made me confider, that a Fool and a wife Man are both alike in the Starting-place, their Birth; and at the Poft, their death.   Only they differ in the race of their Lives: And this begot in me another Reflection, which is, That one may get Wifdom by looking on a Fool.

The next I fhall mention is Mrs. D——, who has a bad face, and a worfe Tongue; and has the Report of a Witch; whether fhe be one or no, I know not, but fhe has ignorance and malice enough to make her one: And indeed fhe has done very odd things, but hitherto fuch as are rather ftrange than hurtful; yea, fome of them are pretty and pleafing; but fuch as I think cann't be done without the *help of the Devil:* As for inftance: She'll take 9 Sticks, and lay 'em acrofs, and by mumbling a few Words, make 'em all ftand up an End like a pair of Nine-Pins; but fhe had beft have a Care, for they that ufe the Devil's help to make fport, may quickly come to do mifchief.   I have been told by fome, that fhe has actually indented with the Devil; and that he is to do what fhe wou'd have him for a time, and afterwards he is to have *her Soul in Exchange:* What pains poor Wretches take to make fure of Hell!

The

The next is Doll— S—der, who uf'd to come often to my Warehoufe and wou'd plague my man *Palmer* more than all my Cuftomers befides: Her life is a perpetual Contradiction; and fhe is made up of "I will" and "I will not": "*Palmer*, Reach me that Book, yet let it alone too; but let me fee't however; and yet 'tis no great matter neither"; was her conftant Dialect in my Warehoufe: She's very Fantaftical, but cann't be call'd Irrefolute; for an Irrefolute Perfon is always beginning, and fhe never makes an End. She writes and blots out again, whilft the other deliberates what to write: I know two Negatives makes an Affirmative, but what her I and No together makes, I know not; nor what to make of it, but that fhe knows not what to make of it herfelf. Her head is juft like a Squirrel's Cage, and her Mind the Squirrel that whirls it round: She never looks towards the End, but only the beginning of things: For fhe will call in all hafte for one, and have nothing to fay to him when he is come; and long, *nay die*, for fome Toy or Trifle, and when fhe has got it, grows weary of it prefently. None knows where to have her a moment, and whofoever wou'd hit her thoughts, muft fhoot flying.

The next is Mrs. ——,[73] who takes as much ftate upon her, as wou'd have ferv'd Six of Queen Elizabeth's Counteffes; and yet fhe's no Lady neither, unlefs it be of Pleafure. Yet fhe looks high, and fpeaks in a Majeftick Tone like one acting the Queen's Part in a Play. She feldom appears twice in a fhape; but every time fhe goes abroad, puts on a different Garb. Had fhe been with the Ifraelites in the Wildernefs, when for *forty years* their Cloaths wax'd not old, it had been punifhment enough for her, to have gone fo long in *one fafhion*. But fhou'd this Ruffling Madam be ftript of her Silken Plumes, fhe wou'd make but a very ordinary figure. For to hide her Age, fhe paints; and to hide her painting dares hardly laugh; Whence fhe has two
counterfeit

---

[73] Mrs. H., fays DUNTON, in "Life and Errors."—ED.

counterfeit Vizards to put off every Night, viz: her *Painting* and her *Modefty*, when fhe lies with her own face, tho' fome fay, not with her own Husband: She was a good Cuftomer to me, and whilft I took her Money, I humour'd her Pride, and paid her (I blufh to fay it,) a mighty Obfervance. The chief Books fhe bought were Plays and Romances; which to fet off the better, fhe wou'd afk for Books of *Gallantry*.

The next is Mrs. T——, whofe Tongue was round like a Wheel, one spoke after another, for there's no End on't: She makes more noife and jangling than the Bells do on a Coronation-Day. It is fome bodies happinefs that fhe is yet unmarried, for fhe wou'd make a Hufband wifh that fhe were dumb, or he were deaf. You wou'd wonder at her matter, to hear her talk; and admire at her talk when you heard her matter; but confidering both together, you'd wonder at neither, but conclude as one did of the Nightingale, That fhe's *Vox, et preterea nihil*, a voice and nothing elfe. To hear her always talking, one wou'd wonder how fhe holds out; but for that, her Tongue moves with as great facility, as leaves wag, when fhaken by the Wind. She uf'd to come to my Warehoufe, not to buy Books, (for fhe talk'd fo much, fhe had no time to read) but that others might hear her talk: fo that (I'm apt to think) had fhe but the Faculty of Talking in her fleep, one might make *the Perpetual Motion* with her Tongue.

And thus, Reader, I have given you the humours of a far different fort of Ladies from the former: And if I have given you *fix* of thefe, for *four* of the other; you muft remember that there are Two Vices for One Vertue. I have not fet their Names down at length, becaufe there is a poffi-bility of their being *reform'd*, and fo I wou'd not expofe 'em. Tho' they are as well known in *Bofton* as if they had been nam'd particularly.[74]

And

---

[74] Part of a page is here miffing in Dunton's manufcript, but at the end is the paffage which ftands in our text, marked with the number of the page.

And thus, Mr. Larkin, having briefly recited my Boſton Viſits, and given you a relation of my Friends and Acquaintance there, I am next to tell you the remarkable Occurrences that fell out whilſt I was in Boſton; and ſo ſhall end this Letter, being Impatient now for a view of the Countrey; but my next Adventure ſhall only be a Ramble to the Neighbouring Villages, (for I am Rambling ſtill) after which I deſign for the Indian Towns.

As Dunton intended to cloſe or divide his Letter at this point, we have made two parts of it, the latter portion being on very different topics from the firſt. We preſerve the enumeration, however, as the Third Letter, ſuch having been the author's plan.—ED.

THE OLD WAREHOUSE IN DOCK SQUARE, BOSTON.

LETTER III.

(*CONTINUED.*)

TO MR. GEORGE LARKIN, PRINTER, AT THE
TWO SWANS, WITHOUT BISHOPSGATE, LONDON.

Boſton, in New-England, March 25, 1686.

NOTHER[75] Occurrence that happened, whilſt I was here, was the Execution of Morgan, which I may ſend you as a Piece of News, for there has not (it ſeems) been ſeen an Execution here this ſeven years. So that ſome have come 50 miles to ſee it: And I do confeſs, Conſidering what ſerious care the two Mathers and Mr. Moody took to prepare the Dying Criminal for Death, the Relation may be worth relateing in my Summer Rambles; and in this Occurrence, I ſhall relate nothing but what I ſaw my ſelf.

And firſt, I went to view the Priſon,[76] in Priſon-Lane; and here

---

[75] At this point Dunton commences an account of the execution of James Morgan, condemned for murder. Concerning this man, SAVAGE records only that a perſon of the name had lived in Boſton, and had children born here, but there is no other reaſon to conclude that the criminal was a citizen here.—ED.

[76] The Priſon ſtood in Priſon-lane, now Court St. DRAKE (p. 635) ſpeaks of the old Stone Jail as ſtanding, in 1754, on a part of the lot now occupied by the Court Houſe. In Bonner's map, 1722, the Priſon occupies this locality exactly.—ED.

here I think it will not be amifs, if I firft give you the
Character of a Prifon: A Prifon is the Grave of the Living,
where they are fhut up from the World and their Friends, and
the Worms that gnaw upon them are their own Thoughts
and the Jayler. 'Tis a Houfe of meagre Looks, and ill
fmells: for Lice, Drink, and Tobacco, are the Compound:
Or, if you will, 'tis the Subburbs of Hell; and the Perfons
much the fame as there: You may afk, as Manippas in
Lucian, which is Nevius, which Thirfites; which the Beggar,
and which the Knight: for they are all fuited in the fame
kind of nafty Poverty. The only fafhion here, is to be
out at the Elbows; and not to be thread-bare, is a great
Indecorum.

Every Man fhews here like fo many Wrecks upon the
Sea: here the Ribs of a thoufand Pound; and there, the
Relicks of fo many Manners is only a Doublet without
Buttons; and 'tis a Spectacle of more Pity than Executions
are. Men huddle up their Lives here, as a thing of no ufe,
and wear it out like an old fuit, the fafter the better; and he
that deceives the time beft, beft fpends it. Men fee here
much fin, and much calamity; and where the laft does not
mortifie, the other hardens: And thofe that are worfe here,
are defperately worfe, as thofe from whom the Horror of
fin is taken off, and the Punifhment familiar. This is a
School, in which much Wifdom is learnt, but it is generally
too late, and with danger; and it is better to be a fool, than
come here to learn it.

Here it was that I faw poor Morgan; who feem'd to
be very forrowful and penitent, and confeffed that he had
in his rage murdered the Man whofe Death and Blood
has been laid to his Charge: He told me that the other
gave him fome ill Language whereby he was provoked,
and that he faid to him, If he came within the door, he
wou'd run the fpit into his Bowels, and he was as wicked as
his Word; and fo confeffed himfelf guilty of Murder.—But
                                                        having

having given you the charaćter of the Prifon, I come next to give you the charaćter of the Jaylor.[77]

A Common and Cruel Jaylor, has the fhape and Form of a Man, but the fiercenefs and Currifhnefs of a Tyger: He was made of the bafeft of the rubbifh of that red Earth of which Man was fafhion'd: Or rather he comes of the Race of thofe Angels that fell with Lucifer from Heaven; whither he never (or very hardly) returns. Of all his Bunches of Keys, not one hath Wards to open that Door. Juftice and Mercy he knows nothing of, but Wrong and Cruelty have been his Conftant Praćtice. He is a Judges Slave, and a Prifoner is his: In this they differ, he is a Voluntary one, but the Prifoner is compell'd. He is the Hang-man of the Law, (with a hard hand) and if the Law gave him all his Limbs perfećt, he wou'd ftrike thofe on whom he is glad to fawn. In fighting againft a Debtor, he is a Creditor's Second, but obferves not the Laws of Duelling, for his Play is foul, and takes all bafe Advantages. His Confcience and his Shackles hang up together, and are made very near of the fame mettal, faving that his Confcience is the hardeft, and hath one property above Iron, for that never melts. He diftils money out of the Tears of the Poor, and grows fat by their Curfes. A Chamber of lowfie Beds, is better worth to him than the beft Acre of Corn-Land in England. Two things are hard to him, nay almoft impoffible, viz: To fave all his Prifoners, that none ever efcape, and to be fav'd himfelf. His Ears are ftopt to the Cries of others, and GOD's to his. And good reafon, for lay the life of a Man in one Scale, and his Fees in the other, he will lofe the firft to find the fecond. He muft look for no mercy (if he defires Juftice to be done him) for he fhews none. And I thinke

he

---

[77] The jailer at this time was probably John Arnold, who held the office a few years later and for a confiderable period. He is named on our earlieft Council record, in 1692, and was difcharged for releafing one of the witchcraft vićtims on a forged warrant, as HUTCHINSON relates, (Hift. Mafs. ii, 61). DUNTON'S remarks however are not perfonal but general.—ED.

he cares the lefs, becaufe he knows Heaven hath no need of fuch as he ; the Doors there want no Porters, for they ftant ever open.

But to return to Morgan, whofe Execution being appointed on the 11th of March, there was that Care taken for his Soul that three Excellent Sermons[78] were preached before him, before his Execution; Two on the Lord's Day, and one juft before his Execution. The firft was preached by Mr. Cotton Mather, who preached upon that Text in *Ifa.* 45:

[78] Dunton's verfion of thefe fermons is quite accurate, and in fome portions is *verbatim.* It feems that Morgan's fpeeches were noted down in fhort-hand, and it is perhaps allowable to imagine that Dunton was the reporter. He certainly feems to have been very much interefted in the proceedings. As a Londoner, an execution can hardly have been a novelty to him, and we muft find fome other reafon for his particular intereft.

The fermons from which the extracts were copied were publifhed with the following titles :

" A Sermon, occafioned by the Execution of a man found Guilty of Murder. Preached at Bofton in N. E. March 11th, 1685-6. Together with the Confef-fion, Laft Expreffion, and folemn Warn-ing of that Murderer to all perfons, efpecially to young men, to beware of thofe Sins which brought him to his miferable End. By Increafe Mather, Teacher of {—} Church of Chrift. The Second Edition. Deut. 19 : 20, 21. Prov. 28 : 17. [7 lines quoted.] Bofton, Printed by R. P. Sold by J. Brunning, Bookfeller, at his Shop at the Corner of the Prifon-Lane, next the Exchange. Anno, 1687."

"The Call of the Gofpel Applyed Unto All men in general, and unto a Condemned Malefactor in particular. In a Sermon, Preached on the 7th Day of March, 1686. At the Requeft, and in the Hearing of a man under a juft

Sentence of Death for the horrid Sin of Murder. By Cotton Mather, Paftor of a Church at Bofton in N. E. The Second Edition. Pfal. 89 : 1. [5 lines quoted.] Printed at Bofton, by Richard Pierce, 1687."

"An Exhortation to a condemned malefactor, Delivered March the 7th, 1686. By Jofhua Moody, Preacher of the Gofpel at Bofton in New-England. Ezek. 33 : 9. Jofh. 7 : 19. Ifa. 55 : 6, 7. [12 lines quoted.] Printed at Bofton, by R. P. Anno, 1687."

The firft fermon occupies pp. 1-36, the fecond, pp. 37-82, and the third, pp. 83-113. There is a preface of two pages, and at the end, pp. 114-124, the printer adds " The Sum and Subftance of what was fpoken with Morgan on his way to his Execution."

Thefe fermons are efpecially worthy of notice, as that by Cotton Mather was the firft of his three hundred and eighty-three publications.

In the MAGNALIA will be found a fhort account of Morgan and his edify-ing fpeeches. Although Cotton Mather feems to have believed in his conver-fion, Increafe Mather pungently fays in the preface to his fermons, " Late re-pentance is feldom true."

We may here add a fact concerning the printer, Jofeph Brunning, which we neglected before. He died 8 April, 1691, and adminiftration was granted his widow, Mary, 25 Aug. following.—ED.

45 : 22, *Look unto Me and be ye faved, all the Ends of the Earth.* He declar'd that when the no lefs unexpected than undeniable Requeft of a Dying Man, who (fays he) now ftands in this Affembly, that he wou'd allow him this morning, a Difcourfe proper to his Uncomfortable Circumftances, was brought to him, he cou'd not think of a more proper Text; Telling the poor Wretch, That he was now liftening to one of the three laft Sermons that ever he was like to fit under before his incounter with the King of Terrors. And then faid, "Poor Man! Do you hearken diligently, and I'll ftudy to make this whole hour very particularly fuitable and ferviceable to you; and methinks a Man that knows himfelf about to take an Eternal Farewel of all Sermons, fhou'd Endeavour to hear with moft Earneft heed. And a little after, "The Faithful and True Witnefs faith unto us, *I will give you reft;* O let the poor fetter'd Prifoner recollect himfelf! James! Thy Name is not excepted in thefe Invitations."

"I am glad for the feemingly penitent Confeffion of your monftrous Mifcarriages, which yefterday I obtain'd in writing from you, and which indeed was no more than there was need of: But it remains yet, that you give your Dying Looks to the Lord Jefus Chrift; for Salvation from all your Guilt, and from all the Plagues in the flying Roll." And a little after, "My requeft unto you is, That you wou'd at this hour think of an Intereft in Chrift.—Surely when the Executioner is laying the Cold Cloth of Death over your Eyes, the Look, with the Shriek of your Soul, will then fay, 'O now a Thoufand Worlds for an Intereft in Jefus Chrift!' Surely a few minutes after that, when your naked Soul fhall appear before the Judgment-Seat of the Moft High, you will again fay, an Intereft in Jefus Chrift, is worth whole Mountains of Maffive Gold!

You have murder'd the Body and (no thanks to you, if not) the Soul of your Neighbour too: And O that the Rock
in

in your Bosom might flow with Tears at such a thought! If the Court shou'd say unto you, Beg hard, and you shall live; O, how affectionate wou'd you be! Poor dying man, The Lord Jesus Christ saith the same thing to you, If thou canst heartily look and beg, thou shalt not be hang'd up among the Monuments of my Vengeance, in Chains for Evermore.

"The sharp Ax of Civil Justice will speedily cut you down; O for a little good Fruit before the Blow! Manifest your penitence for your Iniquities by a due care to excel in Tempers quite contrary to those ill habits and Customs whereby you have heretofore blasphemed the Worthy Name of Christ and Christianity: Especially employ the last minutes of your Life, in giving a Zealous Warning unto others, to take heed of those things which have been destructive unto you. Tell them what wild Gourds of Death they are, by which you have got your Bane; point out before them those Paths of the Destroyer which have led you down So near unto the Congregation of the Dead.

"When the numerous Crowd of Spectators are, three or four days hence, throng'd about the Place where you shall then breathe your last before them all, then do you with the heart-piercing-groans of a deadly wounded Man, beseech of your Fellow-sinners, That they wou'd turn now every one from the Evil of his way. Beseech them to keep clear of ill haunts and ill houses, with as much dread of them, as they cou'd have of lying down in a Nest of poysonous Snakes: Beseech them to abhor all Uncleanness, as they wou'd the Deep Ditch which the abhorred of the Lord do fall into. Beseech of them to avoid all Excess in Drinking, as they wou'd not rot themselves with more bitter Liquors than the Waters of Jealousie. Beseech them to mortifie and moderate all inordinate Passions, as they wou'd not surrender themselves into the hands of Devils, that will hurry them down into deeper Deeps than they are aware of. Beseech them to shun Idle Swearing, as a Prophanity that the God to
whom

whom vengeance belongeth will not permit to go unpunifhed. Befeech them to avoid Curfes on themfelves or others, leaft whilft they like Madmen fo throw about Fire-brands; Arrows, and Death, they bring upon their own heads, as you have done, the things which they are apt to be wifhing. Befeech them to beware of Lying, as they wou'd not be put to need, and Crave, and be deny'd, a drop of Water, to cool their Tongues in the place of Torment. Befeech of them to be as averfe to all ftealing, as they wou'd be to carry coals of Fire into thofe Nefts that they fo feather by their difhonefty. Befeech of them to prize the means of Grace; to fleep at, or keep from fermons no more: To love the Habitation of God's Houfe, and the place where his Honour dwells; left God foon fend their barren, froward fouls to dwell in filence, where there fhall never be a Gofpel-Sermon heard; Never, Never, as long as the Almighty fits upon his Chriftal Throne.

"And when you have given thefe Warnings, upon the Ladder from whence you fhall not come off without taking an Irrecoverable ftep into Eternity; O remember ftill, you give unto Jefus Chrift the Honour of Looking to him for his falvation. Remember, that if you wou'd do a work highly for the Honour of Him, this is The Work of God, that you believe on Him. Even after your Eyes are fo covered, as to take their leave of all fights below, ftill continue Looking unto Him whom you have heard faying, *Look unto me.* And now let the Everlafting Saviour look down in much mercy upon you: O that he wou'd give this Murderer and Extraordinary Sinner, a place among the Wonders of Free Grace! O that this Wretched Man might be made meet for the Inheritance among the Saints in Light; being kept from an unrepenting and deluded Heart, as unquenchable Fire will find fewel in."

This was the Subftance of what Mr. Cotton Mather addreff'd to the Prifoner, in his Sermon in the Morning.

In

In the Evening of the fame Lord's Day, Mr. Joſhua Moodey preach'd before him; his Text was *Iſa.* 12 : 1.—*Tho' thou waſt angry with me, thine anger is turned away.*—He told the Poor condemned Priſoner, That what he had to ſay to him, ſhou'd be under theſe two Heads, 1. By way of Conviction and awakening: 2. By way of Encouragement and Counſel. He told him alſo, That he ſhou'd uſe all Plainneſs and Freedom, taking it for Granted that Dying Men are paſt all Expectation of Flatteries or Complements; and that plain Dealing, which will do the moſt Good, will find the beſt Acceptance: And then, addreſſing himſelf to the Priſoner ſaid:

"Thou ſtandeſt here before the Lord and his People at this Time, as a ſolemn example of that ſacred Text, *Numb.* 32 : 23. *You have ſinned againſt the Lord, and be ſure your Sin will find you out.* This Day is this Scripture awfully fulfilled upon you. You have owned under your hand, that you have lived all your Days in thoſe abominable Sins of Curſing, ſwearing, Lying, Drunkenneſs and Sabbath-breaking; and thoſe that have been acquainted with you, think you have not wrong'd your ſelf in that Confeſſion: Beſides all the other evils your own Heart is privy to.

"You are yet but a young Man, and according to the ordinary Courſe, might have lived many years in this World, had not your over-much Wickedneſs brought you to dye before your time: as *Eccles.* 7 : 17. Not before God's time, but before your time, i. e., before that time which is uſual for Man; whoſe Days are reckoned Threeſcore and Ten, and ſometimes fourſcore years, *Pſal.* 9 : 10.—It is true, we have none of us any leaſe of our Lives, we cannot ſay what may befal us this night: And yet (O amazing madneſs and folly!) how apt are we, if not to boaſt of, yet to lot upon to morrow? How ready to promiſe to our ſelves many years as the fool in the Goſpel did, *Luke* 12 : 20, who well deſerved the name of Fool, had it been for that One Evidence of it only. But

for

for your part, you have your Bounds fet, and told you, beyond which, you cannot pafs; you know at the utmoft, the Date of your Life, and the Day of your Death: You may indeed die fooner, but you muft not live longer; your End is in your View, you have but a few fteps thither, and had not need take any Vain Unprofitable ones.

"You feem to bewail your Sin of Sabbath-breaking: Well, know that you fhall never have another Sabbath to break.— The Lord help you to keep this as you ought.—It is a very awful thing to us to look on you, a Perfon in your Youth, Health, and Strength, Brefts full of Milk, and Bones moiftened with Marrow, and then to think that within fo many Days, this Man, tho' in his full ftrength, muft Dye: And methinks it fhou'd be much more awful to you.—Confider, You have no time to get Sin pardoned, and Wrath turn'd away, (if it be not done already) but between this and Death, into the very Borders, and under the Sentence of which, you now are. In the Grave there is no Repentance, no Remiffion, *Eccles.* 9 : 10. Before four Days more pafs over your head, (and O how fwiftly do they fly away!) you will be entered into an Eternal and Unchangeable ftate, of Weal or Wo; and of wo it will be, if fpeedy, thorough Repentance prevent it not.

" But yet know, That notwithftanding all that has been fpoken, there is yet hope in Ifrael concerning this thing. There is a way found out, and revealed by GOD for the Turning of his Anger even from fuch Sinners. Paul was a Murderer, and yet Pardon'd; Manaffeh made the ftreets of Jerufalem to fwim with Innocent Blood, and yet was forgiven. Nay, the greateft Murtherers that ever were in the world, even thofe that imbrewed their wicked hands in the Blood of the Son of GOD, were many of them, Converted and Reconciled to GOD, and are now in Heaven, beholding the Glory of that Chrift whom they crucified. It is, I confefs, a ftrange way, to leave men to undo themfelves,

thereby

thereby to prevent their being everlaftingly undone. But doubtlefs there have been fuch Examples ;—and who can tell but Thou mayft make one more ?—I am informed that thou didft this morning hear a precious Difcourfe in another Congregation, from that moft fuitable and feafonable Text, *Ifa.* 45, 22. *Look unto me, and be ye faved, all the Ends of the Earth :* Why that is believing, viz : Looking to JESUS for Salvation ; Looking to, and taking him as thy Lord and Saviour : One fuch humble, hearty Look, will fave thee."

Then addreffing himfelf to the Congregation, he faid : " You may not expect to have any come from the Dead to warn you, but here is one that is juft going to the Dead, who bequeaths you this Warning, left you alfo be in like manner hung up as Monuments of GOD's Wrath. I lived near twenty years in this Countrey, before I heard an Oath or a Curfe : But now as you pafs along the Streets, you may hear Children curfe and fwear, and take the great and dreadful name of GOD in vain. This they have learnt from Elder Perfons, but wo to them that taught them, if they repent not.—I remember what Pious Herbert faith, in his Advice to young Men, That the Swearer has neither any fair pretence for doing it, nor Excufe when done, either from Pleafure or Profit, &c., and fays, That if he were an Epicure, he cou'd forbear Swearing.

" And O you Drunkards, Let trembling take hold of you, Efpecially you Drunkards of Ephraim, *Ifa.* 28: 1. I mean Church-Member Drunkards. I wifh there were none fuch, that hear me this Day, who neither are Church-Members now, nor were, till Difmembred for that Sin.

" Sabbath-breaking is likewife a growing Evil among you, and therefore to be teftified againft. Hear this poor condemned Perfon telling you, That he feels this fin now lying as an infupportable Load upon him : And all that are guilty of this Sin, fhall find it fooner or later alike burdenfome to them. It hath been obferved of old, that Religion lives and

dies

dies with the Sabbath. And you now hear this Dying Man bewail his Sabbath-Breaking."

He then faid, "I fhall conclude, in a few words more to this Dying Bloody Sinner":—And then addreffing himfelf to the Prifoner, he faid,—"Poor Man! Confider, That all who live under the Gofpel, are brought to JESUS, *the Mediator of the New Covenant; to the Blood of Sprinkling, that fpeaketh better things than that of Abel.—Heb.* 12 : 24. And thereupon it is prefently added, *vers.* 25, *See that ye refufe not him that fpeaks from Heaven.* Abel's Blood cried for Vengeance upon the Murderer, but Chrift's Blood cries for Pardon, and Chrift himfelf calls on thee, to receive, and not refufe him; unto which Call, if thou yield the obedience of Faith, his Blood will fpeak on thy Behalf. Thy fins fpeak bitter things, old fins, fins of youth, a Courfe of Sin; and this bloody Sin cries aloud, and fpeaks moft bitterly; but that blood of Chrift can out-fpeak, out-cry all thefe. It was from hence, that David, when under the Anguifh of Soul, for his Blood-guiltinefs, expected Pardon, and had it, and fo mayft thou. *Pfal.* 51.

"Let thy heart leap to hear fuch Language of this Blood: Go thy way, and fpend that little time that is left thee, in ftudying the Vilenefs of thy Sins committed, and the mifery unto which thou art thereby expofed, together with the Excellence and precioufnefs of Jefus Chrift, and him cruci-fied, who is ready to fave thee from Sin prefent, and Wrath to come. And tho' thou art not able to come, yet the glorious lifting up of Chrift in the Gofpel, together with the general Invitation unto all that need him, are the means appointed and bleft by GOD, to draw Men to come. Chrift wou'd fain have the Honour of faving fuch a wretched Sinner as thou art: and be thou well affured, that unlefs thou add unto that Sin of fhedding of Mans Blood, the guilt of Refufing and Slighting of Chrift's Blood, thou fhalt not perifh. All the Sins that ever thou haft committed,

fhall

ſhall not damn thee, unleſs thou add Unbelief to all the reſt; viz: The wilful Rejecting of a Tendered Saviour. There is Wrath on thee, but it ſhall not be Everlaſtingly upon thee, if thou believe. It is Unbelief only that makes Wrath abide, *John* 3: *ult.* Other Sins do diſpleaſe, but this only can deſtroy. Look up to Chriſt therefore for the Gift of Faith. The good Lord open thine ear, that thou mayſt be no longer Rebellious, but help thee ſo to hear, as that thy Soul may Live."

This was the ſubſtance of Mr. Moody's Addreſs to the Priſoner; who was remanded to Priſon, where he continued till Thurſday Morning, (the Day of his Execution) and then another Sermon (the laſt he ever heard) was preached before him by the Reverend Mr. Increaſe Mather, juſt before his going to Execution: Of which I ſhall give you the ſubſtance, relating to the Condemned Malefactor, as I have done of the other.—

His Text was, *Numb.* 35: 16.—*And if he ſmite him with an Inſtrument of Iron (ſo that he dye) he is a Murderer: the Murderer ſhall ſurely be put to Death.* His Doctrine from the Text was, That Murder is a Sin ſo Great and Hainous, as that whoever ſhall be found guilty of it, muſt be put to Death by the hand of Publick Juſtice. But here he made an Exception, which was in caſe of a Mans own juſt-Defence, a private Perſon may take away the Life of another; for the Light of Nature teacheth Men ſelf-Preſervation. If a Murderer aſſault him, he may kill rather than be killed. We cannot ſay Abner was guilty of Murder, when he ſlew Aſahel in his own Defence. If a Man be contrary to Juſtice invaded or ſet upon by another, in an hoſtile manner, and there be no other way for him to preſerve his own Life, but by killing the Aſſailant; the Law of Nature, and of all Nations acquit him from the guilt of Murder: But he that has ſhed Blood cauſeleſs, or that has avenged himſelf, is a Murderer, 1 *Sam.* 25: 31.

He

17

He then faid, " This Doctrine juftifieth the Authority here, in refpect of the Sentence of Death which has been paffed on the Murderer who is this Day to be Executed. There is a Man ftanding before the Lord, and amongft his People this Day, who has done juft as my Text expreffeth, he has fmitten his Neighbour, and that with an Inftrument of Iron too, with a cruel Spit made of Iron ; the thing proved by feveral Witneffes ; and the Man that was hurt, dyed by that wound ; and therefore he that has fmitten him is a Murderer, and muft furely be put to Death : Tho' for a long time he denied it, yet fince his Condemnation he has acknowledged it ; and yefterday he confeffed to me that he had in his rage murder'd the Man whofe Death and Blood has been laid to his Charge. He faid the other gave him fome ill Language whereby he was provoked, and he told him if he came within the Doors, he wou'd run the Spit into his Bowels, which the other not regarding, came in, and he did to him as he had faid, fo that he is guilty of Murder.

" This miferable Creature before us acknowledgeth that in his mad paffion he cared not whom he did ftrike : It is not good for them that have lawful Power to ftrike others, to do it in paffion : A moral Heathen, when his fervant had committed a fault that greatly incenfed him, faid to him, ' If I were not angry with thee, I wou'd ftrike thee, but I will ftay till my Paffion is over before I punifh thee.'—The Scripture faith, That a good Man is merciful to his Beaft : they then that make themfelves fport with putting dumb Creatures to mifery, do very finfully : Yet that has .been practiced here of later years in the open ftreets, efpecially on one day in the year : (I mean the Cock-Scalings on Shrove-Tuefday.) To do it at fuch a time is vanity and heathenifh Superftition : Befides, to make fport with exer- cifing Cruelty on dumb Creatures, which had never been miferable had not the Sins of Man made them fo, it is a

wicked

wicked thing, and ought not to be amongft thofe that call themfelves Chriftians.—It was one of Luther's fayings, Cain will kill Abel to the End of the World.—A late Hiftorian reports, That in the kingdom of France within the fpace of Ten years, there were known to be no lefs than fix thoufand Murders committed.

" I know not but that it may be for Edification, and tend to God's glory, if I fhou'd read in this great Affembly, what I received in writing from this dying and diftreffed Creature. It is this which followeth.

"' I, James Morgan, being condemned to dye, muft needs own to the glory of God, That he is Righteous, and that I have by my fins provoked him to deftroy me before my time. I have been a great Sinner, guilty of Sabbath-breaking, of Lying, and of Uncleannefs; but there are efpecially two Sins, whereby I have offended the Great God; one is, that Sin of Drunkennefs, which has caufed me to commit other Sins; for when in drink, I have been often guilty of Curfing, and Swearing, and quarreling, and ftriking others. But the Sin which lyeth moft heavy upon my Confcience, is, That I have defpifed the Word of God, and many a time refufed to hear it preached. For thefe things, I believe God has left me to that which has brought me to a fhameful and miferable Death. I do therefore befeech and warn all Perfons, young Men efpecially, to take heed of thefe Sins, left they provoke the Lord to do to them as he has juftly done by me. And for the further Peace of my own Confcience, I think myfelf obliged to add this unto my Foregoing Confeffion, That I own the Sentence which the Honoured Court has paffed upon me, to be Exceeding juft; in as much, as tho' I had no former grudge and malice againft the Man whom I have killed, yet my paffion at the time of the Fact was fo out-ragious, as that it hurried me on to the doing of that which makes me juftly now proceeded againft as a Murderer.'

" Thus

" Thus does this Miferable Man confefs.—Lett Sinners
hear, and take Warning this Day; This Man now that the
Terrors of GOD have awakened his Diftreffed Soul, bitterly
Complains of Two Sins Efpecially; One is that of Drunkennefs: And indeed Drunkennefs has been a bloody Sin: it
has been the Caufe of many a Murder.   The Man here who
is now flying to the Pit, confeffeth that in his Drink he was
wont to curfe and fwear, and to quarrel and ftrike thofe near
him: And he acknowledged to me that he had made himfelf
grievoufly drunk, the day before he was left of GOD to
commit this Murther which he now muft dye for; yea, and
that he had that very night been drinking to excefs, and
that he was not clear of Drink at the time when he did this
bloody fact.

" It is an unhappy thing that later years a kind of ftrong
Drink called Rum, has been common amongft us, which the
poorer fort of People, both in Town and Countrey, can
make themfelves drunk with.   They that are poor and
wicked too, can for a penny or two pence, make themfelves
drunk: I wifh to the Lord fome Remedy may be thought
of, for the prevention of this evil.—Reverend Mr. Wilfon
once faid in a Sermon, There is a fort of Drink come into
the Countrey which is called Kill-Devil; but it fhou'd be
called Kill Men for the Devil.—If Murder be fuch a Crime
as has been declar'd, then let whofoever has been guilty of
this fin, be humbled for it. As for Interpretative Murder,
many have been guilty of that.—But I hope in all this vaft
Affembly there is none that has been guilty of that Murder,
which by the Law of GOD and of the Land, is a Capital
Crime, excepting one Man; and one fuch Perfon there is
here prefent, unto whom I fhall now apply my felf."

(And then turning to the Prifoner, and addreffing himfelf
to him, faid:) " Do you then hear, that your Soul may live:
This is the laft Sermon that ever you fhall hear: Time was
when you might have heard Sermons, but wou'd not; and
now

now you fhall not hear them, tho' you wou'd. For, as GOD
faid to him, *This Night thy Soul fhall be required of thee;*
fo I fay to you in his Name, This Night thy Soul fhall be
taken from thee: This Night your Soul fhall be either in
Heaven or Hell for ever. You are appointed to dye this
day, and after Death, cometh the Judgment: As foon as
your Body is dead, your Immortal Soul fhall appear before
the Great GOD and Judge of all; and a Sentence of
Everlafting Life, or Everlafting Death, fhall be paffed upon
you.

"I have fpoken fo often to you in private, fince your being
apprehended, that I fhall not need to fay much now: Only
a few Words:—

" 1. Confider what a Sinner you have been; The Sin which
you are to dye for, is as red as Scarlet; and many other
Sins has your wicked Life been filled with. You have been
a ftranger to me; I never faw you; I never heard of you,
until you had committed the Murder, for which you muft
dye this Day; but I hear by others that have known you,
how wicked you have been; and you have your felf confeffed to the World, That you have been guilty of Drunkennefs, guilty of Curfing and Swearing, guilty of Sabbath-
breaking, guilty of Lying, guilty of Secret Uncleannefs; as
Solomon faid to Shimei, *Thou knoweft the Wickednefs which
thine own heart is privy to;* fo I fay to you: and that which
aggravates your guiltinefs not a little, is, That fince you have
been in Prifon you have done Wickedly: You have made
your felf drunk feveral Times fince your Imprifonment;
yea, and you have been guilty of Lying fince your Condemnation.

" 2. Confider what mifery you have brought upon your felf:
on your Body, that muft dye an accurfed Death; you muft
hang between Heaven and Earth, as it were forfaking of
both, and unworthy to be in either. And what mifery have
you brought upon your poor Children? You have brought
an

an Everlafting Reproach upon them. How great will their fhame be, when it fhall be faid to them that their Father was hang'd ? Not for his Goodnefs, as many in the World have been; but for his Wickednefs: Not as a Martyr, but as a Malefactor: But that which is Ten thoufand thoufand times worfe than all this, is, That you have (without Repentance,) brought undoing Mifery upon your poor, yet precious Soul: Not only Death on your Body, but a fecond Death on your never-dying Soul : O tremble at that !

"I remember a Man that was Condemned and Executed in this place fome years ago, that had been a Souldier, and as ftout a fpirited Man as moft in the World, who when he came to die, thus expreffed himfelf to a Minifter that treated with him about his Soul: 'I (faid he) never knew what fear meant, tho' I have been amongft drawn Swords, and before the Cannons Mouth, I feared not Death : But now you tell me of a Second Death, it makes my Soul to fhake within me.'

" The three Sermons which have been preached to you in Publick, fince your Condemnation; the pains which has been taken with you in private, by one or other of the Lord's Servants; all thefe will aggravate your Condemnation, when you fhall be judged again before all the World, at the laft day, if you die Impenitent.

" 3. Confider there is yet a poffibility that your Soul may be faved. Notwithftanding all that has been fpoken to you, do not defpair; Repent, but do not defpair. I wou'd not have you fay as Cain did, My Sin is greater than can be forgiven. The LORD is a merciful GOD: Tho' Men cannot forgive you, GOD can, and he will do it, if you unfeignedly repent, and believe on the LORD JESUS.—But be fure your Repentance be true and fincere. To come nearer to you, I have known fome, more than one, or two, or three, that have been condemned to Die ; and whilft they remained under that Sentence, they feemed very penitent : But they were

afterwards

afterwards pardoned, (for they had not been guilty of Murder, as you have) and fince that, have been as wicked as ever. O then, look to your felf, that you do not diffemble with GOD and Man, and your own Soul too. Do not think you fhall be faved, becaufe good Men have prayed for you, or for the Confeffion of your Sins, which you have now made, or for the fake of any thing but Chrift. And I pray the SON of GOD to have Compaffion on you."

This, Mr. Larkin, is a part of what I heard preached at Mr. Willard's Meeting in an Auditory of near 5000 People; they went firft to the New Church, but the Gallery crack'd, and fo they were forced to remove to Mr. Willard's. They were all preach'd with fo much Awfulnefs, and fo pathetically apply'd to the Poor Condemned Man, that all the Auditory (as well as my felf) were very much affected thereat: And tho' I have been pretty long in the Rehearfal, yet you being an old Diffenter, I did not think the Reading of them wou'd be unacceptable to you. And remember this, I am rambling ftill, tho' it be from one fubject to another.—But before I leave off this fubject, I muft bring Morgan to his Execution, whither I rid with Mr. Cotton Mather, after the Sermon was ended. Some thoufands of the People following to fee the Execution. As I rid along I had feveral glimpfes of poor Morgan, as he went.

He feem'd penitent to the laft: Mr. Cotton Mather pray'd with him at the place of Execution, and conferred with him about his Soul all the way thither, which was about a mile out of Bofton. After being ty'd up, ftanding on the Ladder, he made the following Speech :—

" I pray GOD that I may be a Warning to you all, and that I may be the laft that ever fhall fuffer after this manner. In the fear of GOD I warn you to have a Care of the Sin of Drunkennefs, for that's a Sin that leads to all manner of Sins and Wickednefs: (Mind and have a Care of breaking the Sixth Commandment, where it is faid, *Thou fhalt do no Murder.*)

Murder.) For when a Man is in drink, he is ready to commit all manner of Sin, till he fill up the Cup of the Wrath of GOD, as I have done, by committing that Sin of Murder. I beg of GOD, as I am a dying Man, and to appear before the LORD within a few Minutes, that you may take notice of what I fay to you: Have a Care of Drunkennefs and ill Company, and mind all good Inftruction, and don't turn your back upon the Word of GOD, as I have done. When I have been at a Meeting, I have gone out of the Meeting-Houfe to commit fin, and to pleafe the Luft of my flefh: and don't make a mock at any poor Object of Pity, but blefs GOD, that he hath not left you, as he hath juftly done me, to commit that horrid Sin of Murder.

"Another thing that I have to fay to you, is, To have a Care of that Houfe where that Wickednefs was committed, and where I have been juftly ruined: But here I am, and know not what will become of my poor Soul, which is within a few Moments of Eternity. I have murder'd a poor Man, who had but little time to repent, and I know not what's become of his poor Soul. O that I may make ufe of this opportunity that I have! O that I may make Improvement of this little time, before I go hence, and be no more! O let all mind what I am a faying now, I am a going out of this World! O take warning by me, and beg of GOD to keep you from this Sin, which hath been my Ruine."

After he had been about an hour at the Gallows, and had prayed again, his Cap was pulled over his Eyes, and then having faid, "O Lord, Receive my Spirit; I come unto thee, O Lord; I come, I come, I come"; he was Turned off, and the multitude by degrees difperf'd. I think, during this Mournful Scene, I never faw more ferious nor greater Compaffion.

But from the Houfe of Mourning, I rambled to the Houfe of Feafting; for Mr. York, Mr. King, with Madam Brick, Mrs. Green, Mrs. Toy, the Damfell and my felf, took a Ramble to a place call'd Governour's Ifland, about a mile from Bofton, to fee a whole Hog roafted, as did feveral other Boftonians. We went all in a Boat; and having treated the Fair Sex, returned in the Evening.

Another Occurrence that happened whilft I was here, was, the Arrival of the Rofe Frigot from England, with a New Charter, brought over by one Rundel,[70] a Perfon generally hated by the Boftonians; by this Charter, Major Dudley was made Prefident; a very worthy, honeft, and accomplifh'd Perfon, and every way a Gentleman: infomuch that they cou'd hardly have chofen a better Man in the whole Countrey: He was my particular Friend, and had been Extremely Civil to me, and had done me many Honours fince I came into the Countrey. But they being now to lofe the old Title of Governour and Magiftrates, for Prefident and Council, tho' more Modifh, it wou'd not relifh fo well with Men that had their Liberty for above 60 years.

Mr. Ratcliff[80] was the Parfon that came over with the Charter, who was a very Excellent Preacher, whofe Matter was good, and the Drefs in which he put it, Extraordinary; he being as well an Orator as a Preacher. The next Sunday after he Landed, he preach'd in the Town-houfe, and read Common-Prayer in his Surplice, which was fo great a Novelty to the Boftonians, that he had a very large Audience; and my felf happening to go thither for one, it was told about Town, as a piece of Wonder, That Dr. Annefly's Son-in-Law was turn'd Apoftate: So little Charity have

some

---

[70] The Charter was brought over by Edward Randolph in the *Rofe* frigate, Capt. George. (PALFREY, Hiftory of New-England, iii., 484.) She arrived on the 15th May, 1686.—ED.

[80] This was Robert Ratcliffe, the firft minifter of the Epifcopalian Society which afterwards occupied the Stone Chapel. He undoubtedly went back to England in July, 1689. (See GREENWOOD's Hiftory of King's Chapel, p. 50.)—ED.

fome Men in New-England, for all that have a larger Charity than themfelves. Dr. Bullivant, and Mr. Gouge, and Mr. Tryon, were conftant hearers at this New Church; but for my own part, I went but once or twice at the firft, tho' Mr. Ratcliff (as I have faid before) was an Extraordinary good Preacher.

And now for a Merry Occurrence; Wou'd you Believe your Friend to be a Conjurer? Yet fo, (by reafon of my Trading in Books) a young Lady[81] in Bofton wou'd needs believe me: Mrs. Comfort was concern'd in the Frolick, and to carry on the Jeft, wou'd needs have me tell the Young Lady her Fortune: And inquiring, by the by, of Mrs. Comfort, what her circumftances were, I underftood fhe was in love with a young Gentleman that really lov'd her, but yet courted another, and feem'd very indifferent to her he lov'd. When the young Lady came, fhe told me fhe underftood that I was a Learned Perfon, and by the Knowledge I had arriv'd to, cou'd foretel future Events; upon which, and the Encouragement Mrs. Comfort Wilkins had given her, of my great Civility to all, and efpecially to ftrangers, fhe had done her felf the Honour of giving me a Vifit, in order to be inform'd of the Event of fomething which now very much troubled her.—It is (faid fhe)—'Madam,' faid I, 'I know what it is, 'tis Love:' (for I was afraid fhe wou'd have told me firft, and that wou'd have fpoil'd the beft part of my Fortune-telling) and then remembring that the Delphic Oracles uf'd to be deliver'd in Verfe, I thought I had beft
take

[81] In the "Life and Errors" this young lady is termed Madam WHITE-MORE. It feems very probable that fhe was Frances, daughter of Francis Whitmore, of Cambridge, and was then about fixteen years old. There was a family of Whittemores living in Malden, but the records feem invariably to pre-ferve a fpelling which fhows that the two names were pronounced differently. Befides, in this Malden family we do not find any girl of a fuitable age in 1686 to have been the fubject of fuch a frolic. Francis Whitmore, jr., owned land in Bofton, which he fold in 1692, and may have been living here at this date. If this were his fifter, fhe married within two or three years Jonathan Thompfon, of Woburn, and her great-grandfon was the well known philofo-pher, Benjamin Thompfon, Count Rum-ford.—ED.

take the fame Method: And therefore raifing my Voice, and fpeaking fomewhat Magifterially, I delivered myfelf thus: Madam!

> Neither of Fortune, nor of Love complain,
>   For Love and Fortune both your Friends will prove.
> Tho' his Indifference caufes now your Pain,
>   You fhall at laft Enjoy the Man you love.
>
> 'Tis true, he does a Wandring ftar adore,
>   Which makes a Pretty Twinkling in the Skies;
> • Yet your bright Eyes fhall his loft Love reftore: •
>   For ftars muft Vanifh when the Sun does rife.
>
> You in his heart have the Afcendant now:
>   He only means to try your Conftancy:
> And when he finds you faithful to your Vow,
>   • He at your feet will for his Pardon lie.
>
> But fee you do not ufe him too fevere;
>   When like the Prodigal he does return;
> • Smiles will caufe Love, when Frowns may raife his Fear,
>   • And quench thofe Flames which otherwife wou'd burn.
>
>   But if your Conqueft o'er him, you'd improve,
>   What you fhall gain by Beauty, keep by Love.

When I had deliver'd my Oracle, I made the Lady a bow, which fhe return'd very obligingly, and gave me many Thanks for the trouble fhe had given me; withal telling me, that fhe was furpriz'd to hear me tell her cafe fo plainly; and fince fhe knew what I had faid was true in one part, fhe hop'd it wou'd prove fo in the other likewife; and then thank'd me for my good Counfel at laft, telling me he had got too great an Intereft in her heart to receive any bad Ufage from her. I then defir'd her to conceal what I had done to gratifie her upon Mrs. Comfort's account; affuring
her

• In the "Life and Errors" the four lines here marked ftand refpectively thus:

"Yet your own Charms fhall his loft Love reftore."

"For Pardon, at your Feet he'll proftrate lye."

"Love feeds on fmiles, but Frowns wou'd give defpair,
"And quench thofe Fires, which elfe wou'd Flame and Burn."

her it was a thing I never car'd to practife, nor fo much as to have publickly known. She gave an affurance that fhe wou'd be private, as I had defir'd her, and that none fhou'd know any thing of it from her. And as a Teftimony of her being very well pleaf'd with my performance, fhe afterwards prefented me with a Noble pair of Gloves, which I refufed to accept, which fhe was much troubled at. But I was of Opinion that my Accepting of the Gloves wou'd have been carrying on the Jeft too far. For I knew no more than other Gypfies and Fortune-Tellers, which is juft nothing. But by this you may fee how eafily People may be impof'd upon.[63]

But from Love, I muft make a Tranfition to Arms; and cou'd you think that PHIL., (after the Story of the Ruffles,) wou'd ever make a *Souldier?* Yet fo it fell out: For 'tis their Cuftom here for all that can bear Arms, to go out on a Training Day: But I thought a Pike was beft for a Young Souldier, and fo I carry'd a Pike; and between you and I, Reader, there was another Reafon for it too, and that was, I knew not how to fhoot off a Mufquet. But 'twas the firft time I ever was in Arms; which tho' I tell thee, Reader, I had no need to tell to my *Fellow-Souldiers*, for they knew it well enough by my awkward handling of them. For I

was

---

[63] DUNTON's printed verfion was fo different that we here reprint it. " When I had finifh'd, I made the Lady a Ghoftly Bow, which fhe very obligingly return'd with many Thanks for the Trouble fhe had given me; fhe was very much furpriz'd, fhe told me, to hear her Cafe fo exactly reprefented, and affur'd me, the Gentleman had left her no Power to give him any ill Ufage, whenever he thought fit to become her Humble Servant again. She wou'd have prefented me a Pair of Gloves, which I refuf'd to accept, only defiring fhe'd keep the Matter fecret, in Regard I was very much averfe to lay out my Talent that way, unlefs there was a profpect of doing good. She faid fhe cou'd not be fo ungrateful as to difoblige me in any Kind. However, the fatiffaction fhe receiv'd was too Hot to be kept in her own Breaft; fhe difcover'd it to feveral of her own Companions, who were very Solicitous to fore-know their own Fortunes in the World; but I refuf'd to meddle any more, for the Reputation of a Conjuror is not fo defirable.

" I acknowledge this Frolick to be one of the Errors of my Life: the Young Lady, I fuppofe, might be kept a while from Defpair by't, but that don't juftify the Folly of it."—ED.

was as unacquainted with the Terms of Military Difcipline, as a wild Irifh Man, whom I have heard they ufe to Difcipline at firft, by putting Bread in one Pocket, and cheefe in another, and then bidding them turn to their Bread, and turn to their Cheefe inftead of bidding them turn to the Right and Left, as is ufual; which they did not underftand. But we were even here, for tho' they underftood Arms better than I, yet I underftood Books better than they.

Being come into the Field, the Captain call'd us all into our Clofe Order, in order to go to Prayer, and then Pray'd himfelf: And when our Exercife was done, the Captain likewife concluded with Prayer. I have read that Guftavus Adolphus, the Warlike King of Sweden, wou'd before the beginning of a Battel kneel down devoutly at the head of his Army, and pray to GOD (the Giver of Victory) to give them Succefs againft their Enemies, which commonly was the Event; and that he was as Careful alfo to return thanks to GOD for the Victory. But folemn Prayer in the Field upon a Day of Training, I never knew but in New-England, where it feems it is a common Cuftom. About three of the Clock both our Exercife and Prayers being over, We had a very Noble Dinner, to which all the Clergy were invited.

[84][About this Time, the Tryal of Captain P—— for Infufficiency, made a great Noife in Bofton. In all fuch Cafes the good Wives are loaded with Impudence, &c. But where's the fenfe on't? Women are of the fame Species and Compofition with our felves, and have their Natural Inclinations as well as we. The Inftitution of Marriage has fome Regards to the lawful Pleafures of Senfe, with reference to them, as well as to our felves; and when they Suffer a difappointment of this Nature, why fhou'd they be
reckon'd

---

[84] This paffage ftands in this place in the "Life and Errors" as originally publifhed. There is no reference to it in the prefent Manufcript, but it feems too characteriftic to be omitted, efpecially fince the editor of the reprint, in 1818, has ftricken it from the text without a fingle word of apology.—ED.

reckon'd Impudent, if they but complain?   Befides, in fuch
Cafes, the Man is perjur'd out of his own Mouth, in the
very Form of Marriage.]

And now, Mr. Larkin, having tyr'd you with this long
Letter, 'tis time to draw to a Conclufion; Efpecially having
made good all that I promif'd in the beginning of it.   Befides, I am juft now ready for a Ramble to the adjacent
Towns: For Palmer can fufficiently fupply my place in the
Warehoufe.   And this gives a greater Latitude to my
Rambles: In which I yet obferve fome Method: For as
they that learn to fwim, firft try only within their reach, that
fo they may retreat with fafety, if there be occafion; and
after venture into deeper Waters; So my firft Rambles fhall
be near at hand, to the adjacent Towns; and being by this
means become a little acquainted with the Countrey, I
intend to Ramble further.

But before I end my Letter (as near as I am to it) I muft
defire you to prefent my Service to my Old and true Friend
Mr. James Aftwood:[85] He (you know) was born in this
Countrey, which I think no Small honour to it: For he is
a truly honeft, fober, and Religious Man; and my Fellow-
Sufferer in Excommunication; (being both given to the
Devil (as you alfo were) becaufe we refuf'd to play the Devil
for GOD's fake, and wou'd not help forward thofe Calamities
which

[85] There can be no doubt that James
Aftwood was the fon of James Aftwood,
of Roxbury, born there, as SAVAGE
records, 29 Nov., 1638. The father
died in 1653, and in his will, publifhed
in the Genealogical Regifter, vii., 337,
appointed his wife Sarah executrix.
She refufed, becaufe of her departure
for England, and very probably her fon
James went with her. Of the fon,
DUNTON writes in "Life and Errors:"
"He was my near Neighbor and Intimate Friend for many Years.   He
printed for me near Sixty Books, and
was conftantly engag'd in the *Athenian* *Mercury*. If he had any failing, 'twas
that of a Little Paffion, but 'twas over
in a Word fpeaking; and to make
amends, he was almoft perfect in Charity, Friendfhip, Humility, Juftice, and
every other Vertue; what I fpeak is
from the long Intimacy I had with him.
But I need not inlarge, for fince the
Death of his Son, (Mr. John Aftwood,)
he feems no longer to have any com-
merce with the World, and hath nothing
fo Familiar as a Life that is (by his
Retreat from London to a Country
Village) as it were bury'd in Death."—
ED.

which have now over-taken poor England, by a Popifh King.) He is Induftrious in his Bufinefs, and Confcientious in his Dealing; and one that I hope will do very well, if Mr. Ponder ben't too Ponderous for him. And pray give my refpects alfo to his Son John.

Give my Service alfo (and a great deal of Love to boot) to my very good Friend, that Mirror of Honefty, Mr. John Harris at the Harrow: You know, as well as I, how truly juft and honeft a Man he is: and that it was of him it has been faid,[86]

> If of all honeft Bookfellers, you'll have the Marrow,
> Repair to King John, at the fign of the Harrow.

Nor was he out of the way that beftow'd that Character upon him. As feveral can tell, with whom he has been Partner

---

[86] In his "Life and Errors," DUNTON fays that this couplet was by his "Friend, Mr. Larkin, who being once afk'd, Who was the Honefteft Bookfeller in London, return'd this Extempore Anfwer." "The fame Day He Welcom'd me home from Dublin, he was feiz'd with his Old Diftemper, the Tiffick, &c., which ended his Life in a few Days," DUNTON alfo records "Mrs. Elizabeth Harris. She's the Beautiful Relict of my worthy Friend, Mr. John Harris: Her moft remarkable Graces are Beauty, Wit and Modefty. So pretty a Fabrick was never Fram'd by an Almighty Architect for a vulgar Gueft. He fhew'd the value which he fet upon her Mind, when he took care to have it fo nobly and fo beautifully lodg'd. And to a Graceful carriage and deportment of Body, There is joyn'd a Pleafant Converfation, a moft exact Juftice, and a Generous Friendfhip; all which, as my felf and her fhe-friend can teftifye, fhe poffeffes in the Height of their Perfection." Poffibly connected with this John Harris was Benjamin Harris, of whom DUNTON writes: "He fold a *Proteftant Petition* in King Charles's Reign, for which they fin'd him Five Hundred Pound, and fet him once in the Pillory; but his Wife (like a Kind Rib) ftood by him, to defend her Husband againft the Mobb. After this, (having a deal of Mercury in his Natural Temper,) he travel'd to New-England, where he followed Bookfelling, and then Coffeefelling, and then Printing, but continu'd Ben Harris ftill; and is now both Bookfeller and Printer, in Grace-church Street, as we find by his *London Poft;* fo that his converfation is general, (but never Impertinent,) and his Wit pliable to all Inventions. But yet his vanity (if he has any) gives no Alloy to his Wit, and is no more than might juftly Spring from confcious Vertue; and I do him but Juftice in this part of his Character, for in once travelling with him from Bury Fair, I found him to be the moft Ingenious and Innocent Companion that I had ever met with." After

Partner in above 20 Books. Nor is he only remarkable for his Honefty, but is as much to be commended for feveral other things. Tho' his Stature be fmall, he has a Soaring Soul, and is Mafter of a Vaft Underftanding; and a very thinking Man; his Thoughts always very neat and clean; and his Converfation fo facetious and Entertaining, that I am fure both you and I were very much wont to covet it.

I have yet fomething further to tell you before I conclude, that is, That tho' I have firft broke the Ice, in bringing hither a Cargo of Books; yet by fome Letters I receiv'd by the Rofe Frigot that brought hither the New Charter, I perceive I fhall not be the laft: For Old England is now fo uneafie a Place for honeft Men, that thofe that can will feek out for another Countrey: And this I fuppofe is the Cafe of Mr. Benjamin Harris and the two Mr. Hows, whom I hear are coming over hither, and to whom I wifh a good Voyage. Mr. Ben. Harris, you know, has been a noted Publick Man in England, and I think the Book of Englifh Liberties that you Printed, was done for him and Mr. How: No wonder then that in this Reign they meet with Enemies. Mr. Harris I think alfo Printed the Proteftant Tutor, a Book not at all relifh'd by the Popifh Party, becaufe it is the defign of that little Book to bring up Children in an Averfion to Popery. To fpeak the Truth, Mr. Benj. Harris has had many good Thoughts, tho' he has wanted the Art
of

After this was written, DUNTON evidently quarreled with his friend, and abufes him without limit; amongft other doggerel lines, he writes:

"Slander, *Ned Ward*, confufion, rage and shame,
Attend you to the place from whence you came.
To Tyburn thee let carrion horfes draw,
In jolting cart, without fo much as ftraw," etc.

SAVAGE fays that Benjamin Harris while in Bofton projected a newfpaper, in 1687, which was ftopped on the iffue of one number, and that he returned in 1694 to London. In 1690, he fold Cotton Mather's 'Wonderful Works of God Commemorated,' at the "London Coffee Houfe." In 1693, Cotton Mather's 'Winter Meditations' were "printed and Sold by Benj. Harris, over againft the Old Meeting Houfe." In 1694, Scottow's Narrative was printed by him at "The Sign of the Bible over-againft the Blew Anchor, Cornhill." Thefe however probably mean the fame ftore. THOMAS records that in 1695 Vavafour Harris was a book-feller at the fame place, "oppofite the old Meeting Houfe in Cornhill," and prefumably he was a relative.—ED.

of Improving 'em; and cou'd he fix his Mercury a little, and not be fo volatile, he wou'd do well enough. He advances in years, as well as your felf, and if he can but make a fhift to fcuffle thro' this World, if I ben't mif-inform'd, his W— has taken care for his well-doing in the next, unlefs the Proverb fails.

As to the Two Hows,[87] Job and John (for Job I think is the Elder Brother, tho' John has the moft Mercury) I never heard any thing of 'em, but that they were both Induftrious and honeft Men; and men of very good fenfe, John efpecially, with whom I have moft acquaintance: And always of the Right Side, for the promoting of Englifh Liberties, and the Proteftant Religion: And the caufe of their prefent Sufferings makes me very much Pity 'em; for I am inform'd they have been indicted for Printing a Scandalous and Seditious Libel, and for this have been put by their Trade for three Years, according to the Act for Printing: But I was aftonifh'd to hear that this Scandalous and Seditious Libel, was no other but the Affemblies Catechifm; 'Tis true, they have no reafon to be afham'd of their Suffering, but the Company of Stationers have, who profecuted 'em, and who once laid claim to this Book as their copy; and that they fhou'd indict men for Printing it, as a Scandalous and Seditious Libel, is fuch a thing as certainly a Proteftant Company were never guilty of before! Nor do I know what Plea they can make for themfelves, unlefs it be that of Gratitude. For being Incorporated by Philip and Mary, both Popifh Princes, they thought themfelves bound in Gratitude to their Founders to promote Popery, and fupprefs

the

---

[87] We do not find that thefe brothers John and Job Howe came hither. Yet in "Life and Errors" DUNTON fays of John: "He was a great Sufferer in King James's Reign and has had the Fate of being a *Traveller:* but being an Honeft Man at the bottom, he is bleft where-ever he goes. He is now settled in Grace-Church Street; and being a great Projector, (as we fee by the *London Spyes,* and the *Obfervator,* &c.) is like to encreafe apace." As a traveller he might have vifited New-England, but more probably Holland was the fcene of his exile.—ED.

the Proteftant Religion.   But whither am I Rambled?—If thefe Perfons arrive here before I go hence, I fhall be very glad to fee 'em, and give 'em any affiftance I can, Efpecially the Two Brothers.

Pray give my Love and Service to Mrs. Larkin, the faithful Partner of all your Sufferings, and my refpects to your Son George, and Daughter Lydia.   My kind love to your felf, hoping you will Excufe the trouble of this tedious Epiftle, to which I will now put an End, by fubfcribing my felf, Dear Mr. Larkin,

Your truly affectionate and well-wifhing Friend,

PHILARET.

THE OLD STATE HOUSE, STATE STREET, BOSTON.
Erected A. D. 1748.

LETTER IV.

TO MR. JOHN WOOLHURST,[88] AT HIS HOUSE
IN CLARE MARKET, LONDON.

Dear Coufin!—Not only your Relation to me, is the Son of my Father's own Sifter, but much more our being Contemporary in Years, and Companions to Each other in our Juvenile Sports and Recreations, has made fo deep an Impreffion in my Breft, as neither diftance of Time or Place can ever wear off. And I have often Obferv'd that thofe firft little Friendfhips Children make with their Play-Fellows, are of longer continuance than thofe that are afterwards Contracted. And Methinks the remembrance of our being School-fellows together, between whom there was a little kind of Emulation with refpect to our Learning, (which I remember by that very remarkable token of your Taxing me once with breaking Prifcians Head in making falfe Lattin,) and our being Play-fellows together, both at Refbury and Graham, has ftrangely endear'd you to me.

And therefore that I might Evidence to you that I have carried the remembrance of you, and of our former Inter-courfe with each other, into another World, (for fuch is America,

---

88 John Woolhoufe was the fourth child of Mary Dunton and —— Wool-houfe, as is fhown in the biographical fketch of Dunton.—ED.

America, with refpect to Europe,) I have directed this Letter
to you from thence: For fince we uf'd often in our youthful
years, to fend Letters to each other, tho' but at five miles
diftance, I thought a Letter that came three thoufand miles
might be more acceptable to you: And tho' I doubt not but
you have heard of me fince I rambled into this part of the
World, both by my Deareft Wife, (to whom I write as often
as I can,) and alfo by my Brother Lake, to whom I writ a
large account of my Voyage at Sea, yet I believe a Letter
to your felf, wou'd give you a greater affurance of the
Continuance of my old Friendfhip and Affection for you,
than all thofe fecond-hand Remembrances: Nor do I intend,
my Coufin, that this Letter fhall only be a bare How-do-you;
but fince I know you tinctur'd with that Athenian Itch of
Enquiring after Novelties, I fhall endeavour to fatisfie your
Curiofity, by giving you an Account of fome of the Cuftoms
and Manners of the Natives of this Country; and a little
Narrative of my fhort Rambles to the Countrey Towns
adjacent to Bofton which is the Metropolis of all New-
England. I need not give you an Account of Bofton,
becaufe I have done that already in a Letter to our good
Friend Mr. Larkin, the Printer, who I am very fure will be
glad to oblige you with the fight of it.

After I had a little fettled my Bufinefs, and taken fuch a
furvey of Bofton as I thought convenient, I was minded in
the next place to fee how the Countrey ftood affected; which
being nothing elfe but a great Wildernefs, I was loth to
venture too far at firft; but begun to take a view of it by
fmall Rambles to the Adjacent Towns, an Account of which
fhall be the fubject matter of my Travell-Hiftory; in which,
what I write, you may affure your felf is nothing but Truth,
however the Proverb may abufe poor Travellers (or Ram-
bleres) and give 'em a Licenfe to Lye by Authority.

To begin then, my Coufin; My firft Ramble, was (for I
love to keep a Method, as much at leaft, as can be kept by

a

a Rambler) to Vifit our Captain that brought us over, Captain Thomas Jenner;[89] My felf and three or four Friends with me, fet out from Bofton, about the time that Sol had raif'd his Beams above the Flood, and with his Rays gilded the Mountain Tops. For we were all refolv'd to take the Day before us, and not to make a Toyl of that which we defign'd for Pleafure : The Town where the Captain dwells, and whither we defign'd to Ramble, was Charles-Town : and the Paffage to it is by a Ferry, which I am told is worth about £40 per annum ; and fometimes quickly came to Charles-Town, where the Captain receiv'd us with all the kindnefs and refpect imaginable, and to fpeak the truth, Treated us very genteelly : So that I found it was better being at the Captain's Table a fhoar, than aboard : For on Board, he grutch'd me once a Dumplin, and had like to have beat my Man for bringing it to me ; but here was both Pudding Enough, and all forts of other Varieties ; and to. fhow it was a Sea-Captain's Treat, he crown'd it with a Noble Bowl of Punch.

Dinner being over, and the Punch and other Liquors having exhilerated our Spirits, I defir'd the Captain to take a little walk with me, that I might fee the Town ; with the fituation whereof I was extreamly pleaf'd : For it is fituated upon a narrow Neck of Land, between two. pleafant Rivers, whofe

[89] As to Capt. Thomas Jenner, we learn from an article written by William S. Appleton, Efq., and printed in the *N. E. Hiftorical and Genealogical Regifter* for July, 1865, that he was grandfon of Rev. Thomas Jenner, who came to New-England in 1635, and was fettled at Weymouth and Saco. Returning to England, he lived in Norfolk, but the date of his death is unknown. His fon Thomas was of Weymouth and Charleftown, and had fons John and Thomas. This laft was married in 1655 to Rebecca Trerise, and had nine children. He joined the church of Charleftown in 1681, and the Artillery Company of Bofton in 1673. He was captain of a veffel apparently making regular trips to England, as there are feveral voyages mentioned in letters of that period. He died in England in the autumn of 1686, and his eftate proved infolvent. His widow died 23 Sept., 1732, aged 86. His grandfon, Thomas Jenner, died in Charleftown, and on his tomb are the family arms, of which an engraving will be found in the *Heraldic Journal,* vol. 1., p. 56.—ED.

whofe ftreams on purling Pebbles kept a murmur, and with
their amorous foldings did Embrace the lovely Shore on
either fide the Town; one of thefe Rivers is Namefake to
the Town, and call'd Charles River; and with fuch wanton
kiffes daily greets it, that one wou'd think there was fome
kin between 'em: The other River is call'd Myftick, but
from what Cabala or dark Intent of Fate, this Myftick Name
was put upon the River, is yet to me a Myftery: This River
Myftick runs through the right fide of the Town, and by its
nearnefs to Charles River, makes in one place a very narrow
Neck, On which the moft part of the Town is built: The
Market Place is near the Water-fide; and is encompaff'd
round about with Houfes; from whence two ftreets ftretch
themfelves forth, built with Exact and Curious Symmetry;
And beautify'd extreamly with pleafant Gardens and well-
planted Orchards: Their Meeting-Houfe adorns the North-
fide of the Market, plac'd on the bottom of a little Hill,
which on its back-fide gently over-looks it. The Captain
told me that this Town had belonging to it 1200 Acres of
Arable Land, and 400 Head of Cattel, with as many Sheep:
And that the Inhabitants of the Town had feveral Farms in
the Countrey.

　　I afk'd the Captain if there were any Indians in the Town,
he told me there were fome, but not many: I afk'd him if
he knew 'em; he told me, 'Yes, very well'; 'Then,' faid I,
'Let's go and fee one of 'em, and fee how they'll Entertain
us?' The Captain and my Friends agreed to it, and away
we Rambled to one of their Houfes, which was made of
long Poles fet up, and cover'd with Mats, and on the infide
hung with a fort of Embroider'd Mats, which looks almoft
as well as Hangings: When the Captain, (who was our
Leader) went in, he faluted them with faying, 'What Chear,
Netop,' (Netop in the Indian Language fignifying Friend;)
the Indian very courteoufly thank'd him, and bid us fit
down; which we did; and having difcourf'd a little with him

about

about Countrey matters, and efpecially fhooting with the Bow and Arrows, at which they are very fkilful, the Indian telling us he had often fhot Birds flying; we made fome overtures to be going; but the Indian told us we muft not go till we had Eat; which it feems is a Common Cuftom amongft them, being generally very kind to ftrangers: I was refolv'd to fee their Entertainment, and fo accepted of his Invitation.

Our firft Difh (for we had more than one Courfe) was fome Parch'd meal, as they call'd it, that is, it was a fort of Indian corn parch'd, which is a ready and very wholefome Food, which they eat with a little Water, fometimes hot, and fometimes cold; its tafte is not unlike to that of Coffee; and to thofe that love Coffee eats very pleafantly: That we might not feem unkind guefts, we eat fome of thefe Parch'd Berries, and Commended 'em too, at which the Indian feem'd very well pleaf'd: And told us,[90] That he had travell'd with 200 of his Country-men at once through the Woods, for three or four Days together; and Every Man only carried a little Bafket of this at his back, or elfe a hollow Leathern Girdle of it full about our Middles, and that, with fome Water, was Provifion fufficient for us: 'And with this ready Provifion' (fays he) 'and our Bows and Arrows, we are ready

for

---

[90] At this point we commence one of the moft curious portions of DUNTON's literary plagiarifms. It will be noticed that throughout this letter, he has inferted many interefting details in regard to the Indians, and has reprefented them as being related to him on certain occafions by well-informed friends. *Thefe converfations are entirely imaginary, the text being copied almoft literally* from Roger Williams's "KEY INTO THE LANGUAGE OF AMERICA," printed in London in 1643.

We believe that this book was not reprinted until 1827, fo that DUNTON in 1686 was tolerably fafe from detection,

if indeed he meant more than a literary myftification. In December, 1866, the firft volume of the Narraganfett Club's Publications appeared, containing a reprint of the KEY, admirably edited by J. Hammond Trumbull, late Secretary of State of Connecticut, a gentleman preëminently qualified for the tafk. Our references will be therefore to this edition, and the pagination will be that of the *volume*, and *not* of this *tract*, which is one of four contained in the book.

The remark of the Indian and reply of Capt. Jenner are taken from WILLIAMS, p. 100.—ED.

for War and Travel, at an hours Warning': 'I will affure
you,' anfwer'd our Captain, 'with a fpoonful of this meal, and
a fpoonful of Water Brooks, have I made many a good
Dinner and Supper.'

Our next Courfe (for I told you before we had two) was a
Mefs of Meal Pottage unparch'd; which is, the Indian Corn
beaten and boil'd, and eaten either hot or cold with Milk or
Butter: But ours was cold, and eaten with Milk; tho' he
offer'd to heat fome for us, and do it with Butter; which we,
thanking him, refuf'd. The Indians, for the moft part, eat
this only with water, but we were treated like Perfons of
Quality: Our Captain eat heartily of it, tho' he came from
fo good a Dinner at his own Table; and affur'd us that this
Difh was Exceeding wholefome for Englifh Bodies. And
now, having thank'd the Indian for his kind Entertainment,
we took our Leaves of him. Very well fatisfied with plain-
heartednefs and kindnefs of the poor Indian.

The Captain as we went back, told us, [91] That there were
a fort of People in the Countrey, call'd Mihtukmecha, that
is, Tree-Eaters; Thefe People live between three and four
hundred miles Weft within the Land: They fet no Corn,
but live on the Bark of Chefnuts and Walnuts, and other
fine Trees: They dry and eat this Bark with the fat of

Beafts,

[91] This is from WILLIAMS, p. 101, 102,
103, 105. To account for fo many pages
of the original being cited, we muft
explain that WILLIAMS's book is divided into thirty-two chapters, each
treating of a diftinct topic. In each
chapter he has a vocabulary of words
and phrafes belonging to its fubject, and
on nearly every page a fhort fentence is
introduced of remarks pertinent to the
occafion. DUNTON has brought thefe
brief notes into a connected form,
adding here and there a word to complete the fenfe. He has not however
copied from the book in a continuous
abftract, but taking a chapter has made
his adaptation, and inferted it at fuch a
point in his own letter as feemed fuitable.

It is not impoffible that DUNTON did
receive fome information about the Indians from perfons with whom he converfed, and therefore felt juftified afterward in copying from WILLIAMS, as the
book was confirmed by other teftimony.
Still it is undeniable that he reprefents
other perfons as faying and doing things
which were really faid and done by
WILLIAMS, and has even reprefented as
his own the moral reflections of that
divine.—ED.

Beafts, and fometimes of Men; from whence they are alfo call'd Men-Eaters; they are a ftrong People, and the Terrour of thofe Indians that live near 'em. They generally all take Tobacco, which is alfo a principal part of their Entertainments, tho' we refuf'd it: and it is the only Plant at which the Men labour, the Women it feems managing all the reft. And the Reafons they give for their taking Tobacco, are, firft becaufe it is good againft the Rhume, which they fay caufeth the Toothache, which they are much troubled with, and bear it with great Impatience; and their other Reafon is, becaufe it revives and refrefhes them, which they ftand in need of, drinking nothing but Water.

The Captain further told us, That whofoever cometh in when they are Eating, it is always their Cuftom to offer them to Eat of that which they have, tho' it be but little enough for themfelves. And if any Provifion of Fifh or Flefh be taken by them, they make their Neighbours Partakers with them. Alfo if any Stranger comes in, they prefently give him to Eat of what they have; and tho' it be in the night, and they have nothing ready, they will rife, both the Man and his Wife, and prepare fome Refrefhing for them. Being come back to the Captain's Houfe, he gave us the Parting Bottle, and fo we return'd back again over the Ferry to Bofton.

My fecond Ramble from Bofton was to a Village called Medford,[92] about a Mile and a half from Charles Town: This

---

[92] Medford was undoubtedly a fmall village for many years, though during the early portion of its hiftory it paid a large portion of the taxes of the Colony. This was probably owing to the property there owned by Governor Cradock. Edward Collins bought all of the Cradock property in 1652, and fold much of it to Richard Ruffell in 1656. In 1661, Jonathan Wade bought from Ruffell the manfion-houfe and three-quarters of the land, and probably his fon lived there in 1686. In 1680 the Collins farm was divided between John Hall, Thomas Willis, Stephen Willis, Stephen Francis and John Whitmore. All of thefe were refident in Medford, and with the Brooks, Tufts, Bifhop, Blanchard, Bradfhaw and Seecomb families formed the majority, almoft the whole of the owners of the townfhip for many years.—ED.

20

This was nothing near fo pleafant a Ramble as the other; and that for three Reafons; for firft, the Weather was n't fo good: For tho' the Sun flatter'd me in the Morning, and made me believe it wou'd be a fair day, yet before noon he grew fullen, drew in his exhilerating Beams, and muffl'd up his Face in a Cloud, fo that there was no getting fight of him all the Day after: Nor was the Clouds' obfcuring of the Sun's bright face, the only mifchief that they did me; but to make my Rambling more uncomfortable yet, they pour'd down fuch a Prodigious Shower of Rain upon me, that if I was n't wet to th' Skin, it was becaufe my kinder Fate provided a good Shelter near at hand. For the chief kindnefs I receiv'd at Medford, was to be fhelter'd by it from a Swinging fhower of Rain, which only wet my Upper Garment,—and no more.

But Secondly, Neither was my Company fo good; for I had only with me a young Boftonian for my Guide, who when he faw that it began to rain, turn'd a Deferter, and foolifhly turn'd back again, faft as his Legs cou'd carry him; by which means he was catch'd in all the Shower, whilft I was fhelter'd by making hafte to Medford. Nor thirdly, Did I meet with fuch kind Entertainment at Medford as at Charles Town: For here I had no Acquaintance, but took Sanctuary in a Publick,[93] where there was extraordinary good Cyder, and tho' I hadn't fuch a Noble Treat as at Captain Jenner's; yet with the Cyder and fuch other Entertainment as the Houfe afforded, (together with my Landlord and my Landlady's good Company,) I made a very pretty thing on't.

I afk'd my Landlady whether if the rain continu'd, there was any Lodging to be had, and fhe was pleaf'd to tell me

I

---

[93] We learn from BROOKS's Hiftory of Medford, that about 1690, Major Jonathan Wade built a tavern, which was kept by Nathaniel Pierce. In 1692, Thomas Willis was licenfed, and poffibly as this was the earlieft feffion of the new Court, he may have been licenfed in former years.—ED.

I fhou'dn't want for that, tho' fhe fet up all night her felf; I told her before fhe fhou'd do fo, I'd feek a Lodging out among the Indians: And afk'd my Landlord whether he thought the Indians wou'd entertain me? My Landlord[54] told me there was no need of my going among them, for he had Lodging enough; but as to the Indians Enter-taining of me, he faid that he had often known them (in the Summer time Efpecially) lie abroad themfelves, to make room for Strangers, either Englifh or others. I afk'd him what Beds they had, and he told me either Mats, or elfe Straw; and that when they lay down to fleep, they gener-ally, both in Summer and Winter, made a great Fire, which ferves them inftead of Bedcloaths; and he that finds himfelf a-cold, muft turn to the Fire to warm him; and they that wake firft, muft repair the Fire; For as they have abundance of Fewel, fo they don't fpare in laying of it on. He told me alfo that when they had a Bad Dream, they look'd upon it as a threatening from God, and that on fuch occafions they wou'd rife and fall to Prayer, at any time of the Night.

By this time, the rain was over, tho' it ftill remain'd Cloudy; and therefore I thought it was beft taking Time by the Fore-lock, and go back to Bofton while it held up, there being nothing remarkable to be feen at Medford, which is but a fmall Village, confifting of a few Houfes; And fo paying my Reckoning, I came back to Bofton in good time: For I had not been long at home, before it fell a raining again very hard.

My Third Ramble was to a Town called New-Town, which is fituated three Miles from Charles-Town, on the North Side of the River, a league and a half by Water: This Town was firft intended for a City, and is one of the neateft and beft compacted Towns in the whole Countrey: It has many ftately ftructures, and well-contrived Streets;

Which

Which for handfomnefs and beauty out-does Bofton it felf: The Inhabitants are generally rich, and have many hundred Acres of Land paled with one common Fence,—a mile and half long, affording ftore of Cattel.

You will the lefs wonder, Coufin, at what I have faid about this Town, when you fhall know this Town, that at firft was called New Town, is now made an Univerfity, and called Cambridge, there being a colledge Erected there by one Mr. John Harvard, who gave £700 for the Erecting of it, in the year 1638. I was invited hither by Mr. Cotton,⁎ a fellow of the Colledge, by whom I was very handfomely Treated, and fhewn all that was remarkable in it. He dif-courf'd with me about my Venture of Books; and by his means I fold many of my Books to the Colledge.

Among other Difcourfe that we had, he afk'd me, Who I look'd upon in England to be the beft Authors, and Men of greateft Name and Repute? I told him, This was a very Comprehenfive Queftion; For there were Authors famous in their feveral Faculties, fome for Divinity, others for Philofophy, and fome for the Mathematics; and feveral other Arts and Sciences; and therefore without he was more particular, 'twould be an Endlefs Tafk to anfwer him. He then reply'd he did intend chiefly Divinity; but fince 'twas neceffary for a Scholar to be univerfal in his knowl-edge, fo 'twou'd be neceffary for him to know who were the beft Authors in every feveral Faculty I mention'd: I then told him I wou'd Endeavour to ferve him, as far as my Memory wou'd give me leave: And as to Divinity, in England I muft make a Diftinction between the Eftablifh'd Church-men and the Diffenters.

" The moft Eminent Authors among the Church-Men, or
Conformifts,

⁎This was John Cotton, the fon of Rev. John C., of Plymouth, and grand-fon of the famous Rev. John Cotton, of Bofton. He was born in 1661, was of H. C. 1681, and was minifter of Yar-mouth. From 1681 to 1690 he was Li-brarian of Harvard College.—Ed.

Conformifts, are Dr. Hamond, who has writ very Learned Annotations upon the New Teftament, Dr. Tillotfon, who has writ the Rule of Faith, and feveral Learned Tracts againft the Papifts, and variety of Celebrated Sermons, which are very much efteem'd of, being both a Learned and a very moderate good Man; far from thofe bigotted and high-flown Church-men, who had rather the whole Frame of their Church-Government fhou'd be pull'd down, than part with one fmall Ceremony, tho' it fhou'd be as inconfiderable and unneceffary as that of bowing to the Altar, or the Crofs in Baptifm. The Author of the Whole Duty of Man is (tho' Anonymous) a very celebrated Author, and his Works much in Vogue and well worth buying. Bifhop Sanderfon's Works are alfo very much efteem'd; and Dr. Stillingfleet is very Eminent for Writing his Phanaticifm of the Church of Rome; and had been much better refpected, had he not fallen foul on the Diffenters, and writ his Book of the Mifchief of Separation which has been fufficiently anfwer'd by feveral of the Diffenters again, and the Mifchief of Impofitions made appear to be greater than the Mifchief of Separation. Dr. Patrick is alfo an Author of great Eminency; his Parable of the Pilgrim, and other Practical Difcourfes of his, have fold very well; but his Unfriendly Friendly Debate, never did him any great Credit: For as one wittily fays,

> 'One Scene of Dryden fprings more Noble Fire,
> Than all his Anti-Non-Con Quibling Ire.'

"Dr. Taylor's Life of Chrift, with his book of Holy Living and Dying, and Dr. Cave's Lives of the Apoftles, are all Eminent in their kind. Dr. Barlow, Bifhop of Lincoln, and Dr. Barrow, of Cambridge, are both Eminent Authors; Thefe, Sir, are fome, but not the Tythe of thofe of the Eftablifh'd Church, which Emitted many good Books into the World, and their ftrenuous Writings againft Popery,

even

even in this Reign, are very much to be Commended. Nor
muſt Dr. Sherlock be forgotten, who has gain'd more Reputation by Writing two Practical Treatiſes upon Death and
Judgment, than by all his Polemical Writings.

"But there are alſo, beſides theſe Gentlemen of the Eſtabliſhed Church, ſeveral good Authors alſo among the Diſſenters.
Dr. John Owen, ſometime Vice-Chancellor of Oxford, and
Dean of Chriſt-Church there, has written many Learned
and Elaborate Treatiſes. His Books againſt Socinus, and
Anſwer to the Cracovian Catechiſm, written in Latin, put ſo
great a ſtop to the Spreading of that Errour in Hungary,
that the Proteſtant Churches there, ſent over Meſſengers on
Purpoſe to England, to thank him for the Pains he had
taken therein, declaring at the ſame time the great good
that had been done thereby in that Countrey: His Learned
Exercitations and Expoſition on the Epiſtle to the Hebrews,
is an Excellent Piece, and ſufficiently ſhews his great Learning: His Expoſition alſo of the 130th Pſalm, treating of the
Forgiveneſs of Sins, is a moſt Excellent Book: But ſhou'd
I recite all that he has writ, 'twou'd tire you.

"Dr. Samuel Anneſly, (to whom I have the Honour to be
related as his Son-in-Law,) beſides his being an Excellent
Preacher, is alſo a Famous Author, as his Learned and
Judicious Caſuiſtical Exerciſes, Conſiſting of ſeveral volumes,
do ſufficiently Teſtifie: Beſides ſeveral other of his Works.

"Dr. Bates is alſo a very Eminent Author, and his Works
much Eſteem'd, both of Conformiſts and Nonconformiſts: his
Harmony of the Divine Attribute, his Diſcourſes of the Four
laſt things, and ſeveral other of his Writings, meet with a
general Acceptance. Mr. Stephen Charnock's Learned
Works in two Volumes, are as uſeful for a Divine of any
Perſwaſion, as any Books as I know extant, and have been
as well receiv'd by all men, as they juſtly deſerve. Mr. How
is alſo an Eminent Author among the Diſſenters, as his
Bleſſedneſs of the Righteous, and other good Books by him
                                                    Publiſhed,

Publifhed, fufficiently declare. Dr. Manton's Works in folio, fufficiently declare him an Eminent Author, and fo does Dr. Thomas Goodwin's alfo. Mr. Baxter's many Books (and fome very large ones) have made him well-enough known to the World, and for ought I know, his Name and Memory wou'd have been as facred, had he writ only that firft Excellent Piece of his, call'd the Saints Everlafting Reft. Dr. Collings is alfo an Eminent Author, as his Treatife of Divine Love, and that other of the Actual Providence of God, do well enough declare.

"Nor muft I omit amongft thefe great Names, to mention that of Mr. John Bunyan, who tho' a Man of but very ordinary Education, yet was a Man of great Natural Parts, and as well known for an Author thro'out England, as any I have mention'd, by the many Books he has Publifh'd, of which the Pilgrim's Progrefs bears away the Bell.

"But as I faid of the Church-men, fo I muft of the Dif-fenters, thefe are fcarce a Tythe of the Eminent Authors among 'em. You fee Sir," faid I, "what a Tafk you have put me upon, and therefore if I have been too tedious, and worn your Patience out, you muft thank your felf, fince 'tis the Deference I pay to your Commands that has occafion'd it. But I fhall Difpatch the others quickly.

"As to Philofophy, efpecially Experimental Philofophy, there are the Tranfactions of the Royal Society, publifhed by Dr. Grew; and the Celebrated Works of the Honourable Robert Boyle, Efq., who is alfo as great a Divine as a Philofopher, as his ftyle of the Scriptures, Occafional Re-flections, and his Seraphic Love will Witnefs.

"For Law, Fleta, Bracton, and Cook upon Littleton, are Eminent. There are alfo the Reports of Sir Geoffery Palmer, and divers other Learned Judges, Eminent in their times. Among which Sir Mathew Hale, late Lord Chief Juftice of England, muft not be forgotten, who was the Perfect Pattern of an Upright Judge, and as great a Philofopher and
Divine

Divine as a Lawyer; as Divine Origination of Mankind in Folio, and his Meditations and Contemplations, in Octavo, which are Excellent things, do abundantly Evidence.

"For Phyſick, the Learned Dr. Willett is a Famous Author, and Dr. Salmon by his Diſpenſatory, and ſeveral other Books, is very well known.

"For the Mathematicks, Sir Jonas Moore and Mr. William Leybourn are both very Eminent Authors.

"And for Poetry, the Immortal Cowley, who firſt brought in the uſe of Pindarick Poetry in Engliſh. Beſides whom we have Dryden, Shadwel, Tate, Settle, and ſeveral others, very Eminent Authors.

Nor muſt we here forget to do juſtice to the Fair Sex, Mrs. Katharine Philips having made herſelf deſervedly Famous for her Excellent Poetical Pieces; Mrs. Behn alſo has approved her ſelf a Devotee to the Muſes; and not the leaſt, tho' the laſt, is the Incomparable Philomela; than whom, none has drunk a larger Draught at the Heliconian Spring, or been a greater Favourite of the Muſes."

Mr. Cotton gave me many thanks for the Account I had given him of our English Authors; many of whom he ſaid he had before heard on, and had ſome of their Works; but others of them were till now altogether unknown to him; but now that he knew them, he intended to enlarge his ſtudy with ſome of their Writings. I told him I was very glad I had in any meaſure gratified his Curioſity: And added, That ſince I had given him an Account of ſome of the moſt Eminent of our Old Engliſh Authors, he wou'd by way of Retaliation give me ſome little Account of their New-England Authors, for I did not doubt but there were many that had done worthily in this Countrey.

To this Mr. Cotton reply'd: "That I cou'd not expect New-England cou'd compare with Old, either for the Number of Authors, or the Excellency of their Parts and Endowments; New-England being only a Colony; and all their

Learning

Learning but as fprings from thofe two Fountains in Old England, Oxford and Cambridge: However, we have not been without Excellent Men in this Countrey: And amongft the firft Planters here, Mr. John Cotton, and Mr. Seaborn Cotton, his Son, are defervedly Famous; and Mr. Shepherd for the many Excellent Tracts written by him, has his Praife in all the Churches: The many impreffions that have been made of his Sincere Convert and Sound Believer, both at London, and here at Bofton, fhews what acceptance they have mett with in the World; his Parable of the Ten Virgins alfo, tho' in Folio, has been feveral times printed.

"Nor muft the Famous Mr. Elliot (who is ftill living, tho' very aged,) be Omitted; whofe indefatigable Zeal and Induftry, both by Printing and Preaching, for the Converfion of the Indians, has given Place to none.

"And as to our Modern Authors, the Reverend Mr. Increafe Mather, the Prefent Rector of our Colledge, holds the chief Rank, whofe Univerfal knowledge, both in Divine and Humane Learning, is very well known both in New-England and Old too: And his Worthy Son, Mr. Cotton Mather, does not come much fhort of his Father; and his Works do alfo praife him in the Gate: And to the Honour of our Colledge do I fpeak it, he was brought up in it. And tho' our Colledge does not pretend to compare it felf with any either in Oxford or Cambridge, yet has there been brought up in it fince its Foundation, 122 Minifters; of which Ten are dead, feventy-one remain ftill in the Country, aud Forty-one are removed to England.

"As to the other of our Bofton-Minifters, I believe you have heard 'em, and know 'em to be good Preachers, and men of great Parts; There are alfo feveral eminent Minifters in feveral Parts of the Countrey, but of them, I can give you but a fmall Account, having little Acquaintance with them, and therefore fhall pafs them by."

I then gave Mr. Cotton many thanks for the Trouble I
had

had put him to, and promifed him a Catalogue of my Books as foon as I cou'd write it out, and fo took my leave of him.

As my Friends and I were returning to Bofton, there happened a little Scuffle between an Indian and his Son: and the Boy having received fome Blows from his Father, ran away; at which the Father fell a Crying: I told my Friends, I thought it a great piece of Folly in the Father to Cry for Correcting his Son; To which one of his Friends[96] anfwered, That the Indians were the moft affectionate People to their Relations (and efpecially to their Children,) that were in the World: Infomuch (faid he) that I have known a Father fo extreamly troubled for the lofs of his Child, that for very grief and rage, he cut and ftabb'd himfelf: But this inordinate Affection of the Parents, does only ferve to make their Children Undutiful, bold and fawcy.

He told me he once went into an Indians Houfe, and defir'd him to give him a Cup of Water to drink; the Indian told him he fhou'd have it, and bid his Son, (who was a Lad of about eight years of age,) to fetch fome Water; but the Lazy young Rogue refuf'd it, and wou'dn't ftir: Whereupon (faid he) I told his Father, That if it were my Child, I wou'd make him do what I bid him; and that for refufing it, he ought to be corrected: Upon which the Father took up a ftick to beat him; but the Boy took up another Stick, and flew at his Father: So that the Father was going to lay down his Stick again, and let his Son alone; but upon my perfwafion, faid he, the Father made him fmart a little, and then he went for Water, and threw down his Stick. And the Father acknowledged to me, That Correction was very neceffary for Children; and the neglect of it was the Caufe of their Undutiful Behaviour.

My Friend alfo told me, That there is fuch a Natural Affection in the Indians towards their Brothers, That when one Brother had committed a Murther and fled, they have

Executed

[96] This account of the Indian is from WILLIAMS, pp. 117, 118.—ED.

Executed the other Brother for it. And 'tis common with them for a Living Brother to pay the Debts of a Brother Deceafed. Nor are they lefs kind to their Daughters, who are commonly the moft dutiful; and when Marriageable Virgins, diftinguifh themfelves for fuch, by a becoming Bafhfulnefs, and the falling down of their Hair over their Eyes. There is one thing alfo very commendable among them, and that is, If any Man dies, and leaves fmall Children behind him, the Survivors take care of them, fo that there are no Fatherlefs Children unprovided for, nor any Beggars amongft them.—By that time my Friend had ended his Difcourfe, we were come to Bofton; and after having drank one Bottle of Cyder at George Monks, we parted, and went each to his own home.

My Fourth Ramble, my Coufin, (for you fee I keep reck-oning) was to a town called *Winnifimet,*[97] about a Mile from Charles Town, the River only parting them: There is nothing remarkable to be faid of this Town, fave that it is the laft Town in the ftill Bay of the Maffachufetts: As I was going out of Bofton in the Morning all alone, I met with an Acquaintance who afk'd me whither I was going? I told him I was taking a Ramble to Winnifimet, upon which, he told me he had little to do, and therefore if I wou'd accept of his Company, he wou'd go along with me: Which I very readily did, and fo we went together.

As we went along, we faw two Indian Houfes, one being pretty large and the other a very fmall one: My Fellow-Traveller afk'd me if I knew what that little Houfe was for? I told him No, unlefs it was to lodge a Servant, or put odd things out of the way: He[98] told me I was miftaken; for that little Houfe was made for their Women and Maids to live a-part in, four, five, or fix Days, during the time of their Monthly Sicknefs; Which Cuftom he faid was ftrictly observed

[97] Winnifimet is now called Chelfea. —ED. [98] From WILLIAMS, pp. 120, 121, 123, 124, 125, 126, 127, 128, 132-5.—ED.

obferved through the whole Countrey, and no Male on any
pretence fuffered to come into that Houfe. I then afk'd him
what their Houfes were, and what was generally the Bufinefs
of their Families: Says he, 'I have been often among 'em,
and know their Cuftoms very well;' 'You will,' faid I, 'do me
a pleafure to give me a Relation of 'em.'

'As to their Houfes,' faid he, 'you fee what their outfides
are; They are fupported by long Poles, in number according
to the bignefs they defign it; fome very large ones confifting
of fifty or threefcore Poles, fome more, and fome lefs; but
an Ordinary Houfe has between thirty and forty; thefe
Poles the Men get and pin them in the ground, and then
the Women cover the Houfe with Mats, and afterwards line
it with Embroidered Mats which the Women make, and call
them *Munnotaubana*, or Hangings; which makes a very fair
fhow, and refemble many Mats which I have feen come from
England to hang Houfes with here. And then they have
Burching Bark, and Chefnut Bark, which they drefs finely,
and have a Summer Covering for their Houfes. Two
Families will live very lovingly in a little round Houfe of
about fourteen or fixteen foot over; and fo more or lefs,
according to the bignefs of their Houfes, or the Proportion
of their Families.

'They keep account of the time of the Day by the height
of the Sun; and of the Night, by the height of the Moon
and Stars; by which they can tell, as well as we by Clocks
and Dyals. They are as full of bufinefs as the beft Merchant
in Europe, and as impatient of Meeting with any Obftruction
or hinderance in it. Inftead of fhelves, they have feveral
Bafkets wherein they put all their Houfehold-ftuff; and fome
inftead of thefe Bafkets get great facks made of Hemp,
which will hold five or fix Bufhels, and in them they put
their Houfehold Implements. All their Corn is conftantly
beaten with hand by their Women, who are very laborious,
and have much the hardeft Tafk, for they alfo plant it, drefs
it,

it, and gather it, taking as much pains as any People in the
World, whilſt the Men live at Eaſe, and only follow Hunting,
Fiſhing, or Fowling : So that their Women are the perfect
Reverſe of Europe.   But they have this benefit above our
European Dames, that in bearing of Children, and in the
time of their Labour, their pains are very little and incon-
ſiderable.

  ' They have a great value for knives, whence they call
Engliſh-men Knive-men, from their making of Knives, the
Indians uſing ſharp ſtones formerly, inſtead of Knives and
Hatchets.   Their Houſes are moſt commonly open, their
Door being only a hanging Mat, which when lifted up, will
fall down of it ſelf.   But they begin now to be a little more
refin'd, ſeveral of them having Engliſh Boards and Nails,
with which they now make artificial Doors and Bolts themſelves ; and others of them make ſlighter Doors of Birch or
Cheſnut Bark, which is in much requeſt with 'em : Theſe
Doors they make faſt with a Cord in the Night Time, or
when they go out of Town, and then the laſt that makes faſt
the door goes out at the Chimney, which is a large opening
in the middle of their Houſe.   Their Women ſhew themſelves true Mothers, and Nurſe all their Children themſelves,
except it be ſome very rich or high Woman, and then ſhe
maintains a Nurſe to tend the Child.   Many of them now
begin to be furniſhed with Engliſh Cheſts to put their beſt
things in ; and others when they go out of Town, bring
their Goods to the Engliſh (if they live any thing near :)
And as for their money, they hang it about their Necks,
and lay it under their heads when they ſleep.   They are
generally very contented, for the pooreſt among them will
ſay they want nothing.

  ' Both Men and Women generally take Tobacco, and they
have a Tobacco-Bag, with a Pipe in it, hanging at their
Backs ; Sometimes they make ſuch great Pipes both of
Wood and Stone, that they are two foot long, with Men and
Beaſts

Beafts carved on them; but thefe are very rare among thofe that are here, but are common among the *Mauquduwogs* or Men-Eaters, three or four hundred miles from us. They have an Excellent Art to caft our Pewter or Brafs into very neat and artificial Pipes: The Tobacco they take is of a weak fort, which the Men generally plant themfelves: And yet, as well as they love Tobacco, there are feveral of the Englifh that will out-do 'em in taking it, fo much has that Weed prevail'd.

'They oftentimes remove their Houfes, which they do upon feveral occafions: They commonly Winter in low, Warm Vallies; and when 'tis Spring, and the Weather grows warmer, they remove nearer to their Summer Fields where they plant their Corn.—In the middle of Summer they are extreamly molefted with Fleas, which the duft of the Houfe breeds; this makes 'em on a fudden, to get rid of thofe Troublefome Guefts, remove from that to the other fide of the Field; and fometimes they have Fields a mile or two diftant; and when the Work of one Field is done, they remove Houfe to the other: If any one of their Family happens to dye, they prefently remove to a frefh place, and never return thither again. In time of War, if an Enemy approach, they remove into fome Thicket or Swamp, unlefs they have a Fort to remove to, where they may defend themfelves. Sometimes they remove Houfe for the better Convenience of Hunting and continue there till the Snow begins to lie thick, and then they will remove again to their firft ftation.

'Both Men, Women, and Children, will travel through the Snow, fometimes thirty, nay, fifty or fixty miles. But their great remove is, from their Summer Fields, to warm and thick Woody Bottoms, where they winter. They are very quick in their Motion: For in half a day, nay, fome-times at a few hours warning, they are gone, and the Houfe up elfewhere; efpecially if they have ftakes ready pitch'd

for

for their Matts. I once,' faid he, 'in my Travel lodg'd at a Houfe, in which at my return, I hop'd to have lain again there the next night, but the Houfe was gone in the interim, and I was forc'd to lodge under a Tree. The making of the Poles is the Mens Bufinefs, but the Women make and fet up, take down, order and carry the Mats and Houfehold-Stuff.

'Thus,' fays my Fellow-Traveller, 'I have given you a large account of the Indians Manners and Cuftoms in relation to their Houfes and their Houfe-keeping: which I have heretofore obferv'd in my travels among them.' I acknowledg'd his kindnefs in fo far gratifying my Curiofity, and thank'd him for his Civility and good Company. By this time we were come to the Town, which confifted of fome few Houfes by the Sea-fide, this being the laft Town in the Maffachufets Bay; here my Fellow-Traveller had an Acquaintance and Friend of his that liv'd, which made him fo willing to come along with me, thither it was we went, and met with a hearty welcome: Where after we had ftaid till the Shadows of the Evening were ready to overtake us, we thought it was high time for us to make the beft of our way to Bofton; whither (after having taken our leaves of our Benefactor, and given him many thanks for his kind entertainment,) we went accordingly, and juft came home as Night began to muffle up the Day, and draw her Sable Curtains o'er the Skies.

My Fifth Ramble from Bofton was to a Town now call'd *Lin*, but formerly by the Indians, *Cawguft,*[*] *Saguft, Saugut*: To this Town three or four of my Acquaintance took a Ramble with me, for the day was fo inviting, that none that had any leifure to go abroad, wou'd ftay at home: They were before-hand determin'd to go abroad, fo that I didn't reckon my felf much beholden to 'em for their Company, only they gave me leave to Chufe the place, and I pitch'd upon Lin, being (as I before told you) ftill for New Difcoveries:

---

*The more ufual form was Saugus.—ED.

coveries: They were all very merry but my felf, who was extreamly out of Humour, I knew not why: The ftrange Inquietude I found within, made me fufpeć all was n't well with the dear Partner of my Life, my Iris; and that by reafon of that perfeć Union of Souls, I by a Secret but powerful Sympathy was now the Partner of her Sorrows, tho' I knew 'em not; and this one thought, was caufe enough to fpoil the pleafure of my this Days Ramble, which made me to refleć how poor thofe pleafures are, one thought can fpoil.

However, to divert me, one of the Company[100] wou'd needs give me an account of the Indians manner of Travelling; which he faid was moftly on foot, becaufe they had no Horfes, altho' they coveted them above any other Cattel, but cou'd not come up to the Englifh price, to buy them, and therefore againft their Wills were forc'd to go without 'em. In the time of War they were ufed to make Refuges for their Wives and Children in thick Woods and Swamps, like the Bogs in Ireland; and in the mean time the Men wou'd fight. They are very joyful when they meet any on the Road, and will ftrike fire either with ftones or fticks to take a Pipe of Tobacco, and difcourfe together the while; and there is fome reafon for it, becaufe the Roads are fo much unfrequented. Sometimes a Man fhall meet a lame Man, or an old Man with a Staff; but generally a Staff is a rare fight even in the hand of the Eldeft, their Conftitution is fo ftrong; and yet it is a Rule amongft them, that it is not good for a Man to travel without a weapon, nor alone.

'I once,' faid he, 'travell'd with near 200 Indians, who had word brought 'em of near 700 Enemies in the Way: Yet they all refolved that it was a fhame to fear or go back; and fo they went forward with a purpofe to fight their Enemies, but they did not meet with them, they turning another way. If any Robery fall out in Travel between Perfons of Divers

States,

---

[100] As ufual the friend was WILLIAMS. See pp. 158-162.—ED.

States, the offended State fends for Juftice; and if no Juftice be granted, nor recompence made, they grant out a kind of Letter of Mart, to take fatisfaction themfelves: Yet they are very careful not to exceed, in taking from others beyond the Proportion of their own Lofs; But Murthers and Robberies in this Countrey, are nothing near fo frequent as in Europe.'

My Friend having done, and I being well enough pleaf'd with the Relation he had given me of their Travelling, and obferving their great Juftice, I defir'd him to give me fome account of the Religion of thefe People, that I might know from what Principle they acted : 'I mean,' faid I, 'the Unconverted Indians, and not thofe that are Converted to the Chriftian Religion, (for that I hope we all know,) whom you call Friend Indians.' 'No,' faid my Friend, 'you are miftaken in that; for we call many of the Unconverted Indians Friend Indians, provided they are fuch as live in Friendfhip with us, and are not our declared Enemies. But the Difcourfe of their Religion will engage us now too far, for we are almoft come to Lin; I will therefore referve that difcourfe till we come back again.'

We all agreed to this motion, and in a little Time came to Lin; which is a Town fituated at the Bottom of a Bay without Pullin-Point, fix miles North-Eaft from Winnifimet, near a River, which upon the breaking up of Winter vents it felf with a furious Torrent into the Sea : The Town Confifts of more than an hundred dwelling Houfes, their Meeting-houfe being built upon a level, and defended from the North-Weft Wind, and is made with fteps defcending to it. Tho' it be none of the firft-rate Towns in this Countrey, yet there are many others that are inferiour to it.

Neither my felf nor any of my Friends with me had any Acquaintance there ; fo we went to a Publick Houfe, where we met with good Accommodations : And our Hoft wou'd needs be acquainted with us whether we wou'd or no; he
was

22

was a bold forward fort of a Man, and wou'd thruſt himſelf into our Company, and take up all the Diſcourſe too, which was for the moſt part of his own good Qualities, Knowledge and Underſtanding; valuing himſelf at ſuch a rate that he wou'd have made one of the three Dukes of Dunſtable; and yet wou'd bring Scripture to Apologize for his Impertinence, telling us that a Candle ſhou'd not be hid under a Buſhel; and made ſenſible that he wou'd not hide his, tho' it was but a Snuff, or at beſt but a ruſh Candle; and therefore thoſe few good Qualities he had, he was no Niggard in diſplaying: Some of the Company affronted him ſufficiently, but he took no notice on't, for he thought no vice ſo prejudicial as Bluſhing.

He din'd with us, without being invited, for he needed it not; and his talk at the Table was like Benjamin's Meſs, five times his part to any others; and tho' we often ſhifted the Theme, yet no Argument wou'd ſhut him out for a Quarreller; and rather than be non-pluſt, wou'd fly to Nonſenſe for Sanctuary: For my part I admir'd the addreſs of his humour, and let him alone, for I perceiv'd he wou'd be ſooner daſh'd out of anything than Countenance; and tho' at firſt he ſeem'd very troubleſome, I was at laſt pleaſ'd with him; for I found it was his trade, and that his Words ſerv'd equally for all men, and were all equally to no purpoſe: The beſt thing in him was, that his Troubleſomeneſs made me ſhake off that Indiſpoſition that had lain upon me all Day, and brought me again to a good Humour.

Having ſatisfyed the Cravings of our Stomacks with a good Dinner, and exhilerated our Spirits with ſome good Liquor, and being at laſt wearied with our Landlords Impertinence; We paid our Reckoning, and return'd towards Boſton again. But I had not forgot the promiſe that one of my Fellow-Travellers made me as we came, which was, to give me an Account of the Religion of the Indians, as we came back; which when we had come about half a mile
from

from Linn, I put him in mind of. Whereupon he gave me
the following Account.

'Methinks[101] Atheifts (if any fuch there really be) fhou'd
blufh and be afham'd to deny the being of a GOD, when
even the Heathens themfelves own him; and that he made
the World: Nay, they go higher, and confefs both that GOD
is, and that he is a Rewarder of all them that diligently feek
him. For they will generally confefs that GOD made all;
but then tho' they deny not but the Englifh Mans GOD
made Englifh Men, and the Heavens and the Earth there,
yet they affirm that their Gods made them, and the Heavens
and the Earth where they dwell. I have heard a poor Indian
call up his Wife and Children at break of Day to lament
the lofs of a Child, and with many Tears cry out, O GOD
thou haft taken away my Child, thou art angry with me;
O turn thy anger from me, and fpare the reft of my Children.
And when they are abroad in Hunting, or Fifhing, if they
meet with fuccefs, they acknowledge GOD to be the Author
of it. And in common accidents that happen, as a Fall, or
the like, they will fay, GOD was angry and did it, &c.

'By what I have faid, one wou'd take 'em to be Chriftians,
but they are not, for here is their mifery, they branch their
Godhead into many Gods, which they invocate in their
Solemn Worfhip: As, The Great South-Weft-God, to whofe
Houfe they believe all Souls go; and from whom they fay
their Corn and Beans come: And then they have the Eaftern
God, the Weftern God, the Southern God, the Houfe God,
the Womans God, the Childrens God; not unlike the
Papifts in Europe, who have their He and She Saint Protectors, as St. George, St. Patrick, and St. Dennis; and of
the Female Sex, the Virgin Mary, St. Winnifred, St. Agnes,
&c., to whom they addrefs their Prayers, as thefe poor
Indians do to their feveral forts of Gods. I[102] was once with

an

---

[101] All of this account will be found
in WILLIAMS, pp. 207-220.—ED.

[102] This was Roger Williams, it will
be remembered.—ED.

an Indian young Man who lay a dying, and he called very much upon *Muckquachuckquand*, which thofe about him told me was one of their Gods, which had appeared, as they believed, to the Dying Man fome years before, and bid him call upon him, whenever he was in diftrefs. And as they worfhip thefe fancied Deities, fo they alfo worfhip feveral of the Creatures, in whom they conceive doth reft fome Deity; for they have the Sun God, the Moon God, the Sea God, the Fire God, and feveral others; fuppofing that Deities be in thefe Creatures.

'When I have argued,' faid he, 'with fome of them about their Fire God, they have told me that it cannot be, but that the Fire muft be a God, or Divine Power, that out of a Stone will arife in a Spark, and when a poor Naked Indian is ready to ftarve with Cold, often faves his Life, and dreffes our Food for us; and at other time, if he be angry, will burn the Houfe about us; yea, and if a Spark fall into the dry Wood, will burn all the Countrey about our Ears: So that the Ufefulnefs and Excellency that is in any Creature, makes them worfhip it: And therefore when they fee any Excellency either in Men, Women, Birds or Beafts, they ftraight cry out, *Manitoo!* It is a God! And when they talk among themfelves of the Englifh Ships and great Buildings, of the Plowing of their Fields, and of their reading and Writing, they ufe to fay, *Manitoowock*, They are Gods: Which by the way, is a ftrong argument, that there is a natural Conviction in the Souls of all Men, That GOD fills all things and Places, and that all Goodnefs and Excellency proceeds from him. So that an Atheift muft do violence to his own Nature, before he can race out the Ideas of a Deity out of his Soul.

'But to proceed, and give you a more particular Account of their Cuftoms in their Religion: Their chief Worfhip is at their Publick Feafts and Dances, which are both Publick and Private: And this of two different forts. One is,

in

in Sickneſs, War, Drouth, or Famine; the other is after
Harveſt and Hunting time, when they Enjoy a Calm of
Peace, Wealth, Plenty, and Proſperity. In Sickneſs, the
Prieſt comes cloſe to the Sick Perſon, and performs many
ſtrange Actions about him, and threatens, and ſometimes
conjures out the ſickneſs: For they conceive there are many
Gods, or Divine Powers in the Body of Man, as in his
Pulſe, his Heart, his Lungs, and other parts. They have
been conjectur'd by ſeveral to have been the Deſcendants or
off-Spring of the Ten Tribes of Iſrael,[103] carry'd Captive by
Salmanaſſar, King of Aſſyria, no man knows whither. And
that which gives ſome grounds to this Conjecture, is, That
their Cuſtoms in many things reſembles that of the Iſrael-
ites; for they have ſuch an Exact form of King, Prieſt, and
Prophet, as was in Iſrael. Their Kings and Governours are
called *Sachimauog*, Kings, and *Mauſkowaug*, Rulers, which
do govern them; their Prieſts perform and manage their
Worſhip; and their wiſe Men and Old Men (of which
Number the Prieſts are alſo) whom they call *Taupowauog*,
and theſe make Speeches and Orations, or Lectures to 'em,
concerning Religion, Peace, or War, or indeed any other
matters.

' He or She that makes this Feaſt, or Dance, beſides the
Feaſting of ſometimes forty or fifty, nay, an hundred, or
more, gives alſo a great quantity of money, and all ſorts of
their Goods, according to their Ability, and ſometimes beyond it, to the value of perhaps eighteen pence, or two
ſhillings to one perſon: And the Perſon that receives this
Gift, upon the receiving it, goes out and hollows thrice for
the Health and Proſperity of the Perſon that gave it. By
this

[103] This conjecture of the Iſraelitiſh
deſcent of the Indians may be credited
to DUNTON. WILLIAMS writes (p. 212):
"They have an exact forme of King,
Prieſt and Prophet, as was in Iſrael
typicall of old in that holy Land of
Canaan, and as the Lord Jeſus ordained
in his ſpirituall Land of Canaan his
Church throughout the whole World:
their Kings or Governours called Sachimauog." &c. This certainly gives
no warrant for DUNTON's theory.—ED.

this Feafting, and thofe Gifts, the Devil drives on their Worſhip pleafantly; fo that they will run far and near to aſk who makes a Feaft? One thing is commendable in 'em, and that is, They have a modeft Religious Perſwaſion, not to difturb any Perſon, whether it be themſelves, or the Englifh, Dutch, or any others, in or for their Conſcience and Worſhip.

' The Soul they call *Cowwewonck*, from *Cowwene*, to ſleep, becaufe they fay the Soul works and is active, when the Body ſleeps: They alfo call the Soul *Michachunk*, which ſignifies a Looking-glaſs or clear Refemblance; and indeed, a clear ſight or difcerning, feems very well to agree with the nature of the Soul. They believe that the Souls of Men and Women go to the South-Weft; and that all good Men and Women go to the Houfe of *Cautantouwit*, where they have hopes (as the followers of Mahomet have) to enjoy carnal delights and pleafures: And that the fouls of Murderers, Thieves, Lyars, and bad Men, wander abroad in a reftleſs Condition.

' I was once,[104] where an Englifh Minifter that underftood the Indian Language, fpake thus to a great many Indians, that were gathered together to hear him: " Friends, I will aſk you a Queftion;" they bid him, Speak on: He then faid, " What think you? Who made the Heavens, the Earth, the Sea, and the World?" To this fome faid, *Tatta*, I cannot tell: Others faid *Manitowock*, that is, the Gods: The minifter then aſk'd them, how many Gods there were? They anfwered, There are many, a great many. He then replied,
" Friends,

---

[104] The paffage that follows is a fine ſpecimen of DUNTON's adaptations. WILLIAMS writes (p. 215): " Now becaufe this book (by GOD's good Providence) *may* come into the hand of many fearing GOD, who *may* alfo have many an opportunity of occafional difcourfe of thefe their wild brethren and Sifters. . . . . I fhall propofe fome proper expreffions concerning the Creation . . . . . and particularly theirs alfo, which from my felfe many hundredths of times, great numbers of them have heard," &c. &c. He then gives the phrafes and fupplies the anfwers which the Indians will make. All of this imaginary fcene DUNTON fays happened in the experience of his friend.—ED.

"Friends, It is not fo, you are miftaken, you are out of the way:" (which is a phrafe with which they are much taken; poffibly becaufe it is proper to thofe who are (like them) wandring in the Woods; and fimilitudes do very much pleafe them).

'But the Minifter went on, and faid, " I will tell you fome News : There is only one God, who made the Heavens, the Earth, and the Sea, five thoufand years ago, and upwards. He alone made all things out of nothing : In fix days he made all things : The firft Day he made the Light; the fecond Day he made the Firmament; the third day he made the Earth and Sea; the Fourth Day, he made the Sun and Moon, thofe two great Lights, and all the Stars; the fifth day he made all the Fowl in the Air, and all the Fifh in the Sea ; the fixth day he made all the Beafts of the Field; and laft of all, he made one Man of red Earth, and call'd his Name Adam, or red Earth; and afterward while Adam flept, God took a Rib from him, and of that Rib he made one Woman, and brought her to Adam; and when Adam faw her, he faid, This is my Bone. On the feventh day God refted; and therefore all Englifh Men work fix Days, and on the feventh Day they praife God." At this relation they feemed very much fatisfied; efpecially at the reafon why the Englifh and Dutch (as they had before obferved,) laboured fix Days, and refted the feventh. And fome of them faid, "We never heard of this before ; but our Fathers have told us, That *Kautantowit* made one Man and Woman of a Stone, which he dif-liking, broke them in Pieces, and then made another Man and Woman of a Tree, which were the Fountains of all Mankind."

'After the *Minifter* had made an end of preaching his Sermon, which is too long for me to repeat, (faid my Fellow-Traveller)[105] an Indian told a Sachim that was there, That Souls

---

[105] We here come to another of WILLIAMS'S own experiences ; (p. 219.) "After I had (as farre as my language would reach,) difcourfed (upon a time) before

Souls went up to Heaven, or down to Hell, for, said he, Our Fathers have told us, That our Souls go to the Southweſt. To which the Sachim anſwered, But how do you know your ſelf, that your Souls go to the Southweſt? Did you ever ſee a Soul go thither? The Indian replyed, When did the Miniſter ſee a Soul go to Heaven or Hell? The Sachim anſwer'd again, He hath Books and Writings, and one which GOD himſelf made, concerning Mens Souls, and therefore may well know more than we, that have none; but take all upon truſt from our Fore-Fathers. And the ſaid Sachim, and the Chief of his People diſcourſed among themſelves of keeping the Engliſhmans Day of Worſhip. But whether they did or not, I know not. But by what I have related,' ſaid my Friend, 'you may ſee that the Indians are not an obſtinate or incorigible People, but that there is hopes that in time they all may, as ſome of them have been, be converted, and brought from their Worſhip of many Gods, to the Knowledge of the true GOD, who is bleſſed for ever, and whom to know, is Life Eternal.'

I gave my Friend many thanks for the Ingenious Relation he had made me of the Religion of the Indians, with which I was very much affected; and which I hope will be diverting to you, my dear Couſin. But by this time, we were come to Boſton, where we took leave of each other, and went each to his own Apartment.

My Sixth Ramble was to a Town called *Nantaſcot*: But I wou'd not have you think, my Couſin, that I rambled for Six days together ſucceſſively; that wou'd have been Rambling too much from my Buſineſs: For tho' I left Palmer in my Warehouſe, whom I knew to be a faithful Servant; yet

I

beſore the chieſe Sachim or Prince of the Countrey, with his Archprieſts, and many other in a full Aſſembly; and being night, wearied with travell and diſcourſe, I lay downe to reſt; and before I ſlept, I heard this paſſage: A Qun- nihticut Indian (who had heard our diſcourſe) told the Sachim Miantunnomu, that ſoules went up to Heaven," &c. &c. This was an actual occurrence, here joined to the imaginary one by DUNTON. —ED.

I remembered that as the Masters Eye makes the Horse fat, by honestly cheating the Ostler, who otherwise wou'd have knavishly cheated him, by Wronging the Horse of his Provender; and in like manner I knew that the Masters presence often in the Warehouse both makes the Customers the willinger to come, and the Servant more diligent in attending and accommodating them. Therefore for one day that I rambled abroad, I always took care to stay two days in the Warehouse: For to say Truth, my Cousin,

> Who Profit joyns with Pleasure, gets the Day ;
> He wins the Prize, and bears the Bell away:

But having by this Digression rambled from Nantascot, to which I was a Rambling, 'tis time to get into the way again: Before my Rambling Day came, I always made sure of a Friend or two at least, to ramble with me ; for I never cared to ramble alone, since my Guide serv'd me such a slipery Trick when I rambled to Medford, running away from me, and leaving me to come home alone. My Friends and I therefore having Resolved upon a Ramble to Nantascot, had early notice given us by the Sun, to whom we paid a very great observance, both that 'twas time to rise, and that it was fit weather for us to pursue our Ramble ; which we undertook the more cheerfully, as having an implicit assurance of the Suns good Company along with us, whose all-Enlivening Rays, I always found extreamly exhilerating to my Spirits. Nor had we any Cause to find fault with our Journey, for we found in our way two fathom of Indian Money; which bore our Charges all the Day: Perhaps, Cousin, you may wonder at that Phrase of a Fathom of Money, (as I my self did at first.)

I will therefore here give you a brief Account[106] of the Indians Money which goes Currant among them. You must
know

---

[106] WILLIAMS, pp. 233-237.—ED.

23

know then, that the Indians are ignorant of the Coyns we have in Europe, yet they have given a Name to ours, and call it *Moneaſh*, alluding to our Engliſh money: but tho' they are ignorant of our Coyns, yet they have Money of their own, which is of two ſorts, one white, the other black: The white they make of the ſtem or ſtock of the Periwinckle, which they call *Meteauhock* when all the ſhell is broken off; and of this ſort, ſix of their ſmall Beads, (which they make with holes to ſtring, like Bracelets,) are current with the Engliſh for a Penny: Their black Money, which is inclining to, or looks a little bleùiſh, is made of the ſhell of a Fiſh, which the Engliſh call *Hens*, but the Indians *Poquauhock*, and of this ſort three make an Engliſh Penny. The Black being double the value of the White. It is all made with holes and put upon Strings. They that live upon the Sea-ſide generally are their Coyners, or thoſe that make it; and there it is no Treaſon for a Private Perſon to do it, for as many may make it as will.

For this ſort of Money will the Indians bring down and ſell all their Furs which they take in the Countrey, to the Engliſh, and to the Indians alſo: With this Money the Engliſh, Dutch, and French, trade to the Indians ſix hundred miles in ſeveral parts, (North and South from New-England) for their Furrs, and what ſoever they ſtand in need of from them, as Corn, Veniſon, or any thing elſe. Of theſe Beads 360 put upon a ſtring makes a Fathom, which of the White Money comes to five ſhillings, and of the Black 10ˢ. But ſome years ago, one Fathom of their white money was worth nine, and ſometimes ten ſhillings per fathom; but that which occaſioned the Fall of it, was the Fall of Beaver in England, which it was very difficult to make the Indians underſtand, who thought the Engliſh had cheated them, when for Engliſh Commodities they made them pay ſo much more of their money.

Their white Money they call *Wompam*, which ſignifies
white,

white, and their Black *Suckauhock*, *Sucki* fignifying Black. Both amongft themfelves and the Englifh and Dutch, the Black Penny is two pence white, and the black fathom the value of two Fathom of White: That which we found upon the way happen'd to be all white, and was worth 10*s.* and tho' it was of the worfer fort, we ne'er refuf'd it, but took it as it was. They frequently hang thefe ftrings of money about their Necks and Wrifts, and alfo upon the Necks and Wrifts of their Wives and Children. And I have been told that they make curious Girdles of one, two, three, four and five Inches thicknefs, and more, of this Money, which they wear about their Middles, and as a Scarff about their Shoulders and Brefts, and this fometimes to the value of Ten pounds: And I have alfo been told that their Princes or Sachims make rich caps and Aprons (or fmall Breeches) of thefe Beads thus curioufly ftrung, into many forms and figures; their Black and White being curioufly mixt together.

But having thus far Rambled out of my Way, my Coufin, to give you a defcription of the Indian Money, 'tis time I now return to my Fellow-Travellers, who by this time are come near to Nantafcot: We were fo fair, as to afk all we met, whether they had loft any thing or not, but cou'd find no owner for our two fathom of money, which we were forc'd to fpend in our own defence, fome at Nantafcot, and fome at George Monks, when we came back to Bofton.

Being come to Nantafcot we took a furvey of the Town, which is a Sea-Port, about two Leagues from Bofton, where fhips commonly caft Anchor: near which is Pullin Point, fo called, becaufe the Boats are haled againft the Tide, which is very ftrong. It is the ufual Channel for Boats to pafs into the Maffachufetts Bay. On the South Side of the Paffage there is an Ifland containing about Eight Acres of ground; Upon a rifing Hill within this Ifland is mounted a Caftle. Here 'twas we firft Landed, when I came into the
Countrey;

Countrey: Tho' this Caſtle be no ſtately Edifice, nor very ſtrong, being built with Brick and Stone, yet it commands the Entrance, ſo that no Ship can paſs by without its leave: It is kept by a Captain, under whom is a Maſter-Gunner, and ſome others.

I then next took a tranſient view of Pullin-Point. The Bay is large, and has Boſton in view, as ſoon as you enter into it: It is made by many Iſlands, the chiefeſt of which is the Dear Iſland, which is within a flight ſhot of Pullin-Point: It is called Dear Iſland, becauſe great ſtore of Deer were wont to ſwim thither from the main Land: We then viewed Bird Iſland, Glaſſ-Iſland, State-Iſland, and the Governour's Garden, where the firſt Apple trees in the Countrey were planted, and there alſo was planted a Vineyard: Then there is Round Iſland, ſo called from the figure of it, and laſt of all Noddles Iſland, not far from Charles-Town. Moſt of theſe Iſlands lie on the North-Side of the Bay.

And having now ſatisfied our ſelves with the Pleaſant Proſpect we had, we went to the beſt Houſe we cou'd find in Nantaſcot, and there had a good Dinner, for which we paid a Fathom and a half of our Indian Coyn; and by the length of the Shadows finding the Sun was inclining to his Journeys End, we haſtened to Boſton, whither being come, we went to George Monks (a Noted Publick Houſe there,) and there having melted down the other half Fathom, we parted.

My Seventh Ramble was to *Wiſſaguſet*, the next Town to Nantaſcot, on the South-ſide of the Bay: I had but one Friend that accompanied me in this Ramble; and yet I did not want for Company; for his Converſation was ſo agreable that I was very well pleaſ'd with it. As we went along we fell into a Diſcourſe of the Deers, (which are very numerous in this Countrey,) and of their ſwimming over to Deer Iſland; and my Friend told me that they were not ſo ſubject to be hunted there, as on the main Land; I aſk'd him who it was
that

that ufually hunted them, and he told me it was the Indians:
I told him I had indeed heard that the Indians were great
hunters, but had never heard what fort of Hunting they
uf'd: He told me, If I pleaf'd, he wou'd give me an account
of it; having feen 'em hunt himfelf feveral times: I thank'd
him, and told him he wou'd oblige me much with the
Relation.[107]   He then thus began:

'The Indians have two feveral Ways of Hunting: Firft,
When they purfue their Game, efpecially Deer, of which
there are abundance; thefe they purfue in twenty, forty,
fifty, yea fometimes in two or three hundred in a Company,
as I have feen; when they drive the Woods before them.
A fecond way of Hunting they have is, by Traps of feveral
forts: To which purpofe, after they have obferved in fpring
time and Summer the haunt of the Deer, then about Harveft
they go ten or twenty together, and many times more; and
withal, unlefs it be too far off, their Wives and Children alfo,
where they build up little Hunting-Houfes of Barks and
Bufhes, not comparable to their dwelling-Houfes, and fo
each Man takes his Bounds of two, three, or four miles,
where he fets thirty, forty, or fifty Traps, and baits his Traps
with that Food the Deer loves; and once in two Days he
walks round to view his Traps, of which they are very tender,
where they lie, and what comes at them: For they fay the
Deer, whom the Indians believe to have a Divine Power in
them, will foon fmell, and be gone: And therefore, *Npun-
nowwaumen*, (which is, I muft go to my Traps) is a ufual
Phrafe with them.

'Nor is it without reafon that they are fo careful; for
fometimes when a Deer has been taken in their Traps, they
have found a Woolf there devouring him; and the Wolf
being greedy of his Prey, they have killed the Wolf: Sometimes the Wolf having glutted himfelf with Eating one half,
he leaves the other for his next bait; but the glad Indian
coming

[107] WILLIAMS, pp. 248-252.—ED.

coming in the mean time, prevents him.   But it is not the Wolf alone, that will devour the Deer, but other ravenous Beafts alfo : I remember how a poor Deer, after having been long chafed by a Stout Wolf, was at laft tired, and the Wolf feized upon it, and kill'd it; but in the Act of devouring his Prey, two Englifh Sows, big with Pig, Paft by, and affaulting the Wolf, drove him from his Prey, and devoured fo much of that poor Deer, that the Swine both furfeited, and died that Night.

'When a Deer is caught by the Leg in a Trap, fometimes there it lies a whole day before the Indian comes; and fo the Deer lies a prey to the ranging and ravening Wolf, and other Wild Beafts, but moft commonly to the Wolf, who fiezeth upon the Deer, and robbs the Indian (at his firft devouring) of near half his Prey; and if the Indian comes not the fooner, the Wolf will make a Second Meal, and leave the poor Indian nothing but the Bones, and the torn Deers Skin; Efpecially if the Wolf brings fome of his greedy Companions to this bloody Banquet.   But the Indian being thus difappointed, makes a falling Trap with a great Weight of Stones; and fo fometimes knocks the Wolf on the Head with a gainful Revenge; Efpecially if it be a black Wolf, whofe Skins they greatly prize.   When any Contro-verfie happens between two Indians, or more, whofe a Deer fhall be, they commonly divide it, to prevent quarrelling. And when a Deer, Wolf, or any other Beaft, happens in hunting to run into the Water, and is kill'd there, the fkin is carried to the Sachim or Prince within whofe Territory it was flain : This they call *Pumpom*, that is, a Tribute Skin.'

I gave my Friend many Thanks, for his Relation, but told him they did not hunt for Pleafure, as we did in England, and indeed throughout Europe, where Hunting is counted one of the Nobleft Recreations : He told me 'twas true, they did not hunt with fo much Gallantry, but then it was with

lefs

lefs hazard and more Profit; and as for Pleafure, they took as much to find a Deer in a Trap, as the Europeans did to hunt him down, and then their Profit,' faid he, 'which is the Chief thing they aim at, is confiderable. For they don't only get Winter Provifion for their Families, (they hunting for the fkins moft part after Harveft,) but make a great advantage of the Skins, which they fell both to the Englifh and Dutch, for ready money; and is one of the Chief Commodities which the Merchants Export hence.'

Our difcourfe brought us infenfibly to Wiffagufet, which is a place eafily furvey'd, for it is but a fmall Village, Situate on the South-fide of the Bay, about three miles from a Town call'd Mount Wollefton: There are but few Houfes in it, the Inhabitants for the moft part addict themfelves to Hufbandry, the Soil about the Town being Extraordinary fertile. In this Village we had like to have been hard put to it for a Dinner. But cou'd you think, Coufin, that my Father-in-Law, Dr. Annefly, cou'd help me to a Dinner here? Yet fo it was, for it happened that a Gentleman liv'd in this Village that had feen me in my Ware-houfe in Bofton, and had heard that I was Dr. Annefly's Son-in-law, who paffing by as we were afking for a Public Houfe, told us there was none in the Town: And then afking me whether I was not Dr. Annefly's Son, I told him I had the Honour to be related to him, having married his Daughter: He then defir'd me and my Friend to go along with him to his Houfe, and accept of a fmall Dinner with him: My Friend and I look'd upon it to be no time to compliment, and therefore went at the firft Invitation.

We found there a very good Dinner, and were Treated by the Gentleman very genteelly and Civilly, he being pleaf'd to tell me he was very glad he had an Opportunity to fatisfie his refpects to Dr. Annefly, by whofe Writings he had receiv'd much good, and for whom he had an Extraordinary refpect: (and between you and I, Coufin, I was as

glad

glad on't as he, for otherwife I fhou'd have gone without a good Dinner). And indeed the Dr. is very much efteem'd throughout the whole Countrey. But having Din'd very plentifully, and had as much good Liquor as we car'd to Drink, I gave the Gentleman many Thanks for his great Civility and good Entertainment, telling him I fhou'd be glad to fee him at my Warehoufe in Bofton, we took our leaves on him, and return'd home, very well pleaf'd with our feafonable Treat.

My Eighth Ramble (ftill, Coufin, you fee I am within Reckoning) was to *Braintree*, to which place I had the Company of a Couple of Friends, who were willing to fee Braintree as well as my felf; but not for the fame Reafon: For my Reafon was, becaufe I had a mind to fee it; but theirs was, becaufe they had fome Relations there: Which I was very glad to heare, becaufe by that means I thought we were pretty fure of fecuring a Dinner, which fell out accordingly.

The Wind as we went was pretty high, and the Weather fharp and cold, which occafion'd a Difcourfe among us about the Weather, and made me afk, Why fince New-England is above 12 degrees nearer to the Sun than Old England, it fhou'd yet be colder here fome part of Winter, then it is in England? To this one of my Fellow-Travellers[108] anfwer'd me, 'The Reafon is obvious: All Iflands being warmer than Main Lands and Continents; and England being an Ifland, the Winds in England are Sea-Winds, which commonly are more thick and vaporous, and warmer Winds. But the Northweft Wind, which occafions New-Englands cold, comes over the cold frozen Land, and over many millions of Loads of Cold Snow; And yet,' faid he, 'the pure wholefomenefs of the Air is wonderful, and the Warmth of the Sun fuch in the fharpeft weather, that I have often feen the Indians Children run about ftark naked in the coldeft Days: And

it

[108] WILLIAMS, p. 167.—ED.

it is common for the Indian Men and Women to lye by a fire in the Woods in the Coldeſt Nights.

'And as to the Winds, of all the Winds that blow here, the pleaſanteſt and warmeſt Wind is the Southweſt, which is moſt deſired by the Indians, ordinarily making fair Weather; and therefore they have a Tradition, That to the Southweſt, which they call *Sowwaniu,* the Gods chiefly dwell; and thither the Souls of all their great and good Men and Women chiefly go. This South-Weſt Wind is called by the New-Engliſh the Sea Turn, which comes from the Sun in the Morning, about nine or ten of the Clock Southeaſt, and about South, and then ſtrongeſt Southweſt in the After-noon, and towards Night it dies away. It is rightly called the Sea-turn, becauſe the Wind commonly all the Summer comes off from the North and North-Weſt in the night, and then turns again about from the South in the Day; as Solo-mon ſpeaks of the Vanity of the Winds in their Changes, *Eccles.* 1 : 6.' From this Diſcourſe of my Friend, I reflected, That GOD is wonderfully glorious in bringing the Winds out of his Treaſure, and riding upon the Wings of thoſe Winds in the Eyes of all the Sons of Men in all Coaſts of the World.

By this time we were come to Mount Wolleſton, or Merry Mount, called Maſſachuſets Fields, where one *Chicatabat,* the greateſt Sagamore or Prince of the Countrey formerly liv'd: And here it is that the Town of Braintree is ſeated: Tho' it be near the Sea, yet it is no good Harbour, for no Boat nor Ship can come near it: That which is moſt remarkable in it, is an Iron Mill: To the Weſt of this Town is Naponſet River.

Having view'd the Town, my Friends went to ſee their Relations that liv'd there, who made us ſo very welcome, that we had no reaſon to be diſpleaſ'd with our Ramble, but return'd to Boſton very well Satisfied. And to make my Friends amends for the Treat I had receiv'd upon their

Account

24

Account at Braintree, I told them, That if they wou'd go with me the next week to Dorchefter, I wou'd retaliate their kindnefs, by another Treat which I was fure to have from a Friend of mine there; and that befides, I had a great mind to fee the Town of Dorchefter: They told me they wou'd gladly do it, and fo having appointed a Day, we parted.

My Ninth Ramble, my Coufin, was to the Town of *Dorchefter*; my Friends [met] me in the morning of the fore-appointed Day, according to their Word: We began our Ramble almoft as foon as the Sun began his; and had both good Way and good Weather; the Wind being neither fo high, nor the Weather fo fharp as when we went to Braintree: As we paff'd along, we had the Sea in View, and faw fome Perfons fifhing thereon, which made me fay to my Companions, 'I have already had an Account of the Indians Hunting, and now, to make the way feem lefs tedious, I wou'd defire one of you which beft can, to give me an Account of their way of Fifhing, and what fort of Fifh you have in this Countrey.' Then he that was the beft Spokef-man, and that gave me an Account of the Weather, &c. when we went to Braintree, thus began.

'The way of Fifhing which the Indians ufe, has nothing very remarkable in it to diftinguifh it from that which is uf'd by the Englifh; but the variety of our Fifh may be worth your Knowledge: Which I will therefore give you an account of, as far as my Memory will let me. And becaufe I intend to Name 'em all, I fhall name thofe we have in England, as well as thofe that are peculiar to this Countrey.' I bid him proceed without any further preface.

'The firft,' faid he,[109] 'I fhall name, is the Cod, which is indeed the firft that comes, a little before the Spring; then we have Lampries, which is the firft that comes in the Spring, into frefh Rivers; we have also a Fifh fomewhat like a Herring, but not the same; We have alfo a Fifh call'd

[109] WILLIAMS, pp. 196–202.—ED.

call'd a Baffe, of the head of which the Indians (and the Englifh too) make a very fine Difh, this Fifh having a great quantity of Brains and Fat, which eats as fweet as marrow: We have likewife great quantities of Sturgeon in this Countrey; which for the goodnefs and greatnefs of it, is very much priz'd by the Natives, who upon that fcore refuf'd at firft to furnifh the Englifh either with fo many as they wanted, or fo cheap as they might have been afforded, till the Englifh themfelves got the way of fifhing for them, and now they may have [them] cheap enough. The Indians venture one or two in a Canow (which is a Boat made out of the Body of a Tree, of one intire piece of Wood) and with an Harping Iron, or fome fuch-like Inftrument, ftick this Fifh, and fo hale it into their Canow; and fometimes they take them by their Nets, which they make of Hemp, very ftrong. Which Nets they will fet thwart fome little River or Cove wherein they kill Baffe (at the Fall of the Water) with fharp fticks or Arrows, efpecially if headed with Iron gotten from the Englifh, &c.

'Another Fifh we have is Mackarel; we have alfo Salmon, which the Indians call Redfifh; then we have a fat, fweet Fifh fomething like a Hadock: Bream is another of our Fifh, of which there is abundance, which the Indians dry in the Sun and Smoak, and fome of the Englifh begin to falt; both ways they keep all the year; and it is hoped it may be as well accepted as Cod at a Market; and better too, were it once known, it being a better Fifh; we have likewife a Fifh call'd Sheeps-heads,[110] and good ftore of Eels; Porpufes is another of our Fifh, and we have alfo Whales, which in fome places are often caft up: I have feen fome my felf,' faid he, 'but they were not above fixty foot long, which were counted but fmall ones: The Indians cut them out in feveral Parcels, and give and fend it far and near

---

[110] Mr. Trumbull in his notes to Williams, fays that the Sheeps-head is the Tautog.—Ed.

near among themfelves, for an acceptable prefent ; and as fuch it is taken.

'We have alfo great ftore of Oyfters, Lobfters, and Clams, which laft is a fweet kind of Shelfifh, which all the Indians generally throughout the Countrey delight in, both Winter and Summer; and at low water the Women dig for them : This Fifh, and the natural Liquor of it they boyl, and it makes their Broth and their *Nafaump* (which is a kind of thickened Broth), and their Bread feafonable and favoury, inftead of falt. And becaufe the Englifh fwine will dig and root for thefe clams, wherefoever they come, and watch for the low Water, (as the Indian Women do) therefore of all the Englifh Cattel, the Indians hate the Swine moft, calling them filthy cut-throats; for the truth is, Swine are of a very filthy difpofition, and a Creature good for nothing while it lives; tho'[111] when 'tis dead, it is excellent meat, and far exceeds the beft Pork in England.

'We have alfo in this Countrey Horfe-fifhes, and a little thick fhell-fifh, which the Englifh call Hens, but the Indians *Poquauhock ;* which the Indians wade deep and dive for; and after they have eaten the meat, they break out of the fhell about half an Inch of a black part of it, of which they make their *Suckauhock*, which they account very pretious.

'And then we have a Fifh called the Periwinkle, of which the Indians make their *Wompam*, or White Money : I muft fay this for the Indians,' (continu'd my Friend) 'that the Indians are very induftrious in their Fifhing, watching their Seafons both by Day and Night; it being an Ordinary thing with them to lay their naked Bodies on the cold fhore about a fmall fire of two or three fticks, in the coldeft Night, often going into the Water to fearch their Nets.

'We have alfo here a fort of little Fifh, half as big as fprats,

---

[111] This remark on the fuperiority of American pork may be credited to DUNTON.—ED.

ſprats, very plentiful in the Winter-Seaſon. We have another Fiſh, which we call a Winter-Fiſh,[112] which comes up
in the Brooks and Rivulets, and which ſome call Froſt Fiſh,
becauſe they come from the Sea into Freſh Brooks, in times
of Froſt and Snow: The laſt I ſhall mention, is what we
call a Freſh-Fiſh,[112] which when the Indians take, they are
forc'd to break the Ice in freſh Ponds, where they alſo take
many other ſorts, for the Countrey yields many other ſorts of
Fiſh, beſides thoſe I have mention'd; but I fear I have tir'd
your Patience too much already.'

I thank'd my Friend for his Pains, aſſuring him that I
was ſo far from being tyr'd, that I was very much delighted
with his Relation; and cou'd not but reflect from what he
had ſaid,[113] how many thouſand millions of thoſe under-water
Sea-inhabitants, in all the various Coaſts of the World, ſeem
to exhort the Sons of Men on ſhore, for whoſe uſe they were
made, to adore and magnifie their glorious Maker.

But being not yet come to Dorcheſter, I deſir'd my other
Fellow-Traveller,[114] if it were not too much trouble to him,
to give me a brief account of what ſorts of Beaſts this
Countrey afforded, which were the Inhabitants of their
Woods: He told me 'I ſhall be glad to ſerve you in what I
can, but I can make no long Preamble, and hope you won't
expect it; but as for the Wild Beaſts in the Woods, I think
there are theſe: Wolves good ſtore, and ſome black Wolves,
but not ſo many as the other; and then we have good ſtore
of Beavers, alſo red Foxes and gray Foxes.'

'Hold,' ſaid my other Friend, 'before you proceed any
further, let me ſay ſomething of the Beaver: This is a
Beaſt of Wonder, for he will cut and draw great pieces
of Trees with his Teeth, with which, and ſticks and Earth
together,

---

[112] TRUMBULL calls the "Winter Fiſh" the Tom-Cod; and the "Freſh Fiſh," the Pickerel.—ED.

[113] DUNTON's reflections were only a ſecond-hand, WILLIAMS having already ſaid the ſame. (KEY, p. 202.)—ED.

[114] WILLIAMS, or his double. (KEY, pp. 187–190.)—ED.

together, I have often feen him dam up fair ftreams and Rivers; and upon thefe ftreams thus damn'd up, he builds his Houfe with Stories, wherein he fits at pleafure dry in his Chambers, and either ftays there, or goes into the Water which he pleafes. His Skin is of good Value,[115] and is a very good Commodity both here and in England, the fineft Hats being made of his Furr, which from thence are call'd Beavers.—Now,' faid he to the other, ' Go on again, and I beg your Pardon for interrupting you : '

' I am very glad,' faid he, ' that you help'd me out; for I told you when I begun, you muft expect no Preambles of me : The laft that I nam'd was gray Foxes, of which I have feen feveral; but the Indians fay, They have Black Foxes too, which they have often feen, but cou'd never take; and that makes 'em fay they are *Manitooes*, that is, Gods, Spirits, or Divine Powers; for fo they fay of every thing which they cann't comprehend. Next we have Racoones, Otters, Wildcats, and a Wild Beaft of a reddifh hair, about the big- nefs of a Pig, and rooting like a Pig, which the Indians call *Ockqutchaunnug*.[116] Then we have Squirrels of feveral Colours, and Coneys or Rabbits, which the Indians have a reverend efteem of, and conceive there is fome Deity dwells in it. We have alfo Deer in abundance; we have alfo Horfes, Cows, Goats, Swine, and Dogs. Some of thefe are Beafts of Prey, and others are prey'd upon.'—

My Friend having done, I thank'd him : ' I perceive,' faid I, ' your Wildernefs is a clear Refemblance of the World, where the Great and Rich do for the moft part devour the poor, harmlefs and Innocent, as the Wolves and Wild Beafts purfue and devour the Hinds and Roes.'

This Difcourfe had now brought us to Dorchefter, which lies fix miles beyond Braintree; it is a frontier Town, very

pleafantly

---

[115] This remark about the value of the fkins and the manufacture of hats is doubtlefs Dunton's own.—Ed.

[116] Trumbull fays this is the Wood- chuck.—Ed.

pleafantly feated, ftretching it felf out largely into the Main Land, and well watered with two Small Rivers: her Body and Wings, filled fomewhat thick with houfes, to the Number of above two hundred; beautified with fair Orchards and Gardens, having alfo plenty of Corn-land, and ftore of Cattel. This Town was heretofore efteemed the greateft in New-England, but now gives way to Bofton, which has far out-ftript it. It hath a Harbour for Ships to the North. Having furvey'd the Town to our great fatisfaction, I went with my Two Friends to the Houfe of Deputy Stoughton, who lives here, and who had formerly invited me to his Houfe; which is one of the fineft in all the Town: He exprefs'd himfelf very glad to fee me, in the moft obliging Terms that cou'd be, and told me that both myfelf and Friends were heartily welcome; he fhew'd me all the fine things in his Houfe, Orchard and Garden, which were indeed very ftately; and afterwards, Treated both me and my Friends very Nobly.

He enquir'd of me when I heard from England, and what was the beft News there? I told him there was little good to be expected during that Reign, and that unlefs fome Extraordinary turn of Providence appear'd, things were like to be worfe and worfe. He told me he was of the fame Opinion; but added, GOD was never at a lofs to carry on his own Work. After fome other Difcourfes of this Kind, I took my leave of him, with many Thanks for the Honour he had done me, and fo came back again in the Evening to our old Center, Bofton; being all very well pleaf'd with our that Day's Ramble.

My next Ramble to the adjacent Towns, was to *Roxbury*, whither (for a Particular Reafon) I chofe to go alone. It is but a mile beyond Dorchefter, from whence I might eafily have gone to Roxbury then, but that I had company with me, which I cou'd not genteelly part with, and yet it was not proper for them to go with me. I fet out betimes in the
morning,

morning, and came to Roxbury about Ten a Clock, and then took a view of the Town which is fair and handsome, the streets large and well built, the Inhabitants said to be very rich, their Houses having those necessary Appendages of Orchards and Gardens, and well watered with Springs and small Rivulets, having a Brook running through it called Smelt-River, and a quarter of a mile to the North side of the Town runs Stony-River: It is seated in the bottom of a Shallow Bay, but hath no Harbour for Shipping, tho' Boats may come to it; It hath great store of Land and Cattel belonging to it.

But (that which is) the Glory of Roxbury, as well as of all New-England, is, that the Reverend Mr. John Elliot, (the first Preacher of the Gospel to the Indians,) that Great Apostle and Evangelist of the Indians, lives there. To pay a visit to whom, was the Principal Cause of my Chusing to go thither alone, that so I might have nothing to hinder me in Conversing with him. I had seen him at Boston once, and he then gave me a charge to come and see him at Roxbury, where (as he said) he had something to say to me; which also made me desirous to speak with him alone, that he might speak to me with the greater freedom.

When I came to see him, he receiv'd me with all the Tenderness and respect imaginable, and had me up into his Study; and then he enquir'd of me with all the Expressions of Love and Kindness that cou'd be, how my Father-in-Law, the Reverend Doctor Annesly did? And when I had told him the state of his Health when I left London, he rejoyced very much thereat, and told me he cou'd not have too great a value for so painful a Labourer in the Lord's Vineyard as my Father-in-Law had so many years been, whose Earnest Travail for the Conversion of Souls he had for a long time been acquainted with: Breaking out into this Expression, *Is my Brother Annesly still alive? Blessed be God* that I have heard of his Welfare before I die. And then speaking to me, me, faid, 'Well, Young Man, how goes the Work of Chrift on in England?' I then told him of the Troubles that were there, and how like Popery was to be fet up again.

'No,' faid he, 'it never will, it never fhall: They may indeed attempt it; they have Towering Thoughts, as their Brethren the Babel-Builders had of old, but they fhall never be able to bring their wicked Intentions to pafs; for God will come down, and confound all their Defigns, and make themfelves the Workers of their own Overthrow.' And this he fpake with very good Affurance. 'But,' fays he, 'do the People of God keep up their Meetings ftill? Is the Gofpel preach'd? Does the Work of Converfion go forward? Are Souls brought in to Jefus Chrift? My Bowels,' fays he, yearns after the good of Souls.' I told him, That tho' the Gaols were full of Diffenters, yet the Meetings were as numerous, and as much throng'd as ever. And I had heard my Father fay, That more Members had been added to the Church the laft year than in fome years before.

Mr. Elliot was very well pleaf'd at what I had told, and faid, 'It was a Token for Good, that God had not forfaken his People.' And then, in a way of Triumph, he faid, '*Come down, O Daughter of Babylon! and fit in the Duft; for the Cup fhall pafs over to thee: The Virgin Daughter of Sion hath laugh'd thee to fcorn, fhe hath fhaken her head at thee.* I fee,' faid he 'the fall of Antichrift, which GOD will haften for his Elect's fake.' And then faid to me, 'O labour to get in to the Ark, CHRIST, for there alone you will find Safety.' After which, he prefented me with 12 Bibles in the Indian Language, and gave me a charge to prefent one of 'em to my Father, Dr. Annefly; he alfo gave me Twelve Speeches of Converted Indians, publifh'd by himfelf, to give to my Friends in England: After which, he made me ftay and dine with him, by which means I had the Opportunity of hearing him Pray, and expound the Scriptures with his Family.

After

25

After Dinner, he told me that both for my own, but
especially for my Father's fake, whom he faid he admir'd
above moft Men in England, if his Countenance and
Recommendation cou'd be of any Service to me, I fhou'd
not want it : (And I have already found the good Effects of
it :) And then I took my leave of him, with all thofe
Acknowledgments which I ought to make him for fo great
Favours.   But, my dear Coufin, I cannot yet leave this
Great Man, (for fuch indeed he is.)   I have attempted his
Character, in which, if I am fome thing large, I hope you
will not think much, becaufe I am fure the fubject will
bear it.

He[117] was born in England, but the particular place where,
I know not; tho' perhaps the place of his Nativity was
worthy of the Honour of being Contended for, as that of
the Great Homer; but whatever place had the Honour of
his Birth, it is New-England that with moft Right can call
him hers; for here he drew his beft Breath, and in all
probability will his laft Breath.   He came to New-England
(as I have been informed) in the Month of November, 1631,
among thofe bleffed Planters which came over hither to
Enjoy the free Exercife of the Proteftant Religion, in its
Purity and Power: When he came from England, he left
behind him there, a young and vertuous Gentle Woman to
whom he was contracted, and fhe coming over the year
following, they were married in October, 1632.   And this
Wife of his Youth became alfo the Staff of his Age, and
left him not till about half a year ago.   And

---

[117] Much of this account is taken verbatim from COTTON MATHER'S Life of
Eliot.   The firft edition was printed for
Jofeph Brunning, at Bofton, in 1691;
the third edition was printed in 1694
for John Dunton, in London.   It is alfo
incorporated in the *Magnalia*.

It is certainly to be regretted that we
have no knowledge of the birth-place of
John Eliot, though there is much reafon
to believe that it was Nazing, co. Effex.
He had brothers, Philip, Jacob, and
Francis, and fuch records as are preferved, point clearly to Nazing as the
birth-place of all the family.   He married Ann Mumford or Mountfort, who
died, 22 March, 1687, and by whom he
had feveral children.   Numerous defcendants remain, both of the name of
Eliot and others.—ED.

And I have been told fhe was an Extraordinary Woman for Piety and Vertue, and that at her Death, Mr. Elliot, who very rarely wept, cou'd not refrain from Tears; and that at her Funeral, before a vaft confluence of People, affembled on that occafion, with Tears in his Eyes, he faid, 'Here lies my Dear, Faithful, Pious, Prudent Wife; I fhall go to her, but fhe fhall not return to me!' By her he had fix worthy children; children of a Charaᵭter which may for ever ftop the Mouths of thofe Popifh Blafphemers who have fet a falfe Brand of Difafter and Infamy upon the Off-Spring of a Married Clergy: Tho' if you'll take the words of a Poet, *Do all Breathe fomething more than Common Air.*

This Great Man (for fo I cannot but call him) was Converted very Early; not having known many Turns in the World, before he knew the meaning of a Saving Turn from the Vanity of an Unregenerate State; and one of the Chief Inftruments that Goᴅ was pleafed to make ufe of to that End, was the Venerable Mr. Thomas Hooker, whofe Name among the Churches in New-England, is as an Oyntment poured.

His firft Appearance in the World, after his Education in the Univerfity of Cambridge, was in that difficult and unthankful but very neceffary Employment of a School-Mafter; which he difcharged with great Fidelity.

On his firft arrival in New-England, he foon joyned himfelf to the Church at Bofton; I find 'twas Church-Work that was his Errand hither. Mr. Wilfon, the Paftor of that Church was gone back into England, to perfeᭆ the Settlement of his Affairs; and in his abfence, young Mr. Elliot was he that fupply'd his place.

But 'twas not Bofton was to be his ftation; for having Engaged to fome Chriftian Friends in England, that if they fhou'd come into thefe parts before he fhou'd be in the Paftoral Care of any other People, he wou'd give himfelf to them, and be for their Service; It happen'd that thefe

Friends

Friends Tranfported themfelves hither the year after him, and chofe their Habitation at the Town which they call'd Roxbury: So 'twas in the Orb of that Church that he continu'd as a ftar fix'd for very near Threefcore years, he being now in the 80th year of his Age; and being fo aged, he is often telling his Friends, That he is fhortly going to Heaven, and that he wou'd carry a deal of good News thither with him; he faid, He wou'd carry Tidings to the old Founders of New-England which are now in Glory, That Church Work was yet carried on in New-England; that the Number of their Churches was continually Encreaf-ing, and that the Churches were ftill kept as big as they were, by the Dayly Addition of thofe that fhall be faved. He had once, I hear, a pleafant fear, that the old Saints of his Acquaintance, Efpecially thofe two deareft Neighbours of his, Cotton, of Bofton, and Mather, of Dorchefter, which were got fafe at Heaven before him, wou'd fufpect him to be gone the wrong way, becaufe he ftaid fo long behind them. I fhall attempt to defcribe what was his Magnitude all this while, and how he perform'd his Revolution.

'Tis impoffible to finifh the lively Picture of this Pious and holy Man, without fome Touches upon that Mortification which has accompanied him all his Days: For never did I fee a Perfon more mortified unto all the Pleafures of this Life. He is fo nailed to the Crofs of the Lord Jefus Chrift, that the Grandeurs of this World are unto him, juft what they wou'd be to a dying Man: The meat upon which he lives is *Cibus Simplex*, and homely, but an wholefome Dyet: When he thinks the Countenance of a Minifter looks as if he make too much of himfelf, he will go to him with that Speech, ' Study Mortification, Brother, ftudy Mortification:' And he makes all his Addreffes with a becoming Majefty. The Luft of the Eye is put out by him in fuch a meafure, that it is in a manner all one to him to be Rich or Poor. His Apparel is without any Ornament, except that of Humility:

Had

Had you feen him, Coufin, with his Leathern Girdle, (as I have [11a] fo often, as he comes to the Bofton Lecture,) about his Loyns, you wou'd almoft have thought what Herod fear'd, That John the Baptift was come to Life again. In fhort, he was in all regards a Nazarite indeed, unlefs this one, That long Hair was always very loathfome to him.

He is fo great an Exemplar of Charity, that he that will write of Elliot, muft write of Charity, or fay nothing: His Charity is a Star of the firft magnitude, in the bright Conftellation of his Virtues, and the Rays of it are wonderful, various and extenfive. His Liberality to Pious Ufes, is much beyond the Proportion of his Eftate in the World: Many hundreds of Pounds does he freely beftow upon the Poor. The good People of Roxbury doubtlefs cannot remember, but the righteous GOD will, how often and with what Ardours, with what Arguments he became a Beggar to them for Collections to fupport fuch needy Objects as fall under his Obfervation. The Poor count him their Father, and repair ftill unto him with a filial Confidence in their Neceffities. And yet he cann't perfwade himfelf that he has any thing but what he gives away. He drives a mighty Trade at fuch Exercifes as he thinks will furnifh him with Bills of Exchange, which he hopes after many Days to find the Comfort of in Heaven. He does not put off his Charity to be put in his laft Will, as many do, who therein fhew that their Charity is againft their Will; but is his own Adminiftrator, makes his own Hands his Executors, and his own Eyes his Overfeers. He is alfo a great Enemy to all Contention, and will ring a loud Courfeu-Bell, where-ever he fees the Fires of Animofity. When he hears any Minifter complain that fuch and fuch in their Flocks are too difficult for them, his anfwer always is, Brother, Compofe them; and
Brother,

[11a] All this defcription, as we have faid, is taken from COTTON MATHER; but as he here writes, "Had you feen him with his leathern girdle (for fuch an one he wore)," we may accept DUNTON's teftimony as corroborative on the point.—ED.

Brother, learn the meaning of thofe three little words, Bear, Forbear, Forgive. Indeed, his Inclinations for Peace, makes him fometimes almoft facrifice his Right to obtain it.

I fhall next tell you,[119] Coufin, how this Good man lives in his Family; The Apoftle Paul, reciting and requiring the Qualifications of a Gofpel-Minifter, gives Order, That he be the Hufband of one Wife, and one that ruleth well his own Houfe, having his Children in Subjection with all gravity: His whole Converfation with his Wife, even till her Death, had that Sweetnefs, gravity and modefty beautifying of it, that none came nearer to the Pattern of Zachary and Elizabeth. His Family is a little Bethel, for the Worfhip of GOD is conftantly and exactly maintained in it. No Exorbitancies nor Extravagancies can find a Room under his Roof, nor is his Houfe any other than a School of Piety and Vertue: Which perhaps is the Original of that Tradition that is among 'em, That the Countrey can never perifh, as long as Elliot is alive.

And now you may be fure, Coufin, that I was curious to hear him preach; and of his Preaching, I muft fay, He is a Preacher that makes it his care to give every one their Meat in due Seafon. It is Food, and not Froth, that in his Publick Sermons he entertains the Souls of the People with: He does not ftarve them with Empty and windy Speculations. It is another Property of his Preaching, that there is always much of Chrift in it: And in this he imitateth my Reverend Father, Dr. Annefly,[120] who I believe, never ended a Sermon without Chrift: As 'twas told of Dr. Bodly, That whatever Subject he was upon, when he came to the Application, ftill his Ufe wou'd be, to drive Men to the Lord Jefus Chrift. From hence alfo 'twas, That he ufes to give this Advice to young Preachers, ' Pray let there be much of
Chrift

---

[119] DUNTON ftill continues to follow MATHER clofely, altering but few words.—ED.   [120] The reference to Dr. Annefly is an interpolation by DUNTON.—ED.

Chrift in your Miniftry.' It is obferv'd of him, that he likes that Preaching beft, that hath been well ftudied for; and will very much commend a Sermon, which he perceives has requir'd fome good Thinking and Reading in the Author of it. And yet he likewife looks for fomething in a Sermon, befide and beyond the meer ftudy of Man, for he is for having the Spirit of GOD breathing in it and with it.

An honourable Perfon[121] did once in Print put the Name of an Evangelift upon him; whereupon, in a Letter of his to that Perfon, afterwards Printed, his Expreffions were, ' There is a Redundency where you put the Title of Evangelift upon me; I befeech you to fupprefs all fuch things. Let

[121] This ' honourable Perfon' was undoubtedly Edward Winflow. In Henry Whitfield's " The Light appearing more and more towards the perfect Day, Or, a farther Difcovery of the prefent ftate of the Indians in New-England," 1651, (reprinted by Sabin of New York, 1865,) we find certain letters of Eliot to Winflow. At p. 18, Eliot writes, " A fecond redundance is page 17, (though misfigured and no matter,) where you put the title of Evangelift upon me, which all men take, and you feeme fo to put it for that extraordinary office mentioned in the New Teftament; I do befeech you to fuppreffe all fuch things, if ever you fhould have occafion of doing the like; let us fpeak and do and carry all things with all humility; it is the Lord who hath done what is done, and it is moft becoming the fpirit of Jefus Chrift to lift up Chrift, and our felves lie low; I wifh that that word could be obliterated if any of the books remain." See alfo " Hutchinfon's Collection of Papers," i. 257-259, Prince Society's edition, in proof that this letter was addreffed to Winflow.

Following this trace we find that the occafion when Winflow ufed this expreffion was in a tract reprinted in the Maffachufetts Hiftorical Society's Collections, 3rd Series, vol. iv, p. 89. The tract is entitled " The Glorious Progrefs of the Gofpel amongft the Indians in New-England, manifefted by three Letters, under the Hand of that famous Inftrument of the Lord, Mr. John Eliot, and another from Mr. Thomas Mayhew, jun., both Preachers of the Word, as well to the Englifh as Indians in New-England. Wherein the riches of God's Grace in the effectual calling of many of them is cleared up: As alfo a manifeftation of the hungring defires of many People in fundry parts of that Country after the more full Revelation of the Gofpel of Jefus Chrift, to the exceeding Confolation of every Chriftian Reader. Together With an Appendix to the foregoing Letters, holding forth Conjectures, Obfervations and Applications. By I. D., Minifter of the Gofpell. Publifhed by Edward Winflow. *Mal.* i : 11. London. Printed for Hannah Allen in Popes-head-Alley. 1649."

The particular paffage is on p. 17 of the tract, and p. 89 of the reprint. WINSLOW writes," Another Letter, Courteous Reader, dated in February laft, I received alfo from this our Indian Evangelift (if I may fo terme him)," &c.—ED.

Let us do, and fpeak, and carry all things with Humility.'
His Life has long made it juft for us to acknowledge him
with fuch a Title. I know not whether that of an Evangelift, or one feparated for the Employment of Preaching
the Gofpel, in fuch places where no Churches have hitherto
been gathered, be not an office that fhou'd be continu'd in
our Days: But this I know, by the report of all Men, that
Mr. Eliot does the Service and Bufinefs of fuch an officer.

The Natives[122] of the Countrey, I mean the Indians, have
been forlorn and wretched Heathens ever fince their firft
herding here; and tho' we know not when or how thofe
Indians firft became Inhabitants of this mighty Continent,
yet we may guefs that probably the Devil decoy'd thofe
miferable Salvages hither, in hopes that the Gofpel of the
bleffed JESUS wou'd never come here to deftroy or difturb
his Abfolute Empire over them. But this Good Man, Mr.
Eliot, is in fuch ill terms with the Devil, as to alarm him
with founding the Silver Trumpets of Heaven in his Territories, and has made fome Noble and Zealous Attempts
towards outing him of his ancient Poffeffions here.

I cannot find (upon the beft Enquiry I have made) that
any, befides the Holy Spirit of GOD, firft moved him to the
bleffed Work of being an Evangelift, or Preaching to thefe
Perifhing Indians: 'Twas that holy Spirit which laid before
his Mind the Idea of that which is now on the Seal of the
Maffachufet-Colony: A poor Indian, having a Label going
from his Mouth, with a *Come Over And Help Us:* It was
the Spirit of our LORD JESUS CHRIST which Enkindled in
him a Pity for the dark, dying, damning Souls of thefe
Natives, whom the God of this World has blinded through
all the by-paft Ages. He is none of thofe that make the
Salvation of the Heathen an Article of their Creed, but
(fetting afide the Unrevealed and Extraordinary Steps which
the

---

[122] As might be imagined, this fentence, as well as the preceding, is from
MATHER'S pen.—ED.

the Holy One of Ifrael may take out of his Ufual Paths,) he
thought Men to be loft, if the Gofpel be hidden from them.
All the good Men in the Countrey were glad of his Engage-
ment in fuch an Undertaking: The Minifters efpecially
Encouraged him, and thofe in the Neighbourhood kindly
fupply'd his place, and perform'd his Work, in part, for him
at Roxbury, while he was abroad, labouring among them
that were without.

Hereunto alfo he was further incited by thofe Expreffions
in the Royal Charter, in the Affurance and Protection
whereof, this Wildernefs was firft Peopled, namely, *To win
and incite the Natives of that Countrey to the Knowledge and
Obedience of the only True* GOD, *and Saviour of Mankind.*[120]
And the remarkable Zeal of the Romifh Miffionaries, com-
paffing Sea and Land, that they might make Profelytes,
made his devout Soul think of it with Difdain, that they in
their Countrey fhou'd come any whit behind in their care to
Evangelize the Indians among whom they dwell. But the
Exemplary Charity of this Great and Excellent Perfon in
this Important Affair of the Converfion of the Indians,
cannot be feen in its due luftre, unlefs I make fome Reflections upon the miferable Circumftances which he beheld
thefe forlorn Indians in.

Know then, my dear Coufin, that thefe doleful Creatures
are the verieft Ruines of Mankind, which are to be found
any where upon the face of the Earth: No fuch Eftates are
to be Expected among them, as have been the Baits which
the pretended converters in other Countries have fnapped
at. So poor and miferable was their condition, that one
might fee among them what an hard Mafter the Devil is, to
the moft devoted of his Vaffals. So helplefs they were, that
tho' they had many Iron Mines, there was not a knife, nor
any

[120] " And the Chriftian faith, in our
royal intention, and the adventurer's
free profeffion, is the principal end of
the plantation." This is the remainder
of the quotation as it ftands in Mather's
Magnalia.—ED.

26

any Inftrument of Iron to be found amongft them: So poor, that tho' there be plenty of Gold and Silver Mines, they made their Money of the Shells of Fifhes: So infatuated in their Underftandings, that tho' indeed the Being of a Deity was not quite Eraf'd out of their Souls, yet fo fordid and fottifhly ftupid were they, that they not only worfhip'd the Sun, Moon and Stars, whofe glorious Light, and whofe benign Influences might tempt a Heathen thereunto; but they even defcended fo low, that the Devil himfelf, under the moft abhorr'd and filthy fhapes, became the Objeckt of their Adoration.

Let us in them, my Coufin, here behold the fatal Effeckts of Sin, and the deplorable Ruines of Humane Nature, which tho' Created in fo much Holinefs and Purity, is now miferably Fallen below the very Dregs of the Creation. In this State of gloomy and Cimmerian Night, fat thefe poor Tawny, Black, and Barbarous Indians, when the Great Eliot firft came amongft them: and by the Preaching of the Gofpel brought forth thofe footy Captives of the Devil, into the glorious liberty of the Sons of GOD: For having his Heart inflam'd with a grateful Senfe of the Grate Things GOD had done for him, the love of JESUS having the chief Afcendent in his Soul, he cou'd not reft till he had done his Utmoft to obtain for him the Heathen for his Inheritance, and the uttermoft parts of the Earth for his Poffeffion.

But, Coufin, I muft remember, That I am not writing an Hiftory of his Life, but giving you a brief Charackter of his Excellent Qualifications and admirable Graces: And, tho' you may think I expatiated too much therein, it will be a fufficient Apology, if I tell you, as I truly can, I have not faid the half of what I might: And 'twill be no Hyperbole to tell you, That the moft I can fay, is the leaft that can be faid upon fo great a Subjeckt. From this Perfon, (which is the only thing in the World I have to boaft of) I have had a hearty Welcome into the Countrey; have had Advice, as

my

my Cafe requir'd; and fhou'd I tell you all other Favours I receiv'd from him, I muft write on an Age. In fhort, I cann't but think it a great Happinefs that my Eyes were once bleft with the fight of this Great Man: And the Honour of my having his particular Friendfhip and Countenance during my ftay in America, did me a greater fervice . than can be imagin'd by any that did not know him. I do confefs my felf no Poet, but the Extraordinary Merit of this Great Man, will not let [me] give over this Excellent Theme without writing the following Acroftick:[124]

AN ACROSTICK TO MR. JOHN ELIOT,

Minifter of the Gofpel in New-England, now in the 80th year of his Age:
Anno Dom. 1686.

I n Eliot alone New-England finds
O re richer than in Peru's Golden Mines:
H e in GOD's Grace is Rich beyond Compare:
N ot Pearls nor Rubies half fo precious are:

E ngland (his Birth-place) boaft: And let them fee
L ove like to his does ftill refide in Thee.
I ndians, rejoyce that Eliot e'er came here:
O how Induftrious does he appear,
T hat the True GOD you may both Love and Fear.

And now, my dear Coufin, give me leave to remind you, That my Ramble to Roxbury was the laft Ramble I made to the adjacent Villages: And that therefore I have acquitted my felf of the Promife I made you in the beginning of my Letter, (the length whereof, I hope you will excufe.) My next Ramble fhall be, if GOD permit, farther up into the Countrey among the Indians; of which I fhall give you an Account, if not before, at leaft when I come to London.
Pray

[124] We know at prefent of no one to difpute with DUNTON the authorfhip of this Acroftic.—ED.

Pray give my hearty Love to my Coufin your Wife, and to all elfe that Enquire of my Welfare. And affure yourfelf there is none does more Unfeignedly defire your Profperity and Happinefs, than, Dear Coufin,

Your Affectionate Kinfman,

PHILARET.

---

[100] Since DUNTON has fo much to fay relative to John Eliot, it may not be inappropriate to give here a lift of Eliot's publications, and of the titles of the pamphlets relating to the work of Chriftianizing the Indians here.

In the admirable Biography of John Eliot, contributed by the late Rev. Dr. Convers Francis to Sparks's "Library of American Biography," will be found a lift of eleven pamphlets, relative to the Indian affairs, publifhed between A. D. 1624 and 1671. As will be feen, all but one of thefe have been reprinted, but not in any one volume, or by any one publifher. We therefore give with the titles the reference to the reprints.

I. *(Maſſachuſetts Hiſtorical Society's Collections, 1ſt S. Vol.* viii., *and 2d S. Vol.* ix.) Good Newes from New-England: or, A True Relation of things very remarkable at the Plantation of Plimouth in New-England. Shewing the wondrous providence and goodnefs of GOD, in their prefervation and continuance, being delivered from many apparent deaths and dangers. Together with a Relation of fuch religious and civil laws and cuftoms, as they are in practice amongſt the Indians adjoining to them at this day. As alfo what commodities are there to be raifed for the maintenance of that and other Plantations in the faid country. Written by E. W., who hath borne a part in the fore-named troubles, and there lived fince their firſt arrival. Whereunto is added by him a brief Relation of a credible intelligence of the prefent ſtate of Virginia. London: Printed by J. D., for William Bladen and John Bellamie, and are to be fold at their fhops at the Bible in Paul's Church-yard, and at the Three Golden Lions, in Corn-hill, near the Royal Exchange. 1624.

II. *(Sabin's Reprints, No.* 7.) New-England's Firſt Fruits: in refpect, Firſt, of the (Converfion of Some, Conviction of Divers, Preparation of Sundry) of the Indians. 2. Of the Progreſſe of Learning in the Colledge at Cambridge in Maſſacufets Bay. With Divers other fpeciall Matters concerning that Countrey. Publifhed by the inſtant requeſt of fundry Friends, who defire to be fatisfied in thefe points, by many New-England Men who are here prefent, and were eye or eare-witneſſes of the fame. *Zach.* 4: 10. *Job,* 8: 6, 7. London, Printed by R. O. and G. D., for Henry Overton, and are to be fold at his Shop in Popes-head-Alley. 1643.

III. *(Sabin's Reprints, No.* 9.) The Day-Breaking if not the Sun-Rifing of the Gofpell with the Indians in New-England. *Zach.* 4: 10. *Matth.* 13: 13. Ibid., verfe 33. London, Printed by Rich. Cotes for Fulk Clifton, and are to to bee fold at his fhop under Saint Margarett's Church on New-fifh-ftreet Hill. 1647.

IV. *(Sabin's Reprints, No. 10.)* The Clear Sunfhine of the Gofpel breaking forth upon the Indians in New-England. Or, An Hiftoricall Narrative of God's Wonderfull Workings upon fundry of the Indians, both chief Governours and Common people, in bringing them to a willing and defired fubmiffion to the Ordinances of the Gofpel: and framing their hearts to an earneft inquirie after the Knowledge of God the Father, and of Jesus Christ the Saviour of the world. By Mr. Thomas Shepard, Minifter of the Gofpel of Jefus Chrift, at Cambridge, in New-England. *Ifaiah* 2: 2, 3. London, Printed by R. Cotes, for Bellamy, at the three golden Lions, in Cornhill, near the Royall Exchange. 1648.

V. The Glorious Progrefs of the Gofpel, &c., title already cited in full. See *ante*, p. 199.

VI. *(Maffachufetts Hiftorical Society's Collections, 3d Series, Vol. iv.)* The Light appearing more and more towards the perfect Day. Or, A farther Difcovery of the prefent ftate of the Indians in New-England, Concerning the Progreffe of the Gofpel amongft them. Manifefted by Letters from fuch as preacht to them there. Publifhed by Henry Whitfield, late Paftor to the Church of Christ at Gilford, in New-England, who came late thence. *Zeph.* 2: 11. London, Printed by T. R. & E. M., for John Bartlet, and are to be fold at the Gilt Cup, neer St. Auftins gate, in Pauls Church-yard. 1651.

VII. *(Sabin's Reprints, No. 5.)* Strength out of Weaknefs, Or a Glorious Manifeftation of the further Progreffe of the Gofpel amongft the Indians in New-England. Held forth in fundry Letters from divers Minifters and others to the Corporation eftablifhed by Parliament for promoting the Gofpel among the Heathen in New-England, and to particular members thereof, fince the late Treatife to that effect, formerly fet forth by Mr. Henry Whitfield, late Paftor of Gilford, in New-England. Publifhed by the aforefaid Corporation. *Cant.* 8: 8. London, Printed by M. Simmons, for John Blague and Samuel Howes, and are to be fold at their fhop in Popes Head Alley. 1652.*

VIII. *(Maffachufetts Hiftorical Society's Collections, 3d Series, Vol. iv.)* Tears of Repentance: Or a further Narrative of the Progrefs of the Gofpel Amongft the Indians in New-England: Setting forth, not only their prefent ftate and condition, but fundry Confeffions of fin by diverfe of the faid Indians, wrought upon by the faving Power of the Gofpel: Together with the manifeftation of their Faith and Hope in Jesus Christ, and the Work of Grace upon their Hearts. Related by Mr. Eliot and Mr. Mayhew, two Faithful Labourers in that work of the Lord. Publifhed by the Corporation for propagating the Gofpel there, for the Satisfaction and Comfort of fuch as wifh well thereunto. *Isay.* 42: 3. London: Printed by Peter Cole, in Leaden-Hall, and are to [be] Sold at his Shop, at the fign of the Printing-Prefs in Cornhill, near the Royal Exchange. 1653.

IX. *(Maffachufetts Hiftorical Society's Collections, 3d Series, Vol. iv.)* A Late and Further Manifeftation of the Progrefs of the Gofpel amongft the Indians in New-England. Declaring their conftant Love and Zeal to the Truth: With a readineffe to give Accompt of their Faith and Hope; as of their defires in Church Communion

---

* Sabin fays there were three editions in the fame year, and gives the titles in his reprint.

Communion to be Partakers of the Ordinances of Chrift. Being a Narrative of the Examinations of the Indians, about their Knowledge in Religion, by the Elders of the Churches. Related by Mr. John Eliot. Publifhed by the Corporation, eftablifhed by Act of Parliament, for Propagating the Gofpel there. *Acts* 13 : 47. London : Printed by M. S. 1655.

X. (*Sabin's Reprints, No.* 6.) A further Accompt of the Progreffe of the Gofpel amongft the Indians in New-England, and of the means ufed effectually to advance the fame. Set forth in certaine Letters fent from thence declaring a purpofe of Printing the Scriptures in the Indian Tongue, into which they are already Tranflated. With which Letters are likewife fent an Epitome of fome Exhortations delivered by the Indians at a faft, as Teftimonies of their obedience to the Gofpell. As alfo fome helps directing to the Indians how to improve naturall reafon unto the knowledge of the true GOD. London, Printed by M. Simmons for the Corporation of New-England, 1659.
[This tract Mr. Francis had never feen, but copied an abftract of the title from Rich's Catalogue.]

XI. (*Title copied from Stevens'* NUGGETS.) A Brief Narrative of the Progrefs of the Gofpel amongft the Indians in New-England in the year 1670. Given in By the Reverend Mr. John Eliot, Minifter of the Gofpel there, In a Letter by him directed to the Right Worfhipfull the Commiffioners under his Majefties Great-Seal for Propagation of the Gofpel amongft the poor blind Natives in thofe United Colonies. London, Printed for John Allen, formerly living in Little-Britain at the Rifing Sun, and now in Wentworth Street near Bell-Lane. 1671.
[Of this, Francis wrote that it was a fmall tract of eleven pages, which he had not been able to find,—but that its title was in Rich's Catalogue. We do not know that it has been reprinted.]

As to Eliot's other publications, we have not deemed it neceffary to cite their titles, fince fo many were in the Indian language. In the Eliot Genealogy will be found the following lift, which agrees with Dr. Francis's notes.

In Indian.

1. Indian Catechifm. 1653.
2. The New Teftament. 1661.
3. The Indian Bible, Catechifm, and Pfalms of David in metre. 1663.
4. Indian Pfalter. 1664. (Suppofed to be part of No. 3.)
5. Baxter's "Call to the Unconverted" tranflated. 1664.
6. Indian Grammar. 1666.
7. Indian Logic Grammar. 1672.
8. The Practice of Piety, tranflated. 1685.
9. Indian Primer. 1687.
10. Shepherd's "Sincere Convert" and "Sound Believer," tranflated. 1689.

In Englifh.

11. The Chriftian Commonwealth. 1660.
12. Communion of Churches. 1665.
13. The Harmony of the Gofpels. 1678.
14. An Anfwer to Norcott's Book againft Infant Baptifm.
15. Dying Speeches and Counfels of fuch Indians as dyed in the Lord.

LETTER V.

TO HIS EVER HONORED FATHER,

THE REVEREND DR. SAMUEL ANNESLY,

IN LONDON.

OST Honoured and Reverend Father: Tho' the Providence of GOD has fo order'd things, that I am at this time many hundred Leagues diftant from your fight, yet I am fure I am not out of your Mind; for I am confident there is not one day paffes wherein I am not remembred by you, in your Addreffes at the Throne of Grace: And this I am bold to believe, not only from that Univerfal Charity you have to all Men, which has fhin'd fo illuftrioufly through the whole Courfe of your Life, but alfo as I have the Honour to be related to you, and as I undertook this long (and to me tedious) Voyage, both by your Leave, and under the happy Aufpice of your Solemn Prayers for my Protection and Prefervation in it: Which I have found the good Effects of, in my Deliverance from a Thoufand Dangers which have Threatned me (and through GOD's Goodnefs only Threatned me) fince I faw you laft: On which account (amongft many others) I can never enough Adore that Wonderful Providence that brought me firft to know your Family: Which

makes

makes me recollect how I first saw one of your Daughters,
who pleaf'd my Eye, and in a little time after married another, who engag'd my Heart: The first, indeed, was most
Beautiful and Taking; but the last, most fit for me.   And
tho' I remember I first told you 'twas good to love with
Difcretion, yet I have found by a happy Experience, 'tis the
greateft Difcretion to marry a Suitable Wife.

I have, Sir, often reflected in my long voyage on the Sea,
how you try'd my Love to your Daughter, by your Tunbridge Journey, thereby delaying the Confummation of my
Happinefs; and now 'tis my Turn to try her Love by a long
Ramble to another World: Not that I need a Tryal on't to
fatisfie my felf, who am fo far from Doubt in this particular,
that I am well affur'd we are bound up in one another's
Souls: But that by this fhe has an opportunity to give the
World a more Illuftrious Evidence of that Affection which
yet it is impoffible for any one to know, but thofe that do
poffefs it.

There is a Proverb, Sir, which tells us, *Matches are made
in Heaven;* and if a Man may judge of things either by
antecedent Providences, or fubfequent Events, I dare be
bold to fay that ours was fuch: Why was it elfe that Mr.
Cockeril, (who by the Copies of your Morning Exercifes
became firft confiderable) fhou'd after a long Courtfhip,
ftrengthned by your Approbation, lofe that bright Jewel,
which my felf, affifted by kind Providence, and by your
Favour, have had the Happinefs to gain in a much fhorter·
time?   It is on this Account, Sir, that to this moment I
retain a moft particular and high efteem for all thofe worthy
Inftruments that Divine Providence was pleaf'd to make ufe
of in the making up of this happy Match: Amongft whom
I muft mention with due Honour, my Reverend Uncle, Mr.
Marriot, as he that firft made way for me; and I fhou'd be
Ingrateful, fhou'd I forget my good Friend, Mr. Ifaac Brinley,
who feconded what Mr. Marriot had begun, with good effect;
and

and who was, Sir, fo zealous in the Match, and fo well
fatisfied in the Worth of your Vertuous Daughter, that the
firft time I faw her, ere I had fcarce an opportunity to fpeak
to her, he cry'd out publickly, 'Speak to the Point, Man;'
which put me to the Blufh, and had almoft dafh'd a young
Lover out of Countenance.

(I hope, Sir, that you'll pardon me if I divert you a few
moments, fince it is only the effect of my fincere Affection
to your Daughter, that makes me thus repeat the feveral
Steps by which I was conducted to my Happinefs.) Nor
fhall I ever, Sir, forget, (as there's a Heartinefs peculiarly
proper to you in every thing you do) that you were more
particularly fo in this, as your going to Church with me, and
doing me the Honour there to put into my hand the Greateft
and beft Gift the World cou'd give me, do abundantly
Evidence: I cannot but again acknowledge, Sir, That you
have given me a Gift fo truly valuable, that if the greateft
Queen fhou'd court me to her Bed, and in her Lap bring
me a World of Wealth, I fhou'd refufe the Offer, and think
my felf a Lofer by the Bargain: Nor are thefe Empty
words; your Daughter knows 'tis but a Copy of that which
is Engraven in my Heart. Nor is it any thing but what
you, Sir, Exhorted us both to, when you were pleaf'd to
preach our Wedding Sermon (a Favour which I ever fhall
acknowledge,) wherein, Sir, you were pleaf'd to tell us, Our
Love muft be a Non-fuch-Love; and pardon me, Sir, if I
tell you, We both endeavour that it may be fo.

But I have other things to thank you for, befides my
Wife, (tho' fhe it is indeed that I efteem the Crown of all
my Earthly Happinefs.) I fhou'd be much to blame, fhou'd
I forget your Tendernefs to me, expreff'd on all occafions,
in a peculiar Care both for my Soul and Body: And give
me leave, Sir, I befeech you, to make my boaft of this, (for I
account it worth the boafting of,) That I have yet the
Honour to be efteem'd your Darling Son-in-Law: Which

I

I can attribute to nothing but your Goodnefs; and that you thought the Steps I took to be fo, appear'd more Regular than that of others, as having your Confent in what we did.

But 'tis not, Sir, in England only that I have receiv'd Favours from you; For as your Univerfal Goodnefs has fpread it felf not only thorow England and the Neighbouring Kingdomes, but is diffuf'd even to remoter Worlds, fo it has reach'd America, and here I find its comfortable and benign Influence: Your Works, Sir, have been before me in New-England and obtain'd fo juft and deferved a Reputation, that the Honour I have to be related to you, gives me a free Accefs, and hearty Welcome to the Chiefeft and moft Worthy Perfons in the Countrey: That Great Apoftle of this Countrey, (as he is juftly called here, for that great Care he takes,—like you in England,—almoft of all the Churches,) has Publickly Expreft the mighty Value and Efteem he has for you; and the Countenance which upon your Account, Sir, he has given me here, has been of great Advantage to me. And Mr. Burroughs, one of your old Hearers, (whofe Character I have already given to my good Friend, Mr. Larkin, the Printer, your Neighbour,) thinks he can never enough exprefs his Love to you, but by that Continual Refpect he fhews to me. And once on your Account I met with a good Dinner in a Countrey Town, where I was a Stranger, and muft otherways have gone without one. On your Account, Sir, I have been Treated by the Government at Bofton, and receiv'd no fmall Honours from 'em.

And fince in this Letter I defign to give you an Account of my Ramble to *Natick*, a Town of Converted Indians, I have made choice of you, (and hope you'll pardon the Prefumption,) to direct this Letter to. That I have not writ to you directly before, is not from any Neglect of the Duty I owe you, but becaufe I thought the Subjects I then wrote on, was too light for your more grave and Serious View.
But

But this, Leading me to say something of the Conversion of the Indians, I am very sure it will be acceptable to you as being what you have always labour'd for, and delighted in, I mean the Conversion of Souls: And if, in this relation of my Rambles you find me in any place too light and airy, I doubt not but your wonted Goodness will Pardon it. Upon which assurance (without any further Preface) I shall begin the Relation of my Rambles.

And since I am sure, Sir, that you desire to be informed concerning the Conversion of the Indians in this Countrey, I will give you here a True Account thereof in few Words: It is, (as I am informed,) about forty years since that the Great and Good Mr. Eliot, Pastor of the Church at Roxbury, (about a mile from Boston) even that Mr. Eliot whom I but just before mention'd, who has such a great Esteem and Value for your self, being warmed with a holy Zeal of Converting the Indians, set him self to learn the Indian Tongue, that so he might more easily and successfully open to them the Mysteries of the Gospel; upon account of which he has been (as I have already said, and that not undeservedly) called the Apostle of the American Indians.

This Reverend Person, not without very great Labour and Pains, Translated the Bible into the Indian Language; (Twelve of which he has presented me withal, Charging me to let you have one of them;) he has also Translated several English Treatises of Practical Divinity and Catechisms, into the Indian Tongue. And by the blessing of God upon his Indefatigable Labours, about Twenty six years ago he gathered a Church of Converted Indians, in a Town called *Natick*, being about Twenty miles distant from Boston; These Indians confessed their Sins with Tears, and professed their Faith in Christ, and afterwards they and their Children were Baptized, and they were solemnly joyned together in a Church-Covenant, and the said Mr. Eliot was the first that
administred

adminiſtred the Lord's Supper to them: Tho' afterwards there was ordained for them a Paſtor of their own.

In this Town of Natick, being the firſt formed Town of the Converted (or as they are called, Praying) Indians, there was appointed a General Lecture to be annually kept, and the Lecture to be preached, half in the Indian, and half in the Engliſh Tongue for the Benefit of all that did repair to it: To this Lecture (being kept in the Summer time) it is very uſuall for ſeveral of the Boſtonians (or Inhabitants of Boſton) to go; and I being acquainted with ſome that intended to go thither, and being (you know, Sir,) of a Rambling Fancy, and ſtill for making New Diſcoveries, as alſo becauſe I had a great deſire to be among the Indians, reſolv'd to take that opportunity, and go along with them. And communicating my Intentions to ſome particular Friends of mine here that were of the Fair Sex, (for ſuch I have, Sir, here, and yet without the being falſe to Iris, even in a thought,) they likewiſe did agree to go along with us: And I muſt now divert you, Sir, with a Relation of my Ramble to the Indian Town of Natick, and hope you'll pardon it, altho' it be a Digreſſion from what I principally aim at; and yet 'tis not ſo much a Ramble from it, but that it may be Introductory to it.

The Day of the Natick Lecture being come, and all things being ready for our Journey, I mounted on my ſteed with Madam Brick[126] (the flower of Boſton) behind me, accompanied with Mr. Green and his Wife, Mrs. Toy, the Damſel, Mr. Mallinſon, Mr. King, and Mr. Cook and Mrs. Middleton: With thirty or forty Perſons more unknown, who went on the ſame Errand as we did, *videlicet*, To hear the Natick Sermon preach'd to the converted Indians, as is the uſuall

[126] In his printed "Life and Errors" DUNTON was ungallant enough to write, "When we were ſetting forward, I was forc'd out of Civility and Gratitude, to take Madam Brick behind me on Horſe-Back: 'tis true ſhe was the Flower of Boſton, but in this Caſe, prov'd no more than a Beautiful ſort of Luggage to me."—ED.

ufuall Cuftom every year. Being thus equipp'd, Sir, and my Companions fuch as I have mention'd, (whofe Particular Characters I have given in my Letter to Mr. Larkin,) we fet forward for Natick, the Indian Town, we fet forward through many Woods whofe well-fpread-Branches made a pleafing fhade, and kept us from the Sun's too fcorching heat: Which made me fay to my fair Fellow-Traveller behind me, That we were much beholding to thofe woods for their refrefhing Shade which they afforded us: (of which we then were the more fenfible, becaufe we had but lately rid over fome open Commons.)

Madam Brick told me, that what I faid was very true; 'But,' added fhe, 'if thefe poor Woods afford us fuch a delightful fhade, O what a bleffed fhade is Jefus Chrift, who fkreens us from the Scorching Beams of Divine Wrath; and whom the Scripture reprefents, with refpect to his People, as the Shadow of a great Rock in a weary Land: To fignifie that Comfort and Refrefhing that true Believers find in him:' 'Madam,' faid I, 'you have fpoke true in what you've faid; and yet Chrift is reprefented as a Sun, as well as a Shade:' To this, Mrs. Toy, who rid by us, reply'd, 'He is indeed reprefented both as a Sun and as a Shade, and yet no contradiction: He is a Sun, fhining with the Warm Beams of Love and Grace, to cherifh and revive the Drooping Soul, and as a Shade for the Refrefhment of the Weary and the heavy laden.'

'You are right,' faid Mr. Green, who over-heard us, 'Chrift is fet forth in Scripture, under feveral Denominations, to reprefent to us, that fulnefs that is in him, and to fhew us that there is nothing we can want, but 'tis to be found in him.' 'And fuch a Saviour (faid his Wife) it is we ftand in need of, that is an All-fufficient Good, and adequate to all our wants.' 'And furely,' faid I, 'fuch a Saviour is only Jefus Chrift: He is the great Panpharmacon, who cures all our Difeafes, and fupplies all our Wants; if we want Riches,
he

he exhorts us to buy of him Gold try'd in the Fire; if we want cloathing, he has the only Garment of Salvation; if we are fick, he is the great Phyfician; if we are wounded, he is the Balm of Gilead; if we are hungry, he is the Bread of Life; and if we are thirfty, he can give us Living Waters: And when the Royal Pfalmift wou'd fum up all in a few words, he tells us, He is both a Sun and Shield, and will give Grace and Glory, and no good thing will he with-hold from them that walk uprightly.'

I had fcarce done fpeaking, when Mr. Cook rides up to me, and fays, 'I thought we had been going to Natick to hear a Sermon there:' 'Why fo we are,' faid I: 'Why then,' faid he, 'do you fore-ftall the Market, and make a fermon on the Road?' I told him 'twas no Sermon, but only a difcourfe that happen to be raif'd among us. 'If you'll difcourfe,' fays he, 'pray tell me how I may Court the Damfel, fo as to obtain her?' To this the Damfel anfwer'd, 'You need not be folicitous about your Courting me: I have already, I hope, given my heart to a more worthy Lover: Or, as Mr. Norris in his Mifcellany has it,

A Nobler, a Diviner Gueft,
Has took Poffeffion of my Breft:
He has and does ingrofs it all,
And yet the Room is much too fmall.'

'Well,' fays Mr. Cook, 'if this be all the Comfort you'll give me, I'll e'en Court Mrs. Middleton,' and fo rid on before to *Water-Town*; whither we all came prefently after, and where we alighted and refrefh't our Luggage. And while others were Engaged in Frothy Difcourfes, the Widow Brick and I took a View of the Town, which is built upon one of the Branches of Charles River, very fruitful, and of large extent; watered with many pleafant Springs, and fmall Rivulets: The Inhabitants live flatteringly. Within half a mile is a great Pond divided between the two Towns. A
mile

mile and a half from the Town is a great Fall of Frefh Waters, which convey themfelves into the Ocean through Charles River. 'Tis to this Town (as I'm told) that Mr. John Bayly (whofe Character I fent to my Friend Larkin) will be chofen Paftor. He has a great Efteem for you, and is a valuer of all your Writings, but efpecially of your Sermons of Communion with God.

Having well refrefh'd our felves at Water-Town, we mounted again, and from thence we Rambled through feverall Tall Woods between the Mountains, over many rich and pregnant Vallies as ever eye beheld, befet on each fide with variety of goodly Trees: So that had the moft Skilful Gardner defign'd a fhady Walk in a fine Valley, it wou'd have fallen fhort of that which Nature here had done without him; which is a clear Demonftration that Nature Exceeds Art, and that Art is but a weak and imperfect Imitator of Nature; which has far more Beauty in her Works, than Art can e'er pretend to: Art may (for inftance) delineate the Beauty of a Rofe, and make it very lovely to the Eye, but Nature only gives it Life and Fragrancy.

Whilft I was thus Communicating my Thoughts to Madam Brick that rid behind me: She reply'd, ' If the Productions of Nature are fo excellent, as this Lovely Profpect now before us fhews they are, how much more Excellent and glorious is the God of Nature, the Great Caufe of Caufes! Compar'd to whom all the Sweetnefs, Beauty, and Goodnefs of the Creature, is but as a drop to the Vaft Ocean: And without doubt the Excellency that's in the Creature, was defign'd to lead us to himfelf, as Springs to the Fountain :' The Damfel being by, Reply'd, ' 'Tis only then we make a right ufe of the Creature, when by them our Hearts are drawn forth to adore and magnifie the Great Creator: And therefore, David, having furvey'd the works of Creation, breaks forth into this Pathetical Admiration, How manifold are thy Works, O Lord! In wifdom haft thou made 'em all!'

As

As we rid along that lovely valley I have mention'd, Sir, we faw many lovely Lakes or Ponds, well ftored with Fifh and Beavers: Thefe, they tell me, are the original of all the great Rivers in the Countrey, of which there are many, befides leffer Streams, manifefting the Goodnefs of the Soil, which is in fome places black, in others red, with clay, Gravel, Sand and Loom, and very deep in fome places, as in the Valleys and Swamps, which are low grounds, and bottoms, infinitely thick fet with Trees and Bufhes of all forts; others having no other Shrubs or Trees growing but Spruce, under the Shades whereof we Rambled two or three miles together, being goodly large Trees, and convenient for Mafts and Sail-Yards.

While we were Rambling on under this pleafant Shade of Spruce-Trees, Mr. Cook, a wild young Gentleman, who carried one Mrs. Middleton behind him, (of whom more anon) came riding up to Mr. Green and I, who rid together, faying, 'Come, Gentlemen, methinks we make but a dull Ramble on't: Some of you tell a Story to pafs the time away.' 'Well,' (anfwer'd Mr. Green) 'to pleafure you I will: It is a ftory I was told by a very honeft Englifh Gentleman, who told it for a certain Truth, and faid He knew the Perfons who are the fubject of it: And perhaps fome of you may think it worth the Hearing: The Preface Mr. Green made to his Story, made all refolve with a profound Attention, to be his Auditours. Upon which he thus began:[127] *   *   *   *   *   *   *   *   *   *   *
*   *   *   *   *   *   *   *   *   *   *   *

[We[128] had about Twenty Miles to Natick, where the beft
Accomodations

---

[127] To our profound regret the manu-fcript is here defective, and only a very fmall portion of a ftory about John Bunyan remains. As DUNTON had written part of another ftory to go in this place, it is not uncharitable to imagine that Mr. Green did not narrate a ftory at this particular juncture.—ED.

[128] Although the manufcript is here defective, we are enabled to fupply the miffing paffage from "Life and Errors," as enough remains to fhow the connection.

Accomodations we cou'd meet with, were very courſe. We ty'd up our Horſes in two old Barns, that were almoſt laid in Ruines; however, we cou'd diſcern where they had ſtood formerly. But there was no place where we cou'd beſtow our ſelves, unleſs, upon the Greenſwerd, till the Lecture began.

The Wigwams or Indian Houſes are no more than ſo many Tents, and their way of Building 'em is this: They firſt take long Poles, and make 'em faſt in the ground, and then cover them with Mats on the out-ſide, which they tye to the Poles. Their Fire-place is made in the Middle, and they leave a little Hole upon the Top uncover'd with the Mats, which ſerves for a Chimney. Their Doors are uſually two, and made oppoſite to each other, which they open or ſhut according as the Wind Sits, and theſe are either made of Mats, or of the Barks of Trees. While we were making ſuch Diſcoveries as theſe, we were inform'd that the *Sachim*, or the Indian King, and his Queen, were there. The place, 'tis true, did not look like the Royal Reſidence; however we cou'd eaſily believe the Report, and went immediately to viſit their King and Queen; and here my Courage did not fail as when I wanted my Ruffles,[129] for I ſtept up and kiſſ'd the Indian Queen; making her two very low Bows, which ſhe return'd very civilly. The Sachim was very tall and well limb'd, but had no Beard, and a ſort of a Horſe Face.

The Queen was well ſhap'd, and her Features might paſs pretty well, ſhe had Eyes as black as Jet, and Teeth as white as Ivory; her Hair was very black and long, and ſhe was conſiderably up in Years; her Dreſs peculiar, ſhe had Sleeves of Mooſe-Skin, very finely dreſſ'd, and drawn with Lines of various Colours, in Aſiatick Work, and her Buſkins were

of

tion. In all probability, in this inſtance as in a preceding one, DUNTON took part of his manuſcript for his printed book. The variations are ſlight, and due probably to his own reviſion.—ED.

[129]The matter of his Ruffles has already been explained at p. 30.—ED.

of the fame fort; her Mantle was of fine blew cloath, but very fhort, and ty'd about her Shoulders, and at the Middle with a Zone, curioufly wrought with White and Blew Beads into pretty Figures: her Bracelets and her Necklace were of the fame fort of Beads, and fhe had a little Tablet upon her Breaft, very finely deck'd with Jewels and Precious Stones; her Hair was comb'd back and ty'd up with a Border, which was neatly work'd both with Gold and Silver.]

Having given you, Sir, this account of the King and Queen, it is neceffary that I may fay fomething about their Government. Their Government is altogether Monarchical; and as for thofe Princes whofe Dominions extend further than the Princes Perfonal Guidance will well admit, it is committed into the hands of Vice-Roys, or Lieutenants, who govern with no lefs abfolutenefs than the Princes himfelf: Nothwithftanding, in matters of difficulty, the Prince confults with his Nobles, and fuch whom he Efteems for Wifdom, In which, its wonderful to fee the Majeftick Deportment of the Prince, his fpeech to his Council, and the Grave and Deliberate Difcuffion of any matters that are propof'd for their Advice: After which, what is refolved on by the Prince, or Sachim, is prefently applauded by all, and afterwards Executed with all readinefs.

The Crown (or Government) always defcends to the Eldeft Son, (unlefs in cafe of Ufurpation, which fometimes happens) and not to the Daughter, or any Female, unlefs the Male Line be extinct: For the Indians [have] fuch an high Efteem for the Royal Blood, that if a Prince had iffue by feveral Wives, he fhall fucceed as Heir, who is Royally defcended by the Mother, altho' he be the youngeft: For they look upon his Iffue by a Venter of leffer Quality as not much better than a Nobleman.

Befides their Subjection to the higheft Sachim, to whom they carry Prefents, they have alfo particular Protectors under the Sachim, to whom they carry Prefents likewife;
and

and upon any injury received, and Complaint made, thefe Protectors will revenge it.

Their Nobles are fuch who are defcended from the Blood Royal, or fuch whom the Prince beftows part of his Dominions, with the Royalties thereof, upon: Or elfe fuch whofe Defcent has been from Noblemen, who have been Efteemed fuch, time out of mind.

Their Commons, or Yeomen, are fuch who have no ftamp of Gentility, and yet are efteemed, as having a Natural Right of living within their Princes Dominion, and a Common ufe of the Land, and are diftinguifhed by two Names or Titles, the one fignifying Subjection; the other, Tiller of the Land.

There are alfo another fort of People below thefe; who are defcended from fuch Strangers or Foreigners as heretofore came among them: For tho' the Indians know no Letters, and by confequence can have nothing of Records, yet they have a Tradition from Father to Son, that thefe are the Defcendents of Strangers, and that they are not Priviledged with common Right; but are fubject to the Commons, and are not allow'd to attend the Prince in Hunting, unlefs invited fo to do by the favour of their Prince.

The Indian Princes have no other Revenue than the Prefents brought them by their Subjects; which Prefents are not look'd on as a Kindnefs or Courtefie, but as a due Debt; alfo the Wrecks of the Sea, and the Skins of all Beafts kill'd in the Water, are a Royalty belonging to their Dominions: And this is as much as they need, for in cafe they make War, both People and Eftate are wholly at the Princes Difpofal, and therefore none either demand or expect any Pay. And tho' their Courts are not like thofe of the European Princes, yet is there a fort of Magnificence in it, with refpect to the difference that is between them and their fubjects, which is all that any other Princes with all their Grandeur can boaft of: For their Families and Attend-
ants

ants are well cloathed with the Skins of Moos, Deer, Bear, Beaver, and the like: The Provifions for their Tables are alfo large, as Flefh, Fifh, Roots, Fruits, Berries, Corn and Beans, and all thefe in great Plenty and Variety is always brought by their Neighbouring Subjects; So that thefe Indian Kings live as free from Care, as the greateft Princes in the World.

But tho' thefe Princes Exercife an Abfolute Authority over the People, yet will they not conclude of Laws, Subfidies, or Wars, without their confent; tho' it be not eafily gain'd, for the People are generally averfe to it, and are brought to confent with much perfwafion.

The moft ufual Cuftom amongft them in Executing Punifhments, is for the Sachim to beat, or whip, or put to death with his own hand; to which the common fort moft quietly fubmit: Tho' fometimes the Sachim fends a Secret Executioner, which is one of his Chiefeft Warriors, to fetch off a Head, by Some unexpected blow of a Hatchet, when they have feared a Mutiny by a Publick Execution.

This, Sir, is all that I can fay, as to the Government of the Heathen Indians: As to that of the Converted Indians I fhall give you an Account anon, when I come to fpeak more of their Converfion.

After we had been Entertain'd by the King and Queen, and left them, We were told the meeting was near beginning: Upon which Notice we went to the Meeting, where Mr. Gookins preached upon this Text. *It is appointed unto Men once to dye, and after that, the Judgment:* From which Text he infifted on the certainty of Death, as a Divine Appointment, from which there cou'd be no Efcaping: And that therefore it was the duty of all to prepare for that, which cou'd no way be avoided; and that this fhou'd be done with fo much the greater diligence, becaufe Death is but a Prologue to Enfuing Judgment; and there wou'd be no ftanding in the Judgment without a folemn Preparation

for

for Death: And then fhew'd what this Preparation for Death muft be and wherein it doth confift, which is, in getting an Intereft in Chrift by Faith, and true Repentance; and then in his Application exhorting all Perfons fpeedily to fet about this Preparation for Death, leaft Death fhou'd come upon 'em unawares, When they are not prepar'd, fhewing them the Dreadful Confequence of Dying unprepar'd. And laftly the bleffed condition that thofe were in who were prepar'd for Death whenever it came.

The poor Indians appear'd to me to fit under the Word with great Serioufnefs and Attention, and many of them feem'd very much affected under it.

I remember, Sir, I promif'd at the beginning of my Letter to give you fome account of the Converfion of the Indians; and I will now be as good as my word; But the Account[130] I fhall give you, is what I have received from other hands, becaufe it is of things tranfacted before my coming hither: But I have receiv'd them from fuch undoubted hands, as leaves me no room to queftion the Truth of 'em.

Here, Sir, it will not be amifs to let you know, that the way of living among the unconverted Indians is extreamly barbarous, the Men being moft abominably flothful, and making their poor *Squaws* (for fo they call their wives) do all their Drudgery, and Labour in the Field as well as at Home, planting and dreffing their Corn, and building alfo their Wigwams, (or Houfes) for them. While the Men in the mean time walk about, and take their pleafure; and if they'll condefcend to any Bufinefs, it is that of Hunting; and then they'll go out fome fcores, if not hundreds of them, in a Company, and drive all before them. They continue in a place till they have burnt up all the Wood thereabouts, and then remove their Wigwams, and follow that

therefore

---

[130] This account is from COTTON MATHER's Life of Eliot.—ED.

Wood which they cann't fetch home to themfelves: And therefore thinking all others like themfelves, They fay the Englifh came hither becaufe they wanted firing. They have no knowledge of Arts and Sciences, nor are they underftood amongft them, unlefs juft fo far as to maintain their bruitifh Converfation; which is little more than is to be found among the very Bruits themfelves.

Their divifion of Time is by Sleeps, and Moons, and Winters; and by their lying abroad, they have fomewhat obferved the motion of the Stars: They have very little (if any) Traditions among them worthy of our notice; and Reading and Writing is altogether unknown to them; and yet there is a Rock or two in the Countrey that has unaccountable Characters Engrav'd upon it. The Sum of their Religion is, They believe there are many Gods who made and own the feveral Nations of the World, of which a certain Great God in the South-Weft Regions of Heaven bears the greateft Figure, and commands in Chief.

When they have any great thing to do, they have their folemn affemblies, where after the Ufage of fome Diabolical Rites, the Devil appears to 'em, to inform 'em and advife 'em about their Circumftances; and fometimes there are very odd Events of their making thefe Applications to the Devil; As an Inftance whereof, I have been told, That the Indians in their Wars with the Englifh, being fenfible of a great Inconvenience they fuftained by the Englifhmens Dogs, which wou'd make a fad yelling in the night, when they fcented the Approach of the Indians, they took a Dog and facrific'd him to the Devil: and it was obferved, that after this, no Englifh Dog would bark at an Indian, for feveral months enfuing. This, Sir, was that miferable People that Mr. Eliot propounded to himfelf the faving of! In which he had a double work upon his hands: Firft to make them Men, and then to make them Chriftians: They muft firft be civiliz'd, ere he cou'd hope to make them Saints.

I

I remember, Sir, that I have read that Gregory,[131] Bishop of Rome, seeing some Children of the English Saxons exposed to Sale in the City of Rome, enquired of what Countrey they were, and being told *de Anglis*, he said it was pity that such beautiful Children, whose Countenances were like Angels, shou'd be subjects of the Prince of Darkness; and asking farther of what Province there, was answer'd, *Deira;* ' Then,' said he, ' I will Endeavour that such Angelical Countenances shall be no longer the objects de ira Dei;' and accordingly sent over Austin the Monk to convert the Pagan Saxons.

But Holy Mr. Eliot cou'd see nothing Angelical among these Indians to bespeak his Labour for their Eternal Welfare, for all among them was Diabolical. To think of raising a Number of these hideous Creatures to the Elevations of the Religion of the blessed Jesus, was an Argument of a mighty Faith in the Undertaker, and such was the Faith of Mr. Eliot. You know, Sir, what insuperable Difficulties in the Eye of Reason, you yourself have overcome by Faith, in the Great things you have done in England for the Conversion of Souls (which has so deservedly gain'd you a Universal Esteem among good Men of all Perswasions) and therefore ean the better Judge of this.

I have already told you with what indefatigable Labour and Industry Mr. Eliot apply'd himself to learn their Language, and that he attain'd it to so great a Perfection that he Translated the Bible into it, which considering the Uncouthness of their Language, and the length of their words, was an almost insurmountable Labour: But as he himself writes at the close of his Grammar, *Prayers and Pains through Faith in Christ Jesus, will do anything.* I have also already given you an Account of his Preaching to the Indians, and gathering this Church of Converted Indians at Natick, and
of

---

[131] DUNTON has here enlarged upon MATHER'S reference to Pope Gregory. —ED.

of his Settling of them in a Church-State, according to the Order of the Gospel. Of whom I have this further to say, That as soon as they had felt the Impreffions of his Miniftry, they were quickly diftinguifhed by the Name of Praying Indians; and being Converted, they were quickly for a more decent and Englifh way of Living. For whereas before, they went according to the Cuftom of the Indians, they were now for putting on an Englifh Garb: And here, Sir, I think it will be no digreffion to give you a brief account of the Indians way of Cloathing themfelves.

Their[132] Ordinary Cloathing is a Beafts Skin, or an Englifh Mantle, which only covers their hinder parts, and all their fore-parts from top to Toe, (except their fecret parts, which are covered with a little Apron, after the Pattern of our firft Parents) are open and naked. Their male children go ftark naked, and have no Apron, until they come to Ten or Twelve years of Age; the Females they are fo modeft as to cover with a little Apron of a hands breadth, from their very birth. But their Men often abroad, and both Men and Women in the Houfe, leave off their Beafts Skin, or Englifh Cloth, and fo, (Excepting their little Apron) are wholly naked; yet there is but few of the Women but will keep their Skin or Cloth (tho' loofe) near them, and ready to gather it up about them. Cuftom hath ufed their Minds and Bodies to it, nor does it excite any kind of Wantonnefs in them.

Their coats are made of divers forts of Skins, whence they have their Deer-Skin-Coats, their Beaver-Coats, their Otter-Coats, their Rakoon-Skin-Coats, their Wolves-Skin-Coats, and their Squirrel-Skin-Coats; they have alfo a Coat or Mantle curioufly made of the fineft and faireft feathers of their Turkies, which their old Men make, and is with them as velvet is with us, in Efteem. Within this Coat or

Skin

---

[132] Dunton here reverts to **Williams'** Key, p. 203–205.—Ed.

Skin they creep very contentedly, by day. or night, in the
Houfe or in the Woods; and fleep foundly too, counting it
a great happinefs that every Man is content with his fkin.
They alfo make Shoes and Stockins of their Deer-Skin,
which they tan very well, and is excellent for travel in wet
and Snow; and is fo well tempered with Oyl, that the
Water clean-wrings out; and being hang'd up in their
Chimney they prefently dry without hurt. They have
alfo the Skin of a great Beaft call'd a Moofe, as big as an
Ox, which fome call a red Deer, which they commonly paint
for their Summer Wearing, with variety of Forms and
colours.

They have always a Tobacco-Bag which hangs at their
necks, or fticks at their Girdle, which is to them inftead of
an Englifh Pocket. Our Englifh cloaths are fo ftrange to
them, and their Bodies fo inured to indure the Weather,
that when fome of 'em have had Englifh cloaths, yet in a
fhower of Rain they will rather expofe their fkins than their
Cloaths, and therefore pull their Cloaths off to keep 'em
dry. Several of them whilft they are amongft the Englifh
will keep on Englifh Apparel, but as foon as they come into
their own Houfes and Company, pull off all again.

Having thus, Sir, given you an account of the Indians
Nakednefs and Cloathing, I[133] will now proceed to fay fomewhat more of the converted Indians at Natick, who upon
their being converted, were for conforming themfelves in
their Apparel according to the Cuftom of the Englifh, and
alfo for a more fixed cohabitation: And accordingly in the
year 1652, thofe that before had lived like the Wild Beafts
of the Wildernefs, now compacted themfelves into a Town,
and then firft apply'd themfelves to the forming of their
Civil Government: The General Court for Maffachufetts
Colony at Bofton, (notwithftanding they were always careful
                                                        to

[133] This account is in MATHER's Life   Increafe Mather to Dr. John Leufden,
of Eliot, in the notes to a Letter from   of Utrecht.—ED.

29

to keep thefe Indians fenfible of their fubjection to the Englifh Empire) yet had allowed them their fmaller Courts,
wherein they might govern their own fmaller Cafes and
Concerns after their own particular modes, and might have
their Town orders peculiar to themfelves.

With refpect Whereto, Mr. Eliot on a Solemn Faft made
a Publick Vow, That feeing thefe Indians were not pre-
poffeffed with any Forms of Government, he wou'd inftruct
them into fuch a Form as we had written in the Word of
God, that fo they might be a People in all things ruled by
the Lord. And according he expounded to them the 18th
Chapter of Exodus; and then they chofe Rulers of Hundreds, of Fifties, and of Tens: And there with-all, entered
into the following Covenant: 'We are the Sons of Adam;
We and our Fore-fathers have a long time been loft in our
fins; but now the Mercy of the Lord beginneth to find us
out again; therefore the Grace of Chrift helping us, we do
give our Selves and our Children unto God, to be his People; He fhall Rule us in all our affairs: The Lord is our
Judge, the Lord is our Law-giver, the Lord is our King;
He will fave us; and the Wifdom which God has taught us
in his Book fhall guide us. O Jehovah! Teach us Wifdom,
fend thy Spirit into our Hearts, take us to be thy People,
and let us take Thee to be our God.'

Mr. Eliot has fuch an Opinion about the Perfection of
the Scriptures, that upon this Occafion he expreff'd him
felf thus: "God will bring Nations into diftrefs and Per-
plexity, that fo they may be forced unto the Scripture; all
Governments will be fhaken, that men may be forced at
length to pitch upon that firm Foundation, the Word of
God."

The little Towns of thefe Indians being pitched upon
this Foundation, they utterly abandoned that Polygamy
which had before been common among them: They made
fevere Laws againft Fornication, Drunkennefs, and Sabbath-
breaking,

breaking, and other Immoralities, which they began to lament, and mourn over, after the Eftablifhment of a Church Order among them, and after the feveral Ordinances and Priviledges of a Church-Communion: Which before they were inftated in, a Day was fet apart which they called, A Day of Afking of Queftions, when the Minifters of the adjacent churches, affifted with all the beft Interpreters that cou'd be had, publickly examined a good number of thefe Indians about their Attainments both in Knowledge and Vertue: And after great Satisfaction there received, the Indians were afterwards called to make open Confeffion of their Faith in GOD and Chrift, and of the Efficacy which the Word had upon them for their Converfion to GOD; which Confeffion being taken from their Mouths by able Interpreters, were infpected by the People of GOD, and found much Acceptance with them, which I cannot better relate, than by reciting the Words of the Reverend Mr. Richard Mather, in an Epiftle of his publifhed on this Occafion: His Words are thefe:

" There is fo much of GOD's work among them, as that I cannot but count it a great evil, yea, a great Injury to GOD and his Goodnefs, for any to make light of it. To fee and hear Indians open their Mouths, and lifting up their hands and Eyes in Prayer to the Living GOD, and calling on him by his Name Jehovah, in the Mediation of Jefus Chrift, and this for a good while together; to fee and hear them exhorting one another, from the Word of GOD; to fee and hear them confeffing the name of Chrift Jefus, and their own Sinfulnefs; fure this is more than ufual: And tho' they fpoke in a Language of which many of us underftood but little, yet we that were prefent that Day, we faw and heard them perform the Duties mentioned with fuch grave and fober Countenances, with fuch comely reverence in their gefture, and their whole Carriage, and with fuch plenty of Tears trickling down the Cheeks of fome of them, as did

argue

argue to us, that they fpake with the holy Fear of God; and it much affected our hearts."

At length (as I have mention'd at the beginning) a Church-State was fettled among them; and they entred (as all the Churches in New-England do) into a holy Covenant; wherein they gave themfelves firft unto the Lord, and then unto one another, to attend the Rules and helps, and expect the Bleffings of the Everlafting Gofpel: And holy Mr. Eliot having a Miffion from the Church of Roxbury unto the Work of the Lord Jesus Christ among the Indians, thought himfelf fufficiently authorized unto the performing of all Church-Work about them, and accordingly adminiftred firft the Ordinance of Baptifm, and then the Lord's Supper, unto them.

Thus, Sir, I have given you an Account of the Converfion and Settling of the Church of Natick, through the Bleffing and Power of God, accompanying the Unwearied Labours of Mr. Eliot: between whom and your felf, Sir, there feems to be a great harmony and agreement of Spirit, both in the breathing of your Souls after the Converfion of Sinners, and the Labour and pains you have taken to bring that bleffed Work about.

The Providence of God having placed Mr. Eliot in New-England, his Work lay among the poor Heathen; who tho' Captives to the Devil, yet had not receiv'd or entertain'd any Prejudice againft the Word of God; and his Bufinefs was to perfwade 'em to become Chriftians; but in this, Sir, you had the harder Tafk; for your Province lay in per-fwading Unbelievers, (who thought themfelves Chriftians,) that they were not fo, that thereby you might make 'em fuch; and fure it was a different Work to perfwade thofe Men and Women that they were no Chriftians, that had all along boafted of their Chriftianity; tho' at the fame time as far from being true Believers, as the very Indians: And that Grace that accompanied Mr. Eliot in the Converfion of

them,

them, was not wanting to give Succefs to your Miniftry, in a thorow Converfion of thefe, as Cliff in Kent can witnefs, who tho' fo prejudic'd againft you at Your firft coming thither, as to rife againft you with Spits, and Forks, and even threatening you with Death it felf, yet by the fuccefs · GOD gave to your Miniftry among them, they wou'd afterwards have laid down their lives for you, as appear'd by their loud Cries and Many Fears, when you judg'd your felf obliged to remove from them. The oppofition in your Work, Sir, which you met withal at Cliff, obliges me to give you fome account of the Oppofition that holy Mr. Eliot found in the Converting of the Indians.

The[134] Devil faw his Kingdom was a going down, and his Captives like to be refcu'd from him, and this fill'd him with rage, fo that he ftirr'd up feveral of the Sachims, or Princes of the Indians, againft him; who generally did all they cou'd that their Subjects might not entertain the Gofpel; and the Devil having their Princes on his fide, thereby kept poffeffion of the People too: And the *Pauwaws*, or Devil's Priefts, did all they cou'd to maintain the Intereft of the Devil in this Wildernefs: They were thofe Children of the Devil, and Enemies of all Righteoufnefs, who did not ceafe to pervert the right ways of the Lord. And their Sachims wou'd prefently raife a Storm of Perfecution on any of their Vaffals that fhou'd pray to the Eternal GOD.

And the Reafon of this averfenefs of the Sachims againft the Gofpel, was, That they were afraid it would deprive them of that Tyranny, which they had always Exercifed over their Vaffals: For like the Devil whom they worfhip'd, they held their People in an abfolute Servitude, and rul'd by no Law but their own Will, which left them poor Selves nothing which they cou'd call their own. And now they fufpected that Religion wou'd put a Bridle upon their Ufur-
pations,

---

[134] We are again favored with extracts from Mather, very flightly modified.—
ED.

pations, and oblige 'em to a more equal way of Government: They therefore had the Impudence to addrefs the Englifh, That no motions about the Chriftian Religion might ever be made to 'em.

But Mr. Eliot, tho' fometimes in the Wildernefs without the Company or Affiftance of any other Englifhmen, and has been Treated in a very Threatning and Barbarous manner by fome of thefe Tyrants, has yet been infpir'd with fo much Refolution, as to tell 'em, " I am about the **Great Work of God**, and my **God** is with me, fo that I neither fear you, nor all the Sachims in the Countrey; I'll go on, and do you touch me if you dare": Upon which, the ftouteft of them have fhrunk, and fell before him: And one of them he at length conquer'd by Preaching unto him a Sermon upon the Temptations of our Lord, particularly, the **Temptations** fetch'd from the Kingdoms and Glories of the World.

The Averfation that was in the Great Men among the Indians, was a powerful Obftacle, as I have faid, to the Succefs of Mr. Eliot's Miniftry: But it is very remarkable that feveral of thofe Nations that thus refufed the **Gofpel**, were quickly afterwards fo infatuated as to begin an Unjuft and bloody War upon the Englifh, which iffued in their utter Extirpation. And it has been particularly remark'd in *Philip*, the King-Leader of the moft calamitous War that ever the Indians made upon the Englifh, That Mr. Eliot. made a Tender of the Gofpel to him; but that haughty King refuf'd it with Contempt and Anger; and then taking hold of a Button upon the Coat of the Good Man, told him, ' That he car'd for his Gofpel juft as much as he car'd for that Button.'

But he quickly found the fatal confequence of thus defpifing and refufing the Gofpel: For[135] having cauflefly
broken

---

[135] In the *Magnalia* (Life of Eliot) Mather writes at this point, " It was not long before the hand which now writes, upon a certain occafion, took off the jaw from the expofed fkull of that blafphemous leviathan."—Ed.

broken his League with the Englifh, and plotted a general Infurrection in all the Englifh Colonies, killing, burning, and deftroying the Englifh with the greateft Barbarities imaginable, Divine Vengeance purfued him to that degree, that after the lofs of his Treafure, and of his Wife and Son, whom he was forc'd to leave Prifoners to fave his own Life, and having been hunted like a Savage Beaft through the Woods, for above an hundred miles to and fro, he was at laft forc'd to take Sanctuary upon his own Den at *Mount-Hope*, from whence endeavouring to efcape, he was fhot through the Heart by an Indian of his own Nation; and that Eminent Minifter, Mr. Samuel Lee, is now Paftor to an Englifh Congregation, and founding forth the Praifes of GOD, upon that very fpot of Ground where Philip and his Indians were lately worfhipping the Devil.

Sometimes a more immediate hand of GOD appear'd, making way for Mr. Eliot's Miniftry, by cutting off the Principal Oppofers of the Gofpel among the Indians. Mr. Eliot himfelf relates, that an Affociation of Prophane Indians near Weymouth, in this Countrey, fetting themfelves to feduce the Neighbour Indians from the right ways of the Lord, GOD fent the Small Pox among them, which like a great Plague foon fwept them away, and thereby engaged the reft unto himfelf.

Tho' I am afraid, Sir, that I grieve you by the length of this Relation, yet I muft beg your Patience, whilft I further relate one Attempt made by the Devil to prejudice the Indians againft the Gofpel, which had fomething in it very extraordinary: The Account I had of it is this: While Mr. Eliot was preaching the Gofpel to the other Indians, a Demon appear'd to a Prince of the Eaftern Indians, in a fhape that Refembled Mr. Eliot, or of an Englifh Minifter, pretending to be the Englifh Mans GOD; The Spectre commanded him to forbear the Drinking of Rum, and to obferve the Sabbath Day, and to deal juftly with his Neighbours

bours (all which things had been inculcated in Mr. Eliot's
Miniftry) promifing therewithal unto him, That if he did fo,
at his Death his Soul fhou'd afcend unto a happy place;
otherwife defcend unto mifery; but the Apparition all this
while never faid one word about Chrift, which was the main
Subject of Mr. Eliot's Miniftry.

The Sachim received fuch an Impreffion from the Apparition, that he dealt juftly with all men, (except in the bloody
Tragedies and Cruelties that he afterwards commit on
the Englifh in the Wars;) he kept the Sabbath-day like a
Faft, frequently attending in the Chriftian Congregations; he
wou'd not meddle with any Rum, tho' ufually his Countrey-
men had rather dye than undergo fuch a piece of Self-
Denial; that Liquor has neerly enchanted them. At laft
(and not long fince) this Demon appear'd again unto this
Pagan, requiring him to kill himfelf, and affuring him that
he fhou'd revive in a Day or two, never to dye any more.
He thereupon divers times attempted it, but was ftill prevented by his Friends: But it feems at length, he found a
fair Opportunity for this foul Bufinefs, and hang'd himfelf;
but was deceiv'd in his promif'd Refurrection. But by this
means a ftumbling-block was laid before the miferable
Indians.

Befides the Church of Converted Indians at Natick, there
are in the Maffachufets Colony, four Indian Affemblies,
where the name of the True God and Jefus Chrift, are
folemnly called upon; thefe Affemblies have fome American
Preachers: Mr. Eliot formerly ufed to preach to them once
every fortnight, but now he is fo weakened with Labour and
Old Age, being in the Eighty-third year of his Age, that he
preaches to them but once in two months. There is alfo
another Church of Converted Indians about fifty miles from
hence, called *Mafhippaug;* the firft Paftor of the Church
was an Englifh-Man, who being fkilled in the American
Language Preached the Gofpel to them in their own Tongue:
This

This Englifh Paftor is now dead, and that Church has an Indian Preacher in his ftead.

There are befides that, five Affemblies of Indians Profeffing the Name of Chrift, not far diftant from Mafhipaug, which have Indian Preachers: Mr. John Cotton, Paftor of the Church in Ply[mouth] hath made very great Progrefs in Learning the Indian Tongue, and is very Skilful in it; and preaches in their own Language to the five laft mentioned Congregations every week. Alfo in *Saconct*, in Plymouth Colony, there is a great Congregation of Praying Indians. In fhort, Sir, there are Six Churches of Baptized Indians in New-England, and Eighteen Affemblies of Catechumens Profeffing the Name of Chrift; and of the Indians there are four and twenty who are Preachers of the Word of God: And befides thefe, there are four Englifh Minifters who preach the Gofpel in the Indian Tongue. So greatly has the Word of God prevailed among them.

And now, Sir, that you may fee fomething of the Spirits and Tempers of thefe Converted Indians, and the Effect that the Gofpel has had upon them, I will infert the Dying Speeches of feveral of them, which were given me by Mr. Eliot's own hand, and Publifhed[136] by himfelf; and I am confident (fo much you long after their Converfion) that you will not think your time loft in reading them.

I fhall firft prefix Mr. Eliot's Preface, when he Publifhed them, which begins thus:

'Here be but a few of the Dying Speeches and Counfels of fuch Indians as died in the Lord. It is an humbling to me that there be no more: It was not in my Heart to gather them, but Major Gookins hearing fome of them rehearfed, he firft moved that Daniel fhould gather them in the Language as they were fpoken, and that I fhould Tranflate them into Englifh; and here is prefented what was done that way: Thefe things are Printed, not fo much for Publifhment, as

to

---

[136] We have not feen the original edition, which muft be very rare.—ED.

to fave charge of writing out of Copies for thofe that did
defire them.   JOHN ELIOT.'

1. *Waban* was the firft that received the Gofpel; our firft
Meeting was at his Houfe; the next time we met, he had
gathered a great Company of his Friends, to hear the Word,
in which he had been ftedfaft: When we framed ourfelves
in order, in way of Government, he was chofen a Ruler of
Fifty; he hath approved himfelf to be a good Chriftian in
Church Order, and in Civil Order he hath approved himfelf
to be a Zealous, Faithful, and Stedfaft Ruler to his Death.
His Speech is as followeth.

' I now rejoyce, tho' I be now a dying; great is my Affliction in this World; but I hope that GOD doth fo afflict me,
only to try my praying to GOD in this World, whether it be
true and ftrong, or not; but I hope GOD doth gently call me
to Repentance, and to prepare to come unto him; therefore
he layeth on me great Pain and Affliction. Tho' my Body
be almoft broken by Sicknefs, yet I defire to remember thy
Name, O my GOD, until I dye: I remember thofe Words,
Job xix. 23 to 28. Oh that my Words were now written !
Oh that they were Printed in a Book; that they were
Engraven with an Iron Pen, and Lead, in a Rock for ever !
For I know that my Redeemer liveth, and that he fhall ftand
at the latter Day upon the Earth: and tho' after my Skin,
Worms deftroy this Body, yet in my Flefh I fhall fee GOD,
&c. I defire not to be troubled about matters of this world;
a little I am troubled; I defire you all, my Brethren, and
you my Children, do not greatly weep and mourn for me
in this World; I am now almoft dying, but fee that you
ftrongly pray to GOD; and do you alfo prepare and make
ready to dye, for every one of you muft come to dying:
Therefore confefs your Sins, every one of you, and believe
in Jefus Chrift. I believe that which is written in the Book
of GOD. Confider truly, and repent and believe: Then GOD
                                                      will

will pardon all your great and many fins. GOD can Pardon all your Sins as eafily as one; for GOD's free mercy and Grace do fill all the World. GOD will in no wife forget thofe that in this World do fincerely repent and believe: Verily this is Love, Oh my GOD! Therefore I defire that GOD will do this for me, tho' in my Body I am full of Pain.

· As for thofe that dyed before we prayed to GOD, I have no hope about them. Now I believe that GOD hath called us for Heaven, and there in Heaven are many Believing Souls abiding: Therefore I pray you, do not over-much grieve for me, when I dye in this World, but make yourfelves ready to dye and follow me, and there we fhall fee Each other in Eternal Glory; in this World we live but a little while; therefore we muft be always preparing, that we may be ready to dye. Therefore, Oh my GOD! I humbly pray, receive my Soul, by thy Free Mercy in Jefus Chrift, my Saviour and Redeemer; for Chrift hath dyed for me, and for all my Sins in this World committed. My great GOD hath given me long life, and therefore I am willing to dye. O Jefus Chrift help my Soul, and fave my Soul; I believe that my Sicknefs doth not arife out of the duft, nor cometh at peradventure, but GOD fendeth it, *Job* v. 6, 7. By this Sicknefs GOD calleth me to repent of all my Sins, and to believe in Chrift; now I confefs myfelf a great Sinner; Oh! Pardon me, and help me for Chrift his fake.

' Lord, Thou calleft me with a double calling: Sometimes by Profperity and Mercy, fometimes by Affliction. And now thou calleft me by Sicknefs; but let me not forget thee, O my GOD! for thofe that forget thy Name, thou wilt forfake them: As, *Pfal.* ix. 17. All that forget GOD fhall be caft into Hel; therefore let me not forget thee, O my GOD. I give my Soul to thee, O my Redeemer, Jefus Chrift: Pardon all my Sins, and deliver me from Hell: O do thou help me againft Death, and then I am willing to dye; and

when

when I dye, O help me and receive me.' In fo faying he dyed.

2. *Piambohou*: He was the fecond Man, next *Waban*, that received the Gofpel: He brought with him to the fecond Meeting at Waban's Houfe, many; when we formed them into Government, he was chofen Ruler of Ten; when the Church at *Haffenameffit* was gather'd, he was called to be a Ruler there in that Church; when that was fcatter'd by the War, they came back to Natick Church, fo many as furvived, and at Natick he died.   His Speech as followeth:

'I rejoyce, and am content and willing to take up my Sorrows and Sicknefs; many are the years of my Life; long have I lived, therefore now I look to dye: But I defire to prepare my felf to dye well.   I believe God's Promife, that he will for ever fave all that believe in Jefus Chrift.   O Lord Jefus help me! Deliver me, and fave my Soul from Hell, by thine own Blood, which thou haft fhed for me, when thou didft dye for me, and for all my Sins: Now help me fincerely to confefs all my Sins: O Pardon all my Sins! I now beg in the Name of Jefus Chrift, a Pardon for all my Sins; for thou, O Chrift, art my Redeemer and Deliverer: Now I hear God's Word, and I do rejoyce in what I hear; tho' I do not fee, yet I hear and rejoyce, that God hath confirmed for us a Minifter in this Church of Natick, he is our Watchman.   And all you People dwell with him, both Men, Women, and Children; hear him every Sabbath-Day, and make ftrong your Praying to God; and all you of *Haffaunemefue*, reftore your Church, and Praying to God there. O Lord, help to make me ready to dye, and then receive my Soul: I hope I fhall dye well, by the help of Jefus Chrift: O Jefus Chrift, deliver and fave my Soul in Everlafting Life in Heaven, for I do hope thou art my Saviour, O Jefus Chrift.'   So he dyed.

3. *Old Jacob*: He was among the firft that pray'd to God; he had fo good a Memory, that he cou'd rehearfe the
whole

whole Catechize, both Queſtions and Anſwers: When he gave thanks at Meat, he wou'd ſometimes only pray the Lord's Prayer. His Speech is as followeth:

' My Brethren, now hear me a few Words: Stand faſt, all you People, in your Praying to GOD, according to that Word of GOD. 1 *Cor.* xvi. 13. Watch ye, ſtand faſt in the Faith; quit you like Men, and be ſtrong in the Lord. Eſpecially you that are Rulers and Teachers: Fear not the Face of Man, when you Judge in a Court together; help one another, agree together: Be not divided one againſt another: Remember the Parable of Ten Brethren that held together; they cou'd not be broken, nor Overcome; but when they divided one againſt another, then they were eaſily overcome.

' And all you that are Rulers, Judge Right Judgment; for you do not Judge for Men, but for GOD, in your Courts. 2 *Chron.* xix. 6, 7. Therefore, Judge in the Fear of GOD. Again, you that are Judges, ſee that ye have not only Humane Wiſdom, for mans Wiſdom is in many things contrary to the Wiſdom of GOD, counting it to be fooliſhness: Do not Judge that right which only ſeemeth to be right; and conſider, *Matth.* vii. 1, 2, Judge right, and GOD will be with you, when you ſo do.

' Again, I ſay to you, all the People, Make ſtrong your praying to GOD, and be conſtant in it. 1 *Theſs.* v. 17. Pray continually. Again, laſtly, I ſay to you, Daniel, our Miniſter, be ſtrong in your Work: As *Matth.* v. 14, 16. You muſt bring Light into the World, and make it to ſhine, that all may ſee your good Work, and glorifie your Heavenly Father. Every Preacher that maketh ſtrong his Work doth bring precious Pearls: As *Matth.* xiii. 52. And thou ſhalt have Life Everlaſting in ſo doing. I am near to Death; I have lived long enough; I am about 90 years old: I now deſire to dye in the Preſence of Chriſt. O Lord, I commit my Soul to Thee.'

4. *Antony:*

4. *Antony:* He was among the firſt that prayed to GOD; he was ſtudious to read the Scriptures and the Catechiſm, ſo that he learned to be a Teacher; but after the Wars, he became a Lover of ſtrong Drink: was often admoniſhed, and finally caſt out from being a Teacher. His Dying Speeches follow.

'I am a Sinner, I do now confeſs it: I have long prayed to GOD, but it hath been like an Hypocrite; tho' I was a confeſſing Church-Member, yet like an Hypocrite; tho' I was a Teacher, yet like a Backſliding Hypocrite. I was often Drunk: Love of ſtrong Drink is a Luſt I could not over-come; tho' the Church did often admoniſh me, and I con-feſſed, and they forgave me, yet I fell again to the ſame ſin, tho' Major Gookins and Mr. Eliot often admoniſhed me; I confeſſed, they were willing to forgive me, yet I fell again. Now Death calls for me, and I deſire to prepare to dye well.

'I ſay to you Daniel, beware that you love not ſtrong Drink, as I did, and was thereby undone: Strengthen your Teaching in and by the Word of GOD: Take heed that you defile not your Work, as I did; for I defiled my Teaching by Drunkenneſs. Again, I ſay to you, my Children, Forſake not praying to GOD: Go not to ſtrange places where they pray not to GOD, but ſtrongly pray to GOD as long as you live, both you and your Children. Now I deſire to dye well, tho' I have been a Sinner: I remember that Word that ſaith, That tho' your Sins be many and great, yet GOD will pardon the Penitent, by Jeſus Chriſt our Redeemer. O Lord, ſave and deliver me by Jeſus Chriſt, in whom I believe: Send thy Angels, when I dye, to bring my poor Soul to thee, and ſave my poor ſinful Soul in the Heavenly King-dom.'

5. *Nehemiah:* This very hopeful young Man, going out to hunt with a Companion who fell out with him, and ſtabbed him mortally and killed him: A little was gathered up ſpoke by him, as followeth.

'I

'I am ready to dye now, but knew not of it, even now when I went out of my Doors: I was only going to hunt, but a wicked Man hath killed me: I fee that word is true, He that is well to-day may be dead to-morrow: He that laughed yefterday may forrow to Day. My mifery overtook me in the Woods: No man knoweth the Day and Time when his mifery cometh. Now I defire patiently to take up my Crofs and Mifery: I am but a Man, and muft feel the Crofs. Oh Chrift Jefus, help me: Thou art my Redeemer, my Saviour, and my Deliverer: I confefs my Self a Sinner: Lord Jefus, pardon all my Sins by thine own Blood, when thou diedft for us: Oh Chrift Jefus, fave me from Hell: Save my Soul in Heaven: Oh help me! help me!' So he dyed. The wicked Murderer is fled.

6. *John Owuffumug,* Sen. He was a young Man when they began to pray to GOD; he did not at prefent joyn with them; he would fay to me, 'I will firft fee into it, and when I underftand it, I will anfwer you.' He did after a while enter into the Civil Covenant, but was not entred into the Church Covenant before he dyed; he was propounded to joyn to the Church, but was delayed; he being of a quick, paffionate temper, fome witty littigations prolonged it, till his Sicknefs, but had he recovered, the Church was fatisfied to have received him: He finifhed well. His fpeech as followeth.

'Now I muft fhortly dye: I defired that I might live; I fought for Medicines to cure me; I went to every Englifh Doctor at Dedham, Medfield, Concord; but none could cure me in this World: But O Jefus Chrift, do thou heal my Soul, now I am in great pain: I have no hopes of living in this World; a whole year I have been afflicted; I could not go to the Publick Sabbath-Worfhip to hear GOD's Word: I did greatly love to go to the Sabbath-Worfhip. Therefore I now fay to all you, Men, Women, and Children, Love much and greatly to keep the Sabbath; I have been now

long

long hindred from it, and therefore now I find the worth
of it.

'I fay unto you all, my Sons and children, do not go into
the Woods among Non-praying People; abide conftantly at
Natick: You my Children, and all my kindred, ftrongly
pray to GOD: Love and obey the Rulers, and fubmit unto
their Judgment; hear diligently your Minifters: Be obedient
unto Major Gookins, and to Mr. Eliot, and Daniel. I am
now almoft dead, and I exhort you ftrongly to love each
other; be at peace, and be ready to forgive each other.

'I defire now rightly to prepare my felf to dye; for GOD
hath given me warning a whole year by my Sicknefs. I
confefs I am a Sinner; my heart was proud, and thereby
all Sins were in my heart: I knew that by Birth I was a
Sachim; I got Oxen, and Cart, and Plough, like an Englifh
Man; and by all thefe things my heart was proud. Now
GOD calleth me to Repentance by my Sicknefs this whole
year: O Chrift Jefus, help me, that according as I make my
Confeffion, fo through thy Grace, I may obtain a Pardon
of all my Sins: For thou, Lord Jefus, didft dye for us, to
deliver us from Sin: I hear and believe that thou haft dyed
for many, therefore I defire to caft away all worldly hinder-
ances; my Land and Goods, I caft them by, they cannot
help me now: I defire truly to prepare to dye.

'My Sons, I hope Chrift will help me to dye well: Now I
call you my Sons, but in Heaven we fhall all be Brethren:
This I learned in the Sabbath-Worfhip: All mifery upon
Believers in this World fhall have only Joy and Bleffing in
Jefus Chrift: Therefore, O Chrift Jefus, help me, in all my
Miferies, and deliver me, for I truft in thee. Save my Soul
in thy Heavenly Kingdom. Now behold me, and look upon
me who am Dying.' So he dyed.

7. *John Speen:* He was among the firft that prayed to
GOD; he was a Diligent Reader, he became a Teacher, and
carried well for divers years, until the Sin of Strong Drink
did

did infect us, and then he was fo far infected with it, that he was defervedly laid afide from Teaching. His laft Speeches were as followeth:

'Now I dye, I defire you all my Friends to forgive him that hurt me; for the Word of GOD faith, in *Matth.* vi. 3, 4. Forgive them that have done you wrong, and your heavenly Father will forgive you; but if you do not forgive them, your Heavenly Father will not forgive you: Therefore I intreat you all, my Friends, forgive him that did me wrong:' (for *John Nunufquanit* beat him, and hurt him much, a little before his Sicknefs.) 'Now I defire to dye well, now I confefs all my Sins: I am a Sinner; efpecially I loved ftrong drink too Well; and fometimes I was mad Drunk, tho' I was a Teacher: I did offend againft praying to GOD, and fpoiled my Teaching: All thefe, my Sins and Drunkennefs, O I pray you all forgive me: O Jefus Chrift, help me now, and deliver my Soul; and help me that I may not go to Hell; for thou, O Chrift, art my Deliverer, and Saviour: O GOD, help me; Lord, tho' I am a Sinner, O Lord do not forget me.' And fo he Dyed.

8. *Black James:* He was in former times reputed by the Englifh to be a *Pawaw,* but I cannot tell this: I know he renounced and repented of all his former ways; and defired to come to Chrift, and pray to GOD; and dyed well, as appears in what followeth.

'Now I fay, I almoft dye, but you all my Sons, and all you that pray at *Chabanukongkomuk,* take heed that you leave not off to pray to GOD, for praying to GOD is exceeding good, for praying to GOD is the way that will bring you to the Heavenly Kingdom: I believe in Chrift, and we muft follow his fteps. Efpecially you, my Sons, beware of Drunkennefs; I defire you may ftand faft in my Room, and Rule well: I am almoft now dead, and I defire to dye well. O LORD JESUS CHRIST, help me, and deliver my Soul to dye well.' So he dyed.

Thus,

Thus, Honoured Sir, I have given you an Account of the
Converſion of the Indians; and a Specimen of the Effects
thereof, in the Dying Speeches of them.   I will not pretend
to make Obſervations or Reflections thereon, to you, Sir;
which beſides the Preſumption of it, wou'd be but like
holding a Candle to the Sun.   But I hope I may without
offence, Sir, divert you with what the Divine Mr. George
Herbert, in his Poems called the Church, writes upon this
Subject.

> Religion ſtands on Tip-toe in our Land,
> Ready to paſs to the American Strand
> When height of Malice, and prodigious Luſts
> Impudent Sinning, Witchcraft, and Diſtruſts,
> (The marks of future bane) ſhall fill our Cup,
> Unto the Brim, and make our meaſure up :
> When Sein ſhall ſwallow Tyber, and the Thames
> By letting in them both, pollutes her Streams :
> When Italy of us ſhall have her Wile,
> And all her Callendar of Sins fulfil ;
> Whereby one may foretell what Sins next year
> Shall both in France and England Domineer :
> Then ſhall Religion to America flee,
> They have their times of Goſpel e'en as we.
> Religion always ſides with Poverty ;
> For Gold and Grace did never yet agree.

It now remains, Sir, that I give you an Account of my
Return back from Natick (whither myſelf and ſeveral others
went to hear the annual Lecture, as I have already related)
to Boſton again; and then come to the Concluſion of my
Letter.

To go on then with my Natick Ramble (you ſee, Sir,
Rambling is ſo natural to me, that it makes me ſometimes
Ramble ſo from my Subject, that 'tis hard to get in to't again.)
It was about Four in the Afternoon when the Lecture was
ended.   And we having 20 long miles back to Boſton, were
making the beſt of our way, and therefore Mr. Mallinſon,
one

one of our Company, prefently cry'd to Horfe, to Horfe, which we did accordingly in the fame Order as we came. Difcourfing as we rid of the Sermon we had heard, and of the great Sobriety we obferved in the Converted Indians.

But Mr. Cook one of our Company dropt us, and went another way; and having behind him one Mrs. Middleton (who was of a temper fo fuitable to his, that moft believed they were pretty well match'd) it cauf'd fome of our Company to fay, ' Twas no longer Cook upon Littleton, but Cook upon Middleton now.'

But tho' they were more charitable in their Opinions concerning Phil. and Madam Brick, yet truly Sir, my She-Companion and I loft the reft of our Company in the Wood, being Earneft in difcourfe, and not minding 'em ; and eafily wandring out of the Road, (by a miftake of the neareft way) we fell into a Tract of Land full of Delfs and Dingles, and dangerous Precipices, and other inextricable Difficulties, which might juftly have daunted, yea, quite deterr'd me (for the Night grew on a pace) from Endeavouring to pafs any further : (And by the Way many fuch-like places are to be met with in New-England) but all this did not fright me, for I had now the Flower of Bofton behind me, and did not doubt but the good Angel attending either her or Iris, (two Living Saints worth all the dead ones of the Papifts) wou'd bring us at laft into the right Path ; or at worft, I told her, (fhou'd we have Rambled feven years to find where we were) ·that I was ftill at home in fuch company : And the truth is, not only now, but at other times, I have never been better, than when I have been in fuch a Labyrinth of Difficulties, that I cou'd find no way out by the clue of my own Underftanding.

But at length, we efpy'd Six Horfes ty'd to a Gate, and found they belong'd to our ftragling Friends, who had here put into a Houfe for a Supper of Curds and Cream : And remembering the old Proverb, That the latter End of a

Feaft

Feaft is better than the beginning of a Fray, we alighted, and took part of their Banquet with them. After which, we mounted again for Bofton.

As we rid along, I cou'd not but obferve that one of our Company who was very merry in the morning, was extreamly melancholy all the way home: I took occafion therefore to afk him how he did, and whether he was not well? He told me, As to the health of his Body, he was very well; but, (faid he,) ' I am extreamly troubled in my Mind, that I, who have been brought up in the Profeffion of the Chriftian Religion from my Infancy, fhou'd be no more mov'd under the Preaching of God's Word, than a very ftone, and yet I have this day feen that the poor Indians, who never knew any thing of God till t'other day, (as it were,) melted into Tears under it, and mightily affected with it: Which makes me afraid leaft what our Bleffed Lord threatned the Jews withal, fhou'd be my Portion, when he told them, *Verily I fay unto you, Men fhall come from the Eaft and from the Weft, and from the North, and from the South, and fhall fit down with Abraham, and Ifaac, and Jacob, in the Kingdom of Heaven, and you your felves fhall be fhut out.*'

I told him we had all too much reafon to make thofe Reflections: And that the Fear he had upon him, was a good Prefervative againft the Evil feared; I told him alfo that I believ'd there was nothing more prejudicial to the Souls of Men, than that Miftaken Notion of their being Chriftians from their Infancy, which makes men fo carelefs in looking after Converfions, as thinking they need it not: Whereas it is plain we are all by Nature the Children of Wrath, and without being born again, and made new Crea-tures (that is, converted,) our bleffed Saviour, who is Truth it felf, affures us, we cannot enter into the kingdom of Heaven: But thefe poor Indians being fenfible of their Unconverted State, and their being ftrangers to God, the Word falls with greater Power and Efficacy upon them. He

told

told me, What I had faid was undoubtedly true, tho' he had not before fo well confider'd it.

But after three hours hard Riding, we got fafe home to Bofton, (all but Mr. Cook, who having (as was guefs'd) fome private Bufinefs to Difpatch with Mrs. Middleton, did not come till fome time after us.) And after a Bottle [of] Wine at Mr. Greens, we took leave of each other, and after conducting our Friends of the Fair Sex to their feveral homes, each of us repair'd to his own.

Thus, Sir, having given you an Account of my Ramble to and from Natick, It will be time I put a period to this Letter, having, I am afraid, too long diverted you already from your more weighty Studies. And yet I muft not be fo rude as to conclude, without prefenting my Duty in a kind Remembrance to my Mother-in-Law; whom I have ever efteem'd, as my own Mother, both as fhe was the old Acquaintance of my own Father, at Little Miffenden: and alfo becaufe I have always receiv'd as much Love and Kindnefs from her, as my own Mother cou'd have fhewn me.

And as to your felf, Sir, I am bold to fay, That I owe all the Bleffings of my Life to the many Fafts that you have kept on my Account, and to the many Prayers of my Deareft Wife. And I have this peculiar Bleffing to thank GOD for, above others, That I am not only happy, but that I know my felf to be fo. And tho' I have loft fome hundreds by being bound for my Wives Sifter, yet I have no-body to blame on that account, for 'twas all the Effect of my own pure Choice, being glad of an Occafion to fhew my refpect to your felf; and my Tendernefs to your Daughter, whom I have found the beft of Wives. And were I to act the fame Part again, I fhou'd ftill think I cou'd n't purchafe your Efteem too dear, nor that of any Branch of your Family.

I have only now to acquaint you, That the Reverend and holy Mr. Eliot, prefents his Chriftian and hearty Love to
you,

you, defiring the Continuance of your Prayers for him, while it fhall pleafe GOD to lengthen out his Aged Life. Alfo, the Reverend Mr. Increafe Mather and his Sons, and divers other Minifters, whom I cannot name, do prefent their hearty Love to you. But more efpecially my good Friend Mr. Burroughs, (one of your old hearers) prefents his Cordial Love and Service to you.

This is alfo further to acquaint you, Sir, that I have herewith fent you Six kegs of our New-England Sturgeon, Efteem'd the beft in the World, which I hope will come well to your Hands. And which with my humble Duty to you, begging the Continuance of your Prayers for me, is, Sir, the Earneft requeft of

Your moft obliged, moft humble, and

Moft Dutiful Son-in-Law,

PHILARET.

VIEW OF THE FIRST KING'S CHAPEL IN BOSTON

LETTER VI.

TO MY DEAREST WIFE.

———————

Y ever Deareſt Love! At that great diſtance in which the Providence of GOD has at this time plac'd us from one another, it is a great Satisfaction to me to think, That tho' our Bodies are divided, our Souls are United; and we ſtill live in one another. And we have all a way left us by writing to communicate our Sentiments, our hearts, our very Souls, unto each other: And this I never fail of doing as oft as the going of a ſhip for England, gives me an Opportunity. And tho' ſometimes I take the Advantage of ſuch a convenience to write to others, I never fail of writing to your Self: Of which I hope the many Letters I have ſent you, are a ſufficient Evidence. And in all this, I chiefly gratify myſelf: becauſe my Mind is moſt at eaſe, when you are made the Subject of my Thoughts. My Dear, I do not write thus, to ſatisfie you of the Truth of my Affection, (for never did that Tender Breſt of yours harbour the leaſt ſuſpicious Thought of Philaret) but to acquaint you of that new way of Converſe which Love has found out for us, even without the help of Letters; and this conſiſts only in Sympathy of Souls: You have not one kind thought of Philaret, but
what

what I meet with here; nor do I breathe one figh after my
Iris, but ftraight it flies away to you in England; and at this
diftance we are both made happy, tho' we fcarce know how:
And this, my Dear, is fuch a Myftery, as all the Mafters in
the Art of Love have yet been ftrangers to.   Nor yet will
this be call'd Platonick Love, for that's an Airy thing; but
our Affection centers in Enjoyment.   But I muft change
my Theam, my Dear, and from the thoughts of Love,
defcend to Bufinefs; and tell you how 'tis my Affairs go on
here; for fince you have an Equal Intereft with me in my
Affairs, 'twou'd be unkind not to acquaint you with 'em.

I write to others the Relation of my Rambles, but unto
you, my Dear, I write of Bufinefs: And fo it happens, that
'tis my Bufinefs here to give you a Relation of my Rambles: For having ftock'd the Town of Bofton with my
Books; (fome having bought more, I'm afraid, than they
intend to pay for) and having ftill a Confiderable Quantity
left, Several Gentlemen have given me great Encouragement, (by their Promifes of Affifting me in the Difpofal of
them) to fend a Venture to Salem, (the next confiderable
Town to Bofton in New England) and particularly one Mr.
Sewel,[137] who is a Magiftrate in that Town, has given me
Affurance of a Kind Reception there.   Befides, I am the
more Encourag'd to it, as 'tis in this Town the generous Mr.
Herrick has taken a Houfe; to whom for his Bottle of
Water at Sea, mention'd in my Letter to Brother Lake, I
                                                        was

---

[137] From the feries of very thorough
biographies of the officers of the Effex
Probate Court, furnifhed by A. C.
GOODELL, Jr., Efq., to the Hiftorical Collections of the Effex Inftitute, we learn
(iii. 1-5) that this was Major Stephen
Sewall, great-grand-fon of Henry Sewall,
Mayor of Coventry in 1606. The grandfather and father of Stephen, both
named Henry, came to New-England.
Stephen was born in Baddefly, Co.
Warwick, 19 Aug., 1657, and was
brought here at the age of four years.
In 1682 he married Margaret Mitchell,
and removed to Salem. He was Regifter of Probate and of Deeds, Major in
the militia, and held various other
offices. He died 17 Oct., 1725. He
had feventeen children, one of whom,
Stephen, was Chief-Juftice of the Province.—ED.

was fo much beholden: So that upon thefe confiderations being refolv'd to fend a Cargo thither, I thought it wou'd be firft convenient to go my felf, and fee the Town, and take a Warehoufe there, before I fent my Books. For I defign to intruft Palmer as my Factor; for having trufted much in the adjacent Towns, (efpecially at Connecticot) I cann't be above three Days abfent from Bofton: And having thus refolved to Ramble to *Salem*, it is my Ramble thither, my Reception there, and the Succefs thereof, relating to my Books, that I intend fhall be the Subject of this Letter.

I rambled to Salem all alone, (fave that by an Intercourfe of Souls, my Dear, I had your Company) and upon Byard on Ten Toes too, like a meer Coriat: I fhall fay nothing of the feveral Towns I Rambled through to Salem, defigning to defcribe them in my Ramble to *Ipfwich*: But it may not perhaps be altogether unprofitable to tell you how I employ'd my felf, as I rambled along: For tho' I went by my felf, yet I wanted no Company; for I converf'd with every thing I met with; and cou'd in fome meafure fay with one of the Antient Fathers, I was never lefs alone than when I was alone.

The firft that faluted me in my Rambles was a Curious Bird, whofe Feathers were as various as the colours of the Rainbow; and appear'd very delightful to behold; from whence I cou'd not but reflect, That if God does fo glorioufly adorn the Fowls of the Air, which are here to day, and gone to morrow, and which he has Created for the ufe of Man; how glorious muft the Garments of Salvation be, thofe Robes of Righteoufnefs with which the Saints fhall be cloathed, when they fhall fhine forth like the Sun in the Kingdom of their Father: Here indeed 'tis oftentimes their portion to be cloath'd in Rags, like Lazarus, while the Rich are array'd (like Dives) in purple and fine Linnen: But yet a little while, and the Scene will be chang'd; their
Rags

Rags fhall be turn'd into Robes of Glory, as foon as they fhall be lodg'd in the Bofom of Abraham.

But this Bird that I met with, was not only obfervable for the finenefs of her Feathers, but alfo for the Sweetnefs of her Notes; the pleafant Warbling of her Melodious Airs, expreff'd her Joy for the appearance of the Sun, which then appear'd upon the Mountain tops: From the fweet finging of this Bird, I cou'd not but reflect what an ungrateful Creature Man is, who, (when all Creatures in their feveral kinds, like to this pretty Bird, chaunt forth the Praifes of their great Creator) remains dumb and filent, altho' he was created with the moft proper Organs for Speech, above all other Creatures, that he might therewith found forth the Praifes of his Munificent Maker: But thofe that will not fing Praifes to GOD below, fhall never be admitted to bear a part in thofe Celeftial Anthems that are Sung above.

Tho' the fhining of the Sun in the Morning, promif'd me a fair Day, yet I had not been above an hour upon my Ramble, before The Sun withdrew his Beams, and hid himfelf behind a cloud; which made me very melancholy, and my way uncomfortable: This cauf'd in me a double Reflection: Firft how comfortable a thing it is to have the Sun of Righteoufnefs with healing in his Wings, arife upon the Soul: With what Chearfulnefs and activity does the Soul then run the Race that's fet before it? And how eafie are the hardeft Leffons then made to it? At fuch a time, tho' the Soul walks through the midft of the valley of the Shadow of Death, yet it will fear no Evil: And therefore David cries out, as in an Extafie, on this Account, Bleffed are they, O Lord, that walk in the light of thy Countenance! In thy favour fhall they rejoyce all the Day long.

But then I alfo reflected how uncomfortable a thing it is when GOD with-draws the Light of his Countenance from a gracious Soul: The Darknefs does appear more difmal to him, than if he never had beheld the Light:

It

It makes the wheels of his Chariot move heavily; and tho'
the Soul may keep on his way, it is very uncomfortable.
Thou hidest thy face, says the Pfalmift, *and I was troubled.*
Yet I obferved, that tho' the Sun was hid behind a cloud, he
did not with-draw all his Light, it was Day ftill; and I cou'd
well enough fee my way, tho' it was more uncomfortable
walking: From whence I reflected, That altho' many times
it pleafes God to with-draw the fhinings of his Face from
the Soul, yet it is not left totally in the Dark; it meets with
fecret Supports, and ftill keeps on its way, altho' it travels
uncomfortably: It does not indeed run the way of God's
commandments, as when its heart was Enlarged: But it
keeps going on towards Sion, with its Face thither-ward;
tho' its way lies through the Valley of Baca.

I had not gone half way to Salem, before the Sun was
got again from behind the cloud, and fhin'd forth with more
refplendent Brightnefs than it did before; and fo it continued fhining all the Day after. So that I cou'd not but
admire at the Glory of it: And at the fame time reflect
how bright muft that Glory be, which fhall darken the Glory
of the Sun; and exceed it much more, than the Sun now
does the Smalleft Stars: This Sun, as glorious as it is, muft
fet anon, and then the fable Clouds of Night, will muffle up
the World in Darknefs; but in Heaven the Sun of Glory
fhines for ever, for there fhall be no Night there. This
made me call to mind the Immortal Cowley's Defcription of
Heaven, in his Sacred Poem of the Troubles of David,
where he makes the Glorious Rays of the Sun to be but
dull in Comparifon of the glory of Heaven.[138]

Soon after this, I paft by a great heap of Stones, laid
there, as I fuppofe, to mend the Ways, which ufe to be
exceeding dirty in the Winter: Thefe ftones took up my
Thoughts awhile, which made me think again that fome
Inftruction might be gather'd from 'em: And I confider'd
that

[138] We omit the lines quoted by DUNTON.—ED.

that when the ground is Paved with them, they are laid in the dirt themfelves, and yet keep others out of it: This made me to reflect upon the fad eftate of thofe who preach to others, and are Inftruments of faving of their Souls, and yet themfelves are caftaways. Again: I confider'd that tho' the Rain falls often on the Stones, and multitudes of People daily pafs over 'em, yet there is little or no Impreffion made upon them; fo our Hearts are very obdurate, and hardly wrought upon, notwithftanding we lie under fo many quickning, foftning Sermons, and awakening Providences.

In going along the Woods, I obferved that feveral Arms and Branches of the higheft Trees had been broke off, by the Wind, and lay underneath upon the Ground; whereas the Shrubs that grew below, were out of danger, and all ftanding whole: This made me to reflect what Pains men take to get into great Places, and mount the higheft Pinacle of Honour, when they but thereby make their Falls the greater. While thofe that are but in a low condition, live more fecurely, and are out of Danger. He therefore was much in the right of it, that said,

> Honour's a Bubble ;
> And let blind Fortune where fhe will beftow her,
> Set me on Earth, and I can fall no lower.

With thefe and the like Reflections I entertain'd my felf upon the Road, and about Four of the Clock in the Afternoon, I came to Salem; and found the Town about a mile long, with many fine Houfes in it; and is reputed the next town to Bofton for trade: The Account, my Dear, I have received about the Original of this Town, is, That in the year of our Lord 1628, Mr. John Endicot with a number of Englifh People fat down by Cape Ann, at that place called afterwards *Gloucefter*, but their Abiding Place was at Salem, where they built a Town in 1639, and there they gathered a Church, confifting but of 70 Perfons; but afterwards it
increafed

increafed to 47 Churches in joynt Communion with one another, and in thofe Churches were about 7750 Souls: Mr. Endicot was chofen their firft Governour.

The firft Perfon I went to vifit in Salem, was Mr. Herrick:[130] How kindly he receiv'd a poor Traveller, my Dear, whofe Life he had fav'd at Sea, you may Eafier guefs than I relate. From his Houfe, we went to take a Glafs, and talk over our Sea-Voyage: What we found hard to fuffer, 'twas eafie to recite: Nay, there is a certain kind of Pleafure in the reflecting upon Dangers that are paft. And tho' now it was feveral Months fince, I found the Deliverances we had then, were ftill frefh in his Remembrance. When wee were at the Tavern, among other things, I renew'd my Acknowledgments for his former kindnefs, and drank a kind Remembrance in Wine, to the *Bottle of Water* that had fav'd my Life at Sea; and after that, to Captain Jenner, and our Ships Crew.

I have already told you, my Dear, that Travellers take Pleafure in recounting their paft Dangers; and had you heard how Mr. Herrick was affected with it, I am fure you cou'd have had a great Efteem for him; he fpeaks of you with much Honour and Regard, and I believe we drank your health a dozen times in an hours fitting. From hence he went with me to take a Ware-houfe, which I think ftands very conveniently. Having fettled that Affair, Mr. Herrick wou'd fain have had me lodg'd with him; which I believe I fhou'd have accepted, but that Mr. Sewel, the Magiftrate of Salem I before mention'd, fent me word he fhou'd take it very unkindly if I did not make his Houfe my Quarters: Whereupon, I defir'd Mr. Herrick's Excufe, and lay at Mr. Sewel's, who gave me a Reception worthy of himfelf.

The

[130] SAVAGE fays this was George Herrick, of Salem, who was aged 34 years in 1692, and was Marfhal of Effex during the Witchcraft mania, in which capacity he largely figured. It would feem (*ante*, p. 10) as if Dunton's friend was named Samuel, yet it is only an inference, fince of the two friends mentioned, Roger White certainly did not embark for America.—ED.

The Entertainment he gave me was truly Noble and Generous, and my Lodging fo Extraordinary both with refpect unto the Largenefs of the Room, and Richnefs of the Furniture, as might have Entertain'd a King. So free he was, that had I ftaid a month there, I had been welcome gratis. To give you his Character, in brief, my Dear, He is a Perfon whofe Purfe is great, but his Heart greater; he loves to be bountiful, yet limits his Bounty by Reafon: He knows what is good, and loves it; and loves to do it himfelf for its own fake, and not for thanks: He is the Mirror of Hofpitality, and neither Abraham nor Lot were ever more kind to ftrangers. As he is a Magiftrate, he defires to have his Greatnefs meafur'd by his Goodnefs; and his Care is to live fo, as to be an Example to the People. He wifhes there were fewer Laws, fo that they were better obferv'd; and for thofe that are Mulctuary, he thinks their Inftitution not to be like Briars and Thorns, to catch every thing they lay hold of, but like Sea-marks to avoid the Ship-wreck of ignorant and unwary Paffengers. He thinks him-felf then moft honourably feated, when he gives Mercy the Upper hand; and ftrives rather to purchafe a good Name than Land.

Having flept well in my New Quarters, the next Day I went to pay a Vifit to the Minifters of Salem: (For you know, my Dear, they are generally the greateft Benefactors to Bookfellers; So that my paying them a Vifit, is but in other words to go among my Cuftomers) who were Mr. Higgins,[14] an Antient and Grave Minifter, in his Stature and Phyfiognomy very much refembling your Reverend Father. He is one that knows the Burthen of his calling,

and

---

[14] By Mr. Higgins is meant the Rev. John Higginfon, of Salem. He was born at Claybrook, Co. Leicester, 6 Aug., 1616, and was the oldeft fon of Rev. Francis Higginfon, the well-known clergyman, who came with the colonifts in 1629. Rev. John Higginfon was of Saybrook and Guilford, Conn., but was ordained at Salem in 1660, and died, 9 Dec., 1708, leaving numerous defcendants.—ED.

and makes it [his] bufinefs to Feed, and not to Fleece his Flock. In his Difcourfe there is fubftance as well as Rhetorick; and he utters more things than Words: In controverfal Divinity, he ufes foft words, but hard Arguments; and labours more to fhew the Truth of his Caufe, than his Spleen: His fermon is limited by its Method, and not by the hour-glafs; and his Devotion goes along with him out of the pulpit. He preaches twice on the Lord's Day, and his Converfation is every Days Exercife. I din'd at his Houfe, and he promifes me great Affiftance in my Bufinefs, and Speaks of your Father with a World of Honour. From him, I went to vifit Mr. Noyfe,[141] his Affiftant, who is a hail, lufty Man, appears to be my hearty Friend, and treated me with very much refpect.[142]

Having made thefe Vifits, the next day I went to Dine with Mr. Herrick, who gave me a very handfome and genteel Reception, and treated me with all that was rare in the Countrey, both as to variety of Fifh and Flefh, and Choice of good Wine. In the Afternoon he propof'd to fhew me the Countrey round about Salem; and the next Morning we were to vifit Drinkwater (the Carpenter of the Ship we came to Bofton in) who lives a mile from Salem. Drinkwater was very glad to fee his Two Fellow Travellers, and gave us the welcome of his Houfe. And fo Mr. Herrick and my felf came back again to Salem.

The next morning I took my leave of Mr. Sewel, making my

---

[141] Rev. Nicholas Noyes, b. 1647, of Haddam and Salem, was fon of Nicholas, who was probably born at Choulderton, Co. Wilts. Nicholas, Jr., was ordained as colleague with Higginfon in 1683, was a promoter of the Witchcraft delufion, and died unm. 13 Dec., 1717, fays SAVAGE.—ED.

[142] In the "Life and Errors," DUNTON writes: "From Mr. Higgins[on]'s, I went to vifit Mr. Noyfe, his Affiftant. I fpent feveral agreeable Hours in this Gentleman's Company, which I thought no ordinary Bleffing, for he is all that's delightful in Converfation, fo eafy Company, and fo far from all conftraint, that 'tis a real pleafure to talk with him. He gave me a generous Welcome to Salem: and 'tis no leffening to his Brother Higgins[on], to fay he is in no ways inferiour to him for Good Preaching or Primitive Living."—ED.

my Acknowledgments to him for all his Favours: Who was pleaf'd to tell me, I fhou'd have been more welcome had I made a longer ftay: And renewed his former Promife of giving all the Encouragement he cou'd to my Venture, when it came thither. I then went to take my leave of Mr. Herrick alfo, to whom I efteem my felf very much beholden, for his Generous Treatment and great Civility.[143] And fo having fpent four Days in Salem, to my great fatisfaction, I return'd to Bofton; And having made up a very confiderable Cargo, I fent Palmer with it to Salem: Where he had very good

[143] At this point in the " Life and Errors " we find the following paragraphs, which doubtlefs fhould be in the text:

" I muft alfo remember the great Civilities I met at Salem from Mr. Epes (the moft Eminent School Mafter in New-England): he hath fent many Scholars to the Univerfity in New-England. He is much of a Gentleman, yet has not humbled his Meditations to the Induftry of Complements, nor afflicted his Brain in an Elaborate Leg: (he cannot Kifs his Hand and cry, Madam, Your humble Servant, nor talk Idle enough to bear her Company.) But tho' a School, and the Hermitage of his Study, has made him uncourtly, yet (which is a finer accomplifhment) he's a Perfon of folid Learning; and does not, like fome Authors, lofe his Time by being bufie about nothing, nor make fo Poor a ufe of the World, as to hug and Imbrace it.

" By the frequent Conference I had with him, I found him to be a Perfon of great worth ; he is free from Vice, if ever any man was, for he hath no Occafion to ufe it ; and being a Good Man, is above thofe ends that make Men Wicked. I fhall only add, I lately receiv'd a Letter from Mr. Epes for Two Hundred Pounds worth of Books, but (having given a farewell to trade) I defire this Character may ferve as an Anfwer to it."

" Meeting with fo good Friends in Salem, I began to think my felf at home again ; and could I have put *Iris* out of my mind, I might perhaps have forgot London ; but *Iris* had got fo firm a poffeffion of my Heart, and London fo great a Right to my Friendfhip, that ftill the Name of Native Country bewitch'd me. And 'twas thus with the Firft Planters of this Country, who were ever to their Eightieth Year, ftill pleafing themfelves with Hopes of their returning to England. But 'twas now my Duty (and the Difcharge of my Prefent Duty I thought wou'd help to the better performance of future Duties) to look upon that as my Native Country, where I cou'd thrive and profper. I carry'd about me but Six Ounces of Duft, which I ow'd to our common Mother (for the Chymifts of Cardan found no more in the Afhes of a Calcin'd body) and I did not matter where my Tabernacle was diffolv'd, or where I paid fo fmall a Debt ; all places are alike diftant from Heaven, and having marry'd a kind Wife, I thought it my Duty to provide for her. I did not care whether I met the Sun at his rifing or going down, provided only I cou'd ferve *Iris*. But now *Exit Spoufe*, that is, till I am fetled fo well in Salem as to have nothing to think of elfe."—ED.

good Trading and took Money apace. But not having my Eye over him, I was told he neglected his Bufinefs and fell to fhooting; but quite miff'd the Mark I aim'd at, which was, to have my Books fold, that I might haften to the Arms of my Deareft Expecting, Longing, and Longed for Iris: Whereupon, my Dear, I fent Palmer the following Letter.

Thefe for Samuel Palmer at Salem:

SAMUEL,

When I reflect upon that Fidelity I have found in you hitherto, and that Love you Expreff'd towards me when you voluntarily offer'd to go round the World with me; and when I confider your great care of me in all my Sea-ficknefs, during our long Voyage hither; and after this, your Care and Diligence in all my Bufinefs at Bofton, which you well knew I was fenfible of, and took it very kindly from you: I fay, when I confider all thefe things, I cannot but be extreamly troubled to think that you fhould by your Carelefnefs and neglect of my Bufinefs at Salem, (an Account of which I have receiv'd from feveral hands, of too great a Reputation not to be believ'd) forfeit that good Opinion I have hitherto retain'd of you; and lofe that Reputation in a moment, you have been fo long a building up: That you fhou'd be fo fupine, as not to confider, That 'tis only Perfeverance in well doing, that meets with a Reward.

The Credit and good Name of a Young Man, is more than a Portion; for when that's gone, Money cann't purchafe it: And yet a good Name and Reputation is fuch a tender thing to keep, that it requires abundance of Care and Circumfpection: Remember what Randolph fays about it in his Precepts.

> Thy Credit wary keep: 'Tis quickly gone,
> Being got by many Actions, loft by one.

It is for your fake, Sam, that I am fo much concern'd; for the Injurys you do to me by your Neglect, (tho' very prejudicial

33

dicial to my Affaires, forafmuch as my Return to England depends upon your Difpatch at Salem) is yet but fmall, in comparifon of what you do your felf, which may leave fuch an indelible ftain upon you, as cann't be eafily wafh'd out. And to fhew you that it is your good I aim at, upon your Reformation, and returning to your Bufinefs with your wonted Diligence, I will both Pardon and forget your Fault, tho' I never will forget your love, in venturing your Life with me: And I the rather hope this of you, becaufe I wou'd carry back your good Report to my Reverend Father Dr. Annefly, who recommended you to me, and alfo to your Miftrefs, who has an Extraordinary Efteem for you. And your compliance herein fhall ftill caufe me to continue

Your loving Mafter,

PHILARET.[144]

Upon the Receipt of this Letter, Palmer fent me the following Anfwer.

HONOURED SIR,

I received yours, and having read it, the Remorfe which arofe in my Breft, for offending fo good and indulgent a Mafter, has almoft broke my heart: Since my firft coming to live with you, I acknowledge I have received nothing but Demonftrations of Kindnefs from you: But your laft Letter has been a greater Kindnefs to me, than all that I receiv'd before, for it has brought me to a fight of my Sin, in my Neglect of your Bufinefs, and has reduc'd me to my Duty. Your Goodnefs in Promifing upon my Return, to pardon and forget my Faults, makes me the more fenfible of them, and I hope through GOD's Grace, will caufe me to double

my

---

[144] This letter is figned 'John Dunton' in the "Life and Errors," and is dated "Bofton, April the 4th, 1686." The anfwer is dated "Salem, April the 10th, 1686." Both of them are varied somewhat from the original drafts as here printed. Dunton fays that he inferts them as "a Caution to Eye Servants."—ED.

my Diligence for the time to come; and that I fhall give you fuch evident Tokens of my Repentance for thofe Neglects I have been guilty of, as fhall leave you no room to doubt of the Truth of it. And therefore humbly begging your Pardon for my late Faults, I do faithfully promife that during the Remainder of my Time, I will, by a diligent Applycation to my Bufinefs, Endeavour to approve my felf

Your moft humble and Faithful Servant,

SAMUEL PALMER.

My Dear, I found my Letter to Palmer had the Effect I defir'd, for he afterwards doubled his Diligence, and acquitted himfelf honourably; but does not think of Coming for England, leaft his being concern'd with Monmouth fhou'd rife up in Judgment againft him.

Palmer did not come with me for England, but rambled into another County for 3 years till the ftorm about Monmouth had blown over, and he was out of his time. I gave him a kind Reception and he was welcome to me till his fudden death of a horse.[145]

My Dear, Mrs. Comfort, (my Landlord Wilkins his Daughter) whofe Character I told you was in my Letter to Mr. Larkin, has treated me with a world of kindnefs upon all occafions; and well knowing by all my Difcourfes that I efteem nothing that has not a more than Ordinary value for you, did yefterday deliver into my hands a Noble Looking-Glafs to prefent to you, as an Earneft of her defire to fee a Perfon of whom I have talk'd fo many Tender Things.

I

[145] This is thus narrated in "Life and Errors." "Upon this, Palmer return'd to Bofton, where I fhook hands with him, in Regard he had not the Courage to fee Old England again, for he had been dabbling in Monmouth's Adventure. However, when his Apprenticefhip was expir'd, he ventur'd to come to London, where I receiv'd him with as much Tendernefs, as if he had been my Child, (for I cou'd not forget his Kindnefs to me at Sea) but Sam having a greater Fancy to fhooting then Bookfelling, got a Poft in the Army, and riding to fee his Captain, was drown'd." —ED.

I heard yefterday at Change the News of your Cousin Noyfe's[146] Death, as he was coming from Jamaica hither: And I am much concern'd at the Report, as he was a brave Affertor of Englifh Liberties againft Popery and Tyranny; of which, the Addrefs againft it by the London Apprentices, to Sir Patience Ward, Lord Mayor of London, was a Sufficient Evidence; my felf and he being Two of the Prefenters.

Pray give my humble Duty to Father and Mother, and a kind Remembrance to all other Relations; Particularly to Sifter Sarah Dunton: It will be but a needlefs wafting of Time and Paper to tell you, That I will difpatch my Bufinefs here with all the Application poffible, that I may be once more made happy with your Embraces. For as the Needle touch'd with the Load-Stone can never reft until it Points to its beloved North: So neither can there be any True Repofe Enjoy'd, till in the Arms of Iris, by, my Deareft,

Your ever Faithful

PHILARET.

[146] Nothing has been found concerning this "Coufin Noyes," and what is perhaps worth notice is that no record can be found of George Drinkwater, whom Dunton vifited. The name of Drinker is on our records.—ED.

THE TRIANGULAR WAREHOUSE AT THE TOWN DOCK, BOSTON.

LETTER VII.

TO MY BELOVED SISTER,

MRS. SARAH DUNTON.

Y Dear Sifter: There are many Reafons that crowd in upon me, for the Addreffing this part of my Rambles to your felf; and all appear very cogent: Your more than Ordinary Efteem of me does naturally beget in me that refpect for you which cannot eafily be forgotten; befides your having liv'd with me fome years, has given me an Opportunity of Obferving divers commendable and praife-worthy Qualities in you, which has very much endear'd you to me; Your underftanding fo abftrufe and knotty a part of the Mathematicks as Algebra, fhews you to be a Perfon of a very great Intellect, and one whofe Soul is fufceptive of greater things than thofe.

But there are two Things that Endear me to you more than all the reft; the one is, That very great refpect and efteem that my Deareft Love has always had for you above the reft of my Relations, and the many Endearing things fhe has often faid to me of you. The other, which is yet more Engaging, is, That I very well remember, you were always the beft Beloved Daughter of my Deareft Father;

To

To whofe Pious and happy Memory, I fhall always pay fo great a Deference, as to believe where he lov'd moft, there muft be moft of Merit.

So much for the Reafon of an Addrefs to you in general; and as to my addreffing this part of my Rambles to you in particular, it is, Becaufe this is a Ramble from Bofton to *Plymouth;*[147] to which place I was made the Conductor of one of the Fair Sex; and the Difcourfes with which we whil'd away our Time upon the Road, is a great part of the fubject of this Letter; which how manag'd, is left to your Judgment, as one whom Experience has made capable of giving it: For Women judge of Women's Matters beft.

My Landlady (Mrs. Wilkins) having a Sifter at *Ipfwich*, which fhe had not feen a great while, Mrs. Comfort, her Daughter, (a young Gentlewoman Equally happy in the Perfections both of her Body and Mind,) had a great defire to fee her Aunt, having never been at her Houfe, nor in that Part of the Countrey; Which Philaret having likewife a defire to fee, and being never backward to accommodate the Fair Sex, Profers his Service to wait upon her thither, which was readily accepted by the Young Lady, who knew Philaret fo well, that fhe thought her felf fafe enough under his Protection. Nor were her Parents lefs willing to truft her with him; and Philaret was as careful not to betray his Truft to any Inconvenience.

And now, Sifter, all things being ready for our Ramble, I took my Fair one up behind me, and rid to the River-fide, which tho' it be often and ufually crofs'd in a Canoo, yet I rather chofe to crofs it in a Ferry, having my Horfe with me: Having crofs'd the River, We mounted again, and rid on our way; meeting as we went a long with two or three Indians, who courteoufly faluted us, with, ' What Chear, *Netop?*' Netop in the Indian Language fignifies Friend:

I

---

[147] Thus the Manufcript reads, but Dunton feems never to have vifited the South Shore.—ED.

I return'd their Salutation, and paff'd on; not without obferving that there is a vein of Civility and Courtefie runs in the Blood of thefe Wild Indians, both among themfelves, and towards ftrangers.

As we were Rambling along, I afk'd my Comfortable and Fair-Fellow-Traveller, what her Notions of Marriage were? Mrs. Comfort at firft feem'd furprif'd at the Queftion, and told me fhe did not expect it from me: I then told her, There was nothing in that Queftion but what fhe might very well anfwer: And that fince we were now all alone, and there were no Witneffes of our Words, fhe might do it with the greater Freedom; and that as to my felf, I hop'd fhe had a better opinion of me, and believ'd I had a greater Honour for her, than to take any Advantage of her Words, fo as to Expofe her for them. ' But, Madam,' continu'd I, ' fince we often talk of Marriage and of Love, and you underftand the Words, thefe Words muft convey fome private Notions and Ideas of the things they fignifie, unto your Soul: And what thefe private Notions and Ideas of things are, is that which I wou'd have you be fo free as to relate; this is the Trueft part of Friendfhip, and this is that Unbofoming of our Souls to Each other, by which our Notions of Things are Emprov'd: And whether you will be fo free as to own it or not, I am fure your Thoughts are fometimes Employ'd upon thefe Subjects.'

To this, Mrs. Comfort gave me this Anfwer, ' I believe, Philaret, that as free as you appear from all the Errours of your Sex, you wou'd not wifh your Breft Tranfparent, nor have all the inward Sentiments of your Soul expof'd: There are fome Thoughts there you would not have even your Charming Iris Privy to, as much as you love her; leaft fhe might thereby Difcover fome Obliquity in your fo much boafted Affection. Why fhou'd you then fo rigoroufly require of me to difcover the inmoft Receffes of my Soul, and the moft private Conceptions of things that I have

Lodg'd

Lodg'd there? And even as to Marriage it felf, is it not much more proper for me, who am a Virgin, and know nothing of it, to enquire of you, who having long been married, muft needs know; and fince from what I have obferv'd of you, you are the beft of Hufbands; and from your Words I cannot think but that your deareft Iris is the beft of Wives: I'm fure I cannot Enquire any where with more hopes to be refolv'd, and know the beft of it, than from th' Experience of fo happy and fo bleft a pair.'

' Well, Mrs. Comfort,' reply'd I, ' I fee you'll be too hard for me, and have befides turn'd the Queftion I afk'd you into another, and put it on my felf: For 'twas not fimply what Marriage was that I afk'd you, but what your Private Notions of it were: But fince you have been pleaf'd to put that Complement upon my felf and my Dear Iris, as to make us the Exemplar of a Married Life, I will be fo free as to give you my thoughts of it, that you may afterwards the more freely give me yours. But I fee our Difcourfe has already brought us to Captain Marfhalls, and therefore I fhall adjourn what we have to fay till afterward.' My Fellow-Traveller eafily agreed to my motion, and fo we rid up to Captain Marfhal's Houfe, and there alighted.

This Captain Marfhal[148] is a hearty old Gentleman, formerly one of Oliver's Souldiers, upon which he very much values himfelf: He keeps an Inn upon the Road between Bofton and *Marble-Head:* His Houfe was well-furnifhed, and we had very good Accommodation. I enquir'd of the Captain what memorable Actions he had been in under Oliver, and I found I cou'd not have pleaf'd him better; he

was

---

[148] Capt. Thomas Marfhall is mentioned by NEWHALL in his Hiftory of Lynn, p. 155-7. Still there is a great degree of uncertainty about his identity. SAVAGE confiders him the fame as Thomas M., of Reading, who had children between 1640 and 1655, and at Lynn from 1657 to 1665. He may have been in England between 1648 and 1655. He was fix times a reprefentative from Lynn, and kept a tavern, opened by Jofeph Armitage, on the weft of Saugus river. He died 23 Dec., 1689, and from an affidavit quoted, was aged 67 in 1683. He left two fons and feveral daughters. —ED.

was not long in Refolving me of the Civil Wars at his Fingers' Ends; and if we may believe him, Oliver did hardly anything that was confiderable without his Affiftance; For his good Service at the Fatal Battel of Nafeby, (which gave fuch a Turn to the King's affairs, that he cou'd never after come to a pitch'd Battel,) he was made a Captain; from thence he went to Leicefter, and befieg'd that; then went to York, and afterwards to Marfton-Moor; and in fhort, Rambled fo far in his Difcourfe, that if I wou'd have ftay'd as long as he'd have talk'd, he wou'd have quite fpoil'd my Ramble to Plymouth; and therefore giving Mrs. Comfort to underftand that I begun to be uneafie, fhe very feafonably came into my Relief, and the Captain was forc'd to leave a great part of his Noble Exploits unrelated. My Fellow-Traveller and I, having taken our leave of the Captain, quickly mounted, and went on our Ramble towards Marble-Head.

And now, being all alone again, Mrs. Comfort put me in mind of my Promife to give her an Account what Marriage was. I found fhe cou'd not forget fo pleafing a Subject: For your Sex, my Sifter, how coyly foever they appear to mention fuch Subjects, yet love to hear as much as they can of 'em, and take a Secret pleafure in the Relation; for the Truth of which I appeal to yourfelf.

'Well, Mrs. Comfort,' faid I, 'Since you have put this Tafk upon me, I will Endeavour to acquit my felf as well as I can of it. I do therefore affirm Marriage to be the happieft State on this fide Heaven, that a Man can be in: Nor do I fpeak this as an Empty Notion of my own, but ground it on the greateft and the beft Authority; For if we do but reflect upon the great Inftitutor of it, and the time when, and the place where it was inftituted, nothing can be more obvious: The Inftitutor of it was the great Lord of the Creation, who having framed this glorious Superftructure of the Univerfe out of Nothing, Created Man as the Lord of
it,

it, with a Defign to make him happy: And yet, if Heaven it felf may be believ'd, the Completion of his happinefs confifted in a Married State, GOD himfelf declaring it was not good for Man to be alone; and therefore he provided a meet help for him.

'Nor is the time when Marriage was thus inftituted, lefs confiderable; it was whilft our Firft Parents were cloath'd with all that Virgin Purity and Innocence wherewith they were created. 'Twas at a time wherein they had a bleffed and uninterrupted Converfe and Communion with their Great Creator; and were compleat in all the Perfections both of Mind and Body: 'Twas at a time when they cou'd curioufly furvey the Beauties and Perfections of Each other without fin, and knew not what it was to luft. 'Twas at this happy time that the Almighty Divided Adam from himfelf, and of a Crooked Rib made him a fair and Lovely Bride; and fo by Inftituting Marriage, United Adam to himfelf again, in Wedlock's facred Bands.

'And now the Place where Marriage firft was inftituted, comes next to be confider'd, and that was Paradice, a Place form'd by our Sovereign Maker for Delight and Pleafure: It was a Garden, and muft needs be pleafant; but then if we reflect 'twas the Garden of GOD, it muft needs be fuperlatively fo: 'Twas in the midft of Paradife, the Center of Delight and Happinefs, that Adam was Unhappy, whilft in a Single State; and therefore Marriage may properly be ftil'd The Paradice of Paradice it felf. And where two Perfons of agreeing years and Humours fhall Tye this True Love's Knot, and Enter into Wedlocks facred Bands, their own Experience will tell them more than this. And now, dear Mrs. Comfort, I hope I have made good what I at firft afferted, which was, That Marriage is the happieft ftate on this fide Heaven.'

After fome little filence, Mrs. Comfort told me, That fhe cou'd not expect lefs from me, than fuch an Account of a

married

married ſtate as I have given. 'But if Marriage,' added ſhe, 'be ſuch a happy ſtate as you have repreſented, what means thoſe Inauſpicious Torches Hymen lights at every Wedding? For now we ſee none but unlucky hands link'd in the Wedding Ring; and Tears, and Jars, and Diſcontents, and Jealouſies, (a Curſe as Cruel,) or elſe Barrenneſs, are all the Bleſſings Crown the Genial Bed: And theſe things being every Days Experience, make more Impreſſion on ſuch Minds as mine, than all that fine Harrangue that you have made.'

I cou'd not but confeſs to Mrs. Comfort, That ſuch things are too obvious Every Day; but theſe things cou'd not ſo properly be ſaid to be the Effects of Marriage, but rather the Effects of their Irregularities that enter in a Married State, wîthout attending to the Duties of it.

'Then I perceive,' reply'd Mrs. Comfort ſmartly, 'That Marriage is, as they are that Enter into it; which makes it ſtill extream precarious. And he and ſhe had need be well acquainted with each others humours, before they Tye that Nuptial Knot together, or elſe they may too late, in vain repent it.'

This Diſcourſe had brought us to *Marvail,* or *Marble-Head,* a ſmall Town or Harbour, the Shore Rocky, upon which the Town is built, conſiſting of a few ſcattered Houſes, where they have Stages for Fiſhermen, Orchards and Gardens; half a mile within Land, there is good Paſtures, and Arable Land, very good.

It was about Marriage we had been Diſcourſing as we came a long; and that I think was the Occaſion of my aſking at this Town, of a Friend Indian,[140] what the Cuſtoms of the Indians was, relating to Marriage; and the Account he gave me, was this, That ſingle Fornication they accounted no ſin; but after they were married, it was accounted a very
hainous

---

[140] The 'Friend Indian,' as might be imagined from previous examples, was very familiar with WILLIAMS. See KEY, p. 228–231.—ED.

hainous Crime for either of them to Tranfgrefs, or be found falfe to the Marriage-Bed. That their Marriages were folemnized by the Confent of the Parents, and alfo by Publick Approbation: And that they were Married Publickly, before the Chief Perfons of the Place where they lived. That in cafe either Party were found offending, the Party wronged may put away, or keep the Party offending at their own Pleafure. And if it happens to be the Woman that is found falfe, tho' the Hufband may forgive his Wife, yet will he be folemnly revenged upon the Perfon with whom fhe offended, before many Witneffes, by many Blows and Wounds; and if it be to Death (as fometimes it is) yet the guilty refifts not, nor is his Death revenged. If the like courfe was taken in Europe, there would be both fewer Cuckolds and lefs Cuckold-Makers.

But tho' they are fuch Obfervers of Marriage, yet is not their Number of Wives ftinted, but they may take as many as they pleafe: Tho' the Chief Nation of Indians in this Country, which is the *Narriganfets*, generally Take but one Wife.

Two Caufes they generally alledge for their Plurality of Wives; Firft, Defire of Riches, becaufe the Women bring in all the increafe of the Field; and the Hufband only fifheth and hunteth. Secondly, Their long fequeftring themfelves from their Wives after Conception, until the Child be Weaned, which with fome is long after a year old; for they generally keep their children long at the breft.

The Hufband there buys his Wife, or gives fo many fathom of their money (which is the Shells of certain Fifhes ftrung on a Bracelet) to the Father, or Mother, or Guardian of the Maid. And if the Man be poor that he cann't give anything, his Friends and Neighbours contribute towards the Dowry.

They commonly abound with Children, and increafe mightily; and the Curfe laid upon Women of bringing forth

forth Children in forrow, is mightily moderated to the Indian Women; fo that they have a far more moderate Labour, and a more Speedy and Eafie Delivery than moft of our European Women: Which I believe in a great meafure is occafioned by the hardnefs of their Conftitution; and by their Extraordinary great Labour in the Field, (even above the Labour of Men) as carrying of mighty Burthens, digging Clammes, and getting other Shelfifh from the Sea, and in beating all their Corn in a mortar, &c. Moft of 'em count it a fhame for a Woman to Complain when fhe's in Labour, and many of them are fcarcely heard to groan. It is a common thing among them, to have a Woman merry in the Houfe, and in half an hours time deliver'd and merry again; and within two Days abroad, and after four or five Days at Work.

They frequently put away their Wives for other Occafions befides Adultery; and yet are they not fo fickle but that I have been fhewn many Couples that lived twenty, thirty, and fome forty years together.

From this Account of the Indians Marriage, I made this General Obfervation, my Sifter: That GOD hath Implanted in the Hearts of the Wildeft of the Sons of Men, an high and Honourable Efteem of Marriage, and that the Violation of the Marriage-Bed is abominable; which fufficiently fhews Marriage to be a Divine Inftitution.

Having left Marble-Head behind us, we Rambled towards *New Salem*, four miles North of Marble-Head, and directly in our way to Ipfwich; but having given a large Account of this Place, and of my Ramble thither, and ftaying there for fome time, in a Letter to my Deareft Iris, which you may fee when you pleafe, I fhall fay nothing further of it here, but that having call'd at a Friends Houfe, and refrefh'd our Selves, we Rambled on towards *Wenham;* when by the Way, I thought this a Convenient time for my Fellow-Traveller to perform her Promife, as I had done mine, that

is,

is, to give me her private Notions of Marriage; and what Ideas of it fhe retain'd in her own Breft.

But Mrs. Comfort was, I perceiv'd, a good Proficient in the Art of Wheedling, and wou'd have wheedled me out of the Performance of her Promife, by perfwading me fhe had perform'd it already, in Anfwer to my Difcourfe of Marriage before mention'd: But having convinc'd her that what She then faid was only an Objection to what I had affirm'd, which I had alfo anfwer'd, fhe thus began.

' Since nothing will fatisfie you, Philaret, but my Expofing my felf, by giving you my Private Notions of Marriage, of which we have had fo large an Account from the Indian at Marble-Head, I will run the rifque of being thought an Infipid, rather then Difoblige you, or feem to break that Promife which you only fay I have made, tho' I know nothing of it. That thofe words of Love and Marriage do convey fome peculiar Notions or Ideas to our Souls, as you affirm, is very certain; or elfe our Difcourfe wou'd be altogether unintelligible, and we might as well hold our Tongues, as talk to one another. And 'tis as certain that words convey to us the True Notions of the Things intended by thofe Words; and if fo, what Notion can I have of Marriage, but what the word conveys to me, or what is commonly intended by that Word, which is nothing elfe but the making one of two, or the Uniting of two Perfons in a Married State, fo as Death only can diffolve that Union.

' This, Philaret, is my Private Notion of Marriage, which I think to be Right, as far as I underftand the Word: And this is enough to acquit me of the Promife you Pretend to. But Philaret, that you may fee the Confidence I have in you, and how much freedom I take in your Converfation, I will give you my Private Sentiments concerning Marriage, and they are, That it is a very defirable State; and that there are fuch Charms and fuch Endearing Sweetneffes in the Converfation of an agreeable Hufband, that renders all

other

other Pleafures but naufeous and infipid in comparifon of this: When two Perfons fhall be mutually wrapt up, as it were, in one anothers Soul, and Communicate their very hearts to one another, it muft needs be a Life of great Complacency and Delight; and yet, Philaret, I am not fo great an Admirer of a Married State, as to think 'tis without its Alloys: No, I believe that all thofe fancy'd joys that I have mention'd, are but needful to counter-ballance its Alloys, which are fo many and fo great, as that without fome fuch Endearing Charms as I have mention'd, it wou'd be hardly tolerable; no, tho' a Perfon were fo happy as to meet with a good Hufband; which is fo great a hazard, that 'tis a venturing againft mighty odds to run the rifque on't: For as I'm fure you don't imagine that every Wife you fee wou'd make an Iris; fo neither do I think that fcarce one Husband in Ten Thoufand wou'd prove a Philaret. And therefore fince there is fo great a hazard in getting a good Hufband; and to have a bad one is to be Ruin'd without Remedy, a Single Life is ftill to be preferr'd: Tho' at the fame time this I do declare, that were I fure of having a good Hufband, 'twou'd be the firft thing I fhou'd do to marry him.'

I could not but return my Thanks to Mrs. Comfort, for the Freedom fhe had uf'd in Difcovering her Sentiments to me; affuring her that whatever fhe had faid fhould never be made ufe of to her prejudice; and alfo took notice how much fhe had oblig'd me in the value fhe had put upon my Deareft Iris and my felf; telling her, that howfoever fhe might be miftaken in me, yet my Lovely Iris was a Perfon that I deferv'd all the good thoughts fhe had conceiv'd of her; and that fhe only wanted to know her perfonally to be of my Opinion.

I had juft concluded my Difcourfe, as we came to Wenham, which is an Inland Town, very well watred, lying between Salem and Ipfwich, and confifteth moft of Men of Judgment and Experience in Country Affairs; well ftored
with

with Cattel. At the firft Rife of Ipfwich River, in the higheft part of the Land, near the Head, are the Springs of many Confiderable Rivers; *Shafhin*, one of the moft confiderable Branches of *Merrimack* River; and alfo at the rife of *Miftick* River, are Ponds full of Pleafant Springs.

In this Town of Wenham lives one Mr. Geery;[150] whofe Father is now a Captain in Bofton, in fo delicious a Paradice, that of all the Places in the Countrey, I fhou'd have chofen this for the moft happy Retirement: His Houfe is neat and handfome, fitted with all Conveniencies proper for the Countrey: And does fo abound with every thing of his own, that he has no Occafion to trouble his Neighbours: The lofty fpreading Pines on each fide of his Houfe, are a fufficient Shelter from the Winds; And the Warm Sun fo Kindly ripens both his Fruits and Flowers, as if the Spring, the Summer and the Autumn had agreed together to thruft Winter out of Doors; He entertain'd us with fuch pleafant Fruits, as I muft own Old England is a ftranger to, and amongft all its great Varieties, knows nothing fo Delicious. This Noble Countrey Seat, and that Retirement which feems fo peculiar to it, brought to my Remembrance the fecond Epod of Horace, of the Pleafures of a Countrey Life, which I have here inferted.[151]

This Gentleman's Pleafant Countrey Seat, and good Hufbandry, ftir'd up my Curiofity to inquire into the manners and good Husbandry of the Indians, of which I had this Account given me.[152]

The Indians are very exact and punctual in the bounds of their Lands, belonging to this or that Prince, or private Perfon,

---

[150] As we have before fhown, by 'Geery' is undoubtedly meant Gerrifh. Rev. Jofeph Gerrifh, fon of Capt. William G., was ordained at Wenham in 1673, married Ann Waldron, had feveral children, and d. 6 Jany., 1720. —ED.

[151] And which we have omitted.—ED.

[152] The account, doubtlefs a very exact one, was furnifhed by WILLIAMS, p. 180.—ED.

Perfon, even to a River, or a Brook, &c. and make a firm
Bargain and Sale amongft themfelves for every fmall quantity of Ground they part with.

They have very good Chefnuts, which they call *Wompi-
mineafh,* which they have a peculiar Art of Drying, and fo
preferve them in their Barns for a Dainty all the year:
They dry their Akorns alfo, and in Cafe of want of Corn,
by much boyling they make a good Difh of them. Yea,
fometimes in plenty of Corn, they will eat thefe Akorns for
a Novelty.

They have alfo very good Wallnuts, of which they make
an Excellent Oyl, good for many Ufes, but efpecially for
their Anointing of their Heads. And of the Chips of the
Wallnut Tree (the Bark being taken off) fome Englifh in
the Countrey make Excellent Beer both for Tafte, Strength,
Colour, and inoffenfive operation.

They have the moft Excellent Strawberries in the World:
Which is indeed the Wonder of all the Fruits growing Naturally in thofe Parts: It is of it felf fo Excellent, that an
Eminent Englifh Doctor was wont to fay, That he wou'd
not fay GOD cou'd not have made, but he wou'd fay GOD
never did make a better Berry than this. In fome parts
where the Indians are fettled, I have feen as many as wou'd
freight a good Ship, in a few miles Compafs. Their ufual
way is to bruife them in a mortar, and mix them with meal,
and fo make a very pleafant fort of Strawberry-Bred of
them.

They have alfo another Fruit which they call *Safemineafh,*
in tafte like a Barbary, a fine, fharp, cooling Fruit, growing
in frefh Waters all the Winter. Being made into a Con-
ferve, it is very excellent againft Feavers.

They have likewife Divers forts of Hurtle-Berries, fome
fweet like Currans, fome opening, and fome of a binding
Nature. Thefe Currans are dry'd by the Natives, and fo
preferved all the year; which they beat to powder, and
mingle

35

mingle with their Parch'd Meal, and make a delicate Difh of it, which they call *Sautauthig;* which is as fweet to them as Plum or Spice-Cake to the Englifh.

Tho' the Indians make very pleafant Bread of their Strawberries, having great abundance of them; yet the Englifh exceed them in good Hufbandry, and make an Excellent delicious Wine of their Strawberries, as ftrong and as pleafant as any made of Grapes.

Their Indian Corn (which is of feveral Colours) is very good either boil'd in Milk, or butter'd; and is more agreeable to Englifh Bodies than our Englifh Wheat, which is generally of a binding nature; whereas this keeps the Body in a conftant moderate Loofenefs.

The Women fet, or plant, and weed, and likewife gather and bring in all the Corn into the Barn, and all other Fruits of the Field: Tho' here and there a good Natur'd Man, and one that is fond of his Wife, will help her; which by the Cuftom of the Country he is not bound to do, neither is it any of his work.

When a New Field is to be broken up, they are very fociable and neighbourly; for all the Neighbours, both Men and Women, will freely come and joyn with 'em in the work, to Difpatch it quickly. Sometimes an hundred, or more, will joyn together, on fuch an Occafion. Nor is it only on this Occafion that they will joyn together, but likewife on feveral others, fuch as building their Forts, hunting in the Woods, ftopping and killing Fifh in the River, &c. their United ftrength making difficult things eafie. *Concordia parva res crefcunt, Difcordia magna dilabuntur.*

When their Corn is grown up, they how it, as we do in England; but the Indian Women, tho' they fee daily what Howes the Englifh ufe, will ftill ufe their Natural Howes of Shells and Wood.

When they have gather'd their Corn, they dry it carefully on heaps, laying it on Matts before they barn it up: Cover-
ing

ing it over with Matts at Night, and taking them off the next Day when the Sun is hot. The Woman of the Family will commonly raife two or three heaps of Twelve, fifteen, or twenty Bufhels in a heap; and if She have the help of her Children or Friends it will be much more.

The Indians have alfo their Vine-Apples, which the Englifh from them call Squafhes;[158] they are about the bignefs of Apples, and are of feveral colours. It is a very fweet, wholefome, and refrefhing Fruit.

This Difcourfe had held us fo long, that we both thought it now high Time to profecute our Defigned Ramble to Ipfwich, which was now our next ftage, and to which we wanted but eight miles: As we were riding along, being pleaf'd with Mrs. Comfort's Wit and Ingenuity, and to avoid the tedioufnefs of the Way, I Engaged her again in a new Converfation, thus:

'Well, Mrs. Comfort, Since you find there's fo much difficulty in being well Married, Pray tell me what you think of Platonick Love; a Love fo Sublime, that you may love on to the greateft heights of it, without Danger; a Love refin'd from all that's grofs and Earthy; and divefted of all Carnal affection, fo that it becomes as pure as Æther. This is a Love that you and I may be Engaged in, without a Crime, or the leaft thought of Wrong to my beloved Iris.'

To this Mrs. Comfort reply'd, 'I think 'tis very ftrange to hear a married man commend Platonick Love, fince by his Marriage he has over-thrown the Notion. But in your Circumftances, Philaret, there may be fome allowance given; and in New-England you may pafs with a Platonick Lover: But were you now in London, how foon wou'd you unfay your words, and prove your Love of Iris to be as pure and

as

---

[158] In his note on this paffage in WILLIAMS, (p. 185) TRUMBULL writes: "*Afq.* plural *afquafh*, was a generic name, fignifying that which might be eaten *green* or *raw;* and was probably applied to all the Cucurbitaceæ, or melon-like fruits. The Englifh adopting the plural *afquafh* as a noun in the fingular, formed a new plural, fquafh-es." —ED.

as refin'd, as that Platonick Love to which you now give fo great Elogies: For my part, Philaret, whene'er I love, I will propofe fome End in doing it; for that which has no End, appears to me but the Chimera of a Diftempered Brain: And what end can there be in love of Different Sexes, but Enjoyment? And yet Enjoyment quite fpoils the Notion of Platonick Love: You muft excufe me therefore, Philaret, if I, (ftill paying all the deference I ought, to your far better Judgment) declare my felf againft it, and oppofe real Fruition, in your Platonick Notion.'

To this, I repartee'd, 'Tho' I am very well fatisfied in the Pregnancy of your Wit, yet I can by no means approve of your Judgment, in Oppofition to Platonick Love, which I have fo great an Efteem for, that I can by no means part with it. And fince your Sex are oftener perfwaded by Poetical Compofures, than by down-right Profe, I am refolv'd to attack you that way:' And then I repeated the following verfes.[154]

Mrs. Comfort teftified how highly fhe was pleaf'd with the Copy of Verfes I had Repeated, and affured me that they had almoft made her a Convert to Platonick Love; but our Converfation was interrupted by a Friend Indian's overtaking us, who was a going to Ipfwich as well as we; and becaufe the Evening was pretty far advanc'd, we were glad of his company; who tho' he was on foot, travell'd as faft as our Horfe, and fafter too, or elfe he had not overtook us; and obferving his going, I could not but admire to fee what paths their naked hardned feet had made in that Wildernefs; Even in ftony and rocky Places.

This honeft Indian offered, if we had any thing to carry, to carry it for us. And I obferv'd that for a fmall hire, a

Man   .

[154] It is highly probable that DUNTON did have fome fuch difcourfe during this journey, as he has printed a brief account in his " Life and Errors." Still, as he there varies the poetry quoted, we may fpare our readers three pages of it.—ED.

Man fhall never want Guides who will carry their Provifions for them over Rivers and Brooks, and oftentimes find out Hunting-Houfes, and other Lodgings at night: I have heard of many Englifh that in their Travelling have been loft, who have been found and fuccoured by the Indians very kindly. They are generally very quick on foot; and brought up even from their Mother's Brefts to running; their Legs being ftretch'd and bound up in a ftrange way in their Cradle backward, from their Infancy: Which makes fome of them fo excel in running, that they will run four-fcore or an hundred miles in a Summers Day: and they very often Practice running of Races.

As we went along, I afk'd the Indian what was the occa-fion of his going to Ipfwich? He told me he had fome Money owing him there, which he was going to receive. Upon which I took occafion to afk him, what Method was obferv'd amongft the Indians in Borrowing and Lending of Money, and what courfe they took to recover their Debts? In Anfwer whereto, he gave me the following Account.[166]

'The Indians,' fays he, 'are very defirous to come into Debt, but very negligent in making their Payments; and he that trufts them muft fuftain a Twofold Lofs, Firft, of his Commodity, and fecondly of their Cuftom, as I have found,' fays he, 'by dear Experience: Some indeed are ingenuous, plain-hearted, and honeft; but the moft will never pay, unlefs a Man follow them to their feveral Abodes, Towns, and Houfes, as I my felf have been forc'd to do. The moft common Excufe they make for not paying, and which they think very fatisfactory, is, that they have been fick; becaufe in the time of their ficknefs they give largely to their Priefts, who fometimes heals them by their Conjurations; and alfo at thofe times they keep open Houfe for all to come to help to pray with them, to whom alfo they give money. And this

---

[166] Almoft *verbatim* from WILLIAMS, p. 246-247.—ED.

this they will plead for an Excufe, even when they have not
been fick, on purpofe to deceive and defraud their Creditors.'

The Indian having made an End of what he had to fay,
I told him, If the Cafe were as he reprefented it, I thought
it was very dangerous Trading with them, and that it was a
difficult thing to buy and fell amongft them.

To this the Indian anfwer'd, That if I pleaf'd, he would
give me an Account of the Indians Buying and Selling.   I
told him with all my heart, and that I fhou'd Efteem my felf
oblig'd to him for fo doing.   Whereupon he began thus:

'The [150] Indians among themfelves trade their Corn, Skins,
Coats, Venifon, Fifh, &c. and fometimes come ten or twenty
in a Company to trade among the Englifh.   They have
fome who follow only making of Bows, fome Arrows, fome
Difhes, fome follow Fifhing, fome Hunting, and the Women
make all their Earthen Veffels.   Thofe that live near the
Sea-fide make money, and ftore up Shells in Summer againft
Winter, whereof to make their money.   They all generally
prize a Mantle of Englifh and Dutch Cloth, before their
own wearing of Skins or Furrs; becaufe they are warm
enough, and are lighter.   Cloth of a white colour they don't
care for, but defire to have a fad colour without any White
in it; as fuiting beft with their own natural Temper, which
inclines to fadnefs.

'They have very great difference in their Coyn; fome
will not pafs without Allowance, and fome is made of a
Counterfeit fhell; and their very black counterfeited by
a Stone, and other materials: Yet,' added he, ' I never knew
any of them much deceived; for their danger of being deceived, makes them cautious.   Whoever deals with them
had need of a great deal of Patience, and Wifdom; for they
frequently tell thofe they deal with, You lie, and you deceive
me;

[150] From WILLIAMS, p. 239-245.—ED.

me; which I know are very provoking words. They are mighty cunning in their Bargains to fave a Penny, and very fufpicious that Englifhmen Endeavour to deceive them: Therefore they will beat all Markets, and try all Places, and run twenty, thirty, yea, fometimes fourty miles, and more, and lodge in the Woods, to fave fix pence.

'They will often confefs, for their own Ends, that the Englifh are Richer, and Wifer, and Valianter than themfelves; yet this is for their own Ends, and therefore they add, *Nanoue;* which is, Give me this or that; a fort of begging which they are generally given to, tho' the more ingenuous fcorn it. I have often feen,' faid he, 'an Indian with great quantities of Money about him, beg a Knife of an Englifh Man, who has had never a Penny of Money.

'They are great Admirers of Looking-glaffes; and altho' their Complexions are not fo white and beautiful as the Englifh, yet they love to be looking in thofe Glaffes, as I my felf did, before I became a Friend, or knew how to worfhip GOD; but I now fee that it was nothing but Pride, which will appear in any Colour. And that makes our Women paint their Faces in all forts of Colours. Howes, Hatchets, and Knives, are things much efteem'd among the Indians, and will yield a good Price, and fo alfo will Tobacco Pipes.'

The honeft *Netop*, or Friend Indian, had but juft made an End of his Difcourfe, as we came to Ipfwich: I gave him many thanks for the Information he had given me, and alfo for his good Company, and wou'd have made him drink, but he very thankfully refuf'd it: And fo we parted, he going about his Occafions, and I and my Fair Fellow-Traveller, to Mr. Steward's, whofe Wife was Mrs. Comfort's own Aunt; whofe Joy to fee her Niece at Ipfwich, was fufficiently Expreff'd by the Noble Reception we met with, and the Treatment we found there; which far out-did whate'er we cou'd have Thought: And tho' my felf was but a Stranger to
them,

them, Yet the Extraordinary Civility and refpect they fhew'd me, gave me reafon enough to think I was very Welcome.

It was late when we came thither, and we were both very weary, which yet wou'd not Excufe us from the Trouble of a very Splendid Supper, before I was permitted to go to Bed; which was got ready in fo fhort a time, as wou'd have made us think, had we not known the Contrary, that it had been ready Provided againft we came. Tho' our Supper was extraordinary, yet I had fo great a defire to go to Bed, as made it to me a troublefome Piece of Kindnefs. But this being happily over, I took my leave of my Fellow-Traveller, and was Conducted to my Appartment by Mrs. Stewart herfelf, who Character I fhan't attempt to night, being fo very weary, but referve till to morrow morning: Only I muft let you know that my Apartment was fo Noble, and the Furniture fo fuitable to it, that I doubt not but even the King himfelf has been often-times contented with a worfer Lodging.

Having repof'd my felf all Night upon a Bed of Down, (than which there cou'd be nothing fofter but the Arms of Iris,) I flept fo very foundly that the Sun (who lay not on fo foft a Bed as I did) had got the ftart of me, and rife before me; but was fo kind however as to make me one of his firft vifits, and to give me the *Bonjour;* on which I ftraight got up and dreff'd my felf, having a Mind to look about me and fee where I was: And having took a view of Ipfwich, I found it to be fituated by a fair River, whofe firft Rife from a Lake or Pond was twenty miles up, breaking its courfe thorow a hideous fwamp for many miles, a harbour for Bears; it iffueth forth into a large Bay, (where they fifh for Whales,) due Eaft over againft the Ifland of Sholes, a great place of fifhing; the mouth of that River is barr'd: It is a good Haven Town; their Meeting-Houfe or Church is built very beauti-fully: There is ftore of Orchards and Gardens about it, and good Land for Cattel and Hufbandry.

But

But I remember, Sifter, I promif'd to give you Mrs. Steward's Character, and if I hadn't, yet Gratitude and Juftice wou'd exact it of me: Her Stature is of a middle fize, fit for a Woman; Her Face is ftill the magazine of Beauty, whence fhe may fetch Artillery enough to wound a Thoufand Lovers; and when fhe was about 18, perhaps there never was a Face more fweet and charming: Nor cou'd it well be otherwife, fince now at 33, all you call fweet and ravifhing, is in her Face; which 'tis as great a Pleafure to behold, as a perpetual Sunfhine, without any Clouds at all; and yet all this fweetnefs is joyn'd with fuch attractive vertue as draws all to a certain diftance, and there detains them with reverence and admiration, none ever daring to approach her nigher, or having power to go further off.

She's fo obliging, courteous and civil, as if thofe qualities were only born with her, and refted in her Bofom as their Center. Her Speech and her Behaviour is fo gentle, fweet, and affable, that, whatfoever Men may talk of Magick, there is none Charms but fhe. So good a Wife fhe is, fhe frames her Nature to her Hufbands; the Hiacinth follows not the Sun more willingly, than fhe her Hufband's pleafure. Her Houfehold is her Charge; her care to that, makes her but feldom a Non-refident. Her Pride is to be Neat and Cleanly, and her Thrift not to be Prodigal. And, to conclude, is both Wife and Religious, which makes her all that I have faid before.

In the next place, Sifter, I fuppofe yourfelf will think it reafonable, that unto Mrs. Stewards, I fhou'd add her Hufband's Character; whofe Worth and Goodnefs do well merit it: As to his Stature 'tis inclining to Tall; and as to his Afpect, if all the Lineaments of a Sincere and honeft-hearted Man were loft out of the World, they might be all retriev'd, by looking on his Face: He's one whofe Bounty is limited by Reafon, not by Oftentation; and to make it laft, he deals it difcreetly; as we Sowe our Land not by the

Sack,

Sack, but by the hand-ful: He is fo fincere and upright, that his word and his meaning never fhake hands and part, but always go together: His Mind is always fo ferene, that that Thunder does but rock him a fleep, which breaks other Mens flumbers.   His Thoughts have an Aim as High as Heaven, tho' their Refidence be in the Valley of an humble Heart.   He is not much given to talk, tho' he knows how to do it as well as any Man: He loves his Friend, and will do any thing for him, except it be to wink at his faults, of which he will be always a fevere Reprover: He is fo good a Hufband, that he is worthy of the Wife, that he Enjoys, and wou'd even make a bad Wife good by his Example.[167]

Ipfwich, my Sifter, is a Country Town, not very large, and when a ftranger arrives there, 'tis quickly known to every one: It is no wonder then that the next day after our Arrival, the News of it was carry'd to *Mr. Hubbald,* the Minifter of the Town, who hearing that I was the Perfon that had brought over fo great a venture of Learning, did me the Honour to make me a vifit at Mr. Steward's, where

I

[167] Concerning this Mr. Stewart, not much can be found ; but the records at Salem have been fearched by A. C. Goodell, Jr., who has kindly furnifhed the following facts. He was undoubt-edly the WILLIAM STEWART, of Ipfwich, merchant, whofe inventory was taken 22 Sept., 1693. The following items are interefting : 'Apparell and books, £20 ; cafh and filver plate, £48, 17s. ; 4 beds, bedding, linen, woolen, truncks, and table linen, £48, 7s. ; feveral forts of goods and merchandife in the fhop, £656, 5s. 8d. ; debts due by book, £321, 8s. 8d. ; houfe and barn, orchard and land about it, with Common right be-longing, £300 ; Total, £1,447, 7s. 4d., and debts due from the eftate, £302, 1s. 5d.'

The executrix was the widow Anne Stewart, and there was only one child left, Margaret, aged about 10 years. The fureties were John Stewart and John Harris. This John Stewart went to England the fame year, probably. When the mother was made guardian of the child, 4 Aug., 1696, the fureties were Bartholomew Gedney and John Harris, and 15 Nov., 1697, the widow Anne being dead, Barth. Gedney, judge, &c., appoints himfelf guardian of the orphan. Sept. 2, 1698, the inventory is found of the eftate of Wm. and Anne Stewart, *alias* Anne Gedney. As the firft wife of Col. Barth. Gedney, Judge of Probate, &c., died 6 Jan'y, 1696, it is very probable that he married the widow Anne Stewart.

We may add that we have fhown (*ante* p. 63,) that William Stewart came over with Richard Wilkins, in 1684—ED.

I lay, and afterwards kindly invited me and my Fellow Traveller to his own Houfe, where he was pleaf'd to give us a very handfome Entertainment. His writing of the Hiftory of Indian Warrs, fhews him to be a Perfon of good Parts and Underftanding: He is a fober, grave, and well-accomplifhed Man; a good Preacher (as all the Town affirm, for I didn't hear him) and one that lives according to his Preaching. After fome Difcourfe with him, knowing him to be the Author of the Book called the Indian Wars, I took the Boldnefs to Enquire of him how the Indians manag'd themfelves in their Wars? To which he very courteoufly gave me the following Account.[166]

'When the Indians go to War, and are ready to Engage with their Enemy, they commonly cry out, Fight, Fight, which in their Language is *Juhettcke*: This is the word of Encouragement they ufe, when they animate each other in War: For they ufe their tongues inftead of Drums and Trumpets.

'They alfo make ufe of another word, which is *Numma-yaontam*, which is, I fcorn, or take it in indignation: This is a Common Word, not only in War, but in Peace alfo (their Spirits in naked Bodies being as proud and as high as thofe that are more gallant) from which fparks of their lufts of Pride and Paffion, begin the flame of their Warrs.

'A Drum they call *Popowuttahig;* not [that] they have any fuch of their own making; yet fuch they have from the French; and I once knew a good Drum made among them, in imitation of the Englifh.

'Shott

[166] The Rev. William Hubbard, of Ipfwich, the Hiftorian, is well known. A very good biography is furnifhed by S. G. Drake, Efq., in his edition of the "Hiftory of the Indian Wars." publifhed in two volumes, at Bofton, 1865. Rev. William, fon of William Hubbard, was born at Tendering, Co. Effex, in 1621, was fettled at Ipfwich, in 1656, was twice married, and left iffue. He died, 14 Sept., 1704.

Notwithftanding DUNTON'S affertion that Hubbard gave him this account, we doubt if that clergyman would have fo boldly copied from WILLIAMS, p. 258–264. It may be noticed that DUNTON did not put this fiction in his "Life and Errors."—ED.

'Shott they call *Shottash*, which is a made Word
tho' their Guns they have from the French, and c
many a score to the English, when they are out o
for they know not how to mend them.

'They have their Guards as the Europeans have
once Travelled (in a place that was thought dangero
a great Indian Prince, and his Queen and Children i
pany, with a Guard of near two hundred: Twenty or
Fires were made every Night for the Guard (the Que
Prince in the midst:) And Centinels were set by co
Exact as they are in Europe. And when we tr
through a place where Ambushes suspected to lie, a
Guard, like unto a Life-Guard, compassed (some neare
farther off) the King and Queen, my self and some
English with me.

'They are very copious and Pathetical in Orations
People, to kindle a flame of Wrath, Valour, and Re
from all the Common Places which Commanders use to
on. They have a mighty Faculty of mocking one and
This mocking (between their Great ones) is a great kir
of Wars amongst them; yet I have known some of
Chief Ones say, Why shou'd I hazard the lives of my
cious Subjects, them and theirs, to kindle a Fire whic
Man knows how long and how far it will burn, for the
ing of a Dog?

'The Cry of Fire is very dreadful to them in the Ni
I once lodged in an Indian House full of People, when
sudden the whole company, the Women especially, cried
in Apprehension that the Enemy had fired the Hou
being about Midnight. The House was fired indeed,
not by an Enemy, but by Accident; the men ran up on
House top, and with their naked hands beat out the F
one of them had his Leg scorch'd, and suddenly after t
came into the House again, he undauntedly cut his
with a Knife, to let out the burnt Blood.

'Th

' Their Wars are far lefs cruel and devouring than the bloody Wars in Europe: for feldom twenty are flain in a pitcht Field; partly becaufe when they fight in a Wood Every Tree is a Buckler: And when they fight in a Prifon, they fight with leaping and Dancing, that feldom an Arrow hits: and where a man is wounded, unlefs he that fhot follows upon the Wounded, they foon retire, and fave the wounded Perfon: And yet having no Swords or Guns, all that are flain, are commonly flain with great Valour and Courage; for the Conquerour ventures into the thickeft and brings the Head of his Enemy.'

Mr. Hubbald having done his Difcourfe, I gave him my hearty Thanks, for his Entertaining Relation, and begg'd his Excufe for the Trouble I had given him. And having anfwer'd him fome queftions about the Books I had brought over, and fhewn him a Catalogue of them, which he took very kindly, I took my leave of him, and return'd back with Mrs. Comfort, and Mr. Steward.

The next day I was for another Ramble, in which Mr. Steward was pleaf'd to accompany me, (but I left Mrs. Comfort with her Aunt) and the place we went to, was a Town call'd *Rowley*, lying fix miles North-Eaft from Ipfwich, where moft of the Inhabitants had been Clothiers: But there was that Day a great Game of Foot-Ball to be play'd, which was the occafion of our going thither; There was another Town that play'd againft them, as is fometimes common in England; but they play'd with their bare feet, which I thought was very odd; but it was upon a broad Sandy Shoar, free from Stones, which made it the more eafie. Neither were they fo apt to trip up one anothers heels and quarrel, as I have feen 'em in England.

After their Sport was over, we return'd home, and by the way I enquir'd of Mr. Steward what other Sports or Games the Indians follow'd befides Foot-ball Playing? Upon which, Mr. Steward very readily gave me the following

lowing account;[159] which was very fatisfactory, and fhow'd him to be a very good Man. His Relation was this:

'The Games of the Indians (like thofe of the Englifh) are of two Sorts, Publick and Private; They have a Private, and fometimes a Publick Game, like unto the Englifh Cards; but inftead of Cards, they play with ftrong Rufhes.

'Secondly, They have a kind of Dice, which are Plumb-Stones painted, which they caft in a Tray, with a mighty Noife and Sweating: Their Publick Games are folemnized with the meeting of Hundreds, and fometimes Thoufands; and confift of many Vanities, none of which I durft ever be prefent at, that I might not Countenance and partake of their folly, after I once faw the Evil of them. The Chief Gamefters among them much defire to make their gods on their fide with them in their Games; (as our Englifh Game-fters fo far alfo will acknowledge GOD) therefore I have feen 'em keep as a precious ftone, a piece of Thunderbolt, which is like unto a Chriftal, which they dig out of the ground under fome Tree Thunder-fmitten; and from this ftone they have an Opinion of Succefs; and I have not heard of any of them which have had it, prove Lofers; which I conceive may be Satan's Policy, and GOD's holy Juftice, to harden them, for their not rifing higher from the Thunderbolt, to that GOD who fhoots it.

'When they play Publickly, they have an Arbour or Play-Houfe made of long Poles fet in the Earth four fquare, fix-teen or twenty foot high, on which they hang great ftore of their ftringed Money; and have great ftakings; Town againft Town, and two chofen out of the reft by courfe to play the Game at this kind of Dice, in the midft of all their Abettors, with great fhouting and folemnity: Their Play at Foot-Ball, (which you have now feen) is the moft Innocent of all their Sports, but this they only play at in the Summer time;

---

[159] Mr. Stewart, like DUNTON's other interlocutors, had a marvelous facility of quoting WILLIAMS verbatim. See KEY, p. 254-257.—ED.

time; playing generally Town againft Town; and always on fome broad Sandy Shoar, as now they did; or elfe on fome foft heathy Plot, becaufe of their naked feet, (for you fee they play bare-foot) and tho' they lay great Stakes, yet they feldom quarrel about it. Yet they often regret their great Lofings; which, when fometimes I have told them of, when they have Staked and loft their Money, Cloaths, Houfe, Corn, and themfelves too, if they are fingle Perfons; they wou'd ingenuoufly confefs their folly, being at fuch times weary of their Lives, and ready to make away with themfelves: Which is an Emblem of the horrour of Confcience which poor Sinners walk in at laft, when they fee what woful Games they have played in their Life, and now find themfelves Eternal Beggars.

'They have another kind of Solemn Publick Meeting, wherein they lie under the Trees, in a kind of Religious Obfervation, and have a Mixture of Devotions and Sports. But their chiefeft Idol of all for Sport and Game, is, (if their Land be at Peace) toward Harveft, when they fet up a long Houfe called *Qunnekamuck*, which fignifies Long-Houfe, fometimes an hundred, fometimes two hundred foot long, upon a Plain near the Court, which they call *Kittcickauick*, where many thoufand Men and Women meet; where he that goes in, danceth in the fight of all the reft; and is prepared with Money, Coats, fmall Breeches, Knives, or what he is able to reach to, and gives thefe things away to the Poor, who yet muft particularly beg, and fay, *Cowequetummous*, that is, *I befeech you:* Which Word, (altho' there is not one Common Beggar amongft them, yet they will often ufe, when their richeft amongft them wou'd fain obtain ought by Gift.)

'But I am afraid (faid Mr. Steward) I tire you with my long Relation;' I told him it was fo far from tiring me, that it was very diverting; but I was afraid I gave him too much trouble:

trouble: 'I fhall think nothing fo,' reply'd he, 'that proves a Diverfion to you; but fince I have given you an Account of the Indians Games,' added he, 'I will only make this fhort Obfervation[100] from them, to wit, This Life is a fhort minute, Eternity follows; On the Improvement or Dif-improvement of this fhort minute depends a Joyful or Dreadful Eternity: Yet (which I tremble to think of) how cheap is this invaluable Jewel made, and how many vain Inventions and foolifh paftimes have the Sons of Men found out, to pafs away their Time, and poft over this fhort minute of Life, until like fome pleafant River, they pafs into *mare mortuum*, the Dead Sea of Eternal Lamentation.

Mr. Steward gave me a great deal of fatisfaction by his Difcourfe; and the more, becaufe I found Religion and Real Godlinefs had fo great an Afcendant in his Soul. But his Difcourfe ended juft as we came to Ipfwich Towns End; from whence we were not long a going to his Houfe, where Mrs. Steward had provided us a good Supper, and gave us a hearty welcome home.

You know my Rambling Humour, Sifter, and that I am ftill for New Difcoveries, which made me the next Morning Enquire of Mr. Steward's Servants what other Towns there lay near Ipfwich; (for I had a Months mind that Day to make another Ramble) and they acquainted me that about Seven miles off there was the Town of *Gloucefter*, and that their Miftrefs had a Kinfwoman that liv'd there, and therefore they believ'd fhe wou'd be very ready to go along with me thither.

I was very well pleaf'd with this Information, and prefently went in and told Mrs. Steward, that I was for another Ramble that Day, being for feeing as much of the Countrey as I cou'd: She afk'd me whether I defign'd to Ramble? I told her I defign'd for Gloucefter: 'O,' fays fhe straight,

---

[100] Even this obfervation is WILLIAMS'S.—ED.

ftraight, ' I have a Kinfwoman lives there, I want to fee, and therefore Coufin Comfort and my felf will go a long with you.' I readily accepted of her Kind offer, it being all I wanted; but Mr. Steward, by reafon of fome Bufinefs he had before appointed on that Day, cou'd not go with us, but fent his Chiefeft Man, with one of his beft Horfes, to wait upon his Wife.

The Way we rid was very pleafant; for there the lofty Trees with their proud Spreading Tops, made a refrefhing Shade, and kept us from the Suns too Officious Kindnefs. Befides the conftant Profpect of the Sea on our right hand, brought us fuch cool refrefhing Breezes thence, as made our Journey extream delightful, tho' the Sun fhin'd very hot: I know not what Information Mrs. Comfort had given to her Aunt of me, but fhe was pleaf'd to tell me, She underftood I had a mighty Paffion for *my firft Wife,* and that fhe was a Perfon that deferv'd it; ' But that which I wou'd know of you, (continued fhe,) is, *Whether you have ever* lov'd any before her?' ' Yes, Madam, Many,[161] (anfwer'd I) but none fo well as fhe. Nor do I think that any diminution of my Love for Iris.'

I

[161] DUNTON has confeffed in his "Life and Errors" to numerous youthful admirations, or poffibly flirtations. He began in his thirteenth year by a love for Mrs. Mary Sanders. At London, at Mr. Parkhurft's, he commenced a flirtation with Sufanna S—ing, who lived in the fame houfe. Next came Rachel Seaton, then Sarah Day, of Ratcliffe, Sarah Doolittle and Sarah Brifcow, of Uxbridge.

Whether DUNTON did on this occafion narrate his forrows to Mrs. Stewart, we cannot fay. He did, however, confide them to the public, as the fame ftory is told in his converfation in Ireland, reprinted by Nichols in his fecond volume. There is no mention of a Mrs. Lucy, which feems an afterthought, but the whole is told as belonging to Rachel Seaton. The poem is there printed, and it is explained that DUNTON termed his miftrefs Clara. NICHOLS fays the fame verfes were applied by DUNTON to his publifher, Mrs. S. Malthus, and quotes them in vol. ii, p. 460. He does not apparently notice that as applied to Mrs. Malthus they are parodied.

From the references in DUNTON'S works we may be fatisfied that Rachel Seaton was a real perfon, and the courtfhip was not imaginary.—ED.

37

I told her I admired one Rachel S——, who dyed fome years agoe. For all my other Courtfhips were before I knew her; therefore cou'd be no injury to her; 'but fince She has been mine, I can affirm, I have not had one Thought has ftray'd from her, nor feen the Perfon I cou'd better like than fhe. Not, Madam, that I am fo foolifh as to think that there are none exceed my Iris; I do believe there may be many that every way excell her; but there are none that do fo in my Eye.'

'But, Sir,' faid Mrs. Steward, 'what were thofe Perfons that you courted firft? There muft be fomething that attracted, in 'em; Or elfe a Perfon of your Judgment had never courted 'em at all. I wou'd know therefore from whence your change proceeded.'

'Why truly, Madam,' faid I, 'There was none I courted, but there was fomething I found in 'em, that I thought agreeable. There was one Mrs. —— Lucy I had a mighty kindnefs for; a Venus might have well enough been form'd out of her Perfon, and yet her Wit did far Exceed her Beauty; I took a mighty pleafure in her Company, and becaufe fhe extreamly admir'd Poetry, I made my Courtfhip to the Mufes too, that I might be more grateful to her; and I had the good Fortune to write fomething in her Praife, which met with univerfal Approbation; I firft perfonated them to her, and fhe to her acquaintance.

'But thefe *Poetick Effays* had an Effect different from that which I intended 'em; for I defign'd by 'em only to make my own Addreffes to her the more acceptable; but fhe by fhewing 'em abroad, having a Reputation beyond what fhe had before; began to value herfelf at a higher rate, and treat me with Difdain and Scorn. I wasn't fo blind with gazing on her face or fo charm'd with reading her Letters, but I cou'd fee with what contempt fhe treated me; and feeing, cou'd not but refent it, to that degree, that I thought

'twas

'twas high time to make her low'r her Top-fail; and therefore I foon after fent her the lines I'm going to repeat to you.

> Know, Clara, fince thou'rt grown fo proud,
>   'Twas I that gave thee thy Renown;
> Thou'dft elfe in the *forgotten Crowd*
>   Of Common Beauties liv'd unknown,
> Had not *my Verfe* exhal'd thy Name,
> And Impt it with the Plumes of Fame.
>
> That *Killing Power* is none of Thine:
>   I gave it to thy *Voice, thy Eyes:*
> Thy *Sweets, thy Graces,* all are mine;
>   Thou art my Star, *fhin'ft in my Skies.*
> Then dart not from thy borrow'd Sphere
> *Lightning* on him that plac'd thee there.
>
> Treat me then with *Difdain* no more
>   Left what I made, I Uncreate;
> Let Fools thy *Myftick Forms* adore;
>   *I know thee in thy Mortal State:*
> Wife Poets that wrapt Truth in Tales,
> Know her Themfelves thro' all her Vails.

' Thefe Verfes pluck'd down her Plumes; I underftand fhe Refented 'em very much; which I was not at all troubled at; for her former Difingenuous Carriage had given me enough of her; and fo I left her. And I appeal to you, Madam,' (addreffing my felf to Mrs. Steward) 'whether I hadn't reafon to change.' Mrs. Steward gave her Judgment in my Favour; and expreff'd her felf very well pleaf'd with the Poem I fent her.

We were now come to Gloucefter, which is a pretty little Town. Here it was that the Maffachufets Colony firft fet down, tho' Salem was the firft Town built in that Colony. Here is a very fine Harbour for Ships.

Mrs. Steward's kinfwoman, who was a very obliging Country-Widow, receiv'd us very kindly, and made us very welcome.

While

While Mrs. Steward and Mrs. Comfort were talking with their kinfwoman, my felf and Mr. Steward's Man took a walk about the Town and went down to fee the Harbour; as we were walking along, an Indian comes to me and afks me What News? I told him I was a Stranger there, and knew nothing of any News, but only came to fee the Town. Whereupon the Indian, after a very obliging bow, went his way. This occafion'd me to enquire of Mr. Steward's Man,[162] what was the meaning of it, and whether or no the Indians uf'd to be inquifitive after News? Who gave me this account of it. .

' That their defire after, and delight in News, is as great as the Athenians of old, or any other People at this Day; And that a Stranger that can relate News to them in their own Language, they will ftile him *Manittoo*, a god. Their manner is,' faid he, ' upon any News, to fit round, double, or treble, or more, as their Numbers be: I have feen,' faid he, ' near a thoufand in a round, where half fo many Englifh could hardly have fat: Every Man hath his Pipe of Tobacco, and then there is a deep filence made, and attention given to him that fpeaketh. And many of them will deliver themfelves, either in a relation of News, or in a Confutation, with very fignificant Words, and fuitable Action, commonly an hour, and fometimes two hours together. But they are very impatient, and take it as a great affront, when their Speech is not attended and liftened to. And at the End of his Speech, they commonly fay, You fay true, which are words of great flattery, and conftantly ufed to their Princes at their Speeches; for which, if they be eloquent, they efteem them as gods, as Herod was among the Jews.

' The Indians do often ufe this queftion, Why come the Englifh men hither? And meafuring others by themfelves,

fay,

---

[162] 'Like mafter, like man.' Mr. WILLIAMS. See KEY, p. 142–147.— Stewart's man was alfo well read in ED.

fay, *It is becaufe you want firing.* For they having burnt up the Wood in one place, and having no Draughts to bring wood to them, they are fain to follow the Woods, and fo to remove to a frefh new place for the Woods fake. In a time of War, a Meffenger with News runs very fwiftly; and at every Town the Meffenger comes, a frefh meffenger is fent. He that is the laft, coming within a mile or two of the Court, or Chief Houfe, he hollows often, and they that hear anfwer him, until by mutual Hollowing and Anfwering, he is brought to the place of Audience; where by his means is gathered a great Confluence of People to hear the News.'

I thanked the Man for the Relation he had given me, and made this Obfervation upon it, That the whole Race of Mankind is generally infected with an itching defire of hearing News.

So returning to the Houfe again, we found Mrs. Steward and Mrs. Comfort waiting for us to take Horfe; which (after taking my Leave of the Widow, and thanking her for our kind Entertainment) we quickly did, and came back in very good time to Ipfwich, where Mr. Steward had taken care to have a good Supper ready for us.

The next morning, I was Returning to Bofton, but Mr. Steward was very folicitous to have me ftay that day, and go with him to *Wanafquam*, an Indian Town, where he had fome bufinefs: I confefs he hit me in the right Vein, for I lov'd Rambling dearly, and knew not how to deny him; and therefore was eafily perfwaded to go with him.

Having refrefh'd our felves before we went, by eating a good Breakfaft, we began our Ramble, and had rid almoft half the way to Wanafquam, when on the Road we met an Indian Woman, with her face all over black'd with foot, having a very forrowful and rueful fort of Countenance; and quickly after, two or three Indian Men in the fame black and forrowful Condition, that had I been alone, it wou'd

have

have frightened me. But having Mr. Steward with me, I was well enough : Indeed they all pass'd by us very civilly, saying only *Afcowcquaffum*, which is in Englifh Good morrow to you.

Mr. Steward afk'd me if I had ever feen any of thofe black-fac'd Indians before ? I told him No, and afk'd him what the meaning of it was ? He told me, They had had fome Relation very lately dead ; and that the Blacking of their Faces, was equivalent to the Englifhes going into Mourning for their Relations ; and afk'd me whether I had ever feen an Indian Burial ? I told him No, nor Englifh neither, in New-England, for none had dy'd that I remember'd, fince I came into the Country. Why then, fays he, I'll tell you what the Indian Cuftoms are, in reference to their Dead, and to their Burials.[163]

' Where there is any Body Dead, they generally exprefs it by, *He is in Black*. That is, he hath fome dead in his Houfe : For altho' at their firft being fick, all the Women and Maidens black their Faces with Soot, and other Blackings, yet upon the Death of the fick Perfon, the Father, or Hufband, and all his Neighbours, the Men as well as the Women, wear black Faces, and lay on Soot very thick, which I have often feen clotted with their Tears. This blacking and lamenting they obferve divers weeks, and months ; and fometimes a year, if the Perfon dying be great and Publick. But as they thus abound in Lamentation for the Dead, fo they abound in Confolations to the Living, whom they vifit frequently, bidding them to be of good Chear, which they exprefs by ftroaking the head of the Father, Mother, Hufband, or Wife of the Dead.

' He that winds up, and prepares the Dead for Burial, is commonly one of the moft wife, grave, and well-defcended Men among them. When they come to the Grave they lay the Dead by the Graves Mouth, and then all fit down and
lament ;

---

[163] WILLIAMS, p. 274-277.—ED.

lament; fo that I have feen tears run down the Cheeks of the ftouteft Captains among them in abundance, as well as from little Children; and after the Dead is laid in the Grave, (and in fome parts fome of their Goods caft in with them) they then make a fecond great Lamentation: And upon the Grave is fpread the Mat that the Deceafed Died on, the Difh he eat in, and fometimes a fair Coat of Skin hang'd up upon the next Tree to the Grave; which none will touch, but fuffer it there to rot with the Dead.'

I gave Mr. Steward many Thanks for his Relation; and expreff'd my Acknowledgments to him: But the End of his Story having brought us to the beginning of Wanaf-quam, put an End to our Difcourfe; It is a very forry fort of a Town, but better to come at by Land than by Water: For it is a dangerous place to fail by, efpecially in ftormy weather, by reafon of the many Rocks and foaming Break-ers all about it. We faw feveral other mourning Indians in that Town; and upon Enquiry found that one of the chief Indians in the Town was lately dead and buried.[163]

There was nothing elfe remarkable to be feen in the Town, and therefore as foon as Mr. Steward had done his bufinefs, we return'd back to Ipfwich. And early the next morning, having paid our hearty and repeated thanks to Mr. Steward and his Charming Wife, for the Noble Entertain-ment we had receiv'd from them, my felf and Mrs. Comfort took our leaves, and made the beft of our way for Bofton, where we arriv'd according to our Promife, to the great fatisfaction of my good Landlord and his Wife: Mrs. Com-fort being no lefs pleaf'd with the pleafure of her Journey, than I was with her good Company.

Upon my coming to Bofton, I heard that the Worthily
Famous

---

[163] In the "Life and Errors" DUNTON boldly writes: "We found that one of the Chief Indians in the Town was lately dead, and was to be bury'd that Night. Having never feen an Indian Burial, I ftaid till the Solemnity was over, which was thus performed." He then proceeds to copy the account given by WILLIAMS, and defcribed above.—ED.

Famous Mr. Morton,[164] fo much celebrated in England for
his Piety and Learning, was juft arriv'd from England, and
with him, his kinfman, Dr. Morton the Phyfician: I have
feen his younger Brother often here, and he has the Name
of an Extraordinary Perfon, and no doubt deferves it. Mr.
Morton brought me Letters from my Deareft Iris, by which
I underftand not only that fhe was then in good health, but
that you, my Dear Sifter, were fo too; and your kind
Remembrance to me, which my Iris writes me word of, I
kindly accept, and thank you for.

Mr. Morton did me the Honour to declare he was very
glad to fee me, and I am fure I was as glad to fee him; not
only becaufe he brought me Letters from my deareft Iris,
but becaufe of his own Perfonal Worth: And indeed the
News of his Arrival was received here with Extraordinary
Joy by the People in general; who (to fay the truth,) are all
beholden to him for the great Character he gave of New-
England in London, which was the Chief Motive of my
coming hither. I know it wou'd be Prefumption in me to
draw his character; and yet I cannot but fay fomething of
him, as an Effay towards it.

His Converfation fhews him a Gentleman: For he has
fenfe Enough for a Privy Counfellour, and Soul Great
Enough for a King: And whoever has the honour of his
Company, will quickly be fatisfy'd that he is not only the
Repofitory of all Arts and Sciences, but of the Graces too;
and Will find that for matter, Words, and Manner, he is all
that is delightful in Converfation: His matter is not ftale
and

[164] Rev. Charles Morton, fays SAVAGE,
eldeft fon of Rev. Nicholas M., of
Southwark, near London, was born in
1626, fettled at Blifland, in Cornwall,
was ejected in 1662, and for feveral
years taught in a feminary at Newing-
ton Green. He arrived in Bofton in the
fpring of 1686, and was ordained at
Charleftown in November of the fame
year. He was chofen Vice-Prefident
of Harvard, and died 11 April 1698.
With him came his nephew, Dr. Charles
Morton, who went home in July, 1687;
and the younger brother of the phyfician was undoubtedly Nicholas Morton,
H. C. 1686, who died, 3 Nov., 1689.—
ED.

and ſtudied, but always reſent, and occaſional: for whatever
ſubjeƈt is at any time ſtarted, he has ſtill ſome pleaſant and
pat ſtory for it; nor is he ſtiff and moroſe, but duƈtile and
plyable to the Company; his Diſcourſe is high, but not
Soaring; familiar, but not low; profound, but not obſcure;
and the more ſublime, the more Intelligible and Conſpic-
uous.

His Memory is as vaſt as his Knowledge, which is ſo
great, that in the Firmament of Learning, the Name of
Morton will ſhine like a Bright Star of the firſt Magnitude
to all Poſterity: and as tho' he were the Epitomy both of
Ariſtotle and Deſcartes, he is the very Soul of philoſophy.
Yet tho' he be a very Panaretus, or Magazine of all the vertues, ſo great is his Humility he knows it leaſt of any; and
is as far from Pride as Ignorance: And if we may judge of
a Mans Religion by his Charity, (and can we go by a ſurer
Rule) he is a truly Pious and Religious Man: And being
thus qualify'd, he muſt certainly be the fitteſt to bring up
young Men to the Miniſtry, of any Man in England: And
that this is matter of Faƈt, the many Eminent and Learned
Divines, now Preachers in England, of his bringing up, is a
convincing Teſtimony.

This, Siſter, is that Great Man, by whoſe Inſtruƈtions our
Reverend and Worthy Unkle, Mr. Obadiah Mariott, was ſo
well Qualify'd for the Work of the Miniſtry: You cannot,
Siſter, but remember Mr. Morton, who formerly liv'd at
Newington-Green, but will ſcarce ever return thither, he
ſeeming reſolv'd to Live and Dye here. 'Tis true, he
brought up chiefly the Children of Diſſenters, yet is (as all
good Men are) a Man of Univerſal Charity. But, Siſter,
tho' this be not a Theme ſo proper to entertain you withal,
yet I cou'd not but pay my reſpeƈts to the Worth of this
Great Man. But my next Paragraph will be more agreeable.

In the ſame ſhip with Mr. Morton, came over one Mrs.
Hicks,

Hicks,[166] with the valuable Venture of her own fair Perfon, which went off at an Extraordinary Rate, having married a Gentleman worth £40,000, as is reported. And therefore I don't wonder that fo many fair Ladies venture Themfelves to the Eaft Indies, fince they fucceed fo well, and are a Commodity that makes fuch vaft Returns. By this, Sifter, you fee, That if your Beauty were but Equal to your vertue, I cou'd put you into a ready way of Turning Merchant; but Vertue alone won't do; I confefs vertue is the beft Commodity, yet Beauty in this Market, yields the higheft Price. But where they both meet, as in the Inftance above fpecified, they are the beft cargo that a fhip can carry.

And now, my Sifter, in a few Weeks I hope to take my Leave of this New World, and of my Rambles in it, which have been fill'd with various Adventures: And if you've a defire to know 'em; Then as to what befel me from my taking Boat at Ratcliffe-Crofs (where I parted from you,) to my Arrival at the Ifle of Wight, you may find [in] my Letter from Weft Cowes to my dear Iris: And all the Hardfhips of my Long Sea-voyage, you may find it in my Letter to my Brother Lake. If you wou'd know what welcome I receiv'd at Bofton, and how I manag'd all my Bufinefs there, you'll find it in my Letter to Mr. Larkin; Or if you'd know all the Adventures that I met with in my Rambles to the feveral Adjacent Towns to Bofton, they are contain'd in a Letter to my Coufin Woolhurft: And if you defire to be inform'd of my Ramble to Natick, and the Converfion of the Indians, you may fee it in my Letter to my Father, the Reverend Doctor. My Ramble to Salem, is contain'd in my Laft to Iris, and my Ramble to Ipfwich in this to your felf.

But

---

[166] This was undoubtedly Mary, daughter of Rev. John Hicks, who married Benjamin Browne, of Salem, of a family of diftinguifhed pofition there, and died 26 Dec., 1703. Her husband was a member of the Council, and died 1708. In the "Life and Errors" it is faid fhe married 'a Merchant *in Salem*, worth £30,000.' RANDOLPH, writing July 28, fays Morton had been here about two months.—ED.

But having receiv'd a world of Favours from many friends at Bofton, I gave 'em all a general Treat, but the laft week, at George Monks, the moft noted Publick Houfe in Bofton: which was accepted by my Friends with the fame kindnefs with which it was given. And was done with fo free an air, that 'twas thought lavifh by fome, who like their Predeceffor Judas, were ready to cry, What means all this wafte?

And thus, my Sifter, having acquitted my felf of my Promife, and given you an Account of my laft Ramble in New-England, I muft fubmit it to your Cenfure, who I am fure know how to cover, as well as to obferve, the Faults you find in it. You fee 'tis chiefly a Converfation manag'd with the Fair Sex; and whether I have acquitted my felf well, is what I fhall expect to know from you.

But methinks, Sifter, I begin to be a weary of New-England; For tho' there be good Company, and many good Accomodations, yet 'tis not home, nor is there Iris here. And were it not for the Difpatch of thofe neceffary affairs that lie upon my hand at Bofton, and keeps me here at prefent, I'd be the Meffenger my felf of my own Letter to you. But howfoever, I hope it won't be long ere I fhall follow it. For I have already agreed to go with Captain Leg in the ———. And to my great Satisfaction I hear Mr. Mortimer and Mr. King are to be my Companions for Old England: And O how do I wifh for a quick Paffage! That I might once more Anchor in the Arms of Iris!

As for my Iris, fhe has a Packet from me as well as you, and therefore there's no need to mention her: But when you fee my Brother Lake, give my kind love to him, and let him know I'm well: And do the like to all the reft of our Relations. And now, dear Sifter, till Providence fhall bring me back into Old England, Farewel. And in the meantime reft affured, there's none that more entirely loves you than

Your moft Affectionate Brother,

PHILARET.

LETTER VIII.

TO MR. RICHARD WILKINS IN BOSTON IN
NEW ENGLAND.

NEST Mr. Wilkins: Since you were fo kind as to fee me on Shipboard, and was the laft of my Friends that took their Leaves of me, it will be both rude and Unkind in me, not to give you an Account of my Voyage home: To avoid both which Imputations, I will give a brief Account of my Paffage, with as much Sincerity, and as little Ceremony as may be. Mr. York, Mr. Heath and Mr. Tryon, (and all my Bofton friends) came to our Ship to fhake hands with us, and our Capt. treated 'em with Wine, Beer, Cyder and Neats Tongues, and as foon as ever they took boat again our Capt. ordered all his Guns to fire; at which they all of them (which were about 20,[166]) fil'd the very Heavens with
Hurras

[166] In his " Life and Errors," fome of the twenty friends are named. " I was attended on board by Dr. Bullivant, Mr. Wilkins, Mr. York, Mr. Gouge, Mr. Heath, Mr. Tryon, Mr. Green and fome other of my Bofton friends." He adds at this point the following farewell :

" Kind *Boften* adieu, part we muft, tho' 'tis pity,
But I'm made for Mankind, and all the world is my City.
Look how on the fhore, they hoop and they hollow,
Not for Joy I am gone, but for Grief they cann't follow."

—ED.

Hurras and Shouts, and Shaking of Hats and Gloves, as long as they could fee us.

The Ship I went in, as you well know, was Burthen about 150 Tuns ; and certainly as Tite a Boat as ever Plow'd the Ocean ; and the Mafter, Mr. Samuel Leg,[167] as much a Gentleman as ever put to Sea. Our Ships Crew was very fmall, and we had not fo many in our Paffage to New-England, but we had as few in our Return home : There being only my felf, and Mr. King, and Mr. Mortimer, (whofe charaftcrs I fhew'd you in the Letter I fent to Mr. Larkin,) that were of the Captain's Mefs : But this was never the worfe for us ; For tho' (according to the Proverb) the more the Merrier, yet you know the fewer the better Chear ; Befides our Mefs, there was only Sixteen Saylors to man the Ship.

Shou'd I tell you how great a fit of Melancholy feiz'd me, for a Day or two we were put to Sea, when I call'd to mind your felf and other obliging Friends I had left in Bofton, you wou'd have fcarce believ'd that I lov'd Iris to that degree you thought I did ; but really, Sir, my Love is all Myftery ; for at the fame time I cou'd e'en have dy'd to have feen her ; and yet even then I was dying too for a fight of your felf, and my Friends in Bofton : And tho' this may feem a little Romantick, and look like a Paradox, yet is it eafily Reconcileable, if you will but refleft, That I love Iris as the true Indented Counter-part of my felf, and I lov'd you and the reft of my Friends in Bofton as Perfons for whom I had a kindnefs, and in whofe Converfation I delighted. So then let the Tide of Love fwell ne'er fo high to my Friends ; yet ftill the Love of Iris, like a Spring Tide, over-tops 'em all ; and will have the Afcendant, tho' every Woman in Bofton were as fair a Flower as the Charming Widow Brick.

I am fure I have told you that in our Paffage to New-England,

---

[167] SAVAGE confiders Capt. Samuel Legge as the fon of John Legge, of Marblehead, but he is not named among the children in John Legge's will.—ED.

England we met with fuch Tempestuous and angry Seas, as raif'd our Leaky Veffel Mountain high, and even made our Top-fail tilt the Stars: But in my Paffage home, it was as calm and gentle as if the Guardian Angel of my Iris had fmooth'd the way for my Return to her; and all the Hard-fhips that I met with in my Former Voyage were only the Effects of going from her: For I can tell you now, Sir, what 'tis to have a profperous Gale, and fail with Wind and Tide: Do you yourfelf judge of the hafte we made: I came from Bofton on the Fifth of July and was in London on the fifth of Auguft; which was three months fhorter than my Paffage thither:[108] So that tho' we had but little Company, they were all brifk and jolly: Our Captain was very ferious, and (like a right New-England-Man) went to Prayers duly twice a Day: But Mr. King fung oftener than the Captain prayed; and like a conftant Lover, never could give over Chanting, *All Hail to the Myrtle Shades.*

I have little Elfe to acquaint you with through the whole Voyage, fave only that the good Weather made me very Bountiful to the Seamen, and cauf'd me to dole my Brandy, and the reft of my good Stowage amongft 'em, like any thing.

When I came within fight of our Englifh Coaft, I was fo impatient to have a fight of Iris, that I thought I cou'd have jumpt on fhore, even at feveral leagues diftance: Nor let this feem ftrange to you, Mr. Wilkins; for the nearer things are to their Center, the quicker is their Motion; And even a Tyr'd Horfe, when near his Journey's End, will prick up his Ears, and mend his pace.

The firft Land I faw, was the Lizard; and coming directly up the Channel, we caft Anchor in the Downs; and fo was

                                                                hindred

---

[108] He left the Downs, November 2, 1685, and on the 7th was out of fight of land. He was made " free " of the town of Bofton, 16 Feb., 1686, which was feveral days after his landing. To make out his four months' voyage he muft have dated from Oct. 14th, (fee *ante* p. 9,) when he ftarted for the veffel. —ED.

hindred from calling on an Aftrologer at Newport, who promif'd to tell me the fuccefs of my voyage, when I came back again; which if he cou'd not have done, I cou'd now have done it myfelf, without the help of an Aff-trologer. We lay in the Downs but one Night, and the next day anchor'd at Graves-End, where we lay another Night; And Mr. King and my felf having both a mind to a frefh Bit, only we two went afhore.

And that very Night two Boys belonging to the Ship, having ftolen what they thought convenient, went away with it in the Long-Boat: But tho' I was afhore, I cannot but admire the good Providence of Him that neither flumbereth nor fleepeth, waking on my behalf. I had in my Trunk on Board £400 in filver, which was all the Return I brought home (as you know) of thofe Goods I carry'd to New-England. This Trunk ftood upon a Defk of mine, in which I put my foul Linnen: And thefe two Rogues defigning to rob me as well as others, remov'd my Trunk (wherein was my money) and took away my Defk with my foul Linnen, leaving my Trunk behind them; fo that through the good Providence of GOD, my Lofs was inconfiderable, and they left behind 'em the richeft Price. The Rogues went away with what they had got, and were never heard on after. Thus that good Providence of GOD, that in my going, fo wonderfully Preferv'd my Perfon; as Eminently, in my Return, Preferv'd my Subftance. For both which, and innumerable other Mercies be the Praife and Glory.

The next morning we fail'd up the River of Thames, and caft Anchor near Ratcliff; where taking our Leaves of the Captain and Ships Crews we were fet afhore, and went to our feveral Friends. And I having a Sifter[100] that liv'd at one Mrs. Adams, near Ratcliff-Crofs, I went thither firft, as well to fee her, as to Enquire after the health of Iris. My Sifter

---

[100] In " Life and Errors " fhe is called his fifter Mary.—ED.

Sifter exprefs'd fo unufual a Joy to fee me fafe again after
fo long a Voyage, it cou'd hardly be contain'd within any
Bounds; and carry'd with it fuch an Air of fincere and Un-
diffembled Love, that it will be as hard a matter for her to
make me believe fhe hates me, as it will be for fome in the
World, to make me believe they love me.

After having told me that my Iris was in good Health,
and fome other kind Difcourfes, and my bringing her fome
Recommendations from my Friend Dr. Oaks in New-England, to one Mr. Gilfon at Ratcliff, She wou'd needs bring
me on fome part of my way, and walk'd with me towards
Spittle-Fields; (for I was ftill moving towards the center of
my Happinefs.)   But as Black and White do make up
Chequer Work, fo Clouds and Sunfhine are Inter-weav'd in
all the Concernments of this Life: For my great Joy to fee
my Sifter, foon met with an Alloy, by finding fhe Labour'd
under a Dangerous Melancholy.   But fhe having brought
me into the Fields near White-Chappel, we parted; fhe to
her home at Ratcliff; and for my felf, I flew, faft as the
Wings of Love cou'd carry me, towards my Long'd-for
Iris.

When I came into Spittle-Fields, I went into a Tavern
at the Sign of the Queens Head; and fearing leaft Excefs
of Joy fhou'd prove as fatal to my Iris, as it has done to
fome others, I thought it not convenient to let her know too
fuddenly, and all at once, of my Arrival; and therefore I
firft fent for her Sifter Sudbury; who being come, and
having faluted her, and Enquir'd after the health of all the
Family, I defir'd her to go to Iris, and tell her there was
one wou'd fpeak with her, but conceal the Perfon; which
fhe punctually did; and in lefs time than half an hour
(which yet feem'd unto me a little Age) Return'd again, and
brought along with her a Jewel, which I efteem the Richeft
in the whole World.   At the firft Interview, our mutual
Extafies of Joy fwell'd to that mighty height, (for Sudden
                                                      Joys,

Joys, like Grief, confound at firſt) that Love lock'd up the Organs of our ſpeech, and made us have a kind of ſilent Meeting: But when our Joys wou'd give us leave to ſpeak, (like thoſe that had eſcap'd a Common Shipwreck, and got ſafe to the ſhore,) we then congratulated in the tendereſt manner this our happy Meeting: And talked all thoſe Endearing things to one another, that Love cou'd Dictate to us. And had almoſt forgot our Siſter Sudbury that brought us thus together, who yet became a Partner of our mutual Joys, and was well pleaſ'd to ſee that we were ſo: But we both paid her our Acknowledgments for the kind office ſhe had done us: And having Drunk each others healths, and that of the good Doctor and his Family, (where Iris had remained a Sojourner while I was abſent,) we left the Tavern, and went ſtraight to her Fathers, who gave me ſuch a welcome home, as well became his Generous and Noble Spirit.

·Nor was my Mother leſs ready to receive me with all the Teſtimonies of a Kind reſpect and hearty Welcome: And indeed all the Family (as much as they have forgot me ſince) were equally ſurpriz'd and pleaſ'd to ſee me; each ſtriving who ſhou'd ſhew the moſt affection.[170] ✱ ✱ ✱ ✱ ✱
✱ ✱ ✱ ✱ ✱ ✱ ✱ ✱ ✱ ✱ ✱ ✱

And thus Mr. Wilkins, being got home in ſafety, through GOD's good Providence, and ſafely Anchor'd in the Arms of Iris, you'd think I now might take up my *Quietus eſt*, and give my ſelf a Writ of Eaſe, and reſt contented with having ſeen two Worlds.

[But[171] he that's born to Ramble, muſt purſue his Fate; And I had now a Lawfull Call to take another Ramble from hence to the Low Countries. And what I obſerved in theſe

as

---

[170] We here omit a paragraph relative to his wife's health which DUNTON has eraſed as of no importance.—ED.

[171] The paſſage in brackets is probably an interpolation. Though the letter is not dated, the preſumption is that it was written ſoon after his arrival in London, and before his viſit to Holland. —ED.

39

as well as my New-England Ramble, you will fee both in Print together. But now (as if I had drunk water diftilled from a Woman's Brains) I could not reft till I was on a new Ramble, for now to oblige a Sifter in Law (who I hear has forgot every word on't) I ftaid Ten months in one houfe without once ftirring over the Threfhold, and at the Expiration of that time (to oblidge the fame Sifter in Law) I took a trip to Holland, Flanders, Germany, &c., where after 9 months ftay I return'd for England.]

Having thus given you a full Account of my Voyage home; I muft now take leave to put you in mind of my Affairs at Bofton; which are, you know, intrufted in your hand: which I do not at all doubt you will take all the care you can of. I know men there are very dilatory in their Payments; but yet, had it not been to fee my Iris, I fhou'd have hardly come away, and left £300 in Debts behind me, as I have done. But Mr. Wilkins, that which fatisfies me moft, is this, That I have left the Truft of all with you and fo am fure they are in an honeft hand: For tho' Mr. John Baily gave me £150 Bond to fecure me, I took that only in cafe of Mortality, and look upon your Honefty as the beft Security. The Dull Paymafters of Connecticut will want your Dunning often; and fome in Bofton too, you know will bear the Spur.

But, Mr. Wilkins, I muft beg your Pardon, for methinks to take upon me to give you Directions, is to diftruft your Care; which I am as far from, as the Sun-Rifing's from his going down. But if you pleafe, when you fee any of thofe Perfons that have given me large Orders for Books, Efpecially my Friends of Bofton, Salem, and Harvard Colledge, tell 'em they fhall all be fent in Captain Leg's Ship with whom I came to London.

And do me the Favour likewife to tell Mr. Green the Printer of Bofton, That I have fold the Letters that he fent, but they fall extreamly fhort of his Expectation: And the

New

New Letter I ſhall purchaſe for him will make him greatly my Debtor: But he's an honeſt Man. 'Twas at his Houſe I ſpent my leiſure Hours, and therefore doubt but he'll be as punctual to pay me, as I have been careful to ſerve him.

Pray let me hear from you how you ſucceed in my Buſineſs as often as you can: For, as I have already ſaid, my whole D[ependence] is upon your Care and Honeſty.

My ſelf and my dear Wife do Remember our very kind Love to your ſelf and Mrs. Wilkins: And alſo to Mrs. Comfort: And pray give my Wife's particular Reſpects to Mrs. Comfort, and tell her that ſhe returns her many Thanks for the Looking-Glaſs ſhe ſent her; which[172] . . . . Noble Preſent, yet ſhe eſteems the care the . . . . greateſt Obligation.

Pray gi . . . ſervice to all my Friends in general and in a more particular manner, to the Widow Brick.

And if you have any Buſineſs to do in London, if you pleaſe lay your commands upon me, there is none ſhall be more ready to ſerve you, than, Sir,

Your moſt obliged Friend and Servant,

PHILARET.

[172] The manuſcript is here imperfect.—ED.

VALEDICTORY NOTE.

We cannot perhaps do a better service to Dunton's reputation as an author than to compare the preceding pages with the contemporaneous "Trip to New-England," written by the infamous Ned Ward. As published in 1704 in the volume of his miscellaneous works, it is entitled "A Trip to New-England, with a Character of the Country and People, both English and Indians"; and covers twenty-five pages. It is without a date or a single touch of natural observation which would assure us that the writer had actually visited this country. The style has a great affectation of smartness, which does not palliate the disgusting obscenity of the author. A few anecdotes are given in disparagement of the inhabitants, but not a single fact of the slightest interest or value.

We have not searched the record to see if Ward were actually a resident here, but there is nothing in his book which might not have been gleaned from books or from the idle gossip of drunken sailors who had returned to London from a voyage hither. This book of Ward's and the anonymous libel already cited in our notes, may rank high among the attacks which have been made on Boston and New-England. They are coarser in language, but not more bitter in feeling, than those succeeding attacks which have been made even up to the present day. As compared with Ward, Dunton rises to the dignity of an impartial or even favorable chronicler. His sketches of New-England certainly contain internal evidence of being the work of a resident here, and on the whole his testimony is favorable to the character of the inhabitants. Unlike Ward, whose abuse is so violent as to destroy its effect, the few malicious remarks of Dunton are evidently the result of a momentary spleen, or of a desire to display a fancied wit. To read in Ward the statement—that on selling "an eminent Planter" a shilling's worth of treacle, he protested "he had lived there fifty years and never saw in the whole term, ten pounds in silver money of his own, and yet was rated at a thousand pounds,"—is simply to provoke a belief that the writer told a lie. To read in Dunton the report of long conversations held with his friends, is not a reason to doubt that he had so conversed, but simply to view the exact wording as an author's license.

In brief, Dunton visited Boston, was received by the clergy and reputable citizens with friendship, and wrote a trustworthy account of what he saw. If Ward came here, he was probably familiar with the wharves and sailor boarding-house, not improbably with the whipping-post and jail. No respectable man would have acknowledged his acquaintance, and his parting memorial was a collection of obscenities and falsehoods.

APPENDIX.

APPENDIX A.

THE BLUE ANCHOR TAVERN.

IT has already been fhown at page 85 of this volume that Dunton was a frequent vifitor at George Monck's houfe, the Blue Anchor Tavern. As it was promifed that fomething more fhould be faid about the location of this inn, the following fketch of the ownerfhip of the land has been prepared. The eftates lying near the head of what is now termed State Street, have varied fo little in their boundaries that identification is certain.

It may be noted that Dunton himfelf was refident oppofite the Town Houfe, and that moft of his intimate friends lived in the immediate neighborhood. It was the locality moft familiar to him, and deferves therefore fome attempt at its reconftruction. Commencing, therefore, with the Blue Anchor Tavern, we find that this well-known inn ftood on Wafhington Street, very near the fite now covered by the Tranfcript building. This is evident from the following extracts from deeds on record at Bofton.

In Turner's deed to Monck, it is defcribed as a houfe and land bounded north-weft on the fore ftreet leading towards Roxbury; fouth-eaft on a narrow lane leading towards Mr. Joyliffe's houfe, occupied by Thomas Hill; fouth-weft on lands occupied by Mary Avery, and lands owned by the Widow Woofter; north-eaft on lands of the late elder John Wifwall, and lands of Colonel Nicholas Paige.

March 5, 1695-6, Monck mortgaged thefe lands to Nicholas Paige, and they were mortgaged ftill when he died, in 1698. In 1703, (Deeds, xxi. 369,) his widow, Elizabeth Monck, fold the eftate to James Pitts, and he fold it, (Deeds xxxi. 62) 13 Feb., 1716, with two adjoining tenements on the fouth, to Adam Winthrop and others, Truftees. In this deed the bounds are north-weft on Cornhill, fouth-eaft on Pudding Lane, fouth-weft on J. Campbell, and north-eaft on E. Cooke and Nath. Oliver.

We

We will firſt trace the ſouthern boundary from Avery and Worceſter to Campbell. (Deeds, xix. 71.) Mary, widow of Charles Lidget, (her father was William Heſter, of the borough of Southwark, ſoap-maker, and her brother, John Heſter,) ſells to John Campbell, merchant, "all her tenements in Boſton occupied by Timothy Cunningham, Theodore Perſival and Mary Avery, bounded weſt, on the front, on the ſtreet leading from the Town Houſe towards Roxbury, and meaſur. ing 40 feet; ſouth, by houſe and land belonging to Harvard College, under leaſe to Enoch Greenleaf, meaſuring from ſaid ſtreet to Pudding Lane, 125 feet in a direct line; eaſt, in the rear, by ſaid Pudding Lane, meaſuring from ſaid land let to Greenleaf, to a poſt in a little garden belonging to Widow Wooſter, 19 feet 9 inches in a direct line north; thence in a ſtrait line eaſt and weſt along ſaid garden of Worceſter's, to a poſt or corner of ſaid garden, 18 feet; thence from ſaid corner north and ſouth, in a direct line, along the land of ſaid Wooſter to the land formerly of Robert Turner, now in poſſeſſion of Elizabeth Monck, 34 feet; thence from the corner of Wooſter's houſe, in a direct line eaſt and weſt, along land of ſaid Monck, called the 'Narrow Lane,' adjoining Mrs. Avery on the weſt, 56 feet, 6 inches; thence from the north corner of Mrs. Avery's brick warehouſe in a direct line north to Monck's houſe, the breadth of the lane commonly called 'Turner's Lane,' 4 feet; thence along Monck's houſe on the north, in a direct line, eaſt and weſt, to ſaid ſtreet, 42 feet."

This eſtate was ſold by William Avery and Mary, his wife, relict of John Tappan, to Charles Lidgett.

By Suffolk Deeds, (xix. 203, and xxi. 135,) Conſtance Worceſter, and Conſtance Tuckerman, her daughter, now wife of John Noiles, Jr., fiſherman in 'Brigus be South Newfoundland,' ſold in October, 1699, to John Campbell, their houſe and land, bounded eaſt on Pudding Lane, ſouth on John Campbell, weſt on Campbell and widow Monck, and north on widow Monck.

It ſeems clear, therefore, that between Monck's land and the College eſtate,—a well-known eſtate, now occupied by Little, Brown & Co.,—there was but the Avery eſtate, 40 feet in width on Waſhington Street. The only obſcure points are the location of Turner's Lane, and the adjuſtment of Worceſter's weſtern boundary. Probably her houſe was wholly within Monck's yard, and moſt probably Turner's Lane ran from Pudding Lane, beſide Worceſter's houſe, and ended with Avery's warehouſe.

As to the lots on the north, the adjoining eſtate on Waſhington Street belonged to John Wifwall, whoſe daughter, Mary Emmons, ſold it in 1709 (Deeds, xxiv. 241) to Eliſha Cooke. The houſe and land were "next adjoining to the houſe and land formerly known by the name of the Anchor Tavern, now in poſſeſſion of James Pitts, and bounding thereon ſouth"; weſt on Cornhill Street; north on houſe and land of ſaid Cooke; eaſt on land of Colonel Nicholas Paige.

The next houſe and lot belonged to Eliſha Cooke.   **The**

The corner lot belonged to Colonel Nicholas Paige, who gave it in December, 1714, to Nathaniel Oliver, (Deeds, xxx. 246,) defcribing it as bounded north on King Street, 57 feet ; eaft on John Gerrifh's land, 132 feet ; fouth on E. Cooke and James Pitts ; weft on E. Cook and on Cornhill Street.

The next lot on King Street, now State Street, belonged to John Gerrifh, who fold it, 13 Feb., 1716, (Deeds, xxxi. 66.) It was bounded north on King Street ; eaft on houfe and land of John Burrill, occupied by Jonathan Simpfon ; fouth on land of faid Gerrifh ; weft on Nath. Oliver. It was 22 feet in breadth on King Street, and 104 feet in depth. This as compared with Paige's line of 132 feet, would *feem* to have left a rear lot of 28 feet to Gerrifh, and accounts for his fouth boundary.

The next lot belonged to John Burrill, Jr., of Lynn. He bought it, 11 Dec., 1695, with John Emerfon, of Charleftown, (Deeds, xviii. 32,) of John Rollftone. It was defcribed as the houfe and land formerly of Benjamin Negus, deceafed, bounded north on the High Street againft the Town Houfe, 19 feet 7 inches ; fouth and weft by Nicholas Paige ; eaft by houfe and land of widow Phillips, houfe and land of Jabez Negus, by an old ftable, and 14 feet on the back lane.

The corner lot on King Street and Pudding Lane, belonged to Henry Phillips, whofe widow Mary fold it to her fon, Samuel Phillips, bookfeller, in 1705, (Deeds, xxii. 402.) It was defcribed as a tenement called the Rofe and Crown, bounded north on the broad ftreet over againft the Town Houfe, 41 feet ; eaft on the narrow lane leading to Jofeph Bridgham's, 83 feet ; fouth on houfe of Jabez Negus, 39 feet ; weft on houfe and land of John Rollftone.

Whoever compares thefe lines and meafurements with thofe of the prefent eftates, will be convinced that very little change has taken place within the laft one hundred and eighty years.

APPENDIX B.

MICHAEL PERRY'S INVENTORY.

 HE Hon. John Gorham Palfrey, in the third volume of his admirable History of New England, has noticed John Dunton's vifit here. In a note on page 488, he writes concerning the books which Dunton brought hither: "The reader wifhes that he had put the invoice of them on record. A catalogue of books in demand in New-England at that day would have been a bafis for very interefting confiderations."

Although we cannot do this, we have thought it allowable to publifh here a copy of the Inventory of the eftate of Michael Perry, a Bofton bookfeller, taken A. D. 1700. Not only is the date fufficiently near Dunton's time, but as we have already pointed out, (*ante*, p. 106,) Perry was undoubtedly the fecond husband of Dunton's "Flower of Bofton," the Widow Breck.

SUFFOLK PROBATE RECORDS, VOL. XIV. 287–90—3 1-3 PAGES.

An Inventory of the Eflate of MICHAEL PERRY, *late of Bofton, Bookfeller, deceafed, &c., viz* :

1 Large fol. Bible with Common Prayer and Apoc: £1		1 Bulls Commentary on the 15 Pfalm,		6
1 New body of Geography,	8 ..	3 Flavells mental Errors,		6 ..
2 Cambridge Concordances,	2	2 Rogers on trouble of mind,		6 ..
1 Stapletons Juvenal,	10 ..	4 Flavells compafs Spiritualized,		6 ..
2 Quicks Synodicum,	15 ..	1 Culpeppers Engl: Phy:		3 ..
1 Sturnys Magazine,	12 ..	1 Chrift's tears for Jerufalems unbelief,		6
1 Goldmans Dictionary,	18 ..	1 Dickfon on the Hebrews,		6
1 Leonards hiftory of the Papice,	1 6			1 Cultus

1 Cultus Evangelicus,		3
4 Cares laſt Legacy,		1 ..
1 Fenners Sacrifice of the faithful,		6
1 Ellis Engliſh School,		3
14 Gellebrands Epitome,	1	1 ..
2 Fulfilling of the Scripture,		2 ..
1 Gloſſographia,		6
1 Englands heroical Epiſtles,		6
1 Godfrey of Bulloigne,		6
2 Hiſtory of England,		6 ..
1 Jure maritimo,		6 ..
18 Colſons Kallenders,	1	7 ..
8 do. with Practice,		16 ..
4 Loves art of Surveying,		2 8
1 Morning Exerciſe,		4 ..
1 Plutarchs Lives, 2d Vol.,		1 ..
1 Norwoods Syſtem of Navigation,		6 6
1 Preſtons Liveleſs life,		6
1 Geometrical Seaman,		3
1 Uſe of the Quadrant,		6
1 Forſters Sureties of proportion,		3
2 Sellers practical Navigation,		10 ..
2 Salmons Diſpenſatory,		16 ..
1 ——— Doron medium,		6 ..
12 Strongs Spelling bookes,		12 ..
1 Lives Juſtinian and his Empr:		
1 Innocency and truth,		2
1 Infant Baptiſm vindicated,		3
1 Hodiſdons Sion and Parnaſſus,		3
1 Small Hebrew Bible,		2
1 Whole duty of Man, imperfect,		6
3 Myſtery of husbandry,		2
4 Vincent on Judgement, 15d,	13	9
2 Shour of Earthquakes,		1 ..

2 Mr. Doolittles Funeral Sermon,		8
1 Table concerning the meaſure of time,		2
8 Wakeleys Compaſs rectified,	16	..
1 Vincents converſion of the Soul,		1 ..
20 Youngs Spelling bookes,	16	8
13 Bibles in 12° gilt, N : E : Pſalms,	2 12	..
5 Do. plain do,	15	..
11 Do. in 24° gilt,	2 4	..
1 Smetii,		6
1 Burgus Dicii Logice,	3	..
1 Legrands Philoſophy,	1	..
1 Ovidii Opera, 3 vol.,	6	..
11 Nomenclaturas,	11	..
5 Janua Trilinguis,	15	..
5 ——— Linguarum,	2	6
1 Art of Gardening,		3
2 Vindiciæ Anti Baxteriani,		6
1 Art of drawing Sundials,		2
5 Apology for Congregational Divines,	1	3
1 Balls Aſtro Mathematica,		3
26 Burwoods helps,	1 6	..
23 Doolittles Call,	11	6
1 Young Secretarys Guide,		8
1 Method for guiding reaſon,		2
1 Cordial Endeavours,		2
1 Cares laſt Legacy,		3
1 Conſpiracy againſt Genoa,		4
9 Smiths great Affize,	9	..
1 Lees Joy of Faith,		8
5 Hiſtory of Fortunatus,	3	4
11 Hiſtory of the plott,	2	9
17 Heywoods life,	4	3
4 Lattin bibles at 6s,	1 4	..
7 Owen Of mourning,	1	9
16 Pearce on death,	16	..
3 Pilgrims progreſs with cuts,	3	..

3 Shour

3 Shour of Grace,	1	6
1 Lucius Florus Engl:		2
1 Sincerity and hypocrify, &c,		3
12 Token for mourners,	10	..
1 Chriftian Pilgrim,		6
1 Ifle of Man,		2
8 Vernons Compting houfe,	10	..
3 Seven wife Mafters,	2	..
1 Forme of Sound words,		2
1 Gofpell call in meter,		4
1 Moulins Spiritual Guide,		4
1 Violations of property,		2
1 Piety of Parice,		2
1 Connecticot Election Sermons,		2
1 Enquiry concerning the Trinity in the Godhead,	1	..
1 Alcibiades and Carolina,		6
1 Phillips mathematical manual,	2	..
1 Arrow againft Idolatry,		2
2 Bunian on the Soul,	1	4
16 Baxters call,	13	4
1 Elegancy of Speech,		3
7 Clarks Looking glafs,	1	9
1 Brides longing for her Bridegrooms 2d coming,		2
2 Calamys ark,	2	..
4 Fall and rifeing of St: Peter,	2	..
3 Duty of woman,		6
23 Flavels Saint indeed, 10d,	19	2
2 Howards precious blood,		4
1 Papice glorying in antiquity,		3
5 Life of Q: Mary,	1	3
1 Pharmacopia Hagienfis,		2
1 Saltmarfh Free grace,		2
1 Pearces concern of life,		3
18 Stoddons Paftors charge,	12	..
6 Sion in diftrefs,	1	6
8 Winneys Chriftian choice,	1	4
1 Idiot in 4 books complete,		4

1 Practice of Repentance,		1	4
36 Confcience the beft friend,		12	..
19 Early Religion,		3	2
17 Mr. Bailys life with old Mr. Mathers Sermon,		8	6
19 ditto, without,		6	4
23 Duty of Parents and Children, 5d,		9	7
31 Willards Defertions,		15	6
31 Mathers folly of finning,		12	11
9 Order of Churches,		4	6
5 Willards peril of the times,		2	6
2 Books Bills Lading qt 4qr, both,		7	..
5 Æfops Fables Engl: and Lattin,		10	..
5 Hools Corderius,		10	..
4 Ovid Metamorph:		8	..
6 Tulleys Orations,		9	..
8 Lattin Teftaments,		12	..
7 Virgill,		14	..
12 Accidences,		8	..
15 Cato's, at 10d,		12	6
19 Greek Grammars at 18d,	1	8	6
29 Lattin Grammars at 12d,	1	9	..
14 do. with conftruing books, 16d,	18 8	..	
43 Sententia's, *a* 8d.,	1	8	2
5 Ovid de triftibus,		3	4
1 Thefaurus Poeticus,			3
8 Tulleys Epiftles,		4	..
7 ———— de officiis at 16d,		9	4
9 Æfops Fables,		18	..
8 Corderius,		16	..
8 Accidences,		5	4
1 Syntaxis conftrued,			2
4 Smiths great affize,		4	..
27 Pfalters with Proverbs, 9d,	1	3	3
3 Teftaments,		4	..
28 Primmers,		4	8

3 Pfm

3 Pfm. Books 6 : d in Turkey			
gilt,	7 6		
5 do. bd. in Calfe,	10 ..		
2 do. bd. in red Turk :	4 ..		
9 do. plain,	13 6		
1 do. Bartons,	6		
5 do. by Tate and Brady,	5 ..		
13 Sea Charts,	1 19 ..		
9 packs playing cards,	1 6		
4 Paper books qt 8 qr T : C :			
rd,	12 ..		
11 do. qt 27 qr fml. papr. rd,	1 11 3		
6 do. qt 16 qr T : C :	1 2 ..		
1 do. 4to qt 3qr fmall,	3 ..		
1 9 qr paper fewed into books,	9 3		
21 qr ditto, rd,	15 9		
21 copy books for boys, qt 6 qr,	3 ..		
68 Books in parchment qt 1-2			
qr each, 6d,	1 14 ..		
17 do. qt 16 fheets each, 7d,	9 11		
54 do. bd. in Leather qt 1-2 qr,			
each, 8d,	1 16 ..		
7 do. in Leather, qt 16 fheets,			
S C, 9d,	15 3		
27 beft pencils at 3d,	6 3		
5 pocket books Small bd. in			
Leather,	3 4		
26 do. qt 1-2 qr ordinary paper,			
6d,	13 ..		
19 do. in vellum rd and clafpt,			
16d,	1 5 4		
11 Letter cafes,	11 ..		
23 pr. brafs compaffes, Small			
and large,	1 3 ..		
3 Lead Stand difhes for ink,	1 ..		
68 doz. of Ink hornes, 2s 6d,	8 10 ..		
7 Skins Turkey Leather,	2 2 ..		
2 lb. 1-2 Vermilion,	1 10 ..		
10 Spectacle cafes gilt,	3 4		
13 do. black, not gilt,	3 3		

9 do. wood,	1 6		
4 one foot rules,	4 ..		
2 three foot ditto,	3 ..		
1 two foot do,	1 ..		
11 profpect glaffes great and			
Small,	1 2 ..		
18 do. Lignumvitæ,	13 ..		
109 Ink pots at 4d,	1 16 4		
77 Ink hornes at 2d,	12 5		
13 doz. white Spectacles, 3s,	1 19 ..		
8 doz. & 3 do. black at 4s,	1 13 ..		
200 Quills,	2 8		
100 Epitome of Englifh or-			
thography,	8 4		
168 French Lettr :	14 ..		
152 Remarkable Judgments,	12 8		
31 Warning to the flocks,	1 3		
63 Willards Man of war,	10 6		
13 doz. Affemblys Catechifm,	13 ..		
31 Affemblys do. with proofs,	5 2		
32 Important cafes,	2 8		
32 Willard on morality,	5 4		
2 doz. gilt horne bookes,	2 ..		
1 doz. plain ditto,	6		
36 Chriftians Thank offering,	3 ..		
3 God the guide of Youth,	9		
9 Lamentation of Mary Hooper,	9		
4 Rm. writing paper,	1 8 ..		
2000 Wafers,	4 ..		
30 Collection of papers relating			
to the prefent affairs of			
England,	2 6		
18 Bartons Thankfgiving Ser-			
mon,	1 6		
5 Stevens ditto,	5		
20 Warnings to the unclean,	3 4		
1 1-2 lb. Sealing wax,	3 .		
4 doz. bookes Leafe brafs,	4 ..		
6 Pen knives,	3 ..		
3 Setts of Brafs Letters,	6 ..		
	1 box		

1 box of Book binders tools,	15 ..
1 pr. of money Scales,	1 ..
1 Book binders plow,	10 ..
1 large Prefs,	16 ..
2 do. Small,	8 ..
2 Sewing preffes,	4 ..
4 Common prayer Books, 1 do. Turkey, 1 do. Shaggreene, 1 Mordens Geography, 1 Rawleighs abridgement, 1 Stanhops Kempis, 2 Taylors Contempla:	2 5 ..

Books, &c., in the Chamber, vizt.

60 pocket books fome rd,	3 8 ..
16 doz. gilt horne bookes,	16 ..
38 doz. plain do,	19 ..
12 Rulers,	2 ..
34 doz. White Spectacles, 3s,	5 2 ..
17 doz. wood cafes,	1 14 ..
9 Letter cafes,	9 ..
1 Corderius,	2 ..
14 Accidences, at 8d,	9 4
3 Cato's,	2 6
1 Pearce of Death,	1 ..
2 lb. Holmans Ink powder,	1 ..
2 lb. Sap green,	5 ..
53 Skins writing parchment,	2 13 ..
4 Skins Vellum,	6 ..
6 Parchment Torrells,	4 ..

Books, &c., in the Garretts.

900 Ink pots, at 4d,	15 .. ..
5 Bottoms pack thread,	1 8
536 pieces of parchment for folios, 3d,	6 14 ..
450 Stubs Confcience beft friend, fheets,	1 17 6
18 Rm. Poft paper, 15s,	13 10 ..
4 Law Books Sticht,	4 ..
44 doz. Primmers,	4 8 ..

106 doz. Affemblys Catechifm,	5 6 ..
7 qr painted paper,	1 3
190 Slates,	2 7 6
62 Sheets paft board, 3d,	15 6
88 qr Bills of Ladeing,	4 8 ..
261 pr Clafps for Bibles,	1 .. 11
6 Rm. whited brown paper,	1 10 ..
52 Sheep Skins at 10d,	2 3 4
7 Rm. paper,	2 9 ..
6 doz. Pfalters at 9s,	2 14 ..
7 Calve Skins at 2s 4d,	16 4
9 red Sheep Skins,	13 6
20 bundles of Scale, 2s,	2 .. ..
3 Rm. painted Paper,	12 ..
25 Pfalters qrs. at 5d,	10 5
18 Gumm araback,	18 ..
100 French Lettr:	8 4
7 doz. Willards man of war,	14 ..
2 lead Stand difhes,	8
300 Law Books, qrs,	15 .. ..
28 doz. Black Spectacles,	5 12 ..
16 doz. wood cafes,	1 12 ..
20 doz. Leather do,	3 .. ..
4 doz. gilt do,	16 ..
14 Profpect glaffes, Vellum,	1 8 ..
1 doz. do. ordinary,	4 ..
60 Rm. printing paper, 3s,	9 .. ..
25 Willards peril of the time, 6d,	12 6
25 —— Defertions,	12 6
50 Doolittles call,	1 5 ..
200 do. in qrs, at 3d,	2 10 ..
9 doz. Willard on morality,	18 ..
28 Warning to the Flocks,	1 2
3000 Wafers,	6 ..
225 Pfalm books, qrs, 10d,	9 7 6
2000 Ordinary Quills,	10 ..
300 Primmers, qrs.	1 5 ..
26 doz. Cards, at 2s,	2 12 ..
5 doz. Pfalm bookes, bound, 18d,	4 10 ..

150 Families

150 Families well ordered, 9 qrs, 1d,	12 6	43 Willards fpiritual defcr: bd, 6d.	1 1 6	
25 Order of the Gofpell, qrs, 3d,	6 3	50 Mathers Familys, bd, 5d,	1 .. 10	
125 Spiritual defertions, 9 qrs, 3d,	1 11 3	15 Bailys life, bd, 4d,	5 ..	
		70 Early Religion,	11 8	
30 Mathers folly of Sinning, bd, 5d,	12 6	100 Doolittles Call, bd,	2 10 ..	
		9 Burdwoods helps,	9 ..	
		40 Accidences, 8d,	1 6 8	

Apprifers, ZEC'A TUTHILL.
THO. FITCH.
BENJ. ELIOT.

Prefented by the relict, widow JOANNA PERRY.

Date, *Bofton, January* 23, 1700.

APPENDIX C.

LIST OF THE INHABITANTS OF BOSTON.
1687.

HE earlieſt publiſhed liſt of the inhabitants of Boſton, we believe, is one dated in 1695, which was printed in Nathaniel Dearborn's "Boſton Notions," in 1848. This liſt was taken from the Boſton records; but as printed, its value is much diminiſhed by the alphabetical arrangement adopted. We hope hereafter to print it in its original form. Two earlier liſts, however, have been diſcovered among the Records at the State Houſe, being the valuations for 1687 and for 1688.

From a tranſcript made by W. B. Traſk, Eſq., we now publiſh the earlier liſt, as it contains the names of thoſe inhabitants who were contemporary with Dunton.

The figures placed after many of the names ſignify the number of perſons in the family, aged ſixteen and upwards.—W. H. W.

VALUATION OF PROPERTY—BOSTON, 1687.—BOOK 126, P. 286-306.
MUDDY RIVER, 307. RUMNEY MARSH AND THE ISLANDS, 308.

Francis Hudſon (2)	William Dey	Nathaniell Parkman
Thomas Atckins (2)	Thomas Gutridge	Laurence White
George Hiſcott (2)	Sammuell Rucke, Jun'r	Beniamin Worthyleg
John Hiſcott	Mr. John Pennywell	Robert Moore
Beniamin Williams	Michaell Shutt	Robert Laſh
John Pollen	John White	Francis Whitman
Sammuell Ruck, Sen'r	John Welch	Beniamin Wardle
Mr. Thomas Berrey	William Greenough (4)	John Carter
Hezechiah Hinkſman	Edward Budd	John Wilkins
Nathaniell Hinkſman	John Mattune	John Ranſford

Edward

Edward Collens
Mr. Sammuell Nowell
Percey Clarke
Thomas Eldredge, Jun'r
Sammuell Wakefeild (2)
Mr. William Hobbey
George Hooper
William Clough
Robert Seers
James Smith, Marriner
John Orris (2)
Edward Ransford
Nicolas George
Robert Gammin
William Harris
Jonas Clarke
Thomas Row, faylemaker (3)
John Atwood (2)
Jofeph Williams
George Robifon
Thomas Thurton
John Smith
William Hunt
William Everdon
Daniell Ballerd
William Colman
John Jacobs
Allexander Seers
John Oakey
Thomas Baker (3)
John Jervis, Jun'r
John Stevens
Samfon Waters
Robert Smith
Mr. Humphrey Lifcombe (3)
Mr. Thomas Lifcombe
John Viall
Obediah Gill (3)
William Davis
Major John Richards

Jonathan Howard
Jonathan Bill
Sammuell Burnell
Mr. Robert Bremfdon (2)
John Burredge
Thomas Johnfon
William Downes
Mr. Jofeph Short
Edward Hemfeild
George Nowell
John Roberts
Jobe Chamberlin
Samm'll Greenwood, Jr. (2)
Jofeph Graunt (2)
William Huff
Edward Brecknell
John Pits
Henery Kimbale
John Major
John Merfhale
William Burrows
John Scarlett
Jofeph Tayller
Gabriell Fifhlocke
Sammuell Saxfton (2)
Richard Shut (2)
William Parkeman
Zachariah Davis
Elias Parkeman
John Jervis, Sen'r
William Shute
Aurther Smith (2)
Thomas Hunt (3)
Tymothy Thorneton (2)
Erecte Clesbey
David Robyfon
John Parmenter
John Hulland
George Beard
John Nafh (2)

John Holbrooke (2)
John Leach
Sammuell Bayley, faylemaker
Jofeph Eldredge (2)
Sammuell Greenwood, Sr.
Andrew Elliott
Thomas Edmunds
Charles Hopkins
James Goodwin (3)
John Ammy
Nicolas Stone
Widdow Kellond
Jonathan Jackfon
Widdow Hall
Widdow Hunt
Widdow Greenewood
Widdow Gaurd
Chriftopher Hulland
[   ] Robe
Widdow Haneford
Widdow Cotter
Widdow Blackwell
Mr. Increas Mather
Widdow Margett Smith
William Cundey
Sammuell Hudfon
John Ormes
Widdow Bell
Thomas Goodall
David Cummens
Widdow Groves
David Fauckner
Experience Orris
Richard Tewell
David Edwards
John Gey
Jofeph Gallopp
Benjamin Gallopp
William Dennis

Richard

Richard Whitredge
John Hunt
Benjamin Breeme (2)
Richard Knight
William Trout
Richard Travers (2)
Sammuell Jackſon
Richard Travers, Jun'r
Daniell Turrell, Sen'r (2)
Jonathan Addams (2)
David Addams
Nathaniell Addams (2)
Abraham Addams
David Eddows
Widdow Dowden
Sammuell Burrell
Sammuell Pecocke
Rignall Gregnon
John Wakefeild (2)
Obediah Wakefeild
John Nicols (2)
John Buſhnell (2)
Francis Ellis
Mr. Middlecott
Andrew Marriner (2)
George Hallett
John Worden
Joſeph Arnold
John Langdon, butcher
William Jeffery
John Green
Edward Summers
John Search
Widdow Cundey
Sammuell Phillips
Sammuell Turrell
John Figg *(or Higg)*
Widdow Collicott
Mr. Morton Braer (3)
John Pearce (2)

William Snell
Ellias Kallender (3)
John Endicott (3)
Edward Weeden
John Underwood
Widdow Joules
Mr. Addam Winthropp (2)
Thomas Fox
Robert Fethergill
John Goff (2)
Mrs. Winſley
John Strid
William Mumford
David Copp (3)
Daniell Travers
Thomas Elliott
Obediah Reade
Edward Peggy
Richard Skinner
Gilbert Cardey
James Engliſh
James Graunt
George Loverine
Jno : Farnum
William Johnſon
William Norton
David Norton
Mr. Lauſon, ſhipmaſter
Andrew Dolberry
Andrew Willett
Charles Demerritt
Nicolas Winnopp
Hennery Rawlins
Erecte Hamlin
John Keene (2)
Thomas Kellon
Thomas Beves
Jabes Salter (2)
William Kent (2)
Thomas Warren

Sammuell Dobſon
Jonathan Charles
James Halſey (2)
Robert Lewes
John Clesbey
James Howard
John Commer
Danniell Turell, Jun'r
William Bedlow
Capt. Anthoney Howard (2)
Nathaniell Baker (2)
Edward Mortimore
Mr. John Foſter (2)
Calleb Rawlins
Edward Goodwin
Benjamin Rawlins
Mr. Kerke
John Ketch
John Playſted
John Moore
Thomas Kembale
Sammuell Addams (2)
John Bayley
John Scate (2)
John Barber
William Barrett
Thomas Moore
Edward Worrell
Andrew Stillings
Mathew Atkins
Edmund Mumford
Moſſes Pearce (2)
John Stanbridge
Joſeph Ruſſell (2)
Henery Emes (2)
George Henly (2)
Tymothy Wadſworth
Thomas Cuſhing
John Bearnerd (2)

Thomas

Thomas Bearneard (2)
Daniell Travers, Jun'r
Robert Howard (2)
Thomas Newman
William Roufe
Jofeph Jackfon
William Robey
James Thorneberry
Mathew Joanes
Abraham Gording
John Granton
John Trow
Thomas Gold
Tymothy Prout
Jofeph Prout
Robert Cumbey (2)
Richard Wey (2)
Docter William Hufe
Docter John Clark
Capt. Elifha Hutchifon
Widdow Warren
Sufanah Oliver
Jno : Sneling
Wido Carwithen, alias Rolph
Daved Farnum
Widdow Keene
Widdow Saxton
George Callender
Mary Clarke
Widdow Williams
John Williams, butcher
John Bowden
Oliver Berry
Widdow Tomas
Widdow Anderfon
Widdow Baxter
Deborah Prout
Allexander Plimly
Widdow Webb

Sammuell Norden
Sammuell Slack
Jacolb Huen
Hennery Williams
Tymothy Pratt (2)
Eliathar Blacke
Widdow Puglis
Thomas Walter
Widdow Martine
Gabriell Warner
Thomas Narrowmoor
John Creaffey
Tho : Afhley
John Blake
Jofeph Shaw
John Starr
Grigory Wackcom
James Dowell
William Shipein
Richard Weeden
Nicolas White
Mr. John Jefferd
John Palmer
James Greene
Robert Mare
Sammuell Mansfeil
Richard Ricrafft
[   ] Litherwood, at the pelican
John Bolt
John Champlin
John Waffon
Jofhuah Rawlins
Jofiah Grice
Samuel Grice
John Lawfon
John Barbur
William Boulderfon
George Briggs
Richard Brookes (2)

William Ballentine
John Gepfon
James Rainfthrop
John Courfer
James Adams
Edward Adams
Widow Everell
Jofeph Pearfe
Samuel Walker
Widow Manning
Hugh Mullagin
Thomas Hitchborn
George Hollard, Jun'r
George Thomas (2)
John Sharp
Edmond Draper
Widow Elifa : Thompfon
Nathanael Williams
Ifaac Walker
Thomas Stanbury
Sufanna Walker, widow
Jonathan Champion
John Alden (2)
Sufanna Lendall, widow
Thomas Grofs
John Dyer
Samuel Checkley (2)
John Davis (2)
Jofhua Winfor
Ifaac Lorin
Jacob Randall
Widow Winfor
John Cotta
Jofeph Hiller
Thomas Savage
John Nelfon
Thomas Pembarton
Hannah Prowfe, widow
John Carthew
John Clarke

William

William Palfrey
Edward Lillie
Lancelot Lake
Richard Cheever (3)
David Harris
Gyles Dyer
Mary Milam, widow
Francis Marſhall
John Ballentine
William Long
Elias Heath
John Yorke
John Coomes
John Alcock
Job Prince
Chriſtopher Talbut
Nathanael Jewell
Thomas Paddy
Ebenezar Price
John Walley, Jun'r
John Somes
Robert Perrin
Mary Lake, widow
Thomas Child (2)
Ralph Carter (2)
Robert Johnſon
Samuel Nanney
Samuel Mattocks, Sen'r
Samuel Mattocks, Jun'r
Thomas Biſhop
Ann Checkley, widow
Capt. William Wright (2)
John Coney, Sen'r (2)
Matthew Grofs
Widow Turell
Joſeph Townſend (2)
Widow Rock
Benjamin Backway
Mr. Cotton Mather
Iſaac Jones

Joſeph Callow
Thomas Cooke
Timothy Dwight (2)
Phillip Langdon
John Ricks (2)
Widow Newcombe
Richard Narramore
Henry Godfrey
Lot Gourding
Widow Whitwell
William Smith
Emm Gepſon, widow
William Baſſett
Thomas Barrington
Samuel Johnſon
John Smith
Pilgrim Sympkins
John Hunlock
Thomas Hatherly
Thomas Pennant
Jacob Everitt
Richard Talley
John Tyler
Oliver Tomlyn
John Symons
David Baſſett
Henry Dawſon
Henry Bennett
Edward Evered
John Verniſide
Richard Ellis
Abraham Letherbridge
Jacob Verniſide
Thomas Inglesby
Thomas Gutteridge
William Jones
Samuel Ruggles
John Veren, Sen'r
John Veren, Jun'r
John Webber

John Walley, Sen'r
Richard Preiſt
Joſeph Wing
John Lovering
Henry Mattocks
Richard Muffivant
Conſtantine Sandys
Widow Dickerſon
John Holbrooke
Thomas Veren
William Thwyng
John Gwyn
John Ballentine
John Farnum Tertius (2)
John Aulgar (2)
Samuell Clarke
Thomas Barnes
Edward Crek & 3 men (4)
Edward Watkins
Willi Couch
Johnathan Savige
Joſeph Soper
Jarvis Ballard
Joſeph Bradinge
Thomas Cutler, merchant
James Burges
Capt. Blackwell & 1 man (2)
Robert Purdue
James Webſteir
Sammuel Howard
John Marſhall
John Tuckerman, Ju'r
William Manley
Arthor Hale
John Fairefeld
Bengemen Thrednedell
Bartholme Thrednedle
James Hawkens & man (2)
Ambroſe Dawes

Jobe

Jobe Ingram
Johnathan Dawes
Dauniell Fairefeld
Elliezur Faimden
Thomas Cooper & man (2)
Criftopher Flage
William Paine
Stephen Minor & man
David Stephens
Roger Dubbledaye
Micael Homer
Benjamen Emmones, Sen'r (2)
Jeames Barton & man (2)
John Ruggles & man (2)
Thomas Stedman
John Davis
Benjamen Walker
Richard Inglifh
John Foy
Jonas Clay
William Billings
Hugh Barton
Abraham Smith
John Saffin
John Tuker
Gorg Perfon
Sammuell Ravenfcroft & man (2)
Jeremiah Toye
Jeames Fowele
Richard Lackey
Nathanael Leagit
Ifack Cufins
Francis Foxcraft & man (2)
Richard Rodgers
Peter Clarke
Anthonie Chekley
Andrew Veach

Richard Barrit
John Bonner
William Joyce
Peter Affalli
Thomas Harwod
John Robbinfon
James Tayler & man (2)
Samuell Jacklin & man (2)
Samuell Sparks
John Borland
John Cordner
William Gibfon & 2 men (3)
Grimefton Bowd & man (2)
Thomas Phillipes
Nathaniel Collines
Bartholme Chevers & 2 men (3)
Samuell Lilli & man (2)
John Waker
Samuell Homan
Robbert Shelton
Allin Noletre
Edward Camer
Chriftopher Clark
Thomas Scot
Thomas Duer
Sampfon Duer
Jeames Nesbit
Lewes Allare
John Strang
Joffhua Brodbent
John Tribber
John Horton
Thomas Edwards
William Parfons
John Wooddie & man (2)
James Cooke
Sampfon Stoddard
Jeames Butler

James Sherlock
Jofiah Cobham
Monggoe Craford
Jofhuwaye Cobham
Jemes Webfter
James Marfhall
Charles Salter
Aron Gefferies
Thomas Hamblin
Richard Shering
Elhanon Lion
Thomas Baker
William Turnor
John Jones
William Griges and man
George Cable and man (2)
Edward Allin
James Prier
Obadiah Emmones
Nickcolas Hale
Thomas Madfon, Se'r
Thomas Madfon, Ju'r
Samuell Cahone
Robbert Patin
John Vickcers
Jofeph Vickcers
William Browne
John Birge & 2 men (3)
Henery Ingrum & man (2)
Thomas Hunt & man (2)
Widdow Edfell
Mofes Bradford (2)
John Hill
Nicholas Shapleigh
Thomas Harris (2)
James Worth
Sarah Barrett, als.
Mary Thacher
Widow Harrifon
Anthony Stoddard

William

William Dawes
Thomas Ratlif
James Cooper
Tho : Watkins at ——(?)
Steven Bat at ——— (?)
George Hambleton
David Stephens
Dainel Harrife
John Mulligen
William Laing
James Carne & fhopp
John Edes & houfe
Cornellius Collins
Arnold Collins
Willam Griffin
Bengemen Peck
Sammuel Jones
Willi Willfon
John Holland
Patrick Moyfler
Sammel Marfhall & fonn (2)
Willi Crichfeld
Richard Warner
Dan : Royfe
Jofhua Atwater
Dainell Proctor
James Meers
Will : Bryant
Ben : Mountfort
James Green (3)
Edmont Browne
Returne Waite
John Roberts
Experianc Willis
Michaiel Willis (2)
James Barnes
Humphey Perry
Will : Browne
Mr. [   ] Maine (2)

Ephrem Saile (4)
John Gill
John Lowel (2)
Sufanah Stokes
Eben Pierfe
Tho : Cartor
Tho : Clarke
Coll. Sam'll Shrimpton (2)
Sam'll Hubbert
Georg Hornebuckle
Will : Keen (2)
Jofeph Phillips
Sam'll Plummer (2)
Ifaiah Toy
Chriftor. Crow
Gibfon Farr
Jofeph Rodgers
Tho : Skiner (2)
Eliezer Moody
Tho : Jackfon
Tho : Parris
Daved Jefferies (2)
Michel Perry
Giles Mafter
Will : Lackey
Georg Farwell (2)
Tho : Gutterage
Ben : Harris
Mary Lechfield
John Paintor
Enock Greenleafe (2)
Abigall Dudfon
Edward Hutchinfon
Rodger Killcop
Sam'll Lynde
Margret Thatcher
Mofes Defhan
Will : Crow
Will : Ardall
Dan : Powning

Jofeph Smith
Francis Smith
John Baker
Madam Rebecka Taylor
James Loyde
Mr. [   ] Brockhoven
Tho : Brenly
Will : Brenly
Will : Lamb
Nath : Green
Jno : Gardner
Humpr : Richards
Sam'll Tyly
Bozone Allen (2)
Rob't Prife
John Thwing
Jofeph Peck
Rich : Crifpe
Will : White
Tho : Bulkly
Manaffa Beck
Tho : Beedle
Jno : Doffett, Sen'r
Jno : Doffett, Jun'r
Ezekel Levet
Daved Wailesby
John Weft, Efq.
Petor Haymon
John Bonamy
Tho : Oakes
Ben : Bulifant, Efqr. (2)
Tho : Atkinfon
Richard Procktor
John Rowleftone
Georg Nickafon
Jacob Holloway
Sam'll Button
Humpr : Parfon
Jofeph Allen
Will : Hall

Mary

Mary Swett
Nicholas Backſter
Jos : Thaxter
Will : Gibbons
Joſeph Davis
Georg Dauſon
John Hayward
Mrs. Belengham
Francis Burroughs
Tho : Bludſto
Thaddeus Macarty (3)
John Kilby
John Kilby, Jun'r
Eliakim Hutchinſon, Eſq. (2)[ ] Maſſy y[e] keeper
Georg Eliſton
Joſeph Webb
Dority Hawkins
Habakuck Glover
Ralph Perkins
Tho : Smith
Jotham Grover
Anne Hunt
John Wing
Georg Tomſon
Hen : Sprie
Mary Tyng
John Tuttle
Robert Williams
Richard Reade
John Higgs (2)
Wm : Haberfield
James Woodmanſey
Thomas Kirke
Francis Moſs
Thomas Edwards
John Allen
James Corniſh
Timothy Cunningham
Capt'n Benjamin Davis
Thomas Creeſe

Capt'n Nathll Byfield
Edward Bertles
William Gilbert
Widdowe Smith
Henry Deering
Widdow Geeriſh
Richard Wilkins
David Johnſon
Widdow Egerton
John Linſey
Hudſon Leverett
Joſeph Brunning
John Eyre
James Pemberton
Benjamin Pemberton
James Dennis, Senr.
James Dennis, Junr.
Dennis Mathews
Simeon Meſſenger
Samuel Legg
Jeremiah Bumſtead
Benjamin Negus, Junr.
Widdowe Meſſinger
Abraham Pierce
Richard Chriſtophers
Eliſha Cooke
Madam Leverett
Ezekiel Cheever
Henry Thyte (?)
Arthur Maſon (2)
David Maſon
Abraham Browne
Gamaliel Rogers
John Briggs
Henry Sharp
Bernard Trott
Thomas Tory
Mary Stoddard, Widdowe
Peter Townſend

Benjamin Alford
Richard Bulkley
John Fayerweather
James Allin, Miniſter
Pen Townſend
Humphry Davie
John Davie
Thomas Palmer
Henry Palmer
John Simmons
Joſhua Moody (2)
Joſeph Belknap (3)
John Conny
Thomas Savage
John Tuckerman
Edward Steevens
Simon Lynd, Eſq.
George Pordige (2)
Samuell Pordige
Samuell Bednell
Jeremiah Fitch (3)
Thomas Baker
Simon Daniel (2)
John Royne
Enoch Greenlieffe
Roger Judd
Mary Avery, widdowe
John Cord
Charles Swett
Robert Huſſy
George Monck (2)
Henry Tickner
Thomas Cottle
Thomas Larkin
Thomas Brightman
Henry Brightman
Florence Charty
John Hurd
Sam'll Perine
William Machelaffin

Peter

Peter Barker
Mathew Rea
Jacob Randal
John Hannikin
Joſhua Matſtock
Coll. Nicho: Paige
Thomas Dudley
James Mounteere
Thomas Mallett
[   ] Paige
[   ] Duke
Francis Legare
Warner Werendonke (3)
Andrew Cunningham
Sam'll Phillips (2)
Dunkin Cambell
William Paine (2)
Iſaac Addington
Jabez Negus
John Rawlins
Edward Pery
John Adams
Thomas Thornton
Nicho: King
Simeon Stoddard (2)
Edward Shippen (4)
James Cravin
[   ] Glanvill, at Mr.
———— (?)
Jeremiah Dummer (2)
John Cole
Ebenezar Ruſſell
John Wayte
Coll. Freere
Stephen Werendonke
Thomas Peck
Roger Gilbert
Robert Monkes
Widdowe Man
John Marſhall

Thomas Marſhall (2)
Dan'll Allin
Widdowe Dudley
Epiphras Shrimpton
Wm : Burt
Phillip Finny
Sam'll Johnſon (2)
Sam'll Phillips
Edward Eſtill
Sam'll Landman
David Gwin
Mr. Sam'll Willard
Thomas Smith
John Byre
Widdowe Winſlowe Judith
John Winſlowe
John Alden
Thomas Borenger
John Joyliffe
Rob't Butcher (3)
Ambros Dew
Nath'll Dew
Obadiah Dew
James Maxwell
John Clowe
Samuell Clowe
Joſeph Bridgham (3)
Sam'll Bill
Nath'll Foxe
James Hill, (3)
Sam'll Parris
Richard George
Peter Butler
Charles Lidgett, Eſq.
Mrs. Lewes
Jonath : Bridgham
George Vaughan
Harry Brenning
Tho: Baniſter
Samuell Bayton (2)

Theodor Adkinſon
Timothy Armatage
Edw : Willys
Widd : Whetcombe
Wm : Fiſher
Widd : Froſt
Joſeph Grinliffe
Joſeph Gridlee
Edw : Evens
Henry Ellis
Robert Eable
Richard Draper
Richard Draper
William Denſden
William Howe (2)
Joſeph Hill
Iſack Halem
Henry Calkott
Rich : Jackſon
William James
Joſeph Knight
John King
Henry Lowdor
David Landen (2)
William Fuller
James Floode
John Foſdicke (2)
Rich : Harris
Ambroſe Honywell
Nath : Balſton
Tho : Bligh
John Barrey
Edw : Aſhle
Rich : Corniſh
James Corniſh
Caleb Chaiffin
Tho : Clarke
Ezek : Gardner
Iſack Grigs
Benj : Gillam

Joſeph

Jofeph Lowell, Sen'r
Jofeph Lowell, Jun'r
John Lee
Rich : Lofte
Widd : Langle
Wm : Needham
Rob't Omen
Regnall Odor
Nath : Oliver
Rob't Orchard
Edw : Thwinge
Nath : Thear
Rich : Willy
Rob't Wright
John Winfcome
Tho : Wiborne
John Wear
John Temple
Arther Tanner
Gorge Turfeere
Wm : Slacke
Rowland Stoope
Ralph Striker
John Smith
Tho : Smith, blackfmith
Giles Silvefter
Ebenezer Meffenger
Dan'll Oliver
Hugh Price
Henry Duen
Tho : Davis
John Booker
Abraham Blufh (3)
Jonathan Balfton, Jun'r
Peter Bowden
John Balfton
Jonathan Balfton, Sen'r
Stephen Butler
Sam'll Bridge
Charles Blincoe

John Denfden
Adam Denfden
Jofeph Denfden
Edw : Drinker
Jofeph Day
Sam'll Green
John Greenliffe
Tho : Gretion
James Glaffe
Wm : Holloway, Sen'r (2)
Wm : Holloway, Jun'r
Abraham Harrifon
Jofhua Hubbert
Tho : Meffenger (2)
Jacob Moline
John Mafh, butcher
Henry Munford
John Mafh, currier
[Alexander Bulman]
Edw : Brumfield
Jo : Apleton
Symon Bredftreet
John Baker
John Cooke
Widd : Cooke
John Curbe
Gilbert Cole (2)
David Crutch
Tho : Pound
Jonathan Pollord
Jofeph Parfons
Nath'll Pearce
Danell Quinze
John Melloes
Sam'll Marfhall (2)
Benj : Marfhall
John Robinfon (2)
Tho : Raper
Nath : Renolds
Jofhua Rice

Wm : Robins
Tho : Shipcott
Tho : Smith
Henry Shearloe
Jofeph Stocker
Tho : Stapleford
Tho : Wheler, Sen'or
Tho : Wheler, Juin'or
Widd : Wooddy
Edw : Wanton
Sam'll Wurden
John Pinchin
Sam'll Pearce
John Poole (2)
Widd : Noife
Wm : Phillips
Edmond Perkins
Tho : Peck, Juinor
Edw : Tommas
Rich : Patifhall (2)
John Peck
Tho : Prince
James Pecker
James Penneman
Barth : Sutton
Wm : Smith (2)
Gorge Smith
Widd : Hough
Widd : Stebbins
Peter Sargent (2)
John Salle
John Merriam, Se'or
Ifaack Merriam
Sam'll Merriam
Rob't Sanders
Stephen Sarjent
Henry Stephens
Sam'll Simfon (3)
Jofeph Sowter
John Shawe

Widd :

42

Widd : Sharpe
[   ] Ratliffe
Widd : Pollard
Mathew Darbe
Benj : Merriam
Widd : Parsons, for her weare house at yᵉ dock
Will : Clarke
Tho : Saye
Sam'll Oker
Widd : Elizabeth Winsloe
John Bull
Josiah Fracklin
Wm : King
John Balston
Wm : Rawson
John Pell
Mathias Smith
Capt : Sam'll Sewell (2)
Thomas Cobb
Rich : Cobb
Will : Tudman
Nehamiah Pearce
Joseph Whealer (2)
Joseph Briscoe (2)
Will : Baker (2)
Will : Wallise
Tho : Wallise
John Cowell (2)
Timothy Paydon
Sam'll Gray
Elisha Odlin
John Needham
Jacob Elliott (3)
Soloman Raynsford
Elizabeth Barnes
Tho : Mousett
Widd : Raynsford
David Raynsford

Peter Warren
Wm : Obinson
Tho : Waggett
Alexander Symson
Joseph Symson
Domenick att Alex : Symson's
Tho : Linckhorne
Rob't Sanderson, Se'or
Henry Allen
Rob't Sanderson, Ju'or
Peter Wyer
James Townsend (2)
Laurence Waters
Joseph Hoomes, Se'nor
Joseph Hoomes, Ju'or
Edw : Gouge
Gorge Mathews
John Bennett
Tho : Walker, Sen'or (2)
David Hemes
Tho : Baker
Tho : Walker, Jun'or
John Clowe
John Squire
James White
George Clark
Peter Welcome
Widd : Elliott
Widd : Daves
Tho : Downe
Theophal : Frary (2)
Henry Lilly
James Harris
Widd : Elgason
Satisfaction Belcher
Wm : Pollard
John Belcher
Seth Perre (2)
John Unett

Hugh Drewry
Sam'll Vesee
Eneas Solter (2)
Elizar Holioak
Sampson Sheeffe
James Smith
Moses Payne (2)
Rich : White
John Cornish
John Blake
Tho : Phillips
Joseph Cowell
Edw : Cowell
Hezakiah Usher
John Mason
Sam'll Mason
Michaell Shaller
Sam'll East
Rich : Pearce
Tho : Golde
Wm : Weaver
Mathew Mably
Capt : Roger Clape
Giles Fifeilde
Henry Cole
Isack Goosse (2)
Charles Martarine
James Johnson
Widd : Barnard
Jonathan Wales
Edw : Ellis
John Goodwin
Sam'll Bicknell
John Merriam, Ju'or (2)
John Simkins (2)
Rich : Keats (2)
Ephraim Hall
Anth : Greenhill
Jonathan Francklin, in Wyar's house
Fearnott

Fearnott Shawe
Rob't Browne
John Hewin
John Wilkye
Wm: Middleton

Joſhua Hues
George Hues
Wm: Eſſett
John Mulberre
Iſack White

Rich: Leeke
Ralph Durdent
Sam'll Snow
Henry Wright

MUDDY RIVER VALUATION.

Thomas Gardner, Sen'r
John White, Sen'r
Peter Aſpenall, Sen'r (2)
John Wincheſter, Sen'r
Robert Harris
Thomas Stedman (2)
John Harris
Tymothy Harris
Joſeph Davis
Daniell Harris
Dorman Marrean (2)
Joſiah Wincheſter
Eraſmos Drew (2)
Uriah Clarke
Joſeph White
Thomas Gardner, Jun'r (2)
Joſhua Gardner

Benjamin White
Sammuell Clarke
John Dvoſion
George Baſſtowe
Thomas Woodworth
William Willis
John Parker
Clemment Corbin
Roger Addams
Jonathan Torry
Joſeph Gardner
Nathaniell Stedman and
    Mother
Mathew Miller
Arron Clarke
Widdow Clarke
Ebenezer Heath

Daniell Huley
Joſeph Buckminſter (2)
William Parker
Joſhuah Kibbey
Joſhuah Child
Andrew Gardner
Robert Sharpe
Thomas Boylſtone (2)
Simon Gates
Thomas Burton
John White, Jun'r
Abraham Parker
George Woodward
John Walworth
John Clarke
John Wincheſter, Jun'r
James Parker

VALUATION OF RUMNEY MARSH AND THE ISLANDS, 1687.

James Bill, Sen'r
James Bill, Jun'r
Dean Winthrop
Will: Colmer (3)
John Tuttle
Edward Tuttle
Eliſha Tuttle
Jona: Tuttle

John Floyde
Iſaak Lewes
Sam'll Stocker
Benjamin Muzzey
Ditto Muzzey, Tenant to
    Mr. Page
Teageo Barry
Bryant Bradene

Aron Way (2)
Wm: Ireland
Sam'll Townſend
Jeremy Belcher
John Sentor
Wm: Uſtis
Wido: Maverick
Elias Maverick

John

John Smith
Will : Hafey
John Wifwal
Tho : Chever
Jofeph Bill
Gerfham Davis
Jofeph Hafey
Sam'll Weeden
Sampfon Cole
Abra : Lewes

John Bull
Rob't Renalds
Rob't Muffey
John Pratt
Aphra Benit
Hen : Maier, Long Iland (4)
Eph : Savage, for Hog Iland (2)

Jno : Hore
Coll : Sam'll Shrimpton, Nodle's Iland (3)
Jno : Jackfon at Nodle's Iland
Jno : Pittam at Dere Iland
Nicholas Salfbery at Gov's Iland
Georg Worthylake

INDEX.

Printed in the United States
106105LV00004B/52/A